INTERNATIONAL FINANCIAL ECONOMICS

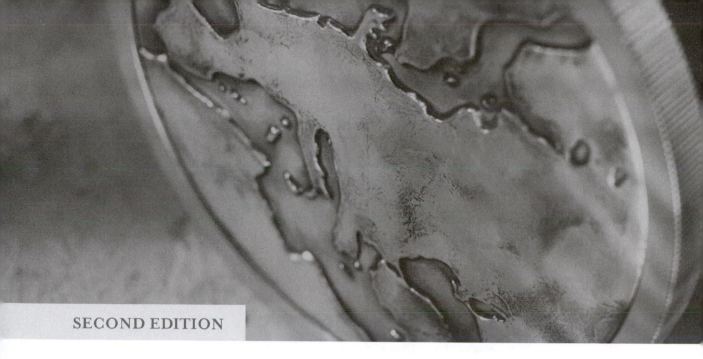

SECOND EDITION

INTERNATIONAL FINANCIAL ECONOMICS

Corporate Decisions in Global Markets

Thomas J. O'Brien

University of Connecticut

New York   Oxford
OXFORD UNIVERSITY PRESS
2006

Oxford University Press, Inc., publishes works that further Oxford University's
objective of excellence in research, scholarship, and education.

Oxford New York
Auckland Cape Town Dar es Salaam Hong Kong Karachi
Kuala Lumpur Madrid Melbourne Mexico City Nairobi
New Delhi Shanghai Taipei Toronto

With offices in
Argentina Austria Brazil Chile Czech Republic France Greece
Guatemala Hungary Italy Japan Poland Portugal Singapore
South Korea Switzerland Thailand Turkey Ukraine Vietnam

Published by Oxford University Press, Inc.
198 Madison Avenue, New York, New York 10016
http://www.oup.com

Library of Congress Cataloging-in-Publication Data

O'Brien, Thomas J.
  International financial economics : corporate decisions in global markets / Thomas J.
O'Brien.—2nd ed.
     p. cm.
  Rev. ed. of: Global financial management. c1996.
  Includes bibliographical references and index.
  ISBN-13: 978–0–19–517504–2
  ISBN 0–19–517504–2 (cloth : alk. paper)
   1. International finance.   2. International business enterprise—Finance.   3. Foreign
exchange.   I. O'Brien, Thomas J. Global financial management.   II. Title.
  HG3881.O263 2005
  685.15′99—dc22

                                                                    2004025888

Printing number: 9 8 7 6 5 4 3 2 1

Printed in the United States of America
on acid-free paper

CONTENTS

*An asterisk preceding a section title designates advanced material that can be omitted without loss of the basic content of an undergraduate course.

PREFACE

I began to teach international finance in 1990. Business school courses in international finance had two models. One was corporate and the other was financial markets, and I preferred for the former. So I tried earlier editions of texts by Madura, Shapiro, and Eiteman and Stonehill the first three times I taught the course.

I found that I wanted a textbook with more foundation in financial economics for topics in FX exposure and overseas valuation. I started to develop my own lecture materials. The best source I found was the *Journal of Applied Corporate Finance*. My lecture notes were published in 1996 as the textbook, *Global Financial Management* (Wiley). About that time, the text by Sercu and Uppal came out. That text has an excellent foundation in financial economics but was above my target level of my course and more detailed than I wanted.

In the meantime, I did some research on the topic of the international cost of capital and cross-border valuation as part of prepping course lectures. At the time of the first edition, I was trying to absorb the international asset pricing literature of Adler, Dumas, Sercu, Stulz, and others. At first I thought that the use of the traditional capital asset pricing model by practitioners would evolve into the use of a two-factor global CAPM as financial markets integrated, with the factors being the world index and a currency index. So I showed how to apply the two-factor global CAPM in the first edition, and I refined this presentation in an article (with Walter Dolde) in the journal *European Financial Management*. But the work of Stulz in 1995 in the *Journal of Applied Corporate Finance* persuaded me that the single-factor global CAPM would be the model that would catch on in practice. So I began to focus my research and overseas valuation chapters on that model.

This second edition of the text and its new title represent the evolved status of my course. The text has been almost completely rewritten. The design of the text is to have one chapter for each of 12 weekly classes in my MBA course at the University of Connecticut. The style of each chapter is to be economical in terms of words and show how to apply the concepts with a few important equations and worked numerical examples. I also try to supply real-world illustrations. By design, the text is not encyclopedic.

MBA students are instructed to read the entire chapter, including the asterisked sections, and work the end-of-chapter problems. The asterisked sections are the ones I would not cover if I were using the text in an undergraduate course at UConn. The text presumes that students have at least taken an introductory course in finance at the MBA or undergraduate level.

Part I, Foreign Exchange Rates, lays a base for Part II, Long-Term Foreign Exchange Exposure. Both Parts I and II are designed to prepare students to get the most out of Part III, International Cost of Capital and Cross-Border Investment Decisions. It is important to me that I stay on pace to cover all of Part III.

Part I contains four chapters on foreign exchange rates. I like doing these four chapters first because the MBA students are usually interested in discussing the topics in class. Chapter 1, Introduction to Foreign Exchange, contains material that I can cover in the first class, knowing that students have not prepared. If a question or comment involves inflation, I tell them we'll cover it the next class, when they have read Chapter 2, Foreign Exchange and Purchasing Power. That chapter covers the connection between FX rates and goods prices, but also discusses deviations between FX rates and purchasing power parity rates.

In the third class, I review Chapter 3, Forward Foreign Exchange. After presenting forward FX contracts and forward FX rates, it is too much to present covered interest arbitrage and covered interest rate parity. So I defer those topics until Chapter 4, Foreign Exchange and Interest Rates. In the fourth class, I also use uncovered interest rate parity (UIRP) to analyze how interest rate changes affect FX rates and cover Siegel's paradox.

After a test over Part I, my course moves on to Part II's four chapters on long-term FX exposure, beginning with Chapter 5, Foreign Exchange Operating Exposure. The ideas in Chapter 5 underlie Chapters 6 and 7. Chapter 6, Debt and Foreign Exchange Exposure, shows the connection between FX operating exposure, denominations of debt, and FX equity exposure. Chapter 7, Currency Swaps, shows the use of currency swaps to hedge FX operating exposure. This orientation is a change from the first edition. Chapter 8, Economic Foreign Exchange Exposure, shows the impact of FX changes on profit-maximizing price and output decisions, including competitive FX exposure. Most of the material in Chapter 8 was not in the first edition.

After a test over Part II, my course moves on to Part III's material on the cost of capital and cross-border investments. Chapter 9, Global Finance and the Cost of Capital, presents the global CAPM and a firm's overall weighted average cost of capital, featuring the case in which some debt is denominated in a foreign currency. Chapter 10, Cost of Capital for Overseas Investments, deals with the cost of capital for overseas investments and divisions, including those in emerging markets. The material in this chapter, including the addition of political risk considerations, was not in the first edition. Chapter 11, Accounting for Foreign Investments and Hedging, shows the accounting implications of foreign investment and FX hedging decisions in light of two Statements of Financial Accounting Standards, SFAS 52 and SFAS 133. This chapter is totally revised from the first edition; students tell me this chapter is tough. Chapter 12, Cross-Border Investment Decisions, finishes the course with an exploration of cross-border investments, including the impact of FX misvaluation on investment and financing decisions. This chapter is also new.

As I expanded the material on the cost of capital and overseas capital budgeting, I discontinued covering currency options in my course. I thought the course had been overweighted in derivatives and financial engineering anyway. Also, options are covered in other courses and the basic idea is the same. So you will have to supplement this text if you want to cover currency options. The same applies to interest rate swaps.

I am grateful for the help of the following people. Paul Donnelly got this second edition off the ground with Oxford University Press, including the new title. I am also grateful to Terry Vaughn, Catherine Rae, and Karen Shapiro for completing the project. I also wish to thank Reid Click (George Washington University) for providing his excellent content review of all twelve chapters. Users of draft chapters who provided helpful suggestions were Shmuel Baruch (University of Utah), Ray Dacey and Michele O'Neill (University of Idaho), Robert Dubil (San Jose State University), and Carmelo Giaccotto and Norm Moore (University of Connecticut). Martin Glaum (Giessen University) was a huge help with Chapter 11. Anna Martin (Fairfield) helped with Chapter 1. Dev Mishra (Memorial University, Newfoundland) helped supply many diagrams, charts, and tables. Patricia Peat provided copyediting that went beyond correcting my grammar and resulted in much better organization and expression. The Oxford University Press copyediting by Brenda Griffing also vastly improved the text. Thanks also to my UConn MBA classes for correcting numerical mistakes in the rough draft.

Thomas J. O'Brien
Storrs, Connecticut

INTERNATIONAL FINANCIAL ECONOMICS

FOREIGN EXCHANGE RATES

Part I introduces foreign exchange rates. The objective is to lay a foundation for the managerial decision topics in Parts II and III.

Chapter 1 presents introductory aspects of FX rates that an instructor can cover in the first three hours of class time even if students have not read the chapter. There are no important equations in this chapter. After some discussion of FX quotation conventions and interpretation of FX rate changes, the chapter discusses FX volatility and FX transaction exposure. Then the chapter reviews some of the important sources of supply and demand pressures on FX rates. Finally, Chapter 1 shows the idea of triangular arbitrage, even though it is unlikely that a manager will ever observe a triangular arbitrage opportunity.

Chapter 2 reviews the connection between FX rates and goods prices. The important concept is purchasing power parity (PPP). However, the chapter also stresses violations of PPP. These ideas seem to naturally lead to a brief review of the evolution of the international monetary system, starting with the gold standard, then the Bretton Woods era, the creation of the euro, and finally the idea of dollarization.

Chapter 3 introduces forward FX rates and forward FX contracts. The chapter covers how to find the profit/loss (the difference check) on a forward FX contract at delivery time and the mark-to-market value of a contract prior to the delivery time. Chapter 3 also presents the use of forward FX contracts to hedge FX transaction exposure and the idea of a synthetic forward FX contract. For graduate students, there is a challenging discussion of financial engineering with currency-linked notes called PERLs.

Chapter 4 begins with the ideas of covered interest arbitrage and the covered interest rate parity (CIRP) no-arbitrage condition. These important ideas would not get the needed attention if they were at the end of Chapter 3. CIRP is compared with the economic theory of uncovered interest rate parity (UIRP). Even though the chapter takes the position that the UIRP condition does not necessarily hold in the real world, the relationship itself is fundamentally very useful. One use is to help examine the impact of interest rate changes on FX rates, as we do in Chapter 4. Another use is seen later, in Part III, when we cover the cost of capital conversion. For the grad students, the chapter presents the problem posed for UIRP by Siegel's paradox.

CHAPTER I

INTRODUCTION TO FOREIGN EXCHANGE

Different national currencies must be exchanged to conduct global business. A *foreign exchange (FX) rate* is, simply, the price of one currency in terms of another. As with stock prices, complex supply and demand forces determine FX rates and cause them to be volatile.

Many companies operate globally, taking raw materials from some countries, producing parts in other countries, assembling in still other countries, and competing to sell final products in markets around the world. Many other companies operate only in their home country or have only limited international operations. For any type of company in today's integrated global economy, the impact of volatile FX rates presents a significant economic challenge to the growth and operations.

This chapter introduces the basics of FX rates and the FX market. We'll also get into the reasons why FX rates are volatile like stock prices and why this volatility is a problem for companies.

FX RATES

The US dollar/British pound FX rate is the price in US dollars of a British pound: 2 $/£ means that $2 will buy 1 British pound. We'll call this the *FX price of the pound*, with the implicit understanding that the pricing is US dollars. The FX rate gives the price of the "denominator currency" in terms of the "numerator currency." Of course, a given FX rate may also be expressed the other way. By taking the reciprocal, the FX rate of 2 $/£ may also be expressed as 0.50 £/$, the FX price of the US dollar in terms of pounds.

The convention in the FX market has been to quote most currencies as the FX price of the US dollar. For example, a quote of 1.60 for the Swiss franc (the "Swissie") implies 1.60 Sf/$ (or 1.60 CHF/USD), and 125 for the Japanese yen means 125 yen per US dollar, or 125 ¥/$ (or 125 JPY/USD). When the FX rate represents the FX price of a US dollar in terms of the other currency, the quotation is said to be in *European terms*, even when the pricing currency involved is not a European currency.

Although most FX quotes are conventionally in European terms, a few are typically quoted in US dollars per unit of the other currency, referred to as *American terms*. This style of quote is the price of the non–US dollar currency in terms of the US dollar. A quote of 1.45 in the case of the British pound means 1.45 US dollars per British pound, or 1.45 $/£ [or 1.45 USD/GBP (Great Britain pounds)]. Other significant currencies usually quoted in American terms include Australian dollars (A$) and New Zealand dollars (NZ$).

Ironically, the most significant currency conventionally quoted in American terms is the euro. For example, a quote of 0.90 for the US dollar/euro FX rate represents 0.90 US dollars per euro or 0.90 $/€ (or 0.90 USD/EUR). The euro is the currency of the 12 countries in the Eurozone, that is, the European Monetary Union (Germany, France, Italy, Spain, Portugal, Belgium, Netherlands, Luxembourg, Austria, Ireland, Finland, and Greece).[1]

The tradition that some FX rates are quoted in European terms and others in American terms may contribute to some initial difficulty in relating to changes in currency values. This text generally cites FX rates following the market conventions, since the sooner you get used to these conventions, the sooner you can comprehend pertinent items in the news.

The notation for an FX rate in this text is the capital letter *X*. To keep things straight, generally we'll follow *X* with a two-currency superscript. Thus, $X^{Sf/\$}$ represents the FX rate in Swiss francs per US dollar, in conventional European terms. Thus, $X^{\$/£}$ would represent the FX rate in US dollars per British pound.

The FX quotes seen streaming on Bloomberg TV and CNBC are quoted following the market conventions, as are the quotes shown in Exhibit 1.1 from the New York Federal Reserve Bank. The FX rates in Exhibit 1.1 are *spot FX rates*, that is, for immediate payment and delivery, which typically means settlement in two business days. The FX

---

[1]Ten more countries joined the European Union on May 1, 2004: Cyprus, Czech Republic, Estonia, Hungary, Latvia, Lithuania, Malta, Poland, Slovakia, and Slovenia. Adoption of the euro normally follows within two years. Member states of the European Union that do not use the euro are Denmark, Sweden, and the United Kingdom. An informative Web site is http://www.wilkiecollins.demon.co.uk/euro/eurocountries.htm.

EXHIBIT 1.1 Federal Reserve Bank of New York Foreign Exchange Rates, October 27, 2003

Currency Area	Unit	FX Rate
Australia*	Dollar	0.7038
Brazil	Real	2.871
Canada	Dollar	1.3107
China	Yuan	8.2767
Denmark	Krone	6.323
European Monetary Union*	Euro	1.1762
Hong Kong	Dollar	7.7541
India	Rupee	45.4
Japan	Yen	108.38
Malaysia	Ringgit	3.80
Mexico	Peso	11.1195
New Zealand*	Dollar	0.6097
Norway	Krone	7.023
Singapore	Dollar	1.743
South Africa	Rand	6.88
South Korea	Won	1183
Sri Lanka	Rupee	94.45
Sweden	Krona	7.725
Switzerland	Franc	1.3159
Taiwan	New Taiwan dollar	33.95
Thailand	Baht	39.99
United Kingdom*	Pound	1.6952
Venezuela	Bolivar	1600

*These rates are quoted in US dollars per foreign currency unit. All other rates are quoted in foreign currency units per US dollar.

rates in Exhibit 1.1 and for other dates can be found at the Web site of the New York Fed (http://www.ny.frb.org/markets/fxrates/noon.cfm). Another useful site for FX information is http://www.oanda.com/index.shtml.

A *cross-rate* is an FX rate between two non–US dollar currencies. A *cross-market* is a market for direct transactions between non–US dollar currencies. If one wants to change euros into yen, for example, one may do so directly in that cross-market. There are relatively deep cross-markets for euros/yen, euros/Swissies, and euros/pounds.

In the absence of a cross-market, the US dollar serves as a *vehicle currency*, meaning that to exchange one non–US dollar currency for another involves two trades, first to exchange one currency into US dollars and then to exchange the US dollars into the second currency. In a vehicle currency system, the cross-rate quote is a *derived* cross-rate. Thus, if the Swiss franc trades at 1.50 Sf/$ and the yen trades at 125 ¥/$, the derived cross-rate would be 125 ¥/$ divided by 1.50 Sf/$, or 83.33 ¥/Sf.

In 2001, over 90% of all spot FX trades involved the US dollar, nearly 38% involved the euro, 23% the Japanese yen, 13% the pound sterling, 6% the Swiss franc, and 2.6% the

EXHIBIT 1.2 Currency Distribution of Reported FX Market Turnover are Percentage Shares of Average Daily Turnover, April 2001 (total = 200%)

US dollar	90.4
Euro	37.6
Japanese yen	22.7
Pound sterling	13.2
Swiss franc	6.1
Swedish krona	2.6

Source: Bank for International Settlements: http://www.bis.org/publ/regpubl.htm.

Swedish krona (Exhibit 1.2). The source of these statistics is the Bank for International Settlements (BIS) triennial survey.

Say you want to convert an amount in dollars, $20,000, to yen, given an FX quote of 125 ¥/$. In this case, you should multiply the amounts, since the dollar symbol in the denominator of the FX rate will "cancel" with the dollar symbol of the currency amount, leaving the units for the answer in the numerator currency symbol of the FX rate, yen: $20,000(125 ¥/$) = ¥2,500,000 = ¥2.5 million.

Now suppose you are given a yen amount of, say, ¥560,000, to convert into dollars at the FX rate of 125 ¥/$. It would make no sense to multiply ¥560,000 by 125 ¥/$ because there is no cancellation of the yen symbol on the currency amount with the denominator currency symbol of the FX rate, the US dollar. To perform the conversion of yen into dollars at an exchange rate expressed in yen per dollar, one can take either of two approaches.

One approach is to reciprocate the FX rate into US dollars per yen, which is 1/(125 ¥/$) = 0.008 $/¥, and then multiply ¥560,000 by the reciprocated rate. Thus, you would have ¥560,000(0.008 $/¥) = $4480. Since the currency symbol of the amount, ¥, cancels with the denominator currency symbol (¥) in the FX rate, the answer is in US dollars.

The second approach is a shortcut. Simply divide ¥560,000 by the quoted FX rate, 125 ¥/$, as in ¥560,000/(125 ¥/$). Now the ¥ symbol in the amount will cancel with the ¥ symbol in the numerator currency of the FX rate, while the denominator currency symbol, $, following the basic algebraic principle that a "denominator of a denominator" goes to the numerator and thus becomes the units for the answer: $4480.

From a country's perspective, an FX rate is said to be in *direct terms* if the home currency is the pricing currency and in *indirect terms* if the foreign currency is the pricing currency. Thus, the FX rate of 2 $/£ is in direct terms from the US point of view. The FX rate of 0.50 £/$ is in indirect terms from the US point of view.

FX RATE CHANGES

If the FX rate for yen goes from 125 ¥/$ to 160 ¥/$, this change represents an increase in the FX price of the US dollar (in yen), as the US dollar is the "denominator currency." We say that the US dollar has appreciated in price when the FX rate goes from 125 ¥/$ to 160 ¥/$. This also implies that the yen has depreciated in its price in terms of the US dollar, from 0.008 $/¥ to 0.00625 $/¥.

Suppose that owing to a net Japanese purchase of US investments, yen are currently being sold for US dollars. Then the buying pressure on the US dollar is causing the FX price of the US dollar to rise. Alternatively, we can say that the FX price of the yen decreases in terms of the US dollar because of the selling of yen. In this case, a *rise* in the conventional FX quote, in ¥/$, represents an appreciation in the US dollar and a depreciation in the yen.

If there is *buying* pressure on the yen, the FX price of the yen increases relative to the dollar, so the FX price of the US dollar declines relative to the yen, and thus the European terms quote declines. For example, an FX rate change from 125 ¥/$ to 119 ¥/$ is a drop in the FX price of the US dollar, that is, a depreciation of the US dollar relative to the yen and an appreciation of the yen relative to the US dollar.

Thinking of an FX rate in terms of the FX price of the "denominator" currency helps if you are new to this subject. In the press, however, you will often see statements like "the yen dropped from 125 ¥/$ to 160 ¥/$" or "the US dollar fell from 1.10 $/€ to 1.25 $/€." Just remember that since the euro appreciates when it goes from 1.10 $/€ to 1.25 $/€, the US dollar depreciates. So it is not incorrect to say that "the US dollar fell from 1.10 $/€ to 1.25 $/€"—just a little confusing at first.

Some reports on FX rates use the terms *devaluation* and *revaluation* instead of depreciation and appreciation, respectively. Devaluation has the same result on an FX rate as depreciation, and revaluation has the same result as appreciation. The difference is that devaluation and revaluation refer to an official change in an FX rate caused by government policy, while depreciation and appreciation imply FX rate changes caused by other market forces. If a central bank intervenes, or even several central banks in a coordinated effort intervene, in the currency market to try to influence the FX price of a currency, this action represents official policy, and the terms devaluation and revaluation would be applicable.

If the spot FX rate for the Swiss franc declines from 1.50 Sf/$ to 1.20 Sf/$, has the Swiss franc depreciated against the US dollar? If the spot FX rate for the euro declines from 1.18 $/€, to 1.03 $/€, has the US dollar depreciated against the euro?

Answers: No to both. The Swiss franc has appreciated. Since one US dollar will buy fewer Swiss francs at 1.20 Sf/$, the FX price of the US dollar has depreciated and the Swiss franc has appreciated. In the second question, the FX price of the US dollar has appreciated and the euro has depreciated.

EXHIBIT 1.3 FX Rate Changes

Country	Currency	AMERICAN TERMS			EUROPEAN TERMS		
		Nov-02	Nov-03	Change FC	Nov-02	Nov-03	Change US$
Canada	C$	0.6364	0.7606	0.1242 ⇑	1.5714	1.3147	(0.2567) ⇓
European Monetary Union	€	1.001	1.1645	0.1635 ⇑	0.999	0.859	(0.140) ⇓
Japan	¥	0.00822	0.00916	0.00094 ⇑	121.63	109.12	(12.51) ⇓
United Kingdom	£	1.570	1.684	0.114 ⇑	0.637	0.594	(0.043) ⇓
Australia	A$	0.561	0.714	0.153 ⇑	1.782	1.401	(0.381) ⇓
Switzerland	Sf	0.682	0.745	0.063 ⇑	1.466	1.342	(0.124) ⇓
New Zealand	NZ$	0.4975	0.6244	0.1269 ⇑	2.010	1.601	(0.409) ⇓

Exhibit 1.3 shows spot FX rates and changes for major foreign currencies (FC) for the year from November 2002 to November 2003.

You can see some changes in FX rates from November 2002 to November 2003 in Exhibit 1.3. Both perspectives are shown, American and European terms. In all cases, the American terms FX quote rose, which represents an appreciation of the non–US dollar currency. Correspondingly, the European terms quote fell, representing a drop in the FX price of the US dollar.

Figures 1.1 through 1.3 depict the movements of three important FX rates from 1997 through November 2003: Figure 1.1 shows $/£, Figure 1.2 shows $/€ (from the year 2000), and Figure 1.3 ¥/$ (also shown in American terms, $/¥).

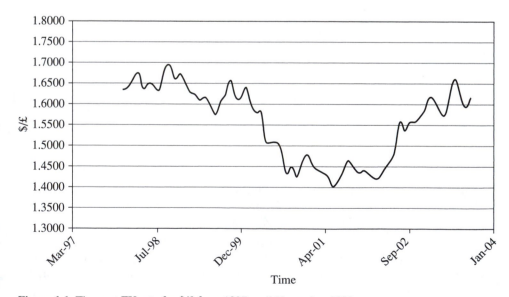

Figure 1.1 The spot FX rate for $/£ from 1997 until November 2003.

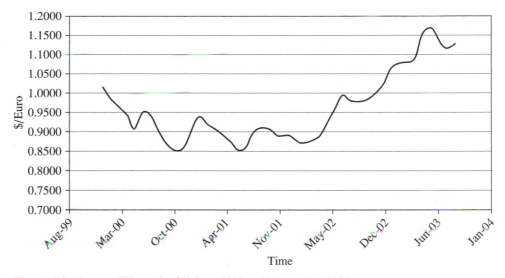

Figure 1.2 The spot FX rate for $/€ from 2000 until November 2003.

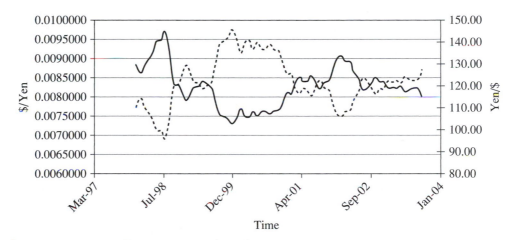

Figure 1.3 The spot FX rate for both ¥/$ and $/¥ from 1997 until November 2003.

FX VOLATILITY AND FX EXPOSURE

As you can see from Exhibit 1.3 and Figures 1.1 through 1.3, FX rates can fluctuate significantly. The tendency for an FX rate to fluctuate is called *FX volatility*. FX volatility implies that while a spot FX rate at the moment is known and observable, we do not know ahead of time what the future spot FX rate for any currency will be. Many try to predict and speculate, but there is always uncertainty about what an FX rate will be in the future.

We measure FX volatility by the standard deviation of annualized percentage changes in the FX rates. For example, an FX volatility of 10% means that the standard deviation of percentage changes in the FX rate is 10% per year.

Exhibit 1.4 contains some estimated FX volatilities. In 2003, for example, the FX volatility of the euro was approximately 9%. As you can see, some currencies are relatively

EXHIBIT 1.4 FX Volatility Estimates

	CURRENCY		VOLATILITY (%)	
Country	Code	Name	9/1/2000	9/1/2003
G8/Eurozone				
Australia	AUD	Dollars	9.50	9.67
Canada	CAD	Dollars	4.73	7.66
Eurozone	EUR	Euro	10.42	9.03
Japan	JPY	Yen	11.62	8.82
Russia	RUB	Roubles	6.02	1.84
United Kingdom	GBP	Pounds	7.29	7.97
Europe (Non-Euro)				
Czech Republic	CZK	Koruny	10.65	10.04
Denmark	DKK	Kroner	10.39	9.01
Iceland	ISK	Kronur	7.08	9.49
Norway	NOK	Krone	8.59	10.20
Poland	PLN	Zlotych	11.25	9.90
Sweden	SEK	Kronor	8.98	9.15
Switzerland	CHF	Francs	10.28	10.10
Latin America				
Argentina	ARS	Pesos	0.39	15.92
Brazil	BRL	Real	9.21	21.45
Chile	CLP	Pesos	6.47	7.98
Colombia	COP	Pesos	7.81	8.46
Mexico	MXN	Pesos	9.01	10.25
Peru	PEN	Nuevos soles	4.50	3.47
Venezuela	VEB	Bolivares	1.45	25.96
Asia/Africa				
China	CNY	Yuan renmibi	0.06	0.18
Hong Kong	HKD	Dollars	0.14	0.05
India	INR	Rupees	2.01	1.50
Indonesia	IDR	Rupiahs	22.78	8.00
South Korea	KRW	Won	5.26	7.31
Singapore	SGD	Dollars	3.86	4.54
South Africa	ZAR	Rand	8.01	17.83

Source: With permission from Justin Pettit and Igor Sokolovsky, "FX Policy Revisited: Strategy & Tactics," Union Bank of Switzerland (UBS) Strategic Advisory Group, October 2003: http://papers.ssrn.com/sol3/papers.cfm?abstract_id=463106

volatile while others are less so, especially in countries whose governments attempt to stabilize the currency in terms of the US dollar. Frequently, especially in developed countries, the FX volatility estimates in Exhibit 1.4 are similar in 2000 and 2003. On the other hand, especially in emerging economy countries, the FX volatility estimates are drastically different in 2000 and 2003. FX volatility fell for Russia and Indonesia. FX volatility for Brazil, Argentina, Venezuela, and South Africa rose.

FX volatility presents a risk for companies that conduct international business and even those that do not. The risk that future FX uncertainty poses to a company is determined by both FX volatility and the company's *FX exposure*, that is, the sensitivity of its financial results to FX changes. Later chapters go into FX exposure in detail; here we introduce the simplest type: *FX transaction exposure*, defined as uncertainty in the home currency value of a contracted foreign currency amount.

Assume that a US company has shipped products to Germany, and the terms call for payment six months from now in the amount of €3000. The US company's receivable may be referred to as a *natural long FX position* in euros, where "long" refers to an inflow (of euros) and "natural" means that the inflow is expected as part of the company's business operations. Since the spot $/€ FX rate six months from now is unknown at the present, the amount of US dollars that the euro receivable will ultimately provide is uncertain. For example, if in six months' time the spot FX rate is 0.96 $/€, the euro inflow will be worth €3000(0.96 $/€) = $2880. If instead the spot FX rate six months from now turns out to be 1.04 $/€, the euro inflow will be worth €3000(1.04 $/€) = $3120. Figure 1.4 depicts the long FX transaction exposure.

FX transaction exposure may be similarly associated with a future payable of an amount of foreign currency that is owed on services received or contracted. Such a payable is called a *natural short FX position* in the foreign currency, where "short" indicates that the situation involves an outflow (of euros). The higher the spot FX price of the foreign

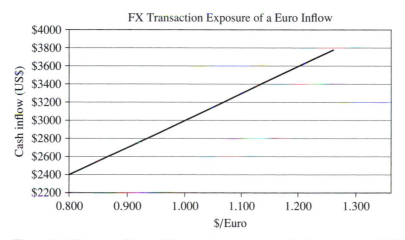

Figure 1.4 The natural long FX transaction exposure of a future receipt of €3000. If the $/€ spot FX rate is 1 $/€, then the cash inflow will be worth $3000. If the $/€ spot FX rate is higher, (e.g., 1.20 $/€), the cash inflow will be worth more in US dollars, $3600.

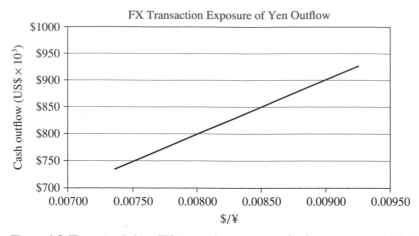

Figure 1.5 The natural short FX transaction exposure of a future payment of ¥100 million. If the ¥/$ spot FX rate is 125 ¥/$ (≡ 0.008 $/¥), then the cash outflow will be $800,000. If the spot FX price of the yen is higher, (e.g., 0.00833 $/¥ = 120 ¥/$), the cash outflow in US dollars will be higher: $833,000.

currency at the time the payment is made, the more base currency is necessary to make the payment. If a US company owes ¥100 million due a year from now, and the spot FX rate turns out to be 125 ¥/$, the US dollars owed will be $800,000. But if the FX price of the yen is higher a year from now, at say 120 ¥/$, the amount of US dollars owed will be higher, $833,000.

Keep in mind throughout the text that "long" and "short" do not refer to time. Instead, being "short X" means you owe X and "long X" means you own X or will be receiving X.

A US exporter has a Swiss franc receivable. If the Swiss franc depreciates in FX price between now and the due date of the receivable, will the exporter be fortunate or unfortunate?

Answer: Unfortunate; the depreciation of the receivable currency implies fewer US dollars for the exporter.

A US importer has a Japanese yen payable. If the US dollar depreciates in FX price (relative to the yen) between now and the due date of the payable, will the importer be fortunate or unfortunate?

Answer: Unfortunate; the depreciation of the US dollar relative to the yen is an appreciation of the yen, and an appreciation of the payable currency implies that the importer will have to pay more US dollars.

FUNDAMENTAL FX SUPPLY AND DEMAND

To see an example of an FX transaction in international trade, assume that Sam's Stores in the United States imports sweaters from Crown Materials Ltd. in England. Naturally, Sam's currency is the US dollar, while Crown's home currency is the British pound. Sam's and Crown must agree on the currency in which the payment is to be made. If Sam's is to send payment in pounds, Sam's must first buy the pounds from a bank in exchange for US dollars. If Sam's is to send payment in US dollars, Crown will exchange those funds with a bank for pounds. If the price of sweaters is fixed in pounds, Sam's will have a natural short exposure to pounds; if the price of sweaters is fixed in US dollars, Crown will have a natural long FX exposure to the US dollar.

In either payment case, there is a *retail FX transaction* between a retail currency user and a bank. Crown's ultimate need for pounds to pay employees and other expenses means a demand in the FX market for pounds and a supply of US dollars. Unless there is a simultaneous source of demand elsewhere in the market for the currency being supplied, at the current FX rate, basic economics tells us that the imbalance between supply and demand will pressure the FX rate to change. In our example, US dollars are being sold for pounds as a result of a US import of British products. Thus, the price of pounds in US dollars, the FX price of the pound, should rise because of the selling pressure on the US dollar and the corresponding buying pressure on the pound. For example, if the FX rate starts at 1.50 $/£, an increase in the FX price of the pound would mean an increase in the FX rate to a number higher than 1.50 $/£, say, to 1.53 $/£. Alternatively, we may say that the FX price of the US dollar will decline relative to the pound.

Retail FX demand originates from other sources besides import/export trade. One example is *foreign direct investment (FDI)* of capital into overseas plant and equipment. A German company wishing to build a plant or buy a plant in Canada needs to exchange euros into Canadian dollars (i.e., buy Canadian dollars with euros) to make the investment.

Another source of retail FX demand is *portfolio investment*, which applies to financial securities, rather than FDI in the form of physical capital. (Technically, the purchase of more than 10% of a company's equity by a foreign investor is classified as FDI rather than portfolio investment.) A Hong Kong manager of a bond portfolio wishing to invest in Japanese bonds needs to exchange Hong Kong dollars into yen to buy the bonds. Upon the liquidation of the bonds, the manager is likely to sell the yen back into Hong Kong dollars. A US company might borrow by selling yen-denominated bonds and FX the proceeds into US dollars to fund US dollar assets. This portfolio trade will cause pressure on the US dollar to appreciate relative to the yen.

Taken together, trade, FDI, and portfolio transactions are fundamental sources of supply and demand for FX transactions. In 2001, the volume of FX transactions for portfolio trades was $329 billion, while the volume of FX transactions by corporate entities for both trade and FDI was $156 billion. Between 1998 and 2001, the volume of FX trading by corporate entities dropped, as treasury departments became more efficient in netting the companies' FX trading internally. On the other hand, the volume of FX trades for portfolio purposes increased as international portfolio diversification increased.[2]

---

[2]See "Review of the Foreign Exchange Market Structure," European Central Bank, March 2003, at http://www.ecb.int/pub/pdf/fxmarketstructure200303.pdf.

Another source of demand for some currencies is as a store of value. In general, nations whose economic policies have promoted economic growth and stability, and controlled inflation, tend to have currencies that appreciate in price over currencies of countries with the opposite policies. The currencies of low-inflation, growth-oriented economies are referred to as *hard currencies*, and the currencies of the weaker, high-inflation economies are referred to as *soft currencies*. There is an additional demand for hard currencies as a basic store of value for individuals, corporations, and governments in soft-currency countries.

INTERBANK FX MARKET

In either of the possible FX transactions in the Sam's/Crown example, a bank provides a retail customer with British pounds in return for US dollars. Unless the bank has an inventory of pounds, the bank itself needs to acquire the pounds for dollars. One candidate is the country's central bank, the Federal Reserve (the Fed) for a US bank or the Bank of England for a UK bank. Another candidate is another bank anywhere in the world. Transactions between relatively large banks are said to take place in the wholesale *interbank (FX) market*. If a bank is a small regional bank without direct trading access to the global interbank market, it may obtain currency from one of the larger interbank participants, possibly through one of a number of established FX brokers. An *FX broker* buys currency in the interbank market and, in turn, sells the currency at a markup to smaller players.

The interbank FX market operates globally, allowing a large number of banks and currency brokers of different nationalities to routinely exchange currencies with each other, with large corporations, and with large fund managers. The need for FX transactions is immense, and the vast interbank market has well over US$1 trillion worth of trades daily. Wholesale interbank FX trading between interbank dealers was about $689 billion in 2001. In the interbank market, no physical paper (banknotes or drafts) changes hands. All transactions take place electronically through an international clearing system. Generally, the FX market is unregulated.

CENTRAL BANKS AND BALANCE OF PAYMENTS

In addition to retail and interbank elements, other important participants in the FX market are central banks and speculators. A country's central bank has an unlimited supply of its own country's currency. In addition, a central bank will maintain balances of *foreign currency reserves (or FX reserves)* of other currencies, obtained over time through transactions in the interbank market.

For example, say the Bank of England has routinely sold pounds to Crown Materials's bank for the US dollars originally sent by Sam's. The Bank of England can either hold the US dollars as FX reserves or trade the US dollars back to the Fed for some of the Fed's existing reserves of British pounds (or for gold or other foreign currency). If Sam's had acquired pounds from its US bank, which in turn had acquired the pounds from the Fed, the Fed would then be holding fewer pounds as part of the inventory of its FX reserves. If the Fed thought its new inventory level was too low, it could buy more pounds in the interbank market or from the Bank of England using gold or US dollars or, for that matter, any other country's currency. Note that if either of the central banks is in the transaction, there is an increase in the *money supply* of pounds, pounds circulating outside the central banking system, and a decline in the money supply of US dollars circulating outside the central bank system.

Whenever a country has a net outflow of currency (including gold), the country has a *balance of payments deficit*. This means that the country's total purchases of foreign goods plus its investments into foreign assets exceed the total purchases of the country's goods by foreigners plus investments by foreigners in the country's assets. The result will be a reduction in the *net FX reserves* held by the country's central bank. The opposite is a *balance of payments surplus*, with a corresponding gain of net FX reserves. If, over a given period of time, the value of all US purchases of British goods and investments is less than the value of British purchases of US goods and investment, the United Kingdom has a balance of payments (BOP) deficit versus the US. And the United States has a BOP surplus versus its trading partner. These ideas are depicted in Figure 1.6.

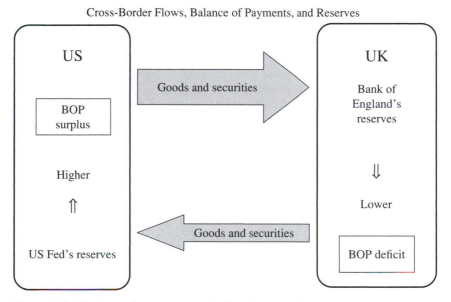

Figure 1.6 A balance of payments surplus for the United States and a balance of payments deficit for the United Kingdom. Britain's total of imports of goods from the United States and investments into the United States exceeds the US total of imports from the United Kingdom and investments into the United Kingdom. The reserves held by the Federal Reserve will increase, and those held by the Bank of England decrease.

A BOP deficit tends to be accompanied by a drop in the FX price of the currency, since the currency is being sold to import goods and/or make overseas investments. Often the United States has had a deficit on trade (imports of goods higher than exports of goods) but a surplus on investment (more foreign investment in the United States than US investment abroad). In this situation, the overseas investment into the United States is said to be "financing the trade deficit" and keeping the US dollar from depreciating. Information about balance of payments may be obtained from the U.S. Department of Commerce's Bureau of Economic Activity (BEA), at http://www.bea.doc.gov/.

The FX transactions of central banks are often routine, as in the example transfer of funds, but at other times they are intended to implement economic policies. In these situations, central banks initiate transactions in the FX market that are large enough to have an influence on the FX rate. This activity is termed *direct intervention*. In the United States, both the Treasury and the Federal Reserve have independent legal authority to directly intervene in the FX market.

In early 2004, a significant direct intervention was conducted by Japan. Japan was buying US dollars with Japanese yen to try to reduce the FX price of the yen. This intervention increases the yen money supply. Sometimes, a central bank will buy or sell long-term securities in the home currency to offset the change in the money supply caused by direct intervention. This process is known as *sterilization*. Sometimes, several central banks act in a coordinated manner to try to influence FX rates to achieve some multilateral policy goals reached by negotiation and compromise.

Direct intervention by central banks may cause FX rates to differ from levels other than what the free market would establish, but it is not the main determinant of FX rates, even when several central banks act in coordination. In fact, the trading volume of the central banks as a whole is very small in comparison to the overall currency market. Central banks influence FX rates but can neither control the global FX market nor totally determine FX rates. Central banks are simply market participants, albeit major ones, in the essentially unregulated interbank market. In addition to direct intervention, central banks may influence FX rates through interest rate policy, which is covered in Chapter 4.

Sometimes the central bank of a less developed country tries to control the FX price of its currency too rigidly. If the currency is freely convertible, this can lead to a currency crisis. Sometimes a government of a less developed country restricts the convertibility of its currency and dictates an *official FX rate*. If this happens, a free market for the currency may spring up. If the government tolerates this free market, it is called a *parallel market*. If not, it is called a *black market*.

The *Bank for International Settlements* is an international organization that fosters cooperation among central banks and other agencies in pursuit of monetary and financial stability. The BIS headquarters is in Basel, Switzerland. Established in 1930, the BIS is the world's oldest international financial organization. Because its customers are central banks, the BIS does not accept deposits from, or provide financial services to, private individuals or corporate entities. The BIS makes available international financial information related to FX rates (http://www.bis.org/index.htm).

SPECULATORS

Another important participant in the FX market is the speculator, who tries to make money on a view about the future direction of FX rates. Naturally, speculators account for supply and demand pressure on FX rates, beyond that fundamentally coming from the retail arena and central banks. Typically, speculators are trader-dealers employed by financial institutions or private operators. George Soros has received much publicity in this regard, particularly in connection with the Asian crisis of the late 1990s. The speculation activity by corporate entities is said to have declined substantially.

Speculators have sometimes tried to figure out when a central bank may be running low on its overall FX reserves, hence unable to defend its own currency in the FX market by using FX reserves to buy it. The speculators will then attack that currency by selling it in large quantity, hastening a crisis and profiting at the expense of one or more central banks. A history of central bank losses to speculators, culminating in a 1992 British pound crisis, may have led central banks to curtail direct intervention in the FX market after 1992.

Some speculators are well informed, while others are not. Trading on good fundamental information will drive an FX rate toward its intrinsic value, or true fundamental value. Trading that is not based on good fundamental information, like trend chasing, may drive FX rates away from intrinsic values. Thus, FX rates are sometimes described as having two components. One component is a permanent component (i.e., the intrinsic value). The other is a transitory component, or deviation from intrinsic value. We can think of an actual FX rate as oscillating around the intrinsic FX value.

In this text, we'll differentiate sometimes between the FX price of a currency and the FX value of a currency. The former relates to the actual FX rate, while the latter relates to the intrinsic value of the FX rate. In the theoretical ideal of an efficient FX market, central banks do not influence FX rates for policy reasons, and irrational speculation such as trend chasing has no impact on FX rates. In an efficient FX market, price and intrinsic value are the same. Despite the distinction we draw between FX price and FX value as actual FX rates versus intrinsic FX rates, you may see the FX value of a currency used in the context of the actual FX rate (i.e., used synonymously with the FX price of the currency). For example, it is common to hear the term "value of the dollar" with reference to actual FX rates.

TRIANGULAR ARBITRAGE

Arbitrage is defined as the simultaneous purchase and sale of essentially the same good at different prices. When a cross-market exists and the direct cross-rate is different from the derived cross-rate, *triangular arbitrage* is possible. For example, assume that the cross-market's direct FX rate for yen/Swiss francs is 80 ¥/Sf at the same time that the yen trades at 125 ¥/$ and the Swiss franc trades at 1.50 Sf/$, implying the derived cross-rate of 83.33 ¥/Sf, found earlier. In this case, triangular arbitrage is possible. The FX price of the Swiss franc, in yen, is lower in the cross-market than in the indirect market using the

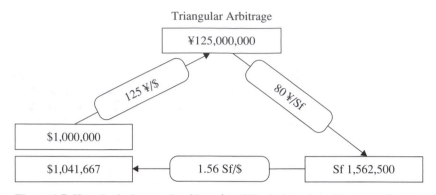

Figure 1.7 Hypothetical example of how $41,667 of triangular arbitrage profit would be possible if one starts with $1 million and can make FX trades at 125 ¥/$, 80 ¥/Sf, and 1.56 Sf/$.

US dollar as a vehicle. Thus, remembering to "buy low and sell high," you should buy Swiss francs with yen directly (at 80 ¥/Sf) and simultaneously sell Swiss francs for yen indirectly (at 83.33 ¥/Sf) using the US dollar vehicle.

Selling Swiss francs for yen indirectly means selling Swiss francs for US dollars and then selling the US dollars for yen. For example, you take 80 yen to buy 1 Swiss franc directly; sell the 1 Swiss franc for US dollars to get Sf 1/(1.50 Sf/$) = $0.667; and then use $0.667 to buy yen at 125 ¥/$, to get $0.667(125 ¥/$) = ¥83.33. You start with ¥80 and ended up with ¥83.33, for an arbitrage profit of ¥3.33.

Maybe this arbitrage will be easier to see if you start with US dollars. The key is that you want to take advantage of a mispricing and buy Swiss francs with yen directly. So the first step is to exchange the US dollars into yen. Say you start with $1 million, and you exchange this amount into ¥125 million. With ¥125 million, you can directly buy Swiss francs: (¥125 million)/(80 ¥/Sf) = Sf 1.5625 million. With Sf 1.5625 million, you can buy (Sf 1.5625 million)/(1.50 Sf/$) = $1,041,667. Your arbitrage profit from these hypothetical transactions is $41,667. This triangular arbitrage strategy is depicted in Figure 1.7.

The potential for triangular arbitrage will tend to enforce the alignment of direct cross-rates with derived cross-rates. In our Swiss franc–yen arbitrage example, the direct purchase of Swiss francs with yen in the direct cross-market will, other things equal, cause the FX price of the Swiss franc (in yen) to appreciate to an FX price higher than 80 ¥/Sf. By the same token, the sale of Swiss francs for US dollars and the purchase of yen with US dollars in the indirect vehicle approach will tend to drive down the FX price of the Swiss franc in US dollars and drive up the FX price of the yen in US dollars. This activity results in a lower derived cross-market FX price of the Swiss franc (in yen) than 83.33 ¥/Sf. Arbitrage activity is likely to continue until the direct cross-rate and the derived cross-rate have converged, at which point no further arbitrage is possible. In reality, the potential for profits from triangular arbitrage results in the situation where no such profits are possible.

Exhibit 1.5 shows some bid-ask FX rates reported on Yahoo on November 15, 2003. At a bid rate, you can buy the numerator currency with the denominator currency. At an ask rate, you can buy the denominator currency with the numerator currency.

EXHIBIT 1.5 Yahoo FX Quotes, November 15, 2003

	¥/$	¥/Sf	Sf/$
Bid	108.00	81.3862	1.3267
Ask	108.12	81.4954	1.3273

Exhibit 1.5 shows real-world spot bid-ask FX quotes observed on Yahoo on November 15, 2003.

Bid: The price at which the numerator currency may be purchased with the denominator currency.

Ask: The price at which the denominator currency may be purchased with the numerator currency.

 We can show that there are no triangular arbitrage opportunities in the real-world quotes in Exhibit 1.5. Let us say that you start with $1 million. You first buy Sf 1.3267 million. With the Sf 1.3267 million, you then buy yen, (81.3862 ¥/Sf)(Sf 1.3267 million) = ¥107.975 million. With ¥107.975 million, you buy US dollars, obtaining (¥107.975 million)/(108.12 ¥/$) = $998,660. You lose $1 million – 998,660 = $1340 with these transactions. This scenario is depicted in Figure 1.8. The next example demonstrates that you would also lose money by going the other route (i.e., first buying yen, then Swiss francs, and finally US dollars).

Start with $1 million. Use the bid-ask quotes in Exhibit 1.5 to buy yen, then buy Swiss francs, then buy US dollars. What is your loss?

Answer: You buy ¥108 million. With this amount, you buy (¥108 million)/(81.4954 ¥/Sf) = Sf 1.3252 million. With this amount, you buy (Sf 1.3252 million)/(1.3273 Sf/$) = $998,439. Your loss is $1 million – 998,439 = $1561.

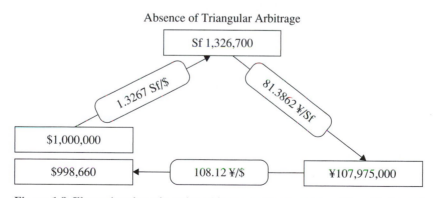

Absence of Triangular Arbitrage

Figure 1.8 Illustration that triangular arbitrage profits are not possible with the real-world bid-ask FX quotes of Exhibit 1.5.

The examples with the FX quotes in Exhibit 1.5 show that triangular arbitrage opportunities do not generally exist in the real world when bid-ask spreads are considered. In the real world, only professional FX traders would have access to the small triangular arbitrage opportunities that temporarily occur. The buying and selling by professional traders pressures the opportunities away as the professionals capture the profits.

For those who are not professional traders, triangular arbitrage is only an instructional concept that is helpful in understanding the implications of the absence of triangular arbitrage opportunities. For example, suppose that we observe FX rates of 1.60 $/£ and 1.15 $/€, and thus we know that the FX rate between pounds and euros must be (1.15 $/€)/(1.60 $/£) = 0.71875 £/€. If the euro depreciates relative to the US dollar to 1 $/€, but the euro/pound FX rate does not change, the pound also must depreciate relative to the US dollar, to (1 $/€)/(0.71875 £/€) = 1.391 $/£. This example demonstrates a unilateral appreciation the FX price of the US dollar relative to the other currencies, perhaps driven by some economic development in the United States. The next example demonstrates a unilateral depreciation in the FX price of the euro relative to the other currencies, driven perhaps by an economic development in the Eurozone.

We observe FX rates of 1.60 $/£ and 1.15 $/€, so we know that the FX rate between pounds and euros must be 0.71875 £/€. If the euro depreciates relative to the US dollar to 1 $/€, but the dollar/pound FX rate does not change, what must the new pound/euro FX rate be?

Answer: (1 $/€)/(1.60 $/£) = 0.625 £/€.

FX INDEXES

Sometimes we want to see how a currency is changing relative to other currencies in general. For example, we may want to know how the FX value of the dollar is doing. For this purpose, we can use an FX index, like a Federal Reserve Board of Governor's (FRBG, or FRB) index of the US dollar price of a basket of foreign currencies. You can find three FRBG FX indexes on the Internet at http://research.stlouisfed.org/fred2/categories/105.

The FRB broad index uses the currencies of a broad group of major US trading partners. The FRB major currency index uses a subset of the broad index currencies that circulate widely outside the country of issue. The weights of FRB index are based on relative importance of each currency in international trade with the United States. The seven foreign currencies and their weights in the FRB major currency index are the Canadian dollar (30.3%), the euro (28.7%), the Japanese yen (25.6%), the British pound (8%), the Swiss franc (3.2%), the Australian dollar (2.6%), and the Swedish krona (1.6%). The third FRBG index uses a subset of the broad index currencies that do not circulate widely outside the country of issue.

The Federal Reserve Bank of Atlanta maintains a different FX index of the US dollar price of a foreign currency basket. The Atlanta Fed Dollar Index includes the Mexican peso (11%), China (5.5%), Taiwan (4.2%), South Korea (4.1%), Singapore (3.0%),

Malaysia (2.3%), Hong Kong (2.1%), Brazil (1.9%), and Saudi Arabia (1.4%). The index is based on trade-weights, but a different perspective is used on trade than with the FRBG indexes. So, the weights on the major currencies are not in the same proportion as the FRBG index weights. The Atlanta Fed Dollar Index weights for the major currencies are Canada (24.6%), Eurozone (16.6%), Japan (15.6%), United Kingdom (5.1%), Switzerland (1.3%), Australia (1.3%), and Sweden (0%).[3]

SUMMARY

This chapter introduces the general subject of foreign exchange (FX) rates and the FX market. An FX rate is the price of one currency in terms of another. The $/€ FX rate is the FX price of the euro in terms of the US dollar, and the ¥/$ FX rate in FX price of the US dollar in terms of yen. The FX price of the euro in terms of the US dollar is the mathematical reciprocal of the FX price of the US dollar in terms of the euro.

FX rates fluctuate with supply and demand pressures, just like stock prices. The volatility of FX rates creates a risk for many companies. The impact of the risk posed by fluctuating FX rates was introduced in the discussion of FX transaction exposure.

The basic supply and demand forces that cause FX rates to fluctuate were discussed, including the activities of central banks and speculators. This discussion covered the relationship between the FX rate and the balance of payments.

Finally, we covered the topic of triangular arbitrage. Given the Sf/$ and ¥/$ FX rates, there is an implied FX cross-rate between Swiss francs and yen. If the actual FX cross-rate differs from the implied FX cross-rate, an arbitrage profit is possible in principle. But since many currency traders are constantly searching for such arbitrage possibilities, the FX rates stay very well aligned, especially from the point of view of those of us who are not currency traders with the lowest transaction costs.

GLOSSARY

American terms: An FX rate quotation expressed as US dollars per one unit of another currency.

Arbitrage: The simultaneous purchase and sale of essentially the same good at different prices.

Balance of payments deficit (surplus): A country in this condition has a net outflow (inflow) of currency, including gold.

Bank for International Settlements (BIS): An international organization that fosters cooperation among central banks and other agencies in pursuit of monetary and financial stability.

---

[3]Detailed discussions of the Atlanta Fed Dollar Index, its revision in 1999, and its differences from the FRBG major currency index are in B. Acree, "Revising the Atlanta Fed Dollar Index," *Federal Reserve Bank of Atlanta Economic Review*, 3rd quarter, 40–51, at http://www.frbatlanta.org/filelegacydocs/acree.pdf.

Black market: Illegal trading in a currency that has an official FX rate dictated by the country's government.

Cross-market: A market for direct exchange of two non–US dollar currencies.

Cross-rate: An FX rate between two non–US dollar currencies.

Devaluation: A decline in the FX price of a currency brought about by official policy.

Direct intervention: The purchase and sale of currencies by central banks to influence FX rates.

Direct terms: An FX rate expressed as the amount of one's home currency price per one unit of a foreign currency.

European terms: An FX rate quotation expressed as the number of units of a currency per one US dollar.

Foreign currency reserves (or FX reserves): Holdings by a central bank in various currencies to facilitate international settlements and provide backing for its own currency.

Foreign exchange (FX) rate: The price of one currency in terms of another.

Foreign direct investment (FDI): Investment into plant and subsidiaries in a foreign country, as distinct from international portfolio investment in securities.

FX broker: One who buys currency in the interbank market and, in turn, sells the currency at a markup to smaller players.

FX exposure: The risk that future FX uncertainty poses to a company.

FX transaction exposure: The uncertainty in the home currency value of a contracted foreign currency amount.

FX volatility: The annualized standard deviation of percentage changes in an FX rate.

Hard currency: A currency that holds its value because the country's economy is strong and growing, experiencing neither severe inflation nor economic deterioration.

Indirect terms: An FX rate expressed as the amount of foreign currency per one unit of one's base currency price.

Interbank (FX) market: The wholesale international market for currency trading between major banks and financial institutions around the world.

Natural long (short) FX position: An inflow (outflow) of a currency is expected as part of the company's natural business.

Official FX rate: An FX rate sometimes dictated by the government of a less developed country whose currency is not freely convertible.

Parallel market: Trading in a currency that is tolerated by a government that has dictated an official FX rate.

Portfolio investment: Investments in financial securities such as stocks and bonds as distinct from foreign direct investment.

Retail (FX) market: The market for currency exchange between banks and retail businesses and investment portfolios.

Revaluation: An increase in the FX price of a currency brought about by official policy.

Soft currency: A currency that loses value because the country's economy is weak and experiencing inflation.

Spot FX rate: Exchange rate for immediate delivery.

Sterilization: A central bank's purchase or sale of long-term securities in the home currency to offset the change in the money supply caused by direct intervention.

Triangular arbitrage: The strategy to exploit the difference between a direct cross-rate and a derived cross-rate.

DISCUSSION QUESTIONS

1. Discuss the roles of the following in the FX market: (a) the need to exchange currencies to conduct international business and for cross-border portfolio investments, (b) policies of national central banks, and (c) speculation.
2. Explain why a currency changes in FX price relative to another currency.
3. Refer to Exhibit 1.4. Why do you think some currencies have higher FX volatility than others?
4. Are you likely to be able to conduct triangular arbitrage? Explain.

PROBLEMS

1. The FX rate for the Swiss franc increases from 1.35 Sf/$ to 1.45 Sf/$. Has the Swiss franc appreciated or depreciated relative to the US dollar?
2. You wish to convert $1000 into British pounds at the FX rate of 2 $/£. What is the amount in pounds?
3. A German exporter has a US dollar receivable. If the euro depreciates in FX price between now and the due date of the receivable, will the exporter be fortunate or unfortunate?
4. A Japanese importer has a US dollar payable. If the US dollar depreciates in FX price (relative to the yen) between now and the due date of the payable, will the importer be fortunate or unfortunate?
5. Assume spot FX rates of 1.50 Sf/$ and 1.50 $/£. What should the direct cross-rate be for Sf/£? If the direct cross-rate is 2.50 Sf/£, describe the triangular arbitrage strategy.

ANSWERS TO PROBLEMS

1. Depreciated
2. £500
3. Fortunate; the depreciation of the euro implies an appreciation of the receivable currency, which means more euros for the exporter.
4. Fortunate; the depreciation of the US dollar relative to the yen implies that the importer will have to pay fewer yen.
5. The direct Swiss franc-pound cross-rate should be 2.25 Sf/£. To execute a "buy-low, sell high" strategy, you would buy pounds with Swiss francs low at 2.25 indirectly (by buying US dollars first): sell pounds high at 2.50 directly into Swiss francs. Starting with US dollars ($1.50), you would buy pounds (£1) with US dollars to sell pounds high directly into Swiss francs (Sf 2.50); sell the Sf 2.50 Swiss francs back into US dollars at 2.25 Sf/$ to get (2.50 Sf/$)/(1.50 Sf/$) = $1.67. The profit is $0.17.

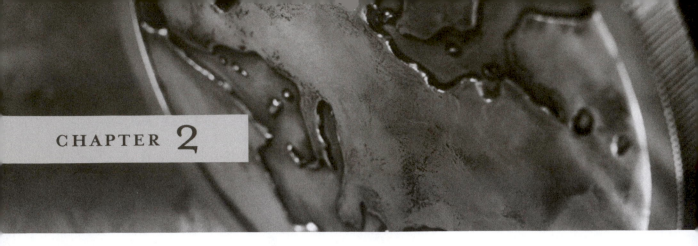

CHAPTER 2

FOREIGN EXCHANGE AND PURCHASING POWER

A driving force of global business is the benefit of international trade. Different peoples, endowed with different ideas and resources, produce different products and produce common products with different degrees of efficiency. Trade can be beneficial to both sides. If, for example, Switzerland has the natural resources to produce watches while the United States has the resources to produce grain, people in both countries can benefit if Switzerland sends watches to the United States in exchange for some grain.

Even if both countries can produce watches and grain, trade can make both better off. This point is relatively obvious if Switzerland can make watches more efficiently than the United States and the United States can grow grain more efficiently than Switzerland, and if transportation costs are not too great.

Even if one country can make both products more efficiently, each may still benefit from specialization and trade, given the economic principle of *comparative advantage*. For example, suppose Switzerland is significantly more efficient in making watches but only slightly more efficient in growing grain. Both Switzerland and the United States could be better off if Switzerland specializes in watches and the United States in grain, because of Switzerland's comparative advantage in making watches. One classic illustration of comparative advantage supposes that you are a better typist than your secretary. Even so, your business is better off if you employ the secretary because you presumably have the comparative advantage in things like understanding international finance.

Let us assume that in the United States the price of a watch is $12 and the price of a bushel of grain is $4. Assume that the price of a watch in Switzerland is Sf 16 and a bushel of grain is Sf 8. Differences in relative prices reflect differences in resources, skills, tastes, and social conditions. Let us see how these relative prices relate to trade and the FX rate.

If the FX rate were above 2 Sf/$, both watches and grain would be cheaper in Switzerland than in the United States, when viewed in the same currency. For example, at an FX rate of 4 Sf/$, the price in US dollars of Swiss watches would be $4 and the price in US dollars of a bushel of Swiss grain would be $2. If the FX rate were below 1.33 Sf/$, both watches and grain would be cheaper in the United States. For example, at 1 Sf/$, a Swiss watch would be $16 and a bushel of Swiss grain would be $8. If the FX rate is between 1 Sf/$ and 2 Sf/$, there is a basis for trade. At 1.60 Sf/$, for example, Swiss watchmakers can export watches to the United States to sell for $10 and the US grain growers can export grain to Switzerland for 5 Sf per bushel (equivalent to $8 per bushel.) We cannot say what the equilibrium FX rate is without additional information. The equilibrium FX rate is the rate that brings the value of the exports and imports of the countries into balance, and thus it depends on demand levels and production capacities.

Despite the benefits of trade, grain producers in Switzerland and watchmakers in the United States would not favor the specialization and trade. They might pressure their governments for trade barriers, a form of *protectionism*. Examples of trade barriers are quotas, tariffs on imports, and government subsidies to domestic producers. In between the no-trade and free trade extremes is a spectrum of trade arrangements. For example, countries can reduce tariffs or increase quotas for trade with specific other countries in mutual preferential trade arrangements.

ABSOLUTE PURCHASING POWER PARITY (APPP)

The price of a tradable commodity in one country should theoretically be equal to the price of the same commodity in another country, after adjusting for the FX rate. The theory is known as the *international law of one price*. When the international law of one price is applied to the representative good or baskets of goods, it is called the absolute purchasing power parity (APPP) condition.

We'll often use a subscript to denote time, in years from the present. Thus $X_0^{\$/£}$ denotes a current spot FX rate, $X_2^{\$/£}$ the spot FX rate two years from now, $X_{0.50}^{\$/£}$ a spot FX rate six months from now, and so forth. Let's use wheat as the representative good. Denoting the price of a bushel of wheat in the United States at time N as $P_N^\$$ and the price of a bushel of wheat in the United Kingdom at time N as $P_N^£$, the APPP condition implies that the spot FX rate at time N *should be* $P_N^\$/P_N^£$, as shown in equation (2.1). The p superscript in $X_N^{p\$/£}$ denotes that the reference is to the spot FX *parity* rate, as opposed to an *actual* spot FX rate, $X_N^{\$/£}$.

Absolute Purchasing Power Parity (APPP) Condition

$$X_N^{p\$/£} = P_N^\$/P_N^£ \qquad (2.1)$$

For example, assume at time N that a bushel of wheat costs $P_N^\$ = \$1.60$ in the United States and $P_N^£ = £1.00$ in England. The APPP condition says that the spot FX rate at time N should be $X_N^{p\$/£} = \$1.60/£1.00 = 1.60$ $/£. At this FX rate, someone in the United States could buy a bushel for \$1.60 or exchange the \$1.60 into £1.00 and purchase a bushel in the United Kingdom for £1.00. Either way, the cost of wheat is the same.

Assume that a bushel of wheat costs \$2.00 in the United States and €3.00 in France (in the Eurozone). What does the APPP condition say should be the FX rate? Express your answer in the form of the accepted FX quotation convention.

Answer: Since the euro FX rate is conventionally expressed in American terms, we want the answer to be in $/€. Thus, $P^\$/P^€ = \$2.00/€3.00 = 0.67$ $/€ is the FX rate that will make a bushel of wheat the same in both economies.

The theoretical argument behind the APPP condition is that if a country's goods were relatively cheap internationally, *goods market arbitrage* would create pressure on both FX prices and goods prices to correct, and to thereby conform to, uniform international prices. Say we fix the FX rate at 1.60 Sf/$ in our example of Swiss watches and US grain. Taking as given the price of a Swiss watch in the United States of \$10 and the price of a bushel of US grain in Switzerland of Sf 5, the APPP condition says that the price of US watches in the United States should drop from \$12 to the price of a Swiss watch, \$10, and the price of a bushel of Swiss grain in Switzerland should drop to the price of a bushel imported from the United States, Sf 5.

FX MISVALUATION

Despite the economic logic underlying the APPP condition, actual FX rates are often not equal to the APPP ideal. The APPP condition assumes that international trade is unencumbered by such frictions as transportation costs and trade barriers (e.g., tariffs, quotas, language/cultural barriers). In reality, these frictions can be significant.

Stickiness in goods prices, in a world where FX rates change continually for many reasons, can also be an explanation for the failure of the APPP condition to describe actual FX rates. To see why, suppose we assume the APPP condition at first holds for wheat prices of $P_0^\$ = \$1.60$ and $P_0^£ = £1.00$. Thus the actual spot FX rate, $X_0^{\$/£}$, is assumed at first to be equal to the theoretically correct APPP rate, $X_0^{p\$/£} = 1.60$ $/£. Let us say that the actual spot FX rate subsequently rises to $X_1^{\$/£} = 2.00$ $/£. (The reason for the rise is not important. Perhaps foreign investors moved funds into British investments, or there was speculation by currency traders.)

Whatever the reason for the actual spot FX change, before any adjustment of wheat prices takes place, a wheat buyer in the United Kingdom will now have the incentive to import wheat from the United States. Given the new actual spot FX rate of 2.00 $/£, it will take £1.00, the equivalent of \$2.00, to buy a bushel of wheat in the United Kingdom but only £0.80, the equivalent of $1.60, to buy a bushel of wheat in the United States. Correspondingly, US wheat buyers will not tend to import any UK wheat, since $1.60 will still buy a bushel in the United States, but will convert to only £0.80, which would buy less than a bushel in the United Kingdom. In principle, goods arbitrageurs could buy wheat in the United States and sell it in the United Kingdom.

Unless and until the actual FX rate changes again or one or both wheat prices adjust to reestablish the APPP condition, the British pound/US dollar FX rate is misvalued in terms of purchasing power. The British pound is *overvalued*, in the sense that the pound can purchase more overseas (in the United States) than the equivalent amount of US dollars can purchase overseas (in the United Kingdom). Correspondingly, the US dollar is *undervalued*.

We can think of the APPP FX rate as a measure of the intrinsic value of the FX rate. An overvalued currency is one whose actual FX price is higher than its APPP FX value. In the preceding example, the time-1 FX price of the pound is 2 $/£ while the APPP FX value of the pound is 1.60 $/£. Thus the pound is overvalued at time 1. Similarly, the time-1 FX price of the US dollar is 0.50 £/$ while the APPP FX value of the US dollar is 0.625 £/$; the US dollar is undervalued at time 1.[1]

The terms *strong* and *weak* are frequently applied inconsistently in FX. Sometimes "strong" is intended to be synonymous with "overvalued" (and "weak" means undervalued); other times, "strong" is used to describe a currency that is appreciating or has appreciated. Confusion may occur if a currency that is undervalued is appreciating (correcting); the currency would be weak in the first sense, but simultaneously strong in the second sense.

THE BIG MAC INDEX

A popular yardstick of FX valuation in terms of purchasing power is the *Economist's* Big Mac Index. This is an index based upon Big Mac prices around the globe that tries to reflect the degree of current FX misvaluation. The *Economist* traditionally published its Big Mac Index annually in April. Now, the Web site http://www.oanda.com/products/bigmac/bigmac.shtml has a current version. Exhibit 2.1 shows values according to FX rates for October 10, 2003.

The first column in Exhibit 2.1 shows local currency prices of a Big Mac; the second converts the local prices into US dollars using the actual FX rates shown in the third column. The average price of a Big Mac in the US is $2.65. The cheapest Big Mac among the countries in Exhibit 2.1 is in China ($1.20); at the other extreme the most expensive is $4.66 in Switzerland. This is another way of saying that the Chinese yuan is the most undervalued currency (by 54.7%), and the Swiss franc the most overvalued (by 76.2%).

The last column shows Big Mac APPP FX rates. For instance, dividing the Japanese price by the American one gives an APPP FX rate of 99.40 ¥/$. The actual FX rate was 111.20 ¥/$, representing a higher FX price of the US dollar, and implying that the US dollar

---

[1]An interesting study of violations of the law of one price for some internationally distributed retail goods (of the IKEA Company) is in J. Haskel and H. Wolf, "The Law of One Price: A Case Study," *Scandinavian Journal of Economics*, December 2001.

EXHIBIT 2.1 The Hamburger Standard: Based on January 15, 2003, Big Mac prices and October 10, 2003, FX Rates

| Country | BIG MAC PRICE | | Actual FX Rate: 1 USD = | Over(+)/Under(−) Valuation against US Dollar (%) | Purchasing Power Price |
	Local Currency	US Dollars			
United States	2.65	2.65	1.00		
Argentina	Peso 3.85	1.33	2.91	−50.1	1.45
Australia	A$3.20	2.23	1.43	−20.4	1.14
Brazil	Real 4.50	1.58	2.85	−40.4	1.70
Britain	£1.99	3.33	1.68*	25.7	0.75
Canada	C$3.20	2.40	1.33	−9.3	1.21
China	Yuan 9.95	1.20	8.29	−54.7	3.75
Euro area	2.75	3.15	0.874	17.9	1.03
Hong Kong	HK$11.25	1.45	7.77	−45.4	4.24
Hungary	Forint 492	2.15	228.94	−18.8	186
Indonesia	Rupiah 16,155	1.89	8529.9	−28.5	6096
Japan	¥263	2.37	111.2	−10.6	99.4
Malaysia	M$5.10	1.34	3.80	−49.5	1.92
Mexico	Peso 22.0	2.00	11.01	−24.6	8.30
New Zealand	NZ$3.95	2.40	1.65	−9.5	1.49
Poland	Zloty 6.30	1.56	4.05	−41.2	2.38
Russia	Rouble 40.00	1.34	29.89	−49.5	15.09
Singapore	s$3.30	1.89	1.75	−28.9	1.24
South Africa	Rand 14.05	2.02	6.96	−23.8	5.30
South Korea	Won 3211	2.71	1187.0	2.0	1211
Sweden	Skr 30.0	3.79	7.92	42.0	11.32
Switzerland	Sfr 6.35	4.66	1.36	76.2	2.40
Taiwan	NT$70.55	2.07	34.09	−21.9	26.62
Thailand	Baht 55.0	1.38	39.94	−48.0	20.75

*US dollars per pound.

Source: The Economist

is overvalued, and the yen is undervalued against the US dollar (by 10.6%), using Big Mac prices as a standard of intrinsic FX value.

Burgers are a flawed measure of APPP value, however, because local prices may be distorted by trade barriers on beef, sales taxes, or big differences in the cost of nontraded inputs such as rents. These reasons could imply that Big Mac APPP FX rates may not be a reliable guide to future FX movements. Yet several academic studies have concluded that the Big Mac index is surprisingly accurate in tracking gradual FX changes over the longer term. Thus, the Big Mac Index may at least give a rough idea of FX intrinsic value relative to goods prices.

Recently, the *Economist* introduced a Starbuck's Latte Index. Since the relative prices of coffee and Big Macs are not the same from country to country, the degree of FX misvaluation differs depending on which good one uses as representative of purchasing power.

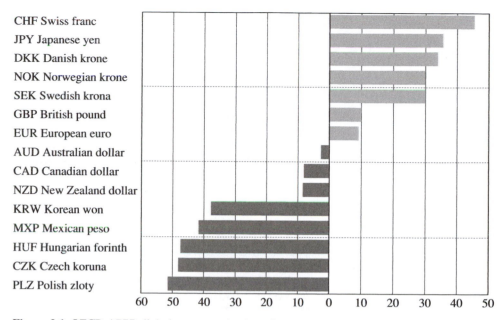

Figure 2.1 OECD APPP: light bars, overvaluation of currency relative to the US dollar; dark bars, undervaluation of currency relative to the US dollar.

(*Source*: OECD, Pacific FX Service, November 11, 2003.)

OECD AND APPP

The *Organization for Economic Cooperation and Development (OECD)* also publishes information on FX valuation by APPP for OECD countries, based on countries' gross domestic product (GDP). The OECD is an international organization that fosters economic development. There are 30 member countries having active relationships with 70 others. The organization is best known for publications and statistics, including individual country surveys and reviews. The OECD promotes rules of the game in areas where multilateral agreement is necessary for individual countries to make progress in a global economy.

Figure 2.1 shows the undervaluation and overvaluation of some currencies (relative to the US dollar) using the OECD approach to APPP. This chart was found on the Web page http://fx.sauder.ubc.ca/PPP.html. This Web page also has an excellent discussion of PPP.

Figure 2.2 uses historical OECD data to compare graphically actual FX rates for the pound and the yen and the corresponding APPP FX rates. One can see how the actual FX rate fluctuates around the APPP FX rate. We can think of the actual FX rates as fluctuating around a measure of intrinsic FX value.

The data for Figure 2.2 were obtained from the OECD Web site, http://www.oecd.org/department/0,2688,en_2649_34357_1_1_1_1_1,00.html.

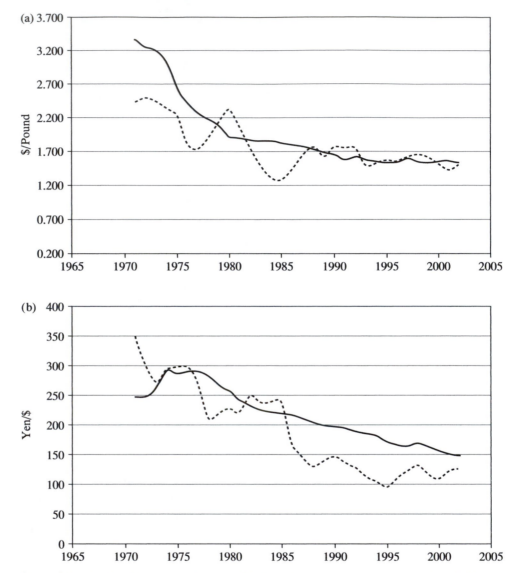

Figure 2.2 PPP of GDP and Annual average FX Rates—for the national currencies of (a) the United Kingdom and (b) Japan: dark curves, average FX rates of the pound (yen); light curves, PPP FX rates.

FX MISVALUATION AND TRADE IMBALANCES

Other things equal, a nation whose currency is overvalued will have high demand for foreign goods and its own goods will be in low demand, implying that a country with an overvalued currency will tend to import more goods than it exports. By definition, a country that imports more than it exports (measured in a currency, i.e., billions of dollars) over a period of time has a *trade deficit*. The opposite of a trade deficit is a *trade surplus*, which is an excess of the monetary value of exported goods over imported goods over a period of time. Trade imbalances can occur for a number of other reasons too, including trade barriers, but FX misvaluations have an impact.

In the situation depicted in Figure 2.3, the actual FX rate is 2.00 $/£ (= 0.50 £/$) but the APPP FX rate is 1.60 $/£ (= 0.625 £/$). Thus the pound is overvalued and the US dollar is undervalued. The UK trade deficit that results is shown by larger imports than exports. The US trade surplus is shown by larger exports than imports.

The high relative demand for products from the country of the undervalued currency (the United States in Figure 2.3), and for that country's currency to buy the products (the US dollar), will tend to result both in higher goods prices in that country and, more immediately, in an appreciation of that country's currency. Of course, the overvalued currency depreciates, and the demand for the country's products is relatively lower, as long as its currency remains overvalued. Thus there is a built-in tendency for FX misvaluations to self-correct.

But how long does this adjustment process take in the real world, where other factors affect FX rates and goods prices all the time? Studies have shown that the adjustment

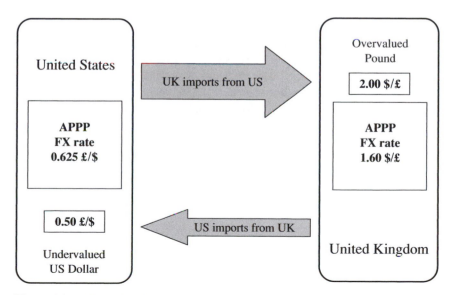

Figure 2.3 APPP and trade flow.

process of FX misvaluations toward APPP is gradual, since so many other factors affect FX rates. As long as the misvaluation between an FX rate and goods prices persists, other things the same, there will be a tendency for the overvalued currency to continue to depreciate and the undervalued currency to continue to appreciate. Some governments try to keep their currency weak as a way to run trade surpluses. This is the strategy that China has followed recently relative to the United States.

Note that a country with a strong economy, with high productivity and growth, may experience a trade deficit as a natural consequence. How? Because of the bright economic scenario, foreign capital is likely to be invested, driving up the spot FX price of the domestic currency. As this happens while goods prices are sticky, the domestic currency becomes overvalued in purchasing power terms. Then a trade deficit may result from the overvalued currency. In this case, the trade deficit does not seem like such a bad thing; it is a natural consequence of an economy experiencing (and expecting) strong productivity and growth.

But a trade deficit does *not* necessarily reflect a strong economy. In the 1990s the Thai baht was overvalued (at least in comparison to Thailand's main Asian trading partners), Thailand had a trade deficit, and the prospects for the economy were illusory. The baht had been supported and stabilized by the Thai central bank for the specific purpose of attracting foreign investment. But the hoped-for economic results of the investment never materialized. As foreign investors began to realize the situation and disinvested, and as the Thai central bank (and other Southeast Asian central bank allies helping Thailand defend the baht, like Malaysia and Indonesia) began to run out of FX reserves, the baht collapsed, starting the Asian currency crisis.

While cases like Thailand's are significant, concern over trade imbalances (deficits and surpluses) has diminished in recent years. One reason is that international business is no longer based on *mercantilism*, where countries vie to win over others in international trade. Instead, in the integrated global economy, countries' economies are interdependent. Trade may become imbalanced at times in this interdependent environment, but this seems to be only part of the natural development of the global economy. Another reason that concern over trade imbalances has subsided somewhat is the global use of hard currencies. For example, US dollars sent to countries outside the United States for imports are not always returned for gold or official FX reserves. Instead, US dollars serve more or less as an international currency. If US officials were to try to create a depreciation of the US dollar to correct a trade deficit, confidence in the US dollar as international currency would drop. Thus, the mercantile view that an undervalued currency stimulates a country's export business may not be relevant in the modern global economy.[2]

---

[2]Several views on the trade deficit are in M. Pakko, "The US Trade Deficit and the 'New Economy'," *Review of the Federal Reserve Bank of St. Louis*, September/October 1999, pp. 11–19, at http://research.stlouisfed.org/publications/review/99/09/9909mp.pdf, and Kenichi Ohmae, "Lies, Damned Lies, and Statistics: Why the Trade Deficit Doesn't Matter in a Borderless World," *Journal of Applied Corporate Finance*, Winter 1991, 98–106.

FEBRUARY 2004

The euro rose by 50% against the US dollar since its low in July 2001. Since January 2002 the euro rose against the greenback by roughly twice as much as the yen, sterling or the Canadian dollar. When the US dollar first started to drop, America's economy was weak, but in February 2004, it was growing far faster than the economies of the euro area and Japan. So why was the US dollar still dropping? Given that stronger growth in America than elsewhere could cause the high US trade deficit to swell still more, a fall in the US dollar is both inevitable and necessary to reduce the deficit by making imports dearer and exports cheaper.

In the past, the US supported a strong dollar, yet today is thriving on a weaker dollar. The lower FX price is boosting exports and profits. As yet, the weaker dollar has not pushed up import prices. Foreign exporters tend to fix their prices in dollars, and have held prices down. Instead, they have trimmed their profit margins. One bizarre result is that some German cars are now almost 30% cheaper in America than they are in Europe. But there is a limit to how much firms can squeeze profits; eventually a falling dollar will push up prices, reducing imports.

The current "strength" of the euro is often exaggerated. As recently as 1995 the currency (as calculated from a basket of the national currencies that preceded it) was trading much higher, at the equivalent of $1.37. The euro's trade-weighted value today is roughly the same as it was at its launch five years ago. In 2002 the European Central Bank (ECB) examined 16 different studies into the fair value of the euro. Most said it lay in the range $1.10–1.20. Surveys suggest that European firms are not yet panicking about the strength of the euro. But one survey found that 90% of larger German manufacturers would have problems exporting at an FX rate above $1.30.

Japan has been intervening in the FX market on an unprecedented scale. Japanese efforts to hold down the yen are annoying European policymakers because it will then require an even bigger rise in the euro to reduce America's current-account deficit. A year ago, when Japan's deflationary economy was still flat, there was a strong case for intervention to hold down the yen. Now Japan's GDP growth is up, the unemployment rate is down, export volume is up, and deflation has eased. A strong yen may be less likely to derail Japan's recovery today than it was in the past because firms' output and profits have become less sensitive to FX swings. So why is the Japanese government intervening on such a vast scale? One reason may be concern about the possible impact on equities if the yen were to dip below a supposed psychological threshold of YEN100. A relapse in the stock market would erode the capital of Japan's shaky banks.

Japan is not the only one trying to resist market forces. The Chinese yuan, the Malaysian ringgit and the Hong Kong dollar are all pegged to the greenback. Other Asian currencies officially float, but their central banks have also been intervening

(continued)

heavily to hold them down. The total reserves of the big four—China, Japan, South Korea and Taiwan—have more than doubled over the past three years, most of it held in American government securities. It is hard to judge the correct value for the Chinese yuan, but there are signs that it is undervalued. One is China's rapidly rising reserves; another is its large surplus on its "basic balance"—the sum of its current-account surplus and the net inflows of long-term capital, such as foreign direct investment. In a free market the yuan would surely rise, helping to spread the burden of the dollar's adjustment. But the Chinese government's priority is to create new jobs as unprofitable state firms are closed down. For that it needs to maintain the currency's competitiveness. Furthermore, until China's shaky banks are shored up, it would be foolhardy to let its currency float. So long as the yuan remains more or less pegged to the dollar, other Asian economies will resist appreciation too.

Most economists expect the US dollar to fall further. Taking the average forecast of seven American and European banks, the euro is expected to trade at $1.32 in 12 months' time, and the dollar to be at YEN101. But it would still not have fallen by enough to make a significant dent in America's current-account deficit. The dollar is still far from cheap: in real trade-weighted terms it remains close to its 30-year average. If the deficit is to shrink, then America's domestic demand has to grow more slowly than that of its trade partners, or the dollar needs to fall further, or a combination of the two. Many economists agree that, even if the American government were to trim its budget deficit (and thus dampen growth in domestic demand), the dollar would need to fall by another 20% in trade-weighted terms in order to achieve a sufficient reduction in America's current-account deficit. To put that figure into context, the dollar fell by over 50% against the D-mark between 1985 and 1987, when America's current-account deficit was smaller. This time the dollar has fallen from its high by just over 30% against the euro.

The problem facing the dollar, therefore, is not that it is too weak, but that it remains too strong. In propping it up, the policies of Asian governments are delaying the necessary adjustment of global imbalances. America is being encouraged to remain profligate for longer. Unlike private investors, Asian central banks care little about the financial return on their US dollar reserves. Their sole concern is to keep their exchange rate stable in order to bolster domestic economic growth.

Source: *The Economist*, February 5, 2004.

RELATIVE PURCHASING POWER PARITY (RPPP)

There is an extension of APPP that has to do with FX movements over time. This dynamic version of purchasing power parity theory relates FX changes to relative inflation rates, where inflation refers to the percentage change in goods prices, is known as the *relative purchasing power parity (RPPP) condition.*

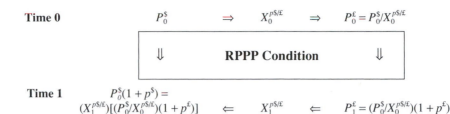

Figure 2.4 Logic flow of the RPPP condition.

Let us continue the US–UK wheat example to explain. Denote the inflation rates in the two countries as $p^\$$ and $p^\pounds$, respectively. If the bushel prices of wheat at time 0 are $P_0^\$$ and $P_0^\pounds$, then new bushel prices of wheat at time 1 are $P_1^\$ = P_0^\$(1 + p^\$)$ and $P_0^\pounds = P_0^\pounds(1 + p^\pounds)$, respectively. It may help to think of the inflation rates as pertaining to a unit of time, say, one year. For example, assume bushel prices at time 0 of $P_0^\$ = \$2.00$ in the United States and $P_0^\pounds = \pounds1.00$ in the United Kingdom, and that the inflation rate in the United States is 6% and in the United Kingdom 3%. Then the new US price of wheat in a year is $\$2.00(1.06) = \$2.12$, and the UK price is $\pounds1.00(1.03) = \pounds1.03$.

The APPP condition says that the spot FX rate at time 0 should be $X_0^{p\$/\pounds} = \$2.00/\pounds1.00 = 2.00$ \$/£, and that the new spot FX rate at time 1 should be $X_1^{p\$/\pounds} = \$2.12/\pounds1.03 = 2.058$ \$/£. Despite the appreciation of the pound (and the depreciation of the US dollar), the pound and the US dollar are correctly valued in terms of wheat prices at both the beginning and ending times. That is, if the APPP condition holds at both times, there is no FX misvaluation in purchasing power terms, despite the change in the nominal FX price of the currencies.

Relative Purchasing Power Parity (RPPP) Condition
FX Rate Form

$$X_1^{p\$/\pounds} = X_0^{p\$/\pounds}\left(\frac{1 + p^\$}{1 + p^\pounds}\right)$$

(2.2a)

To grasp the logic behind equation (2.2a), think in terms of a box with US dollars on the left and pounds on the right, and with time 0 on the top and time 1 on the bottom, as in Figure 2.4. Start at the top left with an amount of US dollars at time 0 that will purchase a bushel, $P_0^\$$. If the APPP FX rate holds at time 0, you can convert this amount into the amount of pounds that will purchase a bushel on the right, $P_0^\pounds = P_0^\$/X_0^{p\$/\pounds}$. Moving down and thus going forward in time, it will take $P_1^\pounds = (P_0^\$/X_0^{p\$/\pounds})(1 + p^\pounds)$ to purchase a bushel in the United Kingdom at time 1. Move back to the left at time 1, converting to US dollars at the time-1 APPP FX rate to get $[(P_0^\$/X_0^{p\$/\pounds})(1 + p^\pounds)](X_1^{p\$/\pounds})$, which must be equal to the time-1 cost of a bushel in the United States, $P_0^\$(1 + p^\$)$. This leads to the FX rate form of the RPPP condition in equation (2.2a).[3]

---

[3]In algebraic terms, after the year has elapsed, the new *spot* FX rate, given that APPP also holds *after* the goods price changes, should be $X_1^{p\$/\pounds} = [P_0^\$(1 + p^\$)]/[P_0^\pounds(1 + p^\pounds)]$. Substitute from equation (2.1) the original FX rate of $X_0^{p\$/\pounds} = P_0^\$/P_0^\pounds$, and we see that the new (time-1) spot FX rate should be $X_0^{p\$/\pounds}[(1 + p^\$)/(1 + p^\pounds)]$. Equation (2.2a) follows.

We can also express the RPPP condition in an equivalent (and popular) percentage form. We compute the percentage change in the FX price of the denominator currency. For example, if the spot FX price of the pound at time 0 is $X_0^{\$/£} = 1.60$ \$/£ and appreciates to 2.00 \$/£, then the percentage change in the spot FX price of the pound is $(2.00$ \$/£ $- 1.60$ \$/£$)/(1.60$ \$/£$) = 0.25$, or 25%. In general, the percentage change in the spot FX price of the pound over the period from time 0 to time N is $(X_N^{\$/£} - X_0^{\$/£})/X_0^{\$/£}$, or $X_N^{\$/£}/X_0^{\$/£} - 1$, and will be denoted $x_N^{\$/£}$. (We will often use lowercase letters to denote percentage variables.)

For now, we add a subscript p to indicate that we are dealing with PPP values. Thus, $x_1^{p\$/£}$ denotes the RPPP percentage change in the FX rate. That is $x_1^{p\$/£} = X_1^{p\$/£}/X_0^{p\$/£} - 1$. Thus an alternative expression of the RPPP condition is in equation (2.2b):

Relative Purchasing Power Parity (RPPP) Condition
Percentage Form

$$1 + x_1^{p\$/£} = \frac{1 + p^\$}{1 + p^£} \tag{2.2b}$$

As seen in the RPPP equation (2.2b), the percentage change in an FX rate is based on the inflation rate differential. To apply equations (2.2a) and (2.2b), assume that the spot \$/€ FX rate at time 0 is 1.15 \$/€ and that the APPP condition holds. Assume that over the next year, the inflation rate in Europe is 5% and in the United States 3%. Using equation (2.2a), the time-1 spot FX rate, according to the RPPP condition, should be $(1.15$ \$/€$)(1.03/1.05) = 1.128$ \$/€. Using equation (2.2b), the percentage change in the \$/€ FX rate, if the RPPP condition holds, should be $x_1^{p\$/€} = 1.03/1.05 - 1 = -0.019$, or -1.9%. That is, the spot FX value of the euro should drop by 1.9%. As a consistency check, we verify the new FX rate found using equation (2.2a) with the percentage FX change found using equation (2.2b): $(1.15$ \$/€$)(1 + x_1^{p\$/€}) = (1.15$ \$/€$)(1 - 0.019) = 1.128$ \$/€.

In this scenario, the euro depreciates from 1.15 \$/€, to 1.128 \$/€, offsetting the higher inflation in Europe. The only way for the APPP condition to hold after the higher goods price increase in Europe is for the US dollar to buy more euros, so the US dollar appreciates and the euro depreciates.

Of course, the RPPP conditions may be expressed in European terms: $X_1^{p£/\$} = X_0^{p£/\$}[(1 + p^£)/(1 + p^\$)]$ and $1 + x_1^{p£/\$} = (1 + p^£)/(1 + p^\$)$.

Remember to put the inflation rate of the numerator currency of the FX expression in the numerator when using equations (2.2a) and (2.2b).

Assume that today's spot FX rate for the Swiss franc is 1.60 Sf/\$. What will be the spot FX rate a year from now, and what will be the percentage change in the FX value of the US dollar, after 5% inflation in Switzerland and 10% inflation in the United States, assuming that the RPPP condition holds?

Answer: Using equation (2.2a), the time-1 FX rate should be (1.60 Sf/\$)(1.05/1.10) = 1.527 Sf/\$. The percentage change in the FX value of the US dollar is found using equation (2.2b): $1 + x_1^{pSf/\$}$ = (1.05/1.10) = 0.9545. Thus $x_1^{pSf/\$}$ = −0.0455.

The RPPP condition is a simple theory of how FX rates *should* move in a system of market-determined FX rates and goods prices, assuming that the APPP condition is valid. Given that the APPP condition does not fit actual real-world spot FX rates, it should not be surprising that researchers reject the RPPP condition as a description of actual short-term FX changes. To see why this can happen, consider a hypothetical two-period example.

Let us say that at time 0, the APPP condition holds and the actual spot FX rate is equal to the APPP FX rate, 1.15 $/€. Assume that over period 1, the inflation rate in Europe is 5% and in the United States 3%. From equation (2.2a), the time-1 spot FX rate, according to the RPPP condition, should be (1.15 $/€)(1.03/1.05) = 1.128 $/€.

Let us say that in period 1 foreign investment into Euroland drives up the spot FX price of the euro, and the spot FX rate moves from 1.15 $/€ to 1.25 $/€. We see that the euro appreciates in period 1 when the RPPP theory says it should depreciate. Thus research with FX data and inflation rate differentials will reject the RPPP theory in period 1, because a force other than goods price change caused the actual spot FX rate change. At time 1, the euro is overvalued and the US dollar is undervalued.

In period 2, we may observe the built-in correction tendency for the overvalued euro to drop in FX price, and for goods prices in the United States to rise in response to the overseas demand created by the undervalued US dollar. Say that in period 2 the inflation rate in the United States is 5% and in Europe is 3%. Thus data from period 2 will show the exact *opposite* situation from that predicted in the RPPP condition: the country with the rise in goods prices (United States) will have the currency that *appreciates* as the demand for the US dollar corrects its undervaluation. So data from period 2 will also reject the RPPP condition. Figure 2.5 shows the dynamics of the example graphically.

In the *theory* of purchasing power parity, FX rates are supposed to adjust immediately to changes in goods prices and vice versa, enforcing the APPP and RPPP conditions. In a country where inflation is high (and thus goods prices are not sticky), and the FX rate is not controlled by the government, the RPPP condition is often a reasonably good description of reality, because the main factor affecting FX rates is inflation. A visit to the http://www.fx4casts.com Web site is instructive. The Web site relates to a service that sells FX forecasts. Of course, one cannot obtain up-to-date forecasts free of charge, but the demos are interesting. Exhibit 2.2 shows inflation rate forecasts.

In other cases, however, there are other factors (especially asset markets) that affect FX rates and goods prices are also sticky. Thus, FX rates often become misvalued in terms of goods prices, and neither APPP nor RPPP is an accurate descriptor of the behavior of *actual* FX rates, especially in the short run, because too many other factors affect FX rates.

Nevertheless, the two PPP conditions depict important factors of correct FX value and are thus useful in FX forecasting. The APPP condition is useful because a deviation from APPP may be forecasted to gradually correct itself. The RPPP condition is useful because inflation rates are somewhat forecastable. Many other factors affect FX rates, but the two PPP conditions are fundamentally important.

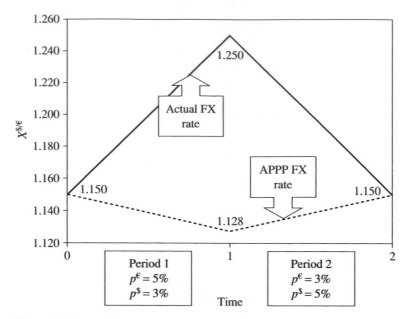

Figure 2.5 Actual FX Rates and PPP FX Rates.

The top line shows the actual spot FX movement. The actual spot FX price of the euro appreciates from 1.15 \$/€ to 1.25 \$/€ during period 1 as a result of US investments into Euroland. The actual spot FX price of the euro depreciates from 1.25 \$/€ to 1.15 \$/€ during period 2 owing to the correction of the FX misevaluation at time 1.

The bottom line shows the RPPP movement, where the spot APPP FX value of the euro depreciates from 1.15 \$/€ to 1.128 \$/€ during period 1, when inflation in Euroland is 5% and in the United States is 3%. The spot APPP FX value of the euro appreciates from 1.128 \$/€ to 1.15 \$/€ during period 2, when inflation in Euroland is 3% and in the United States is 5%.

EXHIBIT 2.2   Inflation Forecasts

Region	ACTUAL			FORECASTS		
	1999	2000	2001	2002	2003	2004
Europe						
Austria	0.5	2.4	2.7	1.8	1.5	1.4
Belgium	1.1	2.7	2.5	1.5	1.5	1.6
Czech Republic	2.1	3.9	4.8	1.8	1.4	3.1
Denmark	2.4	2.9	2.3	2.4	1.8	1.8
Eurozone	1.1	2.1	2.4	2.3	2	1.3
Finland	1.2	3	2.6	1.5	1.7	1.6
France	0.6	1.7	1.6	2	1.9	1.4
Germany	0.5	1.3	2	1.3	1	0.5
Greece	1.9	2.9	3.4	3.6	3.5	3.2
Hungary	10	9.8	9.2	5.3	4.9	4.6
Ireland	1.6	5.6	4.9	4.6	4.4	3.7

EXHIBIT 2.2 *(continued)*

Region	ACTUAL			FORECASTS		
	1999	2000	2001	2002	2003	2004
Italy	1.6	2.5	2.8	2.5	2.5	1.9
Netherlands	2.2	2.4	4.2	3.3	2.9	1.9
Norway	2.3	3.1	3	1.3	2.1	1.6
Poland	7.3	10.1	5.5	1.9	1.4	2.5
Portugal	2.3	2.9	4.4	3.6	3.3	2.6
Romania	45.8	45.7	34.5	22.3	10.5	9.8
Russia	36.4	20.2	18.6	15.1	14.8	12.8
Spain	2.3	3.4	3.6	3.1	3.2	2.4
Sweden	0.3	1.3	2.6	2.4	2.3	1.5
Switzerland	0.8	1.6	1	0.7	0.6	0.5
Turkey	65	55	54	45	28.5	20.1
United Kingdom	2.3	2.1	2.1	2.2	2.6	2.2
Asia						
Australia	1.5	4.5	4.4	3	3	2.4
China	−1.4	0.4	0.7	−0.8	0.5	1
Hong Kong	−4	−3.7	−1.6	−3	−2.5	−1.1
India	3.4	3.8	4.3	4	4.6	5.5
Indonesia	20.5	3.7	11.5	11.9	8.7	7
Japan	−0.3	−0.7	−0.7	−0.9	−0.5	−0.4
Malaysia	2.7	1.5	1.4	1.8	1.5	1.5
New Zealand	−0.1	2.6	2.6	2.7	2.2	2
Philippines	6.6	4.4	6.1	3.1	3.3	4
Singapore	0	1.3	1	−0.4	0.4	0.9
South Korea	0.8	2.3	4.1	2.7	3.2	2.9
Taiwan	0.2	1.3	0	−0.2	−0.1	0.3
Thailand	0.3	1.6	1.6	0.7	1.3	1.4
Americas						
Argentina	−1.8	−0.7	−1.5	26	17.8	9.1
Brazil	8.9	6	7.7	12.5	12.8	7.7
Canada	1.7	2.7	2.5	2.2	2.6	2
Chile	2.3	4.5	2.6	2.8	3.1	2.9
Colombia	9.2	8.7	7.6	7	6.9	6.1
Ecuador	61	91	37	12.5	8.7	6.8
Mexico	12.3	9	4.4	5.7	4.8	3.6
Peru	3.7	3.7	−0.1	1.5	2.2	2.5
United States	2.2	3.4	2.8	1.6	2	1.6
Venezuela	20	13.4	12.3	31.2	41.2	32.1
Other						
Egypt	3.1	2.8	2.3	2.4	2.3	2.5
Israel	5.2	6.5	−1.1	6.9	2.1	4.1
South Africa	5	5.3	4.9	10.1	7.9	5.1

Source: http://www.fx4casts.com/inflation-forecasts.html.

GOLD AND FX RATES

The gold standard for the exchange of currencies began before there were any national currencies, when trade was conducted by barter. The first widely accepted medium of exchange was gold, and merchants began to judge the value of all other commodities in terms of ounces of gold.

At some point, the volume of business transactions outgrew the supply of gold available to serve as a medium of exchange. To solve this problem, those holding large quantities of gold became bankers, printing and circulating paper notes redeemable for gold. The gold notes became a convenient medium of exchange, and when gold was lent to borrowers in the form of paper notes, more in gold notes were in circulation than was represented physically by the gold on hand in banks, "in reserve." Thus, quite a large volume of business transactions could be supported as if there were more gold on hand. The system worked, provided participants had confidence in banks to deliver gold against the notes on demand, and provided not everyone tried to take physical delivery of gold at once.

Eventually, as paper money became nationalized, each country established a central bank to control its paper money supply. The system of paper notes expanded to checks and eventually to electronic balances, on the same principle as the gold reserve system: the physical supply of national paper money could be much lower than the amount circulated in the form of checks and electronic transfers. A bank, as part of a national financial system, is required to hold paper currency reserves and to provide paper money for deposit balances on demand, but the system is based on the notion that all depositors do not need to hold the physical paper money at the same time.

Although it is now impractical, for some time banks were required to redeem paper money for gold on demand. Banks borrowed paper money from the central bank based upon gold deposits. Under this gold standard system, the price at which a central bank would buy or sell gold to banks for paper money was a federal decision. In other words, a free market did not determine the price.

Countries' central banks maintained set prices for gold in their national currencies, and this practice generally dictated FX rates. For example, the United States might set a rate of $20 per ounce of gold, and the British a rate of £4 per ounce. As long as the two nations maintained these set prices for the redemption of gold, the spot FX rate between the national paper currencies (and thus deposit balances) was determined as 5 $/£.

Problems with the gold standard began in the chaotic time of the world wars and the Great Depression. National governments often devalued their currencies relative to gold trying to gain advantage over other countries. For example, the British government might decide to value an ounce of gold at £5 per ounce instead of £4 per ounce. If the United States maintained a gold price of $20 per ounce, the FX price of the pound devalued to 4 $/£. After the devaluation, Britons holding pound balances now would find US products more expensive and would thus buy more at home. By the same token, Americans would find British products less expensive and would tend to import more from Britain. The British might want this result for two reasons: (1) the trade surplus added gold to the British national treasury, and (2) more jobs would be created in their country by the increase in overseas demand for the relatively inexpensive British products.

But the downside was that because people did not want to hold a currency if they thought it might be devalued, they tended to redeem for gold at that country's banks. Central banks of other countries would hold less of the currency as official reserves if there were some suspicion that a foreign central bank would close its gold window or devalue its currency by raising the official price for gold in terms of its own currency.

Eventually, the United States eliminated the national gold standard when it discontinued the redeemability of paper notes for gold. For a while, the United States continued to maintain a fixed dollar price for gold for the settlement of international accounts and for purchase of gold from US citizens. This system, termed the *modified gold standard*, ended in the early 1970s when inflationary pressures forced the United States to quit backing the US dollar with gold, and the price of gold was allowed to find its free market value. Since the end of the gold standard, the world has relied on *fiat money*, so called because it is created by government fiat and backed only by the promises of central bankers to protect its value.

Gold has continued to be a means of settling international trade accounts between countries. If the United Kingdom has a balance of payments surplus with the United States, the Bank of England can then either hold the US dollars as official foreign currency reserves or redeem them at the US Federal Reserve for gold (or for some of the Fed's official reserves of pounds). But many central banks have been reducing their gold reserves in recent years, since gold does not earn interest, whereas foreign currency can be held in the form of interest-bearing securities. Many countries' gold reserves are stored in the vault at the New York Federal Reserve. The use of gold for balance of payment settlement often simply involves the movement of gold bars from one country's gold cubicle to another's.

THE BRETTON WOODS SYSTEM OF PEGGED EXCHANGE RATES (1944–1973)

The Bretton Woods Agreement in 1944 established a system of *pegged FX rates* between countries. The pegged FX rates were maintained by direct intervention by central banks. The stability of the pegged FX rates, it was believed, was a means to promote the international trade that would lead to the world's economic recovery after World War II.

Problems with any pegged FX rate system arise when the FX rates become misvalued in terms of purchasing power, which occurred during the period of the Bretton Woods Agreement. Assume that the $/£ FX rate is initially pegged at a correct APPP rate of 2.00 $/£. Now the United Kingdom experiences high inflation in goods prices. Assume that the price of a bushel of wheat there increases from £1.00/bu to £1.60/bu a year later, while the price of a bushel remains at $2.00/bu in the United States. The APPP condition tells us that the new FX rate should be ($2.00/bu)/(£1.60/bu) = 1.25 $/£, but the actual FX rate is at 2.00 $/£. So the APPP condition does not hold when the price of wheat escalates in the United Kingdom while the actual FX rate stays fixed.

A wheat buyer in Britain will now have an incentive to import wheat from the United States. Given the FX rate of 2.00 $/£, £1.00 will buy a bushel in the US wheat market, compared with £1.60 to buy a bushel in Britain. In principle, goods arbitrageurs could buy wheat in the United States and sell it in the United Kingdom. US wheat buyers will tend not to import any wheat from Britain, since the $2.00 that will still buy a bushel in the United States converts only to £1.00, which will buy less than a bushel in the United Kingdom.

At the new wheat prices, unless the FX rate is allowed to change, the pound and the US dollar are misvalued relative to each other in terms of overseas purchasing power. The pound is overvalued (relative to the dollar) in terms of overseas purchasing power; correspondingly, the US dollar is undervalued (relative to the pound) in terms of overseas purchasing power. Since the actual value of the pound (2.00 $/£) is greater than what it should be (1.25 $/£), the pound is overvalued, so the US dollar is undervalued.

Assume that a country tries to peg its FX rate in terms of the US dollar at a time when the APPP condition holds. But the country experiences higher inflation than the United States. After the inflation, which currency is overvalued, and which is undervalued? Which country is likely to experience a trade deficit and which a trade surplus?

Answers: After the inflation, the foreign currency is overvalued and the US dollar is undervalued. The foreign country is likely to be a net importer of US products and to experience a trade deficit, while the US will be a net exporter and will have a trade surplus.

One can argue that with pegged FX rates there should be pressure on the goods prices to change in such a way that APPP holds. While there might be some such pressure, in fact the frictions and the complexity of international goods trade in the real world make the change very slow. Thus, trade deficits and surpluses are likely to persist for relatively long periods.

We can now understand why the Bretton Woods system of pegged FX rates collapsed in the early 1970s. If two countries are experiencing different inflation rates, but FX rates are held fixed by the pegging arrangement, the country with the higher inflation will lose export markets for its goods because its currency is overvalued. With the loss of export markets, the country's less productive industry will support fewer jobs, and the economy will suffer. Trade deficits in this case would thus signal potential problems for the nation's economy.

Under the Bretton Woods system of pegged FX rates, countries did follow dissimilar national policies on inflation, and some FX rates became misvalued as a result. Some western European countries tried social policies that created high inflation, for example, which with pegged FX rates led to overvalued currencies and trade deficits. At times, these countries had to resort to official devaluation to stimulate their economies and import jobs.

Currency devaluations were contrary to the design of the Bretton Woods system. Currency speculators compounded the problem by using a country's trade deficit figures to actually forecast an eventual devaluation. Then the speculators would sell the endangered currency before the devaluation, creating further pressure for the central bank to devalue. As long as the central bank delayed the inevitable devaluation, speculators were able to sell the currency and then profit at the expense of any central banks that bought that currency.

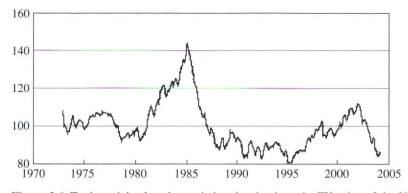

Figure 2.6 Trade-weighted exchange index showing how the FX price of the US dollar has fluctuated against an index of major currencies (March 1973 = 100).
(*Source*: http://research.stlouisfed.org/)

At Bretton Woods, the US dollar was initially pegged at an overvalued rate to both the German mark and the Japanese yen. The purpose was to afford these two countries, which had been the most devastated by World War II, help in rebuilding their economies by making their goods relatively inexpensive in overseas markets. The plan worked so well that the German and Japanese economies became quite powerful by the late 1960s. (Both countries' economic growth was further enhanced by the absence of military expenditures.) Germany and Japan followed very strict anti-inflation policies to ensure economic recovery and development, and when the United States began to experience more inflation in the 1960s, the US dollar became even more overvalued relative to the mark and the yen. The economic consequences of misvalued currencies led the participants of the Bretton Woods Agreement to dispense with the pegging system in the early 1970s and allow free market *floating FX rates*. Figure 2.6 shows how the FX price of the US dollar has fluctuated against an index of major currencies.

In the floating FX rate environment, nations with economic growth, stability, and low inflation will tend to have currencies that appreciate in value relative to countries with the opposite policies. The currencies of strong, low-inflation economies are called *hard currencies*, and the currencies of weaker, high-inflation economies are called *soft currencies*.

In addition to the pegged FX rate system, the Bretton Woods Agreement established the *International Monetary Fund (IMF)*, an organization whose primary functions were originally to oversee the stability of the FX system and to provide assistance to any member country undergoing a short-term international monetary crisis. For example, suppose currency traders at banks decided to sell their inventories of a currency back to the central bank that issued the currency, at the pegged FX rate, and in return receive large quantities of the central bank's gold or FX reserves. If the central bank were to give up too much gold or reserves, confidence in that nation's economy and in its currency would decline both inside that country and outside, possibly precipitating a national or international financial crisis. The IMF's role was to help the beleaguered central bank weather the run by lending it some funds, in the form of international currencies. The IMF was also established to provide short-term monetary assistance to countries trying to develop modern economies for the first time or to rebuild economies after wars or revolutions, including World War II.

Also established at Bretton Woods was the *World Bank*, also known as the *International Bank for Reconstruction and Development (IBRD)*. The function of the World Bank is to provide capital to countries trying to develop or rebuild their economies. Unlike the IMF, the World Bank may issue bonds, in any currency, for purposes of raising capital.[4]

THE EURO

After the collapse of the Bretton Woods system, a number of European countries tried to stabilize their FX rates relative to each other under the *European Monetary System*, starting in 1979. The goal of FX stability was intended to facilitate trade within the European Economic Community. The system involved a composite currency, called the *European Currency Unit (ECU)*, consisting of fixed amounts of 12 member currencies. FX rates were pegged relative to the ECU.

But problems and pressures occurred like those that had led to the end of the Bretton Woods system. Pegging FX rates does not work if some countries control inflation and others do not. Countries with the higher inflation want to devalue their currency when it is overvalued. This defeats the purpose of the pegged FX system.

The system experienced various currency crises. By 1992, the drive for monetary stability led to the *Maastricht Treaty*, in which a number of European nations established the European Central Bank (ECB) and agreed to use a single currency, the euro. This monetary unification was designed to overcome the problem of pegged FX rates that countries can devalue (or leave) at almost any time.

In the years just prior to the introduction of the euro, it was essential to stabilize the FX rates of the existing European currencies. The reason was that the national currencies had to be converted into the euro at a fixed FX rate. To prevent misvaluations, countries participating in the euro had to harmonize their economic policies in terms of growth, inflation, money supply, and so forth.

In 1999 the euro was launched as an electronic currency and finally, in 2002, national currencies were replaced with the euro as legal tender. Denmark, Sweden, and the United Kingdom were the only members of the European Economic Community that did not join the euro. For the members that did join the euro, the uncertainty and transaction costs of exchanging currencies with one another have been reduced, encouraging trade and economic prosperity.[5]

---

[4]For a fascinating account of the FX market and the Bretton Woods conference, especially the role played by Keynes, see Andrew Krieger, *The Money Bazaar* (New York: Times Books, 1992). Another interesting account of the Bretton Woods conference and of the evolution of global markets is in Gregory J. Millman, *The Vandal's Crown* (New York: Free Press, 1995).

[5]For further information about the evolution of the international monetary system, see Chapter 2 of Richard Levich, *International Financial Markets*, 2nd ed. (New York: McGraw-Hill Irwin, 2001).

CURRENCY BOARDS AND DOLLARIZATION

Not all FX pegging is doomed. A number of smaller countries with stable economies are able maintain FX rates that are pegged to a major hard currency. The Hong Kong dollar (HK$) is an example of a currency that has been successfully tied to the US dollar for many years.

The method used by Hong Kong is called a *currency board*. A currency board has four tenets: (1) to prohibit the central bank from printing money that is not backed by reserves of hard foreign currencies; (2) to permit the country's currency to be freely redeemed on demand for hard-currency reserves, a feature called free convertibility; (3) to peg that currency's FX value to a hard currency, often the currency of the major trading partner; and (4) to require the government to maintain responsible economic policies. As FX reserves, the board holds interest-bearing securities in the reserve currency. Estonia and Lithuania also have successful currency boards.

Argentina successfully operated a plan similar to a currency board for a while in the 1990s, but it gave way in early 2002 amidst economic crisis. Argentina had been plagued by high inflation until 1991. In one month in 1989, prices in Argentina rose by nearly 2300%. This kind of inflation caused currency depreciation and discouraged investment. With the currency board plan, inflation was under control by 1992, and Argentina's economy got on track. But the plan failed in the fourth tenet, to require the government to maintain responsible economic policies. By 2002, the inability of the country's politicians to curb government spending and reform labor laws had brought about political and economic chaos.

Dollarization is the replacement of local currency with the US dollar. It may seem like a large loss in prestige for a country to give up its own currency, but this may be acceptable when the alternative is monetary chaos. Ecuador and El Salvador, for examples, have dollarized. Dollarization is a legalization of the natural use of a hard currency as a store of value in soft-currency countries, which is quite frequent.

More information on currency boards and dollarization may be obtained at http://www.dollarization.org/.

*TRADE FINANCE

About half of world trade is carried out using borrowed money, or trade financing. In these circumstances, an exporter of sweaters may worry about shipping on credit to an importer in a different country. The importer would be equally nervous about sending payment in advance. Trade financing begins with a *letter of credit*, which is a document from a financial intermediary that guarantees payment on behalf of the importer, subject to proper delivery of the goods. Letters of credit are typically issued by banks or by institutions specializing in trade credit, *forfaiting houses* also called *forfaiters*.

---

*An asterisk preceding a section title designates material not normally covered in an undergraduate course.

Once the exporter has received the letter of credit, the merchandise-shipping document (bill of exchange) is forwarded to the forfaiter, along with an international draft from the importer for payment to be made at some time in the future, say, 90 days. The forfaiter accepts the draft by stamping it "accepted." The stamped draft is now a *banker's acceptance*, which is a negotiable instrument. The exporter may choose to hold the instrument until its maturity and collect the face value then. Alternatively, the exporter may sell the instrument at any time at a discount in the money market (to another bank, to an insurance company, or to a hedge fund). Later, the importer makes payment for the goods to the forfaiter, which then pays the face value of the acceptance to the holder in the money market. In effect, the money market has been the ultimate source of financing for the international trade. In Chapter 3, we'll say more about the international money market.

The $700 billion trade financing market had traditionally been opaque, highly fragmented, and illiquid, because unlike stock and bond markets, trade financing lacks common standards. There is no one code of market practice, so the documents (letters of credit, insurance, bills of exchange, and invoices) represent a great source of inefficiency. No deal is ever the same as its predecessor, and counterparties differ about what constitutes proper documentation. There is little in the way of historical data, and communication between forfaiters and sellers of trade finance paper is rather basic and unstructured.

A Web-based trade finance exchange, called International Trade Finance Exchange (ITF), experimented with bringing parts of the active trade finance market together at a site online where exporters could list their paper. ITF members would bid for these assets online, using a variety of analytical tools made available by ITF, including digital images of the documentation. The site is no longer active, however. Perhaps this kind of market will reemerge in the future.

SUMMARY

This chapter showed when the current spot FX rate represents a correct FX valuation (in terms of purchasing power) and when the spot FX rate is misvalued in terms of purchasing power and therefore possibly due for a correction.

FX misvaluations tend to have implications for trade imbalances. Other things equal, an overvalued currency leads to a trade deficit, and an undervalued currency leads to a trade surplus.

The chapter also discussed the theoretical relationship between inflation rates and the movement of FX values based on purchasing power. Actual FX rates often deviate from the relative purchasing power parity (RPPP) condition because other factors besides inflation are at work, but RPPP helps us think of how the inflation factor influences FX rates.

We also discussed some historical aspects of the international monetary system related to the purchasing power parity theories, including the gold standard, the Bretton Woods system of pegged exchange rates, and the European Monetary Union. We saw how different national economic policies on inflation will lead to FX misvaluations, and thus trade imbalances, in a system of pegged FX rates. This problem led to the post–Bretton Woods floating FX rate regime in the international market. The problem also helped the evolution of the euro as the one currency of many European countries.

GLOSSARY

Absolute purchasing power parity (APPP): A theory that the price of a tradable commodity in one country should be equal to the price of the same commodity in another country, after adjusting for the FX rate. Also known as the *international law of one price.*

Banker's acceptance: An international draft from an importer for payment to be made at some time in the future, guaranteed ("stamped accepted") by a forfaiter and traded in the money market.

Bretton Woods system: The agreement in effect from 1944 to 1973 in which many nations covenanted to maintain stable, or pegged, FX rates.

Comparative advantage: The economic principle of organizing international production by relative national efficiency, assuming trade is possible.

Currency board: A monetary authority that stabilizes a currency by backing it with hard-currency reserves.

Dollarization: The replacement of a national currency with the US dollar.

ECB: European Central Bank.

European currency unit (ECU): A unit of account that was used before the euro; it was a composite of 12 European currencies.

Fiat money: Currency created by government fiat and backed only by the promises of central bankers to protect its value.

Floating FX rates: FX rates determined by market forces, as opposed to the fixed, or pegged, FX rates under the Bretton Woods system.

Forfaiting house, or forfaiter: A financial institution specializing in trade financing and letters of credit, guaranteeing payment on behalf of an importer, subject to proper delivery of the goods.

International Bank for Reconstruction and Development (IBRD): See *World Bank.*

International Monetary Fund (IMF): An organization established by international agreement to help any member country undergoing a short-term international monetary crisis.

International law of one price: See *Absolute purchasing power parity.*

Letter of credit: A letter from a bank or a forfaiter, guaranteeing payment on behalf of an importer, subject to proper delivery of the goods.

Maastricht Treaty: The agreement in 1992 by a number of European nations that established the European Central Bank (ECB) and the use a single currency, the euro.

Mercantilism: A national strategy to increase wealth at the expense of another country through international trade.

Modified gold standard: A system in the United States, now discontinued, of maintaining a fixed price for buying gold, but not redeeming notes for gold.

Organization for Economic Cooperation and Development (OECD): An international organization that fosters economic development.

Overvalued currency: A currency that can purchase more abroad than at home, given the actual FX rate.

Relative purchasing power parity (RPPP): A theory concept describing how intrinsic FX values change with inflation rates.

Strong currency: An expression with two interpretations: a currency that is overvalued or a currency that has been appreciating.

Trade deficit: The amount by which the value of a country's imported goods exceeds the value of its exported goods.

Trade surplus: The amount by which the value of a country's exported goods exceeds the value of its imported goods.

Undervalued currency: A currency that can purchase more at home than abroad, given the actual FX rate.

Weak currency: An expression with two interpretations: a currency that is undervalued or a currency that has been depreciating.

World Bank: Also known as the *International Bank for Reconstruction and Development (IBRD)*. An international agency that provides capital assistance to countries that are trying to develop or rebuild their economies.

DISCUSSION QUESTIONS

1. Discuss the difference between absolute purchasing power parity (APPP) and relative purchasing power parity (RPPP).
2. Is a weak dollar good, bad, or neutral for US economy? Discuss this question in relation to the following results of a CNBC poll of November 19, 2003; 37% good, 47% bad, 16% neutral.
3. Explain how a currency that is weak in the sense that it has been depreciating could also be strong in the sense that it is overvalued.
4. Discuss the box in the text entitled February 2004.
5. Explain why the pegged FX rates of the Bretton Woods system gave way to floating rates.

PROBLEMS

1. If a bushel of wheat costs \$2 in the United States and ¥350 in Japan, what does the international law of one price (APPP condition) say that the spot FX rate should be?
2. Let the US dollar price of a unit of consumption (thought of as one Big Mac) be \$1 at time 0. What would the price of a Big Mac have to be in pounds for the time-0 spot FX rate of 1.60 \$/£ to represent a correct valuation, given the APPP condition?
3. Let the yen price of a bushel of wheat be ¥150 at time 0 and the US dollar price of a bushel of wheat be \$1 at time 0. Assume that the actual spot FX rate at time 0 is $X_0^{¥/\$} = 150$ ¥/\$. (Thus, in purchasing power terms, the spot FX rate is correctly valued relative to wheat at time 0.) Now assume that inflation is zero in both countries and that the time-1 spot FX rate is $X_1^{¥/\$} = 120$ ¥/\$. At time 1, is there (a) an overvalued yen and an undervalued US dollar, (b) an overvalued US dollar and an undervalued yen, or (c) neither?
4. Assume the same time-0 conditions as in Problem 3. The inflation rate in Japan is 5%, while the inflation rate is 10% in the United States. What would the relative RPPP condition say that the time-1 spot FX rate should be, in conventional European terms?

5. Suppose that, at time 0, the spot FX rate of 1.60 $/£ represents a correct FX valuation in APPP terms. Let the inflation rate between time 0 and time 1 be 30% in the Britain and 10% in the United States. According to the relative RPPP condition, what should be the time-1 spot FX rate?

6. Suppose that at time 0, the spot FX rate of 1.60 $/£ represents a correct valuation in APPP terms. Let the inflation rate in the United Kingdom between time 0 and time 1 be 30%, while US prices drop by 10%. If the spot FX rate goes from 1.60 $/£ to 1.40 $/£ during the same time period, (a) has the pound become overvalued relative to the US dollar, (b) has the US dollar become overvalued relative to the pound, or (c) has neither misvaluation occurred?

ANSWERS TO PROBLEMS

1. 175 ¥/$
2. £0.625
3. a
4. 143.18 ¥/$
5. 1.35 $/£
6. a

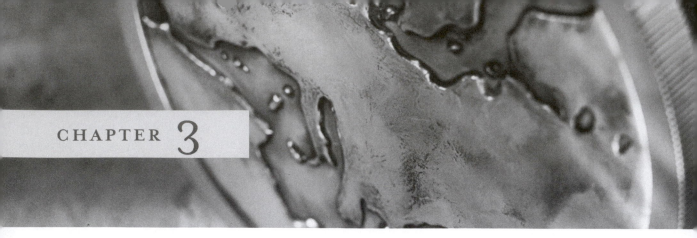

CHAPTER 3

FORWARD FOREIGN EXCHANGE

In a *forward foreign exchange contract*, two parties contract today for the future exchange of currencies at a *forward FX rate*. No funds change hands when a typical forward FX contract originates; funds are exchanged only at the contract's stated future delivery time. Participants in both the retail and interbank sectors of the FX market routinely make forward FX transactions. About 30% of forward FX transactions involve a nonfinancial customer and are typically entered to allow the entity to manage its FX risk.

Like spot FX rates, forward FX rates vary constantly with market activity. The FX market sees an array of market-determined forward FX rates for various delivery horizons, in addition to the spot FX rate. In practice, forward FX rates are quoted for standard periods; one-month, three-month, six-month, and one-year contracts are the most common. Once a forward FX contract has been made between two parties, the forward FX rate *for that contract* is set and does not change. As forward FX rates in the market change, given a contract's set forward FX rate, the contract's market value, called its *mark-to-market (MTM) value*, fluctuates. Prior to the delivery time, a forward FX contract position may be liquidated in the open market at the position's MTM value.

Many banks quote forward FX rates for standard horizons up to 10 years for actively traded currencies. While forward FX quotes of the interbank market are obtainable via Bloomberg and other online financial services, it is not that easy to find quotes on the Internet. Some forward FX quotes may be viewed at a site maintained by the Union Bank

TABLE 3.1 Forward FX Quotes: Sf/$, November 16, 2003

| Expiration | UBS | | OZFOREX | |
	Bid	Ask	Bid	Ask
Spot	1.3273	1.3278	1.32650	1.32750
1M	1.3263	1.3268	1.32550	1.32648
2M	1.3251	1.3258	1.32444	1.32542
3M	1.3241	1.3248	1.32341	1.32443
6M	1.3212	1.3222	1.32054	1.32166
9M	1.3183	1.3194		
1Y	1.3153	1.3166	1.31489	1.31611
2Y	1.2970	1.3060	1.29854	1.30146
3Y	1.2702	1.2953		
4Y	1.2445	1.2813		
5Y	1.2159	1.2669		

of Switzerland (UBS) at http://quotes.ubs.com/, then click on Forex/Banknotes. The Forwards USD link allows you to view some forward FX quotes for many currencies versus the US dollar, except for the Swiss franc. For forward FX quotes for the Swiss franc versus the US dollar, click on Forwards CHF. The Sf/$ forward FX information in the left columns in Table 3.1 was displayed at the UBS site on November 16, 2003. The bid-ask quotes in the two right-hand columns of Table 3.1 are interbank forward FX quotes observed on the same day (a Sunday) from the Ozforex site, http://www.ozforex.com.au/cgi-bin/forwardrates.asp.

The forward FX quotes in Table 3.1 for the Swiss franc versus the US dollar are expressed in conventional European terms. It may help to think of the Swiss franc as the pricing currency and the US dollar as the commodity in which a dealer is making a market. Thus the one-year (1Y) bid/ask quotes imply that UBS is willing to buy one-year US dollars at 1.3153 Sf/$ and sell one-year US dollars at 1.3166 Sf/$. These FX forward rates also represent rates at which UBS is willing to contract today to sell Swiss francs for US dollars for delivery a year from now. UBS agrees to sell one-year Swiss francs for US dollars at 1/1.3153 = 0.7603 $/Sf and to buy one-year Swiss francs with US dollars at 1/1.3166 = 0.7595 $/Sf. The midpoint spot FX rate is 1.32755 Sf/$, while the midpoint one-year forward FX rate is 1.31595 Sf/$. Figure 3.1 is a graph of the UBS forward FX quotes in Table 3.1.

Forward FX contracts are often tailor-made to meet specific user needs. For example, a retail customer wanting a 73-day forward FX contract can get one from a bank. In principle, any two parties may create an informal forward FX contract for any delivery time in the future. In the FX market, forward FX contracts for nonmajor currencies, especially for longer forward horizons, are generally less liquid than for major currencies, resulting in wider dealer bid-ask spreads, and thus higher transaction fees for retail users. Spreads in

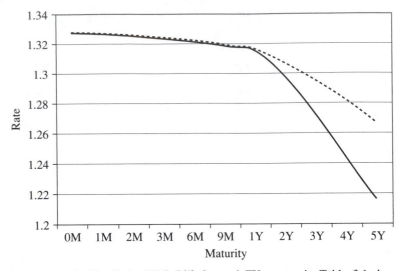

Figure 3.1 Graph of the UBS Sf/$ forward FX quotes in Table 3.1: heavy curve, bid; light curve, ask.

the interbank market are substantially lower than in the retail market. Typically, we'll assume there is sufficient liquidity in the numerical examples to ignore dealer bid-ask spreads.

The notation for a forward FX rate (using US dollars and euros as representative currencies) is $F_N^{\$/€}$, where the subscript denotes the number of years until delivery; N may be a fraction of a year, including longer than one year (e.g., $N = 3.25$ is three years, four months).

If a currency's forward FX price (not the FX rate, but the FX price of the currency) is *lower* than its current spot FX price, the currency is said to be at a *forward discount* (for that specific horizon). Similarly, if a currency's forward FX price is *higher* than its current spot FX price, the currency is said to be at a *forward premium*. Of course, for currencies that are conventionally quoted in European terms, like the Swiss franc, higher FX quotes mean lower FX prices. Thus, in the UBS quotes the US dollar is at a forward discount (relative to the Swiss franc) because the FX price of the US dollar is lower in the forward FX market than in the spot market. The Swiss franc is at a forward premium (relative to the US dollar) for all future delivery times because the FX price of the Swiss franc is higher in the forward FX market than in the spot market.

LONG AND SHORT FORWARD FX POSITIONS

When one has possession of a commodity, one is sometimes said to be *long* the commodity, or have a long position in the commodity. Moreover, as we saw in Chapter 1, one is long something that is a receivable. Similarly, if one owes, or is obligated to deliver, a commodity, one is said to be *short* that commodity.

All forward FX contracts involve two parties. If one contracts forward to buy euros with US dollars, one is said to take a *long forward position in (or on) euros*, with the implicit understanding that the forward FX contract is denominated in terms of US dollars. The other party in the forward FX agreement, with the obligation to deliver (or sell) euros, is said to take a *short forward position in (or on) euros*.

Analyzing forward FX contracts can at first be confusing, as a long position on one currency is a short position on the other currency. It is helpful to standardize the analysis of FX forward contracts by referring to the contract's *size (Z)* in units of the foreign currency (as if it were a commodity), and to the contract's *amount (A)* in units of the pricing currency. The term *size* is meant to convey the idea of a commodity's physical volume, while the term *amount* is meant to convey a monetary amount. To prevent confusion, the pricing currency of a forward FX contact in this chapter will be US dollars unless otherwise stated. Thus, in the example of a forward FX contract on euros, Z is expressed in euros, while A is expressed in US dollars.

A forward FX contract's Z and A can be converted into each other at the forward FX rate, $A^\$ = Z^{€}(F_N^{\$/€})$. If $A^\$$ is \$1000 and the forward FX rate is 1.10 \$/€, then $Z^{€} =$ \$1000/(1.10 \$/€) = €909. This example contract obligates the long euro forward position to receive €909 and pay \$1000 one year after the contract is made. At time 1, the short euro position must deliver €909 and will receive \$1000.

You take a one-year long forward position on Japanese yen at a forward FX rate of 108 ¥/\$. State the cash flow obligations of your long yen forward position, now and a year from now, if the contract amount is \$1000. What is the forward FX contract's size?

Answer: No cash flows now; a year from now, you receive ¥108,000 (the contract's size) and deliver (pay) \$1000.

You take a one-year short forward position on British pounds at a forward FX rate of 1.50 \$/£. State the cash flow obligations of your short forward position on pounds, now and a year from now, if the contract size is £150 million. What is the contract amount?

Answer: No cash flows now; a year from now, you pay £150 million and receive \$225 million (the contract's amount).

DIFFERENCE CHECK SETTLEMENT

There are two ways to settle a forward FX contract at the delivery time: (1) *gross settlement*, through physical exchange of the currencies as indicated by the contract, and (2) *net settlement*, through a *difference check*. Both types of settlement are widely used.

Consider, first, gross settlement. Assume a one-year forward FX contract on euros with $A^\$ = \$1000$ and a forward FX rate of 1.10 \$/€; thus $Z^{€} = €909$. Suppose the spot FX rate at the delivery time of the forward FX contract (a year from now) turns out to be $X_1^{\$/€}$ = 1.12 \$/€. While the short euro position has contracted to pay €909 (and receive \$1000), the spot FX rate of 1.12 \$/€ at time 1 implies that the US dollar value of the €909 would be €909(1.12 \$/€) = \$1018. Thus the €909 that the short euro position is scheduled to pay would be *equivalent* at that time to \$1018. Similarly, the long euro position is scheduled to receive euros that would be worth \$1018 and to deliver \$1000.

Consider, now, a difference check settlement. Given a time-1 spot FX rate of 1.12 \$/€, the long euro position essentially has a net gain of \$18, since the holder is scheduled to receive euros worth \$1018 and deliver \$1000. Similarly, the short euro position has a net loss of \$18, since the party is scheduled to deliver euros worth \$1018 and receive \$1000. Thus, an alternative equivalent to the physical exchange of the *amount* (\$1000) and *size* (€909) at the delivery time is a cash settlement of the net difference in value, given the spot FX rate prevailing at that time. In this case, the settlement would be \$18 [or equivalently \$18/(1.12 \$/€) = €16], from the short euro position to the long euro position. One may also say that at the delivery time, but immediately before the contract is settled, \$18 is the *mark-to-market (MTM)* value of the long euro position, while −\$18 is the MTM value of the short euro position.

If the long euro position actually wants to have the entire €909 for which it contracted, but the forward FX contract is settled via difference check, the \$1000 that would have been physically delivered can instead be combined with the received difference check of \$18 to purchase \$1018/(1.12 \$/€) = €909 in the spot FX market at the delivery time. Either way, through physical delivery, or through spot FX purchase at the delivery time (with the help of the difference check), the long position on euros ends up with €909. The key advantage of the difference check approach is that it avoids the need for both parties to actually have the full funds for the settlement.

The difference check settlement of a forward FX contract always favors the long position on a currency with a higher delivery time FX spot value than forward FX contract value. In the example, the delivery time FX price of the euro is higher at $X_1^{\$/€}$ = 1.12 \$/€ than at $F_1^{\$/€}$ = 1.10 \$/€, and we can see that the long position on euros gained at the expense of the short position on euros.

If the spot FX price of the euro at the delivery time ends up instead lower than the contracted forward FX price, the short position on euros would gain at the expense of the long position on euros. For example, if the spot FX rate were $X_1^{\$/€}$ = 1.05 \$/€ at the delivery time, the spot FX price of the euro would thus be lower than the contracted forward FX price of the euro, 1.10 \$/€. The US dollar equivalent to €909 (the short euro position's obligated delivery) is €909(1.05 \$/€) = \$955. Thus, the long euro position would lose \$45 (= \$1000 − 955), while the short position on euros would gain this amount.

Using \$ to denote the pricing currency and € as the foreign currency, the difference check (or net gain) at the delivery time, expressed in the pricing currency (\$), to the *long* position on the foreign currency (€), is denoted $D_€^{\$}$ and is calculated as follows. First, express the FX rate in *direct terms from the point of view of the pricing currency (\$)*. Next, multiply the contract *size* (in units of the foreign currency) by the difference between the spot FX rate at the delivery time and the contract's forward FX rate. That is:

$$D_€^{\$} = Z^€(X_N^{\$/€} - F_N^{\$/€}) \qquad (3.1)$$

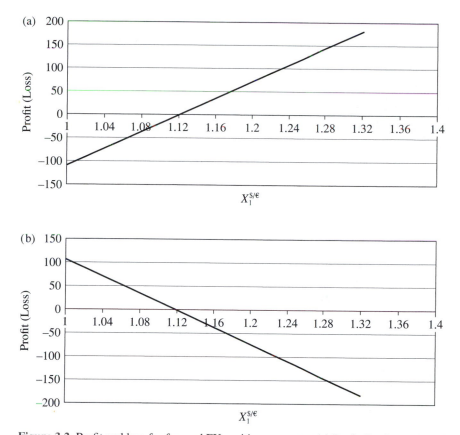

Figure 3.2 Profit and loss for forward FX positions on euros. (a) Profit (loss) on a long forward FX position on euros as a function of the delivery time (time-1) spot FX price of the euro. This is the same as the difference check settlement to the long forward FX position. (b) Profit (loss) on a short forward FX position on euros as a function of the delivery time (time-1) spot FX price of the euro. This is the same as the difference check settlement to the short forward FX position.

Using equation (3.1) in our example with $F_1^{\$/€} = 1.10$ \$/€, if $X_1^{\$/€} = 1.12$ \$/€, the long position on euros would receive $D_€^\$ = €909(1.12\ \$/€ - 1.10\ \$/€) = \$18$. In the second example, where $X_1^{\$/€} = 1.05$ \$/€, the long position on euros would receive $D_€^\$ = €909(1.05\ \$/€ - 1.10\ \$/€) = -\$45$. The negative amount indicates that the long euro position actually would send this amount to the short euro position.

The difference check may also be interpreted as the profit (loss) on the forward FX position. Figure 3.2a shows the profit (loss) on a long position as a function of the delivery time (time-1) spot FX rate. Figure 3.2b shows the profit (loss) on a short position as a function of the delivery time (time-1) spot FX rate.

Applying equation (3.1) with European terms FX quotes is a little tricky, as we demonstrate in an example.

You take a short position in a (US dollar-priced) forward FX contract on Japanese yen at a forward FX rate of $F_1^{¥/\$} = 120$ ¥/\$. Assume that the contract amount is \$1 million. If the spot FX rate for the yen at delivery time is $X_1^{¥/\$} = 100$ ¥/\$, what is your gain (loss) in US dollars on the short yen forward position?

Answer: The contract size is \$1 million (120 ¥/\$) = ¥120 million. To apply equation (3.1), the European terms quotes must be reciprocated into direct terms from the US dollar point of view. The US dollar gain for the long yen position in the forward FX contract, using equation (3.1), is ¥120 million [1/(100 ¥/\$) − 1/(120 ¥/\$)] = ¥120 million [(0.01 \$/¥) − (0.00833 \$/¥)] = \$200,000. Since the gain to the long position is \$200,000, and you took the short position, your loss is \$200,000.

It will be helpful to remember that the *super*script symbol in this text denotes the currency in which a security or contract is priced (or denominated), while the *sub*script symbol denotes the currency to which the contract is exposed. For example, in $D_{\epsilon}^{\$}$ the US dollar is the pricing currency, and the euro is the currency to which the contract is exposed.

FORWARD FX CONTRACTS AND HEDGING FX TRANSACTION EXPOSURE

While forward FX contracts can be used for speculating on the direction of FX changes, one of their important basic functions is *hedging*, or offsetting the risk in other transactions that are affected by FX rate changes.

For example, assume you manage a US company that has shipped products to Germany, and the terms call for payment in three months in the amount of €3 million. The company's receivable represents a natural long position in euros, where "natural" means that the inflow of euros is expected as part of the company's typical or usual business. Since the spot \$/€ FX rate three months from now is unknown at the present, the amount of US dollars that the euro receivable will ultimately provide is uncertain. As discussed in Chapter 1, this uncertainty is called *FX transaction exposure*.

A *short* forward FX position on euros can be used to *hedge* the FX transaction exposure of the natural *long* euro position of the receivable. For example, assume that the three-month forward FX rate is currently 1.04 \$/€. A short FX forward position on euros for a contract *size* of €3 million at the forward FX rate of 1.04 \$/€ would obligate you to deliver €3 million and receive €3 million (1.04 \$/€) = \$3.12 million in return at the delivery time. At the delivery time, you simply flow the €3 million natural receipt through to the counterparty of your forward FX contract (e.g., your bank). Your bank, in turn, gives you the \$3.12 million at that delivery time. [Banks are forward FX counterparties as a fee-based business.] Together, the receivable and the forward FX position result in a guaranteed receipt of \$3.12 million in three months' time. Figure 3.3 depicts the process of hedging the long euro FX transaction exposure with a short FX forward contract on euros.

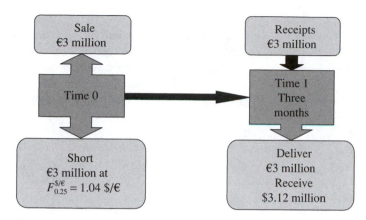

Figure 3.3 Forward FX Hedge: the process of hedging a long euro FX transaction exposure with a short FX forward position on euros.

While you do not receive the $3.12 million until three months later, at least you know now how many US dollars you'll be receiving in exchange for the €3 million you are owed. Actually, your bank may even be willing to give you the discounted value of the $3.12 million today.

The same process may be settled by means of a difference check. For example, if in three months' time the spot FX rate turns out to be 0.96 $/€, the euro receivable will be worth €3 million (0.96 $/€) = $2.88 million. Using equation (3.1), you see that a long FX euro forward position would receive a difference check of €3 million (0.96 $/€ – 1.04 $/€) = –$240,000; this negative amount implies that your short euro forward position would receive $240,000 in settlement from the long euro forward position. Combining the US dollar equivalent of the natural euro receipt, $2.88 million, with the difference check settlement on the short euro forward FX position, the net result is a receipt of $2.88 million + $240,000 = $3.12 million.

Companies may also be concerned about future payables of foreign currency owed on services already received or ordered. The higher the spot FX price of the foreign currency at the time the payment is to be made, the more base currency it will take to make the payment. This payable is a natural short position in the foreign currency. Natural short positions like this are hedged with long positions in (base-currency-priced) forward FX contracts on the foreign currency.

A US company is committed to making a natural yen payment of ¥300,000 in one year. Assume that the current one-year forward FX rate is $F_1^{¥/\$} = 120$ ¥/$. Determine from the forward FX rate the amount of US dollars that may be obtained for certain via a hedge with a forward FX contract. Demonstrate that, if the spot FX rate at the delivery time is $X_1^{¥/\$} = 100$ ¥/$, the difference check hedges the FX exposure.

Answers: At the forward FX rate of $F_1^{¥/\$} = 120$ ¥/\$, the US dollar value of the natural yen liability is ¥300,000/(120 ¥/\$) = \$2500. Thus, $A^\$$ is \$2500, while $Z^¥$ is ¥300,000. Moreover, \$2500 is the US dollar amount that can be locked in in place of an exposed future natural yen payable. If the spot FX rate is $X_1^{¥/\$} = 100$ ¥/\$ at the delivery time, the US dollar value of the yen payable will be ¥300,000/(100 ¥/\$) = \$3000. If one hedges with a \$2500 long yen position in a forward FX contract, the difference check to the long yen forward position, from equation (3.1), will be ¥300,000[1/(100 ¥/\$) − 1/(120 ¥/\$)] = \$500. The company's net US dollar payout, combining the US dollar value of the natural yen payment (\$3000 outflow) and the gain/loss on the long forward FX position (\$500 inflow), is a \$2500 net outflow.

Remember, for a natural FX *receivable* (a natural long position in the foreign currency), you hedge with a *short* forward FX position in the foreign currency. For a natural FX *payable* (a natural short position in the foreign currency), you hedge with a *long* forward FX position in the foreign currency.

TO HEDGE OR NOT TO HEDGE: PEUGEOT-CITROEN IN 2003

Many companies hedge FX exposure and many do not. When the euro appreciated unilaterally in 2003, European multinationals that did not hedge experienced lower profits in euros from foreign currency revenues. In the auto sector, most European carmakers successfully hedged their overseas revenue against a rising euro. One company that did not hedge was the French carmaker, Peugeot-Citroen. The appreciation of the euro wiped out €600 million of Peugeot's profit.

Peugeot's chief financial officer gave the reason that hedging was like gambling. Because hedging locks in a future foreign currency cash flow at a known FX rate, if the foreign currency depreciates, the hedging strategy wins in that the losses are covered, but if the foreign currency appreciates, the hedging strategy loses in that the windfall profits are foregone. In 2003, many European carmakers won and Peugeot lost. But the CFO argued that no one could predict short-term FX movements. Had the euro depreciated, Peugeot would have won and the others would have lost.

One problem with the hedging strategy is that forward FX contracts are often not well understood by the general public. Thus, if a company hedges and forgoes a windfall FX profit, the company's investors may be upset that about the use of the hedging strategy. This is exactly what happened to Peugeot's CFO in 1997; he hedged to protect Peugeot's UK sales against a decline in the FX price of the pound relative to the euro. Investors focused only on the FX losses on the forward FX hedge positions and were shocked.

The lesson learned by the CFO in 1997 was that investors tend to punish ill-advised hedges more severely than those that suffer losses due to lack of hedging. That is, investors have a psychological bias of being less concerned about losses than missing out on what might have been.

Source: Adapted from "Peugeot Won't Budge as Euro Gains Strength," *Wall Street Journal*, November 11, 2003.

Sometimes managers try to hedge FX transaction exposures when they think the FX price will change in the direction that would imply a loss, but not if they forecast an FX change in the direction that would imply a profit. This speculative practice is referred to as *selective hedging*.[1]

THE EUROCURRENCY MARKET

Not so many years ago, banks generally accepted customers' deposits denominated only in the currency of the country in which the bank was domiciled. The situation is different now. Deposit and loan services in major currencies frequently take place outside the geographic area in which a given currency is legal tender, owing to the *eurodollar* concept, which originated in the 1950s. Communist governments, needing US dollars for international trade because their own currencies were not acceptable, feared a potential freeze of their US dollar deposits held at US banks or their foreign subsidiaries. They instead asked some European banks to hold their US dollar deposits. The banks realized they could denominate any deposit in US dollars, pay interest in dollars, and then re-lend the deposited US dollars elsewhere (outside the United States) at a higher rate of interest.

Regular business customers accepted this idea. By the 1960s, it had become common for non–US banks to conduct banking services in US dollars. Because the practice originated in Europe, the term *eurodollar* was coined. Later, as US dollar deposits and loans occurred elsewhere, particularly in Asia, the term *eurodollar* persisted, along with some use of the term *Asian dollar*. In general, "eurodollar" has come to be used for any US dollar-denominated deposit or loan outside the United States.

The eurodollar concept was extended to euroyen, eurosterling, euroSwiss francs, and so forth. In general, the term *eurocurrency* applies to any currency deposit or loan outside the country of the particular currency. Currently, the *eurocurrency market* involves globally traded time deposits and time loans with interest rates in each currency determined by the global market. The term "eurocurrency market" is misleading, since the deposits and loans are neither European nor FX transactions between currencies. And the term has

---

[1]For a discussion of the issues in selective hedging and a survey of the practice in German firms, see Martin Glaum, "The Determinants of Selective Exchange Rate Risk Management— Evidence from German Non-Financial Corporations," *Journal of Applied Corporate Finance*, Winter 2002, 108–121.

become even more misleading with the introduction of the currency called the euro, which has absolutely nothing to do with eurocurrencies. Eurocurrencies are rather traded interest rate instruments, deposits and loans, for which a market is made continuously, globally, with substantial liquidity, and thoroughly integrated with the FX market. At the same time, there is a global interest rate for each currency (for a given horizon). In other words, at a given bank in any country, a borrower of yen from France would pay (more or less) the same interest rate as a borrower of yen from Korea. Eurocurrency deposits and loans are zero coupon instruments.

Suppose a company in any country wants to borrow euros for a year. If the company already has a sufficient line of credit with its bank, it makes a simple call to its banker, and the deal is almost instantaneous. The bank, practically simultaneously, can shop the inter-bank market on a video monitor. If a Japanese bank quotes the best one-year borrowing rate for euros, the company's bank can instantaneously borrow the euros from the Japanese bank and then re-lend them to the retail customer at a markup.

Despite the global nature of the eurocurrency market, its geographic center is, by size and tradition, London. Hence, London banks' eurocurrency quotes are surveyed as a method for obtaining the representative focus of the market. The average of the borrow-ing or "offer" rate is *LIBOR* (the London Interbank Offer Rate), which serves as a daily consensus or index of eurocurrency market interest rates. LIBOR is not just one interest rate. There are many LIBORs, to accommodate different currencies and times to maturity. There is a three-month yen LIBOR, a one-year Swiss franc LIBOR, and so forth. Maturities of one week, three months, six months, nine months, and one year are the most popular in the eurocurrency market, but markets in some eurocurrencies are active for other maturities, including two-year, three-year, five-year, and higher.

The UBS Web site shows LIBOR for a number of currencies for a wide range of maturities. Go to http://quotes.ubs.com/ and click on "Money Market," then "Libor." Table 3.2 shows some one-year LIBORs for various currencies for November 16, 2003. For comparison, the one-year LIBORs for August 10, 2002, are also shown.

Table 3.3 shows some one-year deposit/loan rates quoted on November 16, 2003, obtained at the UBS Money Market site, after clicking on "Deposits". The interest rates show first the rate at which a bank will lend and then the rate at which a bank is willing to

TABLE 3.2 One-Year LIBOR

	Nov-16-03	Aug-10-02
Euro	2.40138	3.43708
GBP (sterling)	4.47500	4.09220
Australian dollar	5.82000	5.03063
Swiss franc	0.60000	1.04667
Canadian dollar	3.01333	2.95667
US dollar	1.49000	1.85375
Japanese yen	0.09375	0.09438

Source: UBS.

TABLE 3.3 One-Year Deposit/Loan Interest Rates, November 16, 2003

Currency	Deposit	Loan
Euro	2.245	2.365
GBP (sterling)	4.309	4.497
Australian dollar	5.593	5.894
Swiss franc	0.410	0.530
Canadian dollar	2.774	3.084
US dollar	1.305	1.425
Japanese yen	−0.134	0.178

Source: UBS.

TABLE 3.4 Deposit/Loan Interest Rates for Swiss Francs and US Dollars, November 16, 2003

Time	SWISS FRANCS		US DOLLARS	
	Deposit	Loan	Deposit	Loan
1Y	0.410	0.530	1.305	1.425
2Y	1.085	1.145	2.065	2.125
3Y	1.540	1.600	2.655	2.715
5Y	2.185	2.245	3.520	3.580
7Y	2.600	2.660	4.075	4.135
10Y	2.995	3.055	4.615	4.675

Source: UBS.

pay for a deposit in that currency. The midpoint of the UBS one-year deposit/loan rate for Swiss francs was 0.47% (less than 1%) on November 16, 2003.

Table 3.4 shows annualized deposit/loan rates for Swiss francs and for US dollars for various maturities.

SYNTHETIC FX FORWARDS AND MONEY MARKET HEDGING

Suppose you conduct three simultaneous transactions, all at time 0: (1) borrow $100 for one year at the interest rate of $r^\$ = 10\%$; (2) exchange the $100 into Swiss francs at an assumed current spot FX rate of $X_0^{Sf/\$} = 1.50$ Sf/$, to get $100(1.50 Sf/$) = Sf 150; (3) put the Sf 150 into a one-year euroSwiss franc deposit yielding $r^{Sf} = 8\%$.

The overall deal involves no *net* cash flow into or out of your pocket at the time of the three simultaneous transactions. But a year from now, you will receive Sf 150(1.08) = Sf 162 from the liquidation of the Swiss franc deposit, and you will have to repay $100(1.10)

= $110 on the US dollar loan. Thus, at time 1, there is an inflow to you of Sf 162 and an outflow from you of $110. This inflow/outflow is the same as if you held an actual long position in a one-year (US dollar-denominated) forward FX contract on Swiss francs, with a contract *amount* of $110, a contact *size* of Sf 162, and a forward FX rate of Sf 162/$110 = 1.473 Sf/$.

In financial markets, a security or instrument that is engineered from other securities or instruments combined is termed a *synthetic*. Your transactions represent a synthetic long forward FX position on Swiss francs. For different diagrams of the process of creating a synthetic long forward FX position on Swiss francs, see Figure 3.4.

You could create a synthetic short forward FX position by reversing the direction of the three simultaneous time-0 transactions. First, borrow Sf 150 for one year at $r^{Sf} = 8\%$, so that Sf 162 will be repaid at time 1. Next, change the borrowed Sf 150 into US dollars at time 0 at the assumed spot FX rate of $X_0^{Sf/\$} = 1.50$ Sf/$, to get $100. Finally, place the

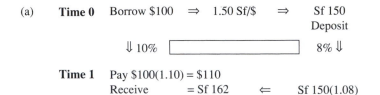

(a)   **Time 0**   Borrow $100 $\Rightarrow$ 1.50 Sf/$ $\Rightarrow$ Sf 150
                                                                              Deposit

        $\Downarrow 10\%$ [   ]   8% $\Downarrow$

      Time 1   Pay $100(1.10) = $110
                   Receive   = Sf 162 $\Leftarrow$ Sf 150(1.08)

Synthetic forward FX rate: $F_1^{Sf/\$} =$ Sf 162/$100 = 1.473 Sf/$

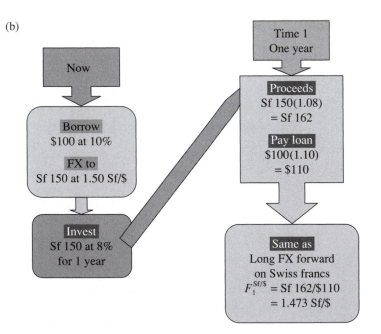

(b)

Now

Time 1
One year

Borrow
$100 at 10%

FX to
Sf 150 at 1.50 Sf/$

Invest
Sf 150 at 8%
for 1 year

Proceeds
Sf 150(1.08)
= Sf 162

Pay loan
$100(1.10)
= $110

Same as
Long FX forward
on Swiss francs
$F_1^{Sf/\$} =$ Sf 162/$110
= 1.473 Sf/$

Figure 3.4 A synthetic long FX forward position. (a) Process of creating a synthetic long forward FX position on Swiss francs. (b) Flowchart of the process.

$100 at time 0 into a one-year deposit at the interest rate of $r^\$ = 10\%$, to end up with $110 at time 1. In effect, you have created a contract that involves no *net* cash flow (into or out of your pocket) at time 0, but it obligates you to pay Sf 162 and receive $110 at time 1. Thus, you have manufactured a synthetic short position in a one-year forward FX contract on Swiss francs with a forward FX rate of Sf 162/$110 = 1.473 Sf/$.

At time 0 you borrow $1000 in time-1 face value at a 6% US dollar interest rate ($r^\$$), exchange the borrowed proceeds into British pounds at the spot FX rate of $X_0^{\$/£} = 1.60$ $/£, and place the pounds in a one-year deposit at $r^£ = 8\%$. How many pounds will you receive from your sterling deposit at time 1, and what is the synthetic forward FX rate?

Answers: The time-0 proceeds from the US dollar loan are $1000/1.06 = $943.40, which FXs to $943.40/(1.60 $/£) = £589.62. The time-1 liquidation of the sterling deposit is £589.62(1.08) = £636.79. The synthetic forward FX rate is thus $1000/£636.79 = 1.57 $/£.

You can use a memory device to prompt understanding of a synthetic forward FX position: *the direction of the spot FX exchange in the synthetic is the same as in the actual forward FX position.* Thus, a synthetic long forward FX position on Swiss francs involves a spot FX purchase of Swiss francs. Once you know the direction of the spot FX transaction of the synthetic, the loan/deposit directions fall into place. Since you need US dollars to buy the Swiss francs in the spot FX market, you must *borrow* US dollars; after the spot FX, you have Swiss francs, which you must deposit. For a mental check, you can think that at the delivery time, you will receive the Swiss francs as proceeds from the deposit and use US dollars to repay the loan, the same basic delivery time cash flows in an actual long forward FX position on Swiss francs.

Using y to denote "synthetic", the synthetic forward FX rate can be computed directly via equation (3.2):

Synthetic Forward FX Rate

$$F_N^{ySf/\$} = X_0^{Sf/\$} \left(\frac{1 + r^{Sf}}{1 + r^\$} \right)^N \tag{3.2}$$

Using the assumptions in the example, where $N = 1$, equation (3.2) yields that the synthetic forward FX rate is $F_1^{ySf/\$} = 1.50$ Sf/$ (1.08/1.10) = 1.473 Sf/$.

Assume the one-year US dollar interest rate is 6%, the one-year British pound interest rate is 8% and the spot FX rate is $X_0^{\$/£} = 1.60$ $/£. What is the synthetic forward FX rate using equation (3.2)?

Answer: (1.60 $/£)(1.06/1.08) = 1.57 $/£.

The use of synthetic forward FX contracts to hedge FX transaction exposure is referred to as a *money market hedge*. You can hedge a future receivable, for example, by borrowing the foreign currency and converting the borrowed proceeds into the base currency today; later you use the receivable cash flow to repay the borrowed foreign currency amount.

The balance sheet disadvantage of money market hedging with synthetic forward FX positions via loans and deposits is that the practice tends to inflate corporate balance sheets. That is, the deposit must be carried as an asset and the loan must be shown as a liability. While the two items offset each other in value, their mere presence on the balance sheet will alter the financial ratios that external analysts calculate to assess a company's creditworthiness. An actual forward FX contract does not produce any untoward balance sheet implications.

Why would anyone want to construct a synthetic forward FX position instead of simply using an actual forward FX position? The answer is that if the synthetic forward FX rate is better than the actual forward FX rate (considering transaction costs), a synthetic forward FX position would be preferred, as long as the user can tolerate the balance sheet implications of the synthetic approach.

For example, suppose the actual one-year forward FX rate is 1.46 Sf/$ and the synthetic forward FX rate is 1.47 Sf/$. If you want a long forward position on Swiss francs, which would be more advantageous, the actual FX forward or the synthetic FX forward?

The answer is whichever position allows the forward purchase of Swiss francs at the better rate with the fewest US dollars, that is, at the lower FX price of the Swissie. Thus, the synthetic should be the choice for a long forward FX position on Swiss francs, rather than the actual FX forward. If you want to establish a short forward FX position on Swiss francs, the better choice would be via the *actual* forward FX contract, *not a synthetic* short forward FX position. The reason is that it is more advantageous to sell Swiss francs at 1.46 Sf/$ than at 1.47 Sf/$.

It is useful to think of a US dollar-denominated forward FX contract on Swiss francs as equivalent to a deposit in Swiss francs and a simultaneous borrowing of US dollars. We can express this equivalence in symbolic form by denoting a long US dollar-denominated forward position on Swiss francs as $F_{Sf}^{\$}$, a zero coupon Swiss franc deposit as T^{Sf} and a zero coupon US dollar deposit as $T^{\$}$. [Recall our convention of using a superscript to denote the pricing currency.] An amount borrowed is simply the negative of an amount deposited (or loaned), so the borrowing of US dollars would be denoted $-T^{\$}$. Thus we have the statement of equivalence:

$$F_{Sf}^{\$} \equiv T^{Sf} - T^{\$} \qquad (3.3)$$

Equation (3.3) is not an equation you plug numbers into. Rather, it is simply a symbolic statement of equivalence of the forward FX position on Swiss francs with a deposit in Swiss francs financed by borrowing in US dollars. Alternatively, it is said that a long forward FX position on Swiss francs is equivalent to a long Swiss franc zero coupon note and a short US dollar zero coupon note.

A short forward position on Swiss francs can be expressed symbolically as $-F_{Sf}^{\$}$ and is equivalent to $T^{\$} - T^{Sf}$. You can see this by multiplying both sides of equation (3.3) by "minus one." This helps us think about a short forward FX position on Swiss francs as equivalent to a long US dollar zero coupon note and a short Swiss franc zero coupon note.

MARK-TO-MARKET VALUE OF A FORWARD FX CONTRACT

The *mark-to-market (MTM) value* of any position is the present value (PV) of the future inflows minus the present value (PV) of the future outflows. To mean anything, this valuation must be consistently expressed in one specific currency. When the components are in different currencies, as is the case in a forward FX contract, the present value of each component is first found in its own currency, using interest rates applicable to that currency. Then the current spot FX rate can be used to convert the PVs into the MTM value expressed in one currency.

The MTM value of a forward FX contract on Swiss francs can be found by netting the PVs of the forward contract's future cash flows, using the current spot FX rate to combine the two PV components into a common currency. As equation (3.3) tells us, a long forward position on Swiss francs is equivalent to owning a Swiss franc receipt and owing a US dollar payment. The Swiss franc receipt is the forward contract's *size*, Z^{Sf}, and the US dollar payment is the contract's *amount*, $A^{\$}$.

For example, suppose three months (1/4 year) has elapsed since a one-year forward FX contract was established at the forward FX rate of 1.46 Sf/$. Assume a contract *amount* of $A^{\$} = \$100,000$; thus the contract *size* is $Z^{Sf} = $ Sf 146,000. Assume that now the annualized nine-month interest rate is 6% in Swiss francs and 9% in US dollars. Assume further that the spot FX rate at this time is 1.55 Sf/$. The present value of the Sf 146,000 receipt is Sf $146,000/(1.06)^{0.75} = $ Sf 139,760, which at the spot FX rate of 1.55 Sf/$ is equivalent to Sf $139,760/(1.55 \text{ Sf}/\$) = \$90,166$ in US dollars. The present value of the $100,000 owed is $\$100,000/(1.09)^{0.75} = \$93,741$.

A long forward FX position on Swiss francs to receive Sf 146,000 in nine months (with PV in US$ of $90,166 now) and to pay $100,000 in nine months (with PV of $93,741 now) thus has an MTM value in US dollars of $90,166 - 93,741 = -\$3575$. The negative MTM value in this case represents an amount that the long forward position on Swiss francs would have to pay to liquidate the position to someone else in the market, given that the spot FX rate is 1.55 Sf/$. The MTM value of the long position on Swiss francs is negative mainly because at 1.55 Sf/$, the spot FX price of the Swiss franc is substantially lower than at the contract's forward FX rate of 1.46 Sf/$. Also, changes in interest rates since the time the forward contract originated will have an influence on a forward FX contract's MTM value.

A short forward position on Swiss francs, with contract *size* of Sf 146,000, pays Sf 146,000 and receives $100,000 nine months from now, and thus has an MTM value today of $\$93,741 - 90,166 = \$3575$. This MTM value represents what the short forward position on Swiss francs would receive through liquidating the position in the market. The short forward position on Swiss francs benefits from the low spot FX price of the Swiss franc (1.55 Sf/$), relative to the contract's forward FX rate (1.46 Sf/$).

In general the MTM value, in US dollars, of a *long* forward position on Swiss francs is the present value in US dollars of the Swiss franc receipt minus the present value of the US dollar payment. This value is given by equation (3.4), where n represents the number of years left until the delivery time of the forward FX contract that had N years till delivery when it originated.

$$M_{Sf}^\$ = X_0^{\$/Sf} \frac{Z^{Sf}}{(1 + r^{Sf})^n} - \frac{A^\$}{(1 + r^\$)^n} \qquad (3.4)$$

As usual, the *super*script symbol denotes the currency in which a security or contract is denominated, while the *sub*script symbol denotes the exposure currency. So in $M_{Sf}^\$$, the US dollar is the pricing currency for the forward FX contract and the MTM value is exposed to changes in (the FX price of) the Swiss franc. The MTM value of a long forward FX position on Swiss francs, $M_{Sf}^\$$, is priced in US dollars. The first term on the right-hand side is the present value of the contract's Swiss franc receipt, adjusted into US dollars at the current spot FX rate, and the term after the minus sign is the present value of the contract's US dollar payment.

For example, consider again the forward FX contract that originated as a one-year contract at the forward FX rate of 1.46 Sf/\$. Recall the assumptions: that three months after origination the spot FX rate is 1.55 Sf/\$, the annualized nine-month interest rates are 6% in Swiss francs and 9% in US dollars. First, reciprocate the current spot FX rate of 1.55 Sf/\$ into direct terms from the US dollar point of view, to get 1/(1.55 Sf/\$) = 0.64516 \$/Sf. Then equation (3.4) says that the MTM value of the long position on Swiss francs, with $Z^{Sf} =$ Sf 146,000 and thus $A^\$ = \$100,000$, should be (0.64516 \$/Sf)(Sf 146,000/$1.06^{0.75}$) − $\$100,000/1.09^{0.75} = -\$3575$. The MTM value of the short position is just the negative of the MTM value to the long position. The MTM value of the short position on Swiss francs should be \$3575.

A year ago you took a two-year long euro forward position with a contract amount of $A^\$ =$ **\$100. Assume that the two-year forward FX rate was $F_2^{\$/€} = 1.164$ \$/€. Thus the contract size is $Z^€ = \$100/(1.164$ \$/€) = €85.91. At present, with a year left until the delivery time, assume that the spot FX rate is 1.05 \$/€, the one-year US dollar interest rate is 6.20% and the one-year euro interest rate is 3.60%. What is the MTM value now of the long forward FX position taken a year ago?**

Answer: Using equation (3.4), the MTM value of the long position on euros is (1.05 \$/€)(€85.91/ 1.036) − \$100/1.062 = −\$7.09.

FX SWAPS AND FUTURES

A forward FX transaction is often part of an *FX swap*, which is the simultaneous spot sale (or purchase) of currency against a forward purchase (or sale) of approximately an equal amount. When not part of an FX swap, a forward FX transaction is called an *outright* forward.

The FX swap market has the highest daily volume of the FX market. In 1995, FX swap transactions accounted for about half of the \$1.5 billion daily FX market turnover. FX swaps are usually very short-term contracts. The great majority (71%) have a maturity of less than a week.

FX swaps are typically used to reduce exposure to short-term FX changes. Suppose a US trader wants to invest in seven-day pound certificates of deposit (CDs). The trader buys spot pounds, uses them to purchase the CDs, and then sells pounds forward in a single FX swap transaction. The swap simultaneously provides the trader the funds to buy the CD and provides protection against a depreciation of the pound during the life of the CD.

In basic concept, an *FX futures contract* is both like and unlike a forward FX contract. Like a forward contract, a futures contract is an obligation by two parties to exchange currencies at a set delivery time at a contract-specified rate. Unlike forward FX contracts, which are the instruments of the vast over-the-counter currency market, FX futures contracts are traded on particular exchanges in the world. To be traded on an exchange requires that contracts be standardized for ease of secondary market liquidation. For this reason, FX futures contracts have standardized delivery *dates*, rather than standardized maturities of FX forward contracts. For example, a three-month forward FX contract may be originated at any time in the FX market for settlement in three months, but FX futures contracts that are available offer delivery on only certain days of certain months. Another difference is that futures contracts are cash-settled every day, since the market-determined futures exchange rate fluctuates.

Because forwards and futures are similar, financial arbitrage between exchange-traded FX futures contracts and interbank forward FX contracts should keep FX futures contract rates near forward FX rates for the same horizon. Actually, volatile daily interest rates and the marking-to-market feature may cause FX futures rates to differ slightly from forward FX rates.

FX futures contract trading accounts for such a small portion of FX contract trading that we concentrate on forwards and do not differentiate the two. Technically, the text deals with forward FX contracts, but you could substitute "futures" for "forwards," and the general mechanics and valuation methods would still apply to a close approximation.

*PERLS

PERLs, for *principal exchange rate–linked securities*, pay principal in US dollars but in variable amounts linked to the FX price of a currency, or to a complex formula of values of multiple currencies. PERLs were designed to allow US savings banks, insurance companies, and other institutions to indirectly invest in foreign currency instruments despite restrictions against doing so directly. PERLs have ultimately been sold to a wide array of institutions and wealthy individuals.

Our example is a simple PERL that makes no coupon payments, but the principal repayment at maturity is linked to the FX rate for the Thai baht. The issuer states that the PERL is technically denominated in US dollars to enable holding by the target buyers. The PERL is an easy sell to the unsophisticated: it promises a high yield and states that it is a US dollar-denominated security. Of course, the principal repayment is only technically in US dollars; the principal amount is based on a formula involving the spot FX price of the baht a year later.[2]

---

[2]This kind of deal is described in Frank Partnoy, *Fiasco* (New York; Penguin, 1999). The PERL was sold prior to the Asian crisis, when Thai monetary authorities were using high baht interest rates to artificially prop up the FX price of the national currency.

Time 0 $900.90 Proceeds of PERL

US dollar zero coupon note + *One-year short forward on baht*

⇓   **PERL**   ⇓

Time 1: Pay $1000   + Bt 25,000($X_1^{\$/Bt}$ – 0.04 $/Bt)

Time 1   PERL Pays $1000 + Bt $25,000(X_1^{\$/Bt} - 0.04$ \$/Bt) = Bt 25,000

Figure 3.5 The cash flows of the PERL.

Assume that the one-year PERL has a face value of $1000, except that the US dollar principal repayment may be more or less than $1000 according to the formula: $1000 + Bt $25,000(X_1^{\$/Bt} - 0.04$ \$/Bt). Thus the payoff is above $1000 if the spot FX price of the baht is higher at the note's maturity than 0.04 $/Bt (25 Bt/$), and vice versa. The PERL is equivalent to a US dollar zero coupon note with face value of $1000, plus a long forward FX position on baht at a customized forward FX rate of 25 Bt/$ and contract *size* of Bt 25,000. The PERL buyer gets the equivalent of a US dollar zero coupon note plus a long forward FX position on baht. The PERL issuer sells the equivalent of a US dollar zero coupon note plus has an embedded short position on the baht forward FX contract.

Let us say that the PERL advertises that it is a US dollar-denominated note that pays a yield of 11%, even though the going one-year US dollar zero coupon interest rate is only 6%. The proceeds from the PERL are $1000/1.11 = $900.90 (Figure 3.5).

The PERL structure can also be viewed as a synthetic baht zero coupon note. We can see this by rearranging equation (3.3) to get $T^{\$} + F_{Bt}^{\$} \equiv T^{Bt}$, using baht in place of Swiss francs. The PERL issuer sold the equivalent of a one-year baht zero coupon note. Just as a synthetic forward FX contract can be created from zero coupon instruments, a synthetic zero coupon position in baht was created for the PERL buyer. The total payoff in US dollars on the PERL can be reexpressed as Bt $25,000(X_1^{\$/Bt})$. That is, the total payoff in US dollars is also equivalent to the payoff in US dollars on a one-year baht zero coupon note with a face value of Bt 25,000.

Since the PERL issuer sets a high customized forward FX price of the baht in the embedded forward contract, the synthetic baht zero coupon note pays a lower interest rate than the going market interest rate on actual baht zero coupon notes. Some buyers might have been willing to accept a below-market baht interest rate as a concession to be able to own the equivalent of a baht zero coupon note when restrictions would otherwise prohibit this investment. Another possibility is that buyers might have been deluded, thinking that the stated interest rate is a true US dollar interest rate (and better than the going rate).

The PERL issuer is likely to want to hedge the baht exposure with an actual long forward FX position on baht. The issuer thus engineers his short baht zero coupon note position into a short synthetic US dollar zero coupon note position. We see this by rearranging equation (3.3) to get $-T^{\$} \equiv -T^{Bt} + F_{Bt}^{\$}$, which says that an issued US dollar zero coupon note is equivalent to an issued baht zero coupon note plus a long forward FX position on baht. Since the short forward baht position embedded in the PERL is at a customized rate, the effective US dollar interest rate on the engineered US dollar zero coupon note is below market.

Time 0 $900.90 Proceeds US dollar zero coupon note (6%)

Time 0	$900.90	Proceeds PERL +	*One-year long forward on baht*
	⇓ **5.06%**	⇓	⇓
Time 1	$946.50 = $1000 + Bt 25,000$(X_1^{\$/Bt} - 0.04\ \$/Bt) -$ Bt 25,000$(X_1^{\$/Bt} - 0.03786\ \$/Bt)$		

Time 1 $954.95 = $900.90(1.06) Payment on US dollar zero coupon note

Figure 3.6 The cash flows of the synthetic US dollar zero coupon note structured from the PERL and the long forward position on baht.

Say that the PERL issuer receives $900.90 proceeds from issuing the PERL with a stated face value of $1000 and interest rate of 11%. Assume that the PERL issuer simultaneously takes a one-year long forward FX position on Bt 25,000 (the contract *size*) at the forward FX rate of 26.415 Bt/$. At time 1, the issuer will pay $1000 + Bt 25,000$(X_1^{\$/Bt} -$ 0.04 \$/Bt)$ on the PERL, and will receive Bt 25,000$(X_1^{\$/Bt} - 0.03786\ \$/Bt)$ on the long forward FX position. The issuer knows at the time of the issue that its net payout at time 1 is actually a certain amount in US dollars, of $1000 - Bt 25,000(0.04 \$/Bt - 0.03786 \$/Bt) = $946.50. In effect, the long forward FX position with the issued PERL is a synthetic US dollar zero coupon note with a face value of $946.50 and proceeds of $900.90. The issuer's effective interest rate paid (in US dollars) is $946.50/$900.90 − 1 = 0.0506, or 5.06%, wereas the going rate on actual one-year US dollar zero coupon notes is 6.00%. Figure 3.6 shows the cash flows of the synthetic US dollar zero coupon note structured from the PERL and the long forward position on baht.

Figure 3.7 is a flowchart of the process of combining the issued PERL with an actual long baht forward position to create a synthetic US dollar zero coupon note.

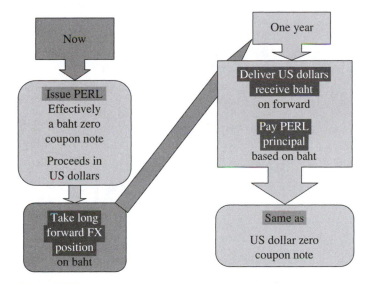

Figure 3.7 Flowchart showing how combining the PERL with a long forward FX position on baht creates a synthetic US dollar zero coupon note for the PERL issuer.

Suppose a one-year PERL is based on the Brazilian real, for a stated $1000 of face value and sells to yield 10%. The PERL promises to pay the face value of $1000 + Re 2000[$X_1^{\$/Re}$ − 0.50 $/Re]. Assume that the spot FX rate is 2 Re/$, and the going US dollar one-year interest rate is 6.50%, while the Brazilian real one-year rate is 11.20%. Assume the actual one-year forward FX rate is 2.088 Re/$, or 0.479 $/Re. If the PERL issuer hedges the FX exposure with a long forward FX position on real, what is the PERL issuer's effective US dollar interest rate on its synthetic US dollar zero coupon note?

Answer: By issuing the PERL and simultaneously taking a long forward FX position on real, with Z^{Re} = Re 2000, the issuer has a net time-1 outflow of $1000 + Re 2000($X_1^{\$/Re}$ − 0.50 $/Re) − Re 2000($X_1^{\$/Re}$ − 0.479 $/Re) = $958. Since the note is sold to yield 10% on principal of $1000, the proceeds are $1000/1.10 = $909.09. The effective interest rate paid on the synthetic US dollar zero coupon note is $958/$909.09 − 1 = 0.0538, or 5.38%, below the going rate on an actual US dollar zero coupon note of 6.50%.

SUMMARY

This chapter covered the basic mechanics of taking long and short positions in forward FX contracts. It examined an important motivation for corporate use of forward FX contracts: the hedging of unwanted FX transaction exposure to exchange rate fluctuations.

The net settlement of forward FX contracts involves a difference check. The difference check may be viewed as the profit (or loss) on the contract. We showed how to compute the difference check.

We described the eurocurrency market for traded time deposits and loans. We also covered the financial engineering of synthetic forward FX contracts through spot FX transactions combined with eurocurrency deposits and loans.

The chapter introduced the concept of the mark-to-market (MTM) value of a forward FX position between the position's origination and delivery time.

Finally, we revealed the financial engineering methods behind the use of synthetic foreign currency notes called PERLs.

GLOSSARY

Amount (in a forward FX contract): The number of units of the pricing currency in a forward FX contract.

Difference check: A means of cash settlement on a forward FX contract that avoids physical delivery. Also called a *cash-settled unwind*.

Eurocurrency: A time deposit or time loan in a currency, traded globally at market interest rates.

Eurodollar: A time deposit or time loan in US dollars, traded globally at market interest rates.

Forward FX contract: A contract between two parties for the future exchange of currencies at a *forward FX rate*.

FX futures contract: Essentially the same as a forward contract, but with some distinctions, especially the feature of daily settlement, referred to as marking-to-market.

FX swap: The simultaneous sale (or purchase) of spot foreign exchange against a forward FX purchase (or sale) of approximately an equal amount of the foreign currency.

Gross settlement of a forward FX contract: Settlement of a forward FX contract through physical exchange of the currencies at the delivery time as indicated by the contract.

Hedging: The use of a financial instrument to reduce or eliminate uncertainty about future cash flows.

LIBOR: The London Interbank Offer Rate, an index of the interest rate in the market for deposits and loans of a given currency and a given maturity.

Long forward FX position on currency X: Receives currency X at contract delivery date and delivers the contract's pricing currency.

Mark-to-market (MTM) value: The market value of a position that has not been liquidated and with time remaining until maturity.

Money market hedge: The use of currency deposits and loans to create synthetic forward FX contracts to hedge FX exposure.

Natural long position in a foreign currency: The holding or receivable of the foreign currency as part of normal operations.

Natural short position in a foreign currency: An obligation to pay the foreign currency as part of normal operations.

Net settlement of a forward FX contract: Settlement of a forward FX contract through a difference check at the delivery time.

Outright forward: A forward FX transaction that is not part of an FX swap.

PERLs: An abbreviation for *principal exchange rate–linked securities*, which pay principal in US dollars, in variable amounts linked to the value of a currency, or to a complex formula of values of multiple currencies.

Selective hedging: The practice of hedging FX exposure when the FX price is forecasted to change in the direction that would imply a loss, but not if the forecast is in the direction that would imply a profit.

Short forward FX position on currency X: Obligated to deliver currency X at contract delivery date and receive the contract's pricing currency.

Size (in a forward FX contract): The number of units of the foreign currency in a forward FX contract.

Synthetic: An equivalent to a security that is created, or engineered, from other existing securities.

DISCUSSION QUESTIONS

1. Explain why a company might want to take a long position on a foreign currency in a forward FX contract.
2. Explain the advantage of the difference check settlement relative to physical delivery.

3. Assume a company wants to go long a forward FX contract on a foreign currency. Explain how a synthetic long forward position can be constructed.
4. Explain the advantage of an actual forward FX position over a synthetic forward FX position in terms of a user's balance sheet.
5. Why do investors want PERLs and why do companies want to issue PERLs? Explain the basic idea rationalizing each tendency.

PROBLEMS

1. You take a one-year short forward FX position on euros at a forward FX rate of 0.9375 $/€. State the cash flow obligations of your short euro forward position, now and a year from now, if the contract *amount* is $2 million. What is the contract *size*?
2. You take a one-year long forward FX position on Swiss francs at a forward FX rate of 1.50 Sf/$. State the cash flow obligations of your long forward position on Swiss francs, now and a year from now, if the contract *size* is Sf 150 million. What is the contract *amount*?
3. You take a one-year short position in a (US dollar-denominated) forward FX contract on yen at a forward FX rate of $F_1^{¥/\$} = 130$ ¥/$. The contract *amount* is $1 million. If the spot FX rate for the yen a year from now is $X_1^{¥/\$} = 120$ ¥/$, what is the US dollar gain (loss) on the short forward position on yen? *Hint*: This is the same as the difference check to (from) the long yen position.
4. You take a long position in a two-year (US dollar-denominated) forward FX contract on British pounds at a forward FX rate of 1.60 $/£. The contract *amount* is $2 million. If the spot FX rate for the pound two years from now is $X_2^{\$/£} = 2.00$ $/£, what is your gain (or loss) on the contract in US dollars?
5. A US company has to make a natural British pound payment of £9 million in three months. Assume the current three-month forward FX rate is $F_{0.25}^{\$/£} = 1.75$ $/£. Determine from the forward FX rate the US dollar value of the liability that can be locked in by dealing in the forward FX market. Show how this locked-in amount results if the forward FX contract is settled via a difference check at the delivery time, if the spot FX rate at that time is 1.50 $/£.
6. Assume the one-year eurocurrency interest rate for euros is 5% and the one-year eurodollar rate is 3.50%. The spot FX rate is 1.25 $/€. What is the synthetic one-year forward FX rate?
7. You established a short two-year forward FX contract on yen a year ago at a forward FX rate of 112 ¥/$. The contract's *amount* is $1 million and the delivery time is a year from now. The current one-year spot FX rate is 102 ¥/$. The one-year US dollar interest rate is currently 6.50% and the one-year yen interest rate is currently 2%. What is the MTM value of your short forward position on yen? That is, how much would you receive (or have to pay) if you liquidated the forward FX position in the market today?
*8. Suppose a one-year PERL is based on the Brazilian real, for a stated $1000 of face value, and sells to yield 9%. The PERL promises to pay the face value of $1000 + Re 4000($X_1^{\$/Re}$ − 0.25 $/Re). Assume that the spot FX rate is 4 Re/$, and the going US dollar one-year interest rate is 6%, while the Brazilian real one-year rate is 11%. Find the PERL issuer's effective US dollar interest rate on a synthetic US dollar zero coupon note. Assume that the one-year forward FX rate is 4.19 Re/$.

---

*Problems marked with an asterisk are for MBA students; undergraduates need not attempt them.

ANSWERS TO PROBLEMS

1. No cash flows now; a year from now, you pay €2.133 million (the contract *size*) and receive $2 million.

2. No cash flows now; a year from now, you receive Sf 150 million and pay $100 million (the contract *amount*).

3. −$83,333

4. $500,000

5. $15.75 million

6. 1.232 $/€

7. The long forward position on yen would have a MTM value of (¥112 million/1.02)/(102 ¥/$) − $1 million/1.065 = $0.1375 million, that is, $137,500.

*8. By issuing the PERL and simultaneously taking an actual long forward FX position on real, with $Z^{Re} = $ Re 4000, the issuer has a net time-1 outflow of $1000 + $ Re $4000(X_1^{\$/Re} - 0.25 \ \$/Re) - $ Re $4000(X_1^{\$/Re} - 0.2387 \ \$/Re) = \$954.80$. Since the note is sold to yield 9% on principal of $1000, the proceeds are $1000/1.09 = $917.43. The effective interest rate paid on the synthetic US dollar zero coupon note is $954.80/$917.43 − 1 = 0.0407, or 4.07%, below the going rate on an actual US dollar zero coupon note of 6%.

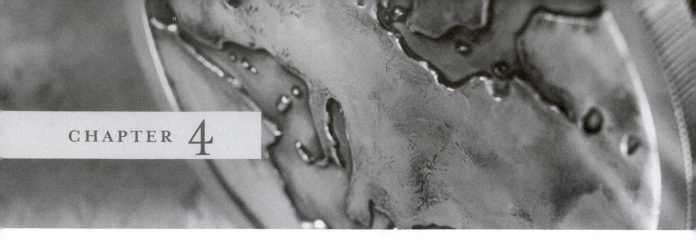

CHAPTER 4

FOREIGN EXCHANGE
AND INTEREST RATES

This chapter covers two relationships that are similar in that both involve FX rates and interest rates. But the two relationships are conceptually different. The first is the *covered interest rate parity (CIRP)* condition. As you will see, the CIRP condition is a no-arbitrage condition. This means that if the CIRP condition is violated, an arbitrage profit is available. The basic idea is that the actual forward FX rate should be equal to the synthetic forward FX rate constructed from a loan, a spot exchange transaction, and a deposit. Otherwise, a pure arbitrage profit could be obtained by a trading technique called *covered interest arbitrage*. Since this trading technique is relatively easy, the CIRP condition is reliably a very close approximation of reality.

The second is the *uncovered interest rate parity (UIRP)* condition. The UIRP condition is an economic theory rather than a no-arbitrage condition. The basic idea is that the actual forward FX rate should be equal to the market's expected spot FX rate. This economic relationship cannot be enforced by arbitrage. It is difficult to assess whether real-world data fit the UIRP theory, and many economists think not. Nevertheless, you'll see that the UIRP condition is a useful tool to help us think about how FX rates respond to changes in interest rates. The chapter also explains a mathematical problem with the traditional UIRP condition known as *Siegel's paradox*.

COVERED INTEREST ARBITRAGE

You know that arbitrage involves buying a claim for one price and selling essentially the same claim simultaneously for a higher price. An arbitrage strategy is theoretically possible across the spot FX, forward FX, and eurocurrency (interest rate) markets. The basic idea is that the actual forward FX rate, $F_1^{Sf/\$}$, should be equal to the synthetic forward FX rate. Otherwise, a pure arbitrage profit could be obtained by a technique called *covered interest arbitrage*.

For example, assume that one-year eurocurrency interest rates are $r^{Sf} = 8\%$ and $r^{\$} = 10\%$; that the spot FX rate is 1.50 Sf/\$; and that the actual one-year forward FX rate is $F_1^{Sf/\$} = 1.46$ Sf/\$. The synthetic one-year forward FX rate is $F_1^{ySf/\$} = X_0^{Sf/\$}[(1 + r^{Sf})/(1 + r^{\$})] = 1.50$ Sf/\$(1.08/1.10) = 1.473 Sf/\$. We will see how covered interest arbitrage is possible in this case because the actual forward FX rate of 1.46 Sf/\$ is not equal to the synthetic forward FX rate of 1.473 Sf/\$.

To see how to capture the arbitrage profit from this misalignment of the FX rates and interest rates, note that today's actual forward FX value of the US dollar at 1.46 Sf/\$ is *lower* than the synthetic forward FX value of the US dollar, 1.473 Sf/\$. You want to "buy low and sell high." Thus your arbitrage strategy will involve selling Swiss francs forward at the actual forward FX rate of 1.46 Sf/\$ and simultaneously buying Swiss francs forward at the synthetic forward FX rate of 1.473 Sf/\$. To sell Swiss francs in an actual FX forward is the same as taking an actual short forward position on Swiss francs. Such a position, with a contract *size* of Sf 1.46, will obligate you to deliver Sf 1.46 and receive $1.00 a year from now.

In the arbitrage strategy, the actual short forward FX position on Swiss francs should be counterbalanced with a synthetic long forward position on Swiss francs. In the synthetic long position on Swiss francs, you are buying Swiss francs forward at a lower FX value of the Swiss franc (1.473 Sf/\$) than you are selling Swiss francs forward through the actual FX forward contract.

The synthetic long Swiss franc position involves borrowing US dollars, using them to buy Swiss francs, and then depositing the Swiss francs. You are going to do this in such a way as to be able to extract the arbitrage profit at time 0. To do this, think about how much you need to deliver against the actual forward FX position, Sf 1.46. You will need to end up with this amount when you liquidate the Swiss franc deposit of the synthetic position. Since you want the deposit to yield Sf 1.46 a year from now, you must deposit the present value of Sf 1.46 at time 0, which is Sf 1.46/1.08 = Sf 1.352. At the current spot FX rate of 1.50 Sf/\$, you thus need $0.9013 at time 0. Now consider the time-1 US dollar receipt on the actual forward contract, $1. You borrow the present value of $1 as part of the synthetic contract, knowing that the actual forward FX receipt will provide the loan repayment amount. That is, you borrow the present value of $1.00, which is $1/1.10 = $0.9090. Of the $0.9090 proceeds, you only need $0.9013 to do the rest of the transactions of the synthetic forward position. The remainder is the arbitrage profit, $0.9090 minus $0.9013 = $0.0077. Table 4.1 lays out the calculations.

If the actual forward FX rate instead were 1.49 Sf/\$, given that the synthetic forward FX rate is still 1.473 Sf/\$, you would reverse the arbitrage process. In this case, you want

TABLE 4.1 Covered Interest Arbitrage Cash Flow

	TODAY		IN ONE YEAR	
	Sf	**US$**	**Sf**	**US$**
Enter actual forward FX contract—short Sf	0	0	−1.46	1.00
Borrow $1.00/1.10 = $0.909	**0**	**0.9090**	0	−1.00
Spot FX $0.9013 US$ to Sf at 1.50 Sf/$	1.352	−0.9013	0	0
Deposit Sf 1.46/(1.08) = Sf 1.352	−1.352	0	1.46	0
Arbitrage profit (today)		**+0.0077**		

to buy Swiss francs in the actual forward FX market at 1.49 Sf/$ and simultaneously sell Swiss francs at the higher synthetic forward FX value of the Swiss franc, 1.473 Sf/$.

For example, you take a long FX forward position on Swiss francs with contract *size* of Sf 1.49 at the actual forward FX rate of 1.49 Sf/$. You figure out how much you can borrow today against the future receipt of Sf 1.49, which is Sf 1.49/1.08 = Sf 1.38. At the spot FX rate of 1.50 Sf/$, you can spot-exchange the Sf 1.38 into $0.9198. Next note how much you need to deliver on the actual forward contract, $1. You will be depositing the present value of $1, which is $1/1.10 = $0.909. You can thus walk away at time 0 with the arbitrage profit of $0.9198 minus $0.9090 = $0.0108.

The future cash flows of the actual long forward FX position on Swiss francs are covered by the synthetic: the proceeds of Sf 1.49 from the actual forward FX contract repays the Swiss franc loan, while the obliged $1 delivery in the actual forward is covered by money from the US dollar deposit.

COVERED INTEREST RATE PARITY (CIRP)

As we have seen, an arbitrage opportunity is available, one way or another, unless the actual forward FX rate equals the synthetic forward FX rate, that is, unless $F_1^{Sf/\$} = F_1^{ySf/\$}$ $= X_0^{Sf/\$}[(1 + r^{Sf})/(1 + r^\$)]$. This equality is referred to as the *covered interest rate parity (CIRP) condition*. Equation (4.1a) is expressed for the general case of N years and in FX rate form (as opposed to a percentage form shown later).

Covered Interest Rate Parity (CIRP) Condition
FX Rate Form

$$F_N^{Sf/\$} = X_0^{Sf/\$} \left(\frac{1 + r^{Sf}}{1 + r^\$} \right)^N \tag{4.1a}$$

Equation (4.1a) is expressed with the forward FX rate on the left-hand side of the equation. Under this arrangement, *the interest rates in the numerator and denominator should match the numerator and denominator currency symbols in the superscript of*

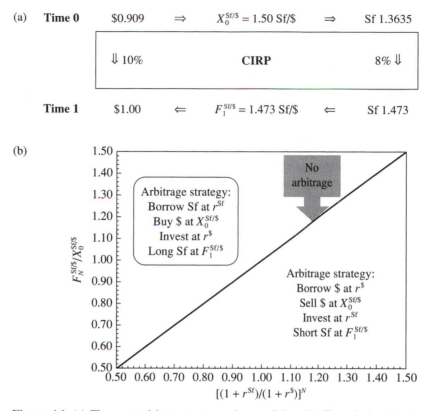

Figure 4.1 (a) The covered interest rate parity condition. (b) The relationship between covered interest arbitrage and the CIRP condition.

the FX quote. The FX rates expressed in equation (4.1a) are in European terms, as is conventional for the Swiss franc. For FX rates that are quoted in American terms, like the US dollar/euro FX rate, the interest rate in the numerator of the CIRP condition will be for the US dollar.

For the Swiss franc example, given the spot FX rate of $F_1^{Sf/\$} = 1.50$ Sf/\$, $r^{Sf} = 8\%$, and $r^\$ = 10\%$, equation (4.1a) shows that the forward FX rate should be 1.473 Sf/\$, or else there is an arbitrage opportunity. When the synthetic forward FX value of the US dollar is too high, in comparison to the actual forward FX value, arbitrageurs will buy Swiss francs in the forward FX market and sell Swiss francs in the spot FX market (in the synthetic transactions) to capture the arbitrage opportunity. This buying low/selling high pushes the spot FX value of the Swiss franc/dollar lower and the forward FX value higher, until the arbitrage opportunity is eliminated, and equation (4.1a) holds with actual FX spot and forward rates. Figure 4.1a depicts the CIRP condition, and Figure 4.1b describes the relationship between covered interest arbitrage and the CIRP condition.

> **Assume that the actual one-year forward FX rate for the Japanese yen is $F_1^{\yen/\$} = 100$ ¥/\$, and the actual current spot FX rate is $X_0^{\yen/\$} = 106$ ¥/\$. Assume the one-year euroyen interest rate is $r^{\yen} = 2\%$, while the one-year US dollar eurocurrency interest rate is $r^{\$} = 6\%$. Is an arbitrage profit available? If so, show how to perform the arbitrage, and find the amount of time-0 arbitrage profit (in US dollars) that can be made via covered interest rate arbitrage for an actual forward FX contract amount of \$1000.**
>
> *Answers: Equation (4.1a) tells us that the forward FX rate should be (106 ¥/\$)(1.02/1.06) = 102 ¥/\$. Since the actual forward FX rate is given to be 100 ¥/\$, there is an arbitrage opportunity. Since the US dollar should be selling for 102 ¥/\$ in the forward FX market (given the other information), but is actually selling for 100 ¥/\$, the actual forward FX value of the US dollar is too low relative to the synthetic. To "buy low and sell high," the arbitrage will involve buying US dollars (shorting yen) in the actual forward FX market and selling US dollars (going long yen) in the synthetic forward FX market. Thus you take an actual short forward FX contract on yen with $A^{\$} = \$1000$ and thus $Z^{\yen} = \$1000(100$ ¥/\$$) = ¥100,000$. You need to deposit ¥100,000/1.02 = ¥98,040 to cover the short forward yen position's delivery obligation of ¥100,000, so you will need to buy ¥98,040 in the actual spot FX market at 106 ¥/\$, with ¥98,040/(106 ¥/\$) = \$925. You take a US dollar loan with time-0 proceeds of \$1000/1.06 = \$943.40, knowing you will be receiving \$1000 from the actual forward FX position. The arbitrage profit is \$943.40 − 925 = \$18.40.*

Let us see how well the CIRP condition of equation (4.1a) fits with the actual one-year UBS data from Tables 3.1 and 3.4. In Table 3.1 the UBS spot FX bid is 1.3273 Sf/\$ and the spot FX ask is 1.3278 Sf/\$, so we will use the midpoint, 1.32755 Sf/\$. Also in Table 3.1, the UBS one-year forward FX bid is 1.3153 Sf/\$ and the ask 1.3166 Sf/\$, so we'll use the midpoint, 1.316 Sf/\$. In Table 3.4, the one-year Swiss franc deposit rate is 0.41% and the loan rate is 0.53%, so we'll use the midpoint, 0.47%. Also in Table 3.4, the one-year US dollar deposit rate is 1.305% and the loan rate is 1.425%, so we'll use the midpoint, 1.365%. The CIRP condition in equation (4.1a) says that the forward FX rate should be 1.32755 Sf/\$(1.0047/1.01365) = 1.3158 Sf/\$. This answer is extremely close to the actual one-year forward FX rate of 1.316 Sf/\$, especially given that we ignore transaction costs and dealer spreads and use midpoints of four indicative (not live) quotes. This numerical example illustrates that the CIRP condition in equation (4.1a) is a good description of reality for the currencies of developed countries.

Another way to look at the CIRP condition is by thinking of an FX swap. Recall that an FX swap is the simultaneous spot FX trade against a simultaneous forward FX trade in the reverse direction. For example, you put on an FX swap by spot-exchanging US dollars into euros, and simultaneously take a one-year short forward position on euros with a size equal to the time-0 amount of euros plus one year's worth of interest. The assumption is that the euros resulting from the spot FX trade are invested at a competitive euro interest rate. You are basically lending US dollars today, and the US dollars you get back a year later should provide the US dollar interest rate. For the forward FX rate in the FX swap to be consistent with the two interest rates and the current spot FX rate, the CIRP condition needs to hold.

It would be nice for us readers if we were the only ones who understood the CIRP condition and how to put on the covered interest arbitrage strategy. Actually, both CIRP and the arbitrage strategy are well known in FX markets. Moreover, covered interest arbitrage is relatively easy and inexpensive for interbank FX traders in many cases. For these reasons, one would expect traders to pounce on even minor deviations from the CIRP condition, with the arbitrage trading then causing the deviation to quickly disappear. Thus we generally observe that the CIRP condition in equation (4.1a) holds very closely, especially in the case major liquid currencies. Indeed, empirical testing of equation (4.1a) for actively traded currencies of developed countries confirms that the CIRP condition is very accurate.

That said, we have seen cases of covered interest arbitrage activities in the currencies of less-developed countries. The accompanying box gives one example, Northstar Corporation. The PERLs example in Chapter 3 is also a form of covered interest arbitrage.

NORTHSTAR'S PESO ARBITRAGE

In mid-1993, a US multinational, Northstar, arbitraged the forward FX market between US dollars and Mexican pesos. Northstar borrowed US dollars from its lead commercial bank at the prime interest rate of 6%, spot-FXed the US dollars into pesos at the rate of 3.11 Pe/$, and then invested the proceeds into peso-denominated Mexican government bills yielding about 16%. Effectively, Northstar created a *synthetic* long forward FX position on pesos. That is, if Northstar borrowed $1000, spot-FXed into Pe 3110, and deposited the Pe 3110 for a year at 16%, it would end up with Pe 3110(1.16) = Pe 3607.60 and an obligation to repay $1000(1.06) = $1060. This strategy represents a synthetic long forward FX position on pesos with a synthetic forward FX rate of (3.11 Pe/$)(1.16/1.06) = 3.40 Pe/$.

Northstar's bank was quoting an *actual* forward FX rate at a lower forward discount than represented by the synthetic forward FX rate. Say, for example, that the actual forward FX rate quote was 3.30 Pe/$. Northstar was covering its long synthetic forward positions on pesos (at 3.40 Pe/$) by going short actual peso forward contracts (at 3.30 Pe/$). Northstar was thus practicing a form of covered interest arbitrage by selling pesos forward (actually) at 3.30 Pe/$ while simultaneously buying them forward (synthetically) at 3.40 Pe/$.

The arbitrage was made possible when the Mexican government attempted to support the FX value of the peso via a high peso interest rate. The market then quoted a low-discount actual forward peso in the expectation that the peso would not depreciate to the extent implicit in the interest rates in the synthetic forward FX rate. This kind of arbitrage is generally not available in the market for FX of developed countries that do not try to control their currency values.

Source: Adapted from Laurent Jacque and Gabriel Hawawini, "Myths and Realities of the Global Capital Market: Lessons for Financial Managers," *Journal of Applied Corporate Finance*, Fall 1993, 81–90.

CIRP IN PERCENTAGE FORM

It is common to express the forward FX premium or discount of a currency as an annualized percentage deviation from the spot FX value. The annualized percentage premium in an N-year forward FX rate, f_N, is generally calculated as $f_N = [(F_N - X_0)/X_0]^{1/N}$. For a one-year forward FX rate, the percentage is simply $f_1 = [(F_1 - X_0)/X_0]$. For example with the one-year Swiss franc/US dollar spot FX rate midpoint of 1.32755 Sf/$ and the one-year forward FX rate midpoint of 1.316 Sf$ (see the preceding section), $f_1^{Sf/\$} = (1.316$ Sf/$ $- 1.32755$ Sf/$)/(1.32755$ Sf/$) = -0.0087$, or -0.87%. In this example, $f_1^{Sf/\$}$ is negative, and since the FX rates express the FX value of the US dollar (the denominator currency), the one-year forward FX value of the US dollar is at a 0.87% discount. You can verify that the US dollar is at a forward discount by noting that the forward FX rate of 1.316 Sf/$ represents a lower FX value of the US dollar than the spot FX rate of 1.32755 Sf/$. The Swiss franc is at a forward premium.

The percentage form (annualized) of the CIRP condition is shown in equation (4.1b).

Covered Interest Rate Parity (CIRP) Condition
Percentage Form—Annualized

$$1 + f_N^{Sf/\$} = \frac{1 + r^{Sf}}{1 + r^{\$}}$$

(4.1b)

We see that a currency is at a forward FX discount if its interest rate is higher than the other currency, as in the case here of the US dollar, for which the November 16, 2003, one-year interest rate midpoint of 1.365% is higher than the one-year Swiss franc interest rate midpoint of 0.47% (see the preceding section). By the same token, a currency is at a forward FX premium if its interest rate is lower than the other currency. The Swiss franc was at a one-year forward FX premium on November 16, 2003, because the interest rate in Swiss francs was higher than the interest rate in US dollars. Thus the interest rate differential is another way of looking at the CIRP condition.

It is also the case that $f_1^{Sf/\$}$ is approximately equal to the linear difference between the one-year interest rates in Swiss francs and US dollars, which (rounded) is $0.47\% - 1.365\%$ $= -0.895\%$. In this way, the percentage forward premium/discount currency *approximately* reflects the linear interest rate differential, in that $-0.87\% \approx -0.895\%$. According to this linear approximation, the percentage form CIRP condition is in equation (4.1c).

Covered Interest Rate Parity (CIRP) Condition
Percentage Form—Linear Approximation

$$f^{Sf/\$} = r^{Sf} - r^{\$}$$

(4.1c)

In equation (4.1c), the first interest rate, with the implicit positive sign, is the numerator currency of the FX rate expression, while the interest rate with the negative sign is the denominator currency.

Assume the one-year interest rates for the US dollar and the euro are 6.8 and 3.5%, respectively. (1) Use equation (4.1b) to find the one-year forward/premium discount on the euro in annualized percentage terms. Then, with the approximate CIRP condition in equation (4.1c), find the linear approximation to the one-year forward premium/discount on the euro.

Answers: (1) $f_1^{\$/€} = (1 + r^\$)/(1 + r^€) - 1 = 1.068/1.035 - 1 = 0.0319.$ *(2) Approximately,* $f_1^{\$/€} = r^\$ - r^€$ $= 0.068 - 0.035 = 0.033.$

UNCOVERED INTEREST RATE PARITY (UIRP)

While today's spot FX rate is observable and given, the spot FX rate for future times is unknown today. We use the concept of an expected spot FX rate, even though true expected spot FX rates are not observable. According to one economic theory, the consensus expectation of FX market participants is equal to the true expected future spot FX rate, and the forward FX rate (the synthetic forward FX rate if an actual forward contract is not traded) is equal to the true expected spot FX rate.

Let the true expected spot rate at time N be $E(X_N^{*\,Sf/\$})$, where the asterisk conveys the idea that the expectation is the true expectation. The logic behind the theory that $F_N^{Sf/\$} = E(X_N^{*\,Sf/\$})$ is the efficient market argument; that is, that alert traders will quickly exploit any profit opportunities, and that their trading will force the forward FX rate to be aligned with the expectation. If $F_N^{Sf/\$} \neq E(X_N^{*\,Sf/\$})$, there is a speculative profit opportunity. If the US dollar has a lower forward FX value than the expected future spot FX value, it is a no-brainer to go long forward US dollars. Traders will lock in a low price today for buying US dollars in the future, and then profit from the higher realized value of the US dollar at that future time.

Since CIRP is empirically reliable, the assertion that $E(X_N^{*\,Sf/\$}) = F_N^{Sf/\$}$ is the same saying that $E(X_N^{*\,Sf/\$}) = X_0^{Sf/\$}[(1 + r^{Sf})/(1 + r^\$)]^N$. This theory is called the uncovered interest rate parity (UIRP) condition. The term "uncovered" is used because the condition is assumed to result from trading activity other than covered interest arbitrage. The UIRP condition is also called the *international Fisher equation* or the *Fisher open equation*, after the economist Irving Fisher. The FX rate form of the UIRP theory is shown in equation (4.2a). Just as in the CIRP condition, r^{Sf} and $r^\$$ in equation (4.2a) represent the annualized interest rate on a zero coupon eurocurrency instrument in Swiss francs and US dollars, respectively, between now and time N.

Uncovered Interest Rate Parity (UIRP) Condition
FX Rate Form

$$E(X_N^{*\,Sf/\$}) = X_0^{Sf/\$}\left(\frac{1 + r^{Sf}}{1 + r^\$}\right)^N \tag{4.2a}$$

Figure 4.2 shows an example of the UIRP condition where $N = 1$, $r^{Sf} = 0.04$, $r^\$ = 0.06$, $X_0^{Sf/\$} = 1.60$ Sf/\$, and $E(X_1^{*\,Sf/\$}) = 1.57$ Sf/\$. By following the arrows in Figure 4.2, you can see how two paths will get you from \$1 at time 0 to \$1.06 at time 1. One path is to deposit

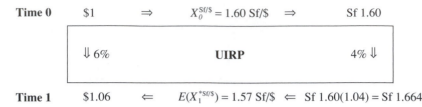

Figure 4.2 The uncovered interest rate parity condition, where $N = 1$, $r^{Sf} = 0.04$, $r^{\$} = 0.06$, $X_0^{Sf/\$} = 1.60$ Sf/\$, and $E(X_N^{*Sf/\$}) = 1.57$ Sf/\$. The UIRP condition holds because $E(X_1^{*Sf/\$}) = 1.57$ Sf/\$ $= 1.60$ Sf/\$$[(1.04)/(1.06)]$.

$1 in a US dollar account earning a 6% interest rate. The second path is to convert the
$1 to Sf 1.60 at the spot FX rate of 1.60 Sf/$, then invest Sf 1.60 in a Swiss franc account
earning 4% to have Sf 1.664 at time 1, and convert the Sf 1.664 back into US dollars. If
you convert back at 1.57 Sf/$, you end up with $1.06. The UIRP condition holds because
$1(1.06) = $1(1.60 Sf/$)(1.04)/(1.57 Sf/$), which is the same as saying that 1.57 Sf/$ =
1.60 Sf/$[(1.04)/(1.06)].

Under the theory of UIRP, the true expected rate of change in the FX rate is equal
to the interest rate differential. The currency with the higher interest rate is expected to
depreciate (just as the currency with the higher interest rate is at a forward discount under
CIRP). This result can seem counter intuitive, but remember that UIRP theory assumes
that the current spot FX rate is already in equilibrium, in the sense that all potential profit
opportunities have already been exploited. If the currency with the higher interest rate
were expected to appreciate, meaning that the currency with the lower interest rate is
expected to depreciate, money everywhere would shift from the low interest rate currency
to the high interest rate currency. Movement like this would cause the spot value of the
high interest rate currency to rise until equilibrium was reached, whereupon money would
quit shifting. In equilibrium, we assume the spot FX value of the high interest rate currency
has already been bid up high enough that the expected future depreciation of the currency
leaves investors indifferent between interest-bearing deposits in the two currencies.

**The one-year interest rate in US dollars is 7% and in yen is 2%. Informed FX market
participants expect the spot FX rate to be 104 ¥/$ a year from now. What is the spot FX rate
now if the UIRP condition holds?**

*Answer: You want to find $X_0^{¥/\$}$ such that $E(X_1^{*¥/\$}) = 104$ ¥/\$ $= X_0^{¥/\$}[(1 + r^{¥})/(1 + r^{\$})] = X_0^{¥/\$}[(1.02)/(1.07)]$. Thus, $X_0^{¥/\$} = 109.10$ ¥/\$. Note that if the UIRP holds, the currency with the
higher interest rate, the US dollar, is expected to depreciate.*

The UIRP condition is a simple theory of how asset markets affect FX rates. The
UIRP may be called an *equilibrium* condition, in the sense that if the condition does not
hold, there will be economic pressure for the variables in the UIRP to change until it does
hold. Since FX flows for investment purposes are larger than for international goods trade,

it seems reasonable that the UIRP theory could be more likely to hold than the PPP theory in Chapter 2. Indeed, FX rates that are affected by investment flows may cause PPP not to hold.

The economic logic is clear enough, but whether the UIRP fits real-world data is a question. Empirical studies that are designed to test the UIRP theory check whether the forward discount or premium is a good predictor of actual future FX rate movements. The results for developed countries, however, are often the opposite of what the UIRP relationship would predict. That is, on average, currencies at a forward premium (lower interest rate) have tended to depreciate in FX value, exactly the opposite of the UIRP prediction. Similarly, currencies at a forward discount (higher interest rate) have on average appreciated, contrary to the UIRP prediction. This situation is known as the *forward premium puzzle*.

For example, the euro was at a forward premium (there were lower euro interest rates than US dollar interest rates), and the euro depreciated in 1999–2000. Thus, the empirical evidence that has been reported generally supports the notion that FX rates are often *not* in equilibrium. One reason is likely to be the market's inability to reflect the true expected future spot FX rate. Perhaps high interest rates reflect a level of investment that has not yet caught up to a strong economic outlook, so the higher-interest currency is undervalued from the perspective of anticipated investment returns.

The forward premium puzzle evidence from the academic empirical studies is consistent with a common speculative strategy called a *currency carry trade*, or often simply a *carry trade*. In this trade, a speculator will borrow in a low interest rate currency and deposit the exchanged proceeds into a high interest rate currency. The speculator has laid out no capital, basically creating a synthetic long forward FX position on the high interest rate currency. If the market were in equilibrium under the UIRP condition, the speculator would not expect to profit because the high interest rate currency presumably would decline. So a speculator doing a carry trade, and many do, believes that the market is not in equilibrium. The evidence from the empirical studies suggests that on average this kind of speculation has been profitable, at least for developed counties.[1]

The UIRP relationship is thus very different from the CIRP as an empirical reality. CIRP is a no-arbitrage financial relationship; if it is violated, traders can earn immediate profit through an easy and inexpensive arbitrage using traded instruments and no risk. For this reason, the CIRP condition reliably fits actual data for currencies of developed countries. The UIRP condition by contrast is an economic theory; it is based on much more vague and less realistic notions. And we have found the UIRP is not supported by empirical research. It is fundamentally different from the CIRP condition.

---

[1]See R. Bansal and M. Dahlquist, "The Forward Premium Puzzle: Different Tales from Developed and Emerging Economies," *Journal of International Economics*, 2000, 115–144. This study reports that the forward premium puzzle mainly occurs between developed countries and mainly when the US dollar has the higher interest rate. This study also reports that the UIRP prediction, a decline in FX value of a currency with the higher interest rate, is more reliable when an emerging market country is involved. This would be expected, since higher interest rates are more likely to reflect higher inflation rates in emerging market countries.

Let the he notation $E(x_N^{*Sf/\$})$ represent the expected (annualized) percentage change in the value of the US dollar (relative to the Swiss franc), between now and time N, given the UIRP condition holds. We might say that the asterisk denotes the efficient market assumption that FX market is in equilibrium with the interest rate market. The percentage form UIRP is thus equation (4.2b).

Uncovered Interest Rate Parity (UIRP) Condition
Percentage Form—Annualized

$$1 + E(x_N^{*Sf/\$}) = \frac{1 + r^{Sf}}{1 + r^{\$}} \qquad (4.2b)$$

The corresponding linear approximation in terms of the annualized percentage forward premium or discount is shown in equation (4.2c).

Uncovered Interest Rate Parity (UIRP) Condition
Percentage Form—Linear Approximation

$$E(x_N^{*Sf/\$}) = f_N^{Sf/\$} = r^{Sf} - r^{\$} \qquad (4.2c)$$

Assume the one-year interest rates for the US dollar and the euro are 6.8 and 3.5%, respectively. (1) Find the one-year expected percentage change in the FX value of the euro assuming the UIRP condition holds. (2) Then, with the approximate UIRP condition in equation (4.2c), find the linear approximation to the one-year expected percentage change in the FX value of the euro.

Answers: (1) $E(x_1^{*\$/\epsilon}) = (1 + r^{\$})/(1 + r^{\epsilon}) - 1 = 1.068/1.035 - 1 = 0.0319$, or 3.19%.
(2) Approximately, $E(x_1^{*\$/\epsilon}) = r^{\$} - r^{\epsilon} = 0.068 - 0.035 = 0.033$, or 3.3%.

Even though the UIRP condition does not fit actual FX data, it is useful for three reasons. First, the interest rate differential has some partial FX forecasting power when it is used in FX forecasting models in combination with several other factors, even though the interest rate differential by itself is not a reliable forecaster. Second, the UIRP condition is useful in cost of capital estimation. Actually, the UIRP condition ignores the idea of risk, but we will address this issue later in the text, when a risk-adjusted version of the UIRP is used in cost of capital estimation. Third, the UIRP condition provides a logical model to analyze the general idea of how interest rate changes affect FX rates, as we do next.

INTEREST RATE CHANGES AND FX RATES

We now use the UIRP model to address the following question: if an interest rate suddenly changes, what will be the impact on the spot FX rate? For this purpose, it is necessary to use the FX rate form of the UIRP in equation (4.2a) and not either one of the percentage forms. You will see the reason shortly.

We start with the assumptions that the one-year $r^{Sf} = 4\%$, the one-year $r^{\$} = 6\%$, and the current spot FX rate $X_0^{Sf/\$} = 1.60$ Sf/\$. We assume the UIRP condition holds, so that the true expected spot FX rate for a year from now is assumed to be $E(X_1^{*Sf/\$}) =$ 1.60 Sf/\$(1.04/1.06) = 1.57 Sf/\$. Suppose that suddenly the one-year Swiss franc interest rate rises from 4% to 4.50%. What do you expect to happen to the spot FX rate?

There are two polar extremes of theory on how an interest rate change affects FX rates. They are referred to as the *asset market theory* and the *Fisher theory*. The basic distinction is that interest rate changes are driven by changes in expected inflation in the Fisher theory but not in the asset market theory. The result is that interest rate changes affect the expected FX rate under the Fisher theory, while the spot FX rate is not affected. Under the asset market theory, the interest rate change affects the spot FX rate, and the expected FX rate is not affected.

Asset Market Theory

Current Spot FX Rate Responds; Interest Rate Change Driven by Something Other Than Inflation Change

Fisher Theory

Expected FX Rate Responds; Interest Rate Change Driven by Inflation Change

Let's first look at the asset market theory. Suppose, for example, that the sudden increase of 50 basis points in the Swiss franc interest rate from 4% to 4.50% occurred because productive Swiss firms suddenly experienced a demand for more capital. In this case, the asset market theory applies because the interest rate change is not driven by a change in inflation expectations. The result is that the spot FX value of the Swiss franc will immediately appreciate.

The reason is that capital in the asset market will flow rapidly into the Swiss franc to capture the high potential that Swiss investments seem likely to offer. If $E(X_1^{*Sf/\$})$ stays at 1.57 Sf/\$, the new spot FX rate that will reestablish the UIRP condition, given the new Swiss franc interest rate of 4.50%, can be found using equation (4.2a), 1.57 Sf/\$ = $X_0^{Sf/\$}(1.045/1.06)$ implying the new $X_0^{Sf/\$}$ = 1.592 Sf/\$. In this case, the spot FX value of the Swiss franc rises, since the spot FX rate changes from 1.60 Sf/\$ to 1.592 Sf/\$, when the Swiss franc interest rate suddenly rises from 4% to 4.50%.

Figure 4.3 shows the asset market theory. The spot FX rate at time 0 printed in bold type is the UIRP variable that responds to the interest rate change in the asset market theory.

A similar scenario occurs if the increase in the Swiss franc interest rate is due to an increase in the Swiss discount rate by the Swiss central bank. Often, an increase in the

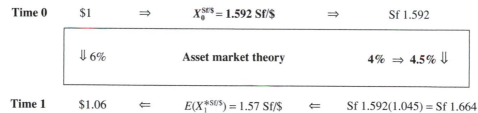

Figure 4.3 Asset market theory, showing the UIRP condition, where $N = 1$, $r^{Sf} = 0.045$, $r^{\$} = 0.06$, $X_0^{Sf/\$}$ = 1.592 Sf/\$, and $E(X_N^{*Sf/\$})$ = 1.57 Sf/\$. The UIRP condition holds because $E(X_1^{*Sf/\$})$ = 1.57 Sf/\$ = 1.592 Sf/\$[(1.045)/(1.06)].

short-term interest rate by a central bank is designed to help raise the spot FX value of the currency. The higher interest rate attracts foreign investors; movement of funds into the currency results in buying pressure on the currency and causes the spot FX value of the currency to increase. If the central bank's interest rate policy causes the one-year Swiss franc interest rate to rise from 4.0% to 4.5%, the new spot FX rate will be the same as the one we just calculated, 1.592 Sf/$.

Now let's look at the Fisher theory. Assume that the cause of the sudden interest rate increase, from $r^{Sf} = 4\%$ to 4.50%, is new information about a sudden rise in the anticipated Swiss inflation rate. In this case, there is (theoretically) *no* immediate reaction in the spot FX market. Instead, the increase in inflation will dictate a lower expected future FX value of the Swiss franc. You can see this by recalling the absolute purchasing power parity (APPP) ideas of Chapter 2.

Before the increase in the anticipated inflation rate and the Swiss franc interest rate, the Swiss franc was expected to increase in FX value gradually, from a spot FX rate of 1.60 Sf/$ today to 1.57 Sf/$ a year from now. If the anticipated Swiss inflation rate suddenly increases, the expectation of the Swiss franc's future FX value will be revised downward from the current expectation of 1.57 Sf/$. Given that the spot FX rate remains at 1.60 Sf/$, we know from the UIRP condition in equation (4.2a) that the new expected future FX rate is 1.60 Sf/$(1.045/1.06) = 1.58 Sf/$. This represents a lower FX value of the Swiss franc than in the previous expectation, 1.57 Sf/$.

Figure 4.4 shows the Fisher theory, where the expected FX rate at time 1 (boldface type) is the UIRP variable that responds to the interest rate change.

Because the interest rate increase is due to a revision of inflation expectations, the impact of the interest rate change is on the expected FX rate for the future, not on the spot FX rate today. While the spot FX value of the currency can depreciate quite quickly between time 0 and time 1 in high-inflation countries, this dynamic is different from the one we are looking at here, which is the immediate impact of an interest rate *change*.

Perhaps now you can see why the FX rate form of the UIRP condition in equation (4.2a) must be used in the analysis of interest rate changes, not the percentage change forms in equations (4.2b) or (4.2c). The simple reason is that there is no way to examine where the impact takes place in either of the percentage forms of the UIRP condition. It might be in the spot FX rate, in the expected future FX rate, or in some combination. So the FX rate form of the UIRP condition in equation (4.2a) must be used.

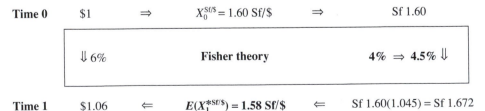

Time 0 $1 $\Rightarrow$ $X_0^{Sf/\$} = 1.60$ Sf/$ $\Rightarrow$ Sf 1.60

    $\Downarrow 6\%$ **Fisher theory**   **$4\% \Rightarrow 4.5\% \Downarrow$**

Time 1 $1.06 $\Leftarrow$ $E(X_1^{*Sf/\$}) = 1.58$ **Sf/$** $\Leftarrow$ Sf 1.60(1.045) = Sf 1.672

Figure 4.4 Fisher theory, showing the UIRP condition where $N = 1$, $r^{Sf} = 0.045$, $r^{\$} = 0.06$, $X_0^{Sf/\$} = 1.60$ Sf/$, and $E(X_1^{*Sf/\$}) = 1.58$ Sf/$. The UIRP condition holds because $E(X_1^{*Sf/\$}) = 1.58$ Sf/$ = 1.60 Sf/$[(1.045)/(1.06)].

Assume that the spot FX rate for the British pound is currently 1.60 $/£. Assume initially that the one-year US dollar interest rate is 5% and that the 1-year sterling rate is 10%. Now let the one-year US dollar interest rate stay at 5% and assume that the one-year sterling interest rate jumps instantaneously to 12%. (1) Use the UIRP condition in equation (4.2a) to determine what FX rate change occurs, assuming the asset market theory. (2) If the change in the sterling interest rate is due to revised inflation expectations (Fisher theory), what is the impact on the spot FX rate?

Answers: (1) Given the UIRP condition, the original equilibrium expected FX rate is (1.60 $/£)(1.05/1.10) = 1.527 $/£. If the sterling interest rate suddenly jumps to 12%, the new time-0 equilibrium spot FX rate is (1.527 $/£)/[(1.05/1.12)] = 1.63 $/£. This answer means that the equilibrium spot FX value of the pound is higher (1.63 $/£ vs 1.60 $/£). This spot FX change takes place "instantaneously." Since the predicted FX value of the pound one year from now is unchanged and is still 1.527 $/£, then over the next year, the pound is still predicted to depreciate gradually to 1.527 $/£. At the new spot FX rate of 1.63 $/£, however, the pound is now predicted to depreciate by a greater amount between time 0 and time 1. The new predicted gradual depreciation of the pound is consistent with the fact that the interest rate on sterling deposits is higher than on US dollar deposits. (2) If the sudden rise in the sterling interest rate is due to a revision of inflation expectations, the current spot FX rate is theoretically unchanged, but the expected future FX value of the British pound is revised downward to (1.60 $/£)(1.05/1.12) = 1.50 $/£.

Underlying the Fisher theory is the assumption that the real rate of interest is the same across countries. Using a linear approximation, the real rate of interest is the nominal rate of interest minus the inflation rate. Thus in the United States, the real rate of interest would be $r^{\$} - p^{\$}$, and in Switzerland, the real rate of interest would be $r^{Sf} - p^{Sf}$. Equating the two real rates results in the *international Fisher effect*, $r^{\$} - p^{\$} = r^{Sf} - p^{Sf}$.

The impact of an interest rate change may be more complex than either the asset market theory or the Fisher theory can explain. The interest rate change can simultaneously affect other economic variables that are not explicit in the UIRP condition. In some cases, an interest rate increase can slow an economy (perhaps by design of the monetary authorities). If so, investors may revise their expected future FX value of the currency downward without thinking in terms of inflation. This result could in turn affect the spot FX rate. If there is a strong perceived impact on the economy and the expected future currency value is very strong, the increased interest rate could also lead to a decline in the current spot FX value.

Canada experienced this kind of effect in the early 1990s. The Bank of Canada raised short-term interest rates, intending to defend the Canadian dollar, but the market out there perceived the interest rate hikes as being so negative for the Canadian economy that the spot FX value of the Canadian dollar actually fell in response. In 2000, the FX value of the euro fell when the European Central Bank (ECB) announced it would raise short-term interest rates. The market expected the move to hinder economic growth (see box "August 2000").

In the United States, a rise in interest rates in 1994 was coupled with a decline in the value of the US dollar. The reason turned out to be that, as interest rates rose and bond values fell, foreign investors in long-term US bonds decided to get out of the US bond market. Of course, their sale of US dollars into other currencies caused the spot FX value of the US dollar to plunge. The consequent depreciation of the US dollar was then further reason for squeamish foreign investors to pull out.

In summary, the impact of a change in an interest rate depends on (1) the cause of the interest rate change and (2) the anticipated collateral impact of the change on other economic variables that relate to FX rates.

AUGUST 2000

The euro tumbled to its lowest ever against the yen and was just shy of a record against the dollar on concern an expected interest rate increase by the European Central Bank tomorrow may hinder economic growth. Europe's currency declined to 88.82 US cents from 89.22. The euro has depreciated against the dollar for 14 of its 19 months in existence.

The British pound, meantime, slid to a seven-year low against the dollar of $1.4465 on speculation the Bank of England won't push up its benchmark interest rate again, following four increases in the past year. Credit Suisse Group's proposed acquisition of US-based Donaldson, Lufkin & Jenrette Inc. for $13.4 billion in cash and stock is also weighing on the euro and Swiss franc. The company will need to buy dollars, selling euros and possibly Swiss francs to finance the cash component of the deal. "Corporate flows are heading into the US and that seems to be the main factor" for the dollar's strength against European currencies, said John Parker, who helps oversee 1.8 billion pounds ($2.61 billion) at Pavilion Asset Management in Brighton.

Meantime, ECB policy-makers are expected to boost the benchmark interest rate from 4.25 percent tomorrow, according to 39 of 42 analysts surveyed by Bloomberg News yesterday. Eighteen of those 42 economists forecast a 25 basis-point rise, and 21 predicted a half-point move. A rate increase, aimed at capping price gains, would be the central bank's sixth since November. Inflation among the region's 11 nations sped passed the bank's 2 percent target for a second month in July.

While the prospect of rising interest rates tends to support a currency as deposit rates offer better returns, higher borrowing costs can also make it hard for companies to finance their investments, crimping profits and economic growth. "The ECB is in a Catch-22 situation," said Mike Moran, an economist at Standard Chartered Bank. "If it tries to be more aggressive, the growth picture may turn sour, which is the last thing the euro needs."

The euro's 23 percent decline against the dollar, and 29 percent loss against the yen, since its debut on Jan. 4, 1999, stems mostly from the strength of the US economy, analysts said. Record US growth continues to lure foreign investors to dollar-based financial assets, especially as there's little evidence of accelerating inflation.

The Federal Reserve left key rates on hold at 6.5 percent this month, a nine-year high.

Source: Bloomberg.

FEBRUARY 2004

Despite dropping in FX value for two years, the FX value of US dollar remained too high. Previous falls in the dollar's exchange rate have pushed American bond yields up as foreign investors have demanded a bigger reward to compensate for the increased exchange-rate risk. This drop, however, has so far been painless with bond yields staying remarkably low. Ten-year Treasuries, for example, are currently yielding 4.1%, slightly less than the yield on comparable German bonds.

In 2003, Asian central banks financed well over half of both America's current-account deficit and its budget deficit. At their recent pace of intervention, Japan and China could buy enough Treasury bonds this year to more than cover the American government's new borrowing needs. This would allow America to continue borrowing recklessly without the usual warning sign of rising bond yields.

Not only do artificially low bond yields appear to offer false signals that America's budget deficit is no cause for concern, but by holding down mortgage rates (which are linked to bond yields) they are also prolonging an unsustainable boom in consumer spending and borrowing. This benefits America in the short term, but allows even bigger imbalances (in the shape of domestic debt and foreign liabilities) to build up in the long term. To contain these debts will eventually require a far sharper collapse in the dollar, a steeper rise in bond yields, and a harder economic landing.

Source: The Economist.

FX FORECASTING

No one can forecast exactly what a future FX rate will be any more than anyone can forecast stock prices or interest rates. But many managers would like to base decisions on a best guess about future FX rates, derived from available economic and financial information. We learned about two variables that can be useful in forming FX forecasts in Chapter 2. One was the predicted inflation rate differential. The other was the extent of current deviation from absolute purchasing power parity. We have learned about two more potential factors in this chapter. One is the interest rate differential, or alternatively, the forward FX rate. Based on past data, one might predict FX rates to appreciate less than suggested by a forward premium and to depreciate less than suggested by a forward discount. The other variable was predicted changes in interest rates. Of course, no one can predict interest rate changes reliably, but many like to think they can at least predict the future direction.

There are other factors that must be considered: balance of payments, national income, economic growth, and so forth. Generally, managers may want to obtain forecasts from their company's economics department. An alternative is to use the research of investment banks. For an example, see the Merrill Lynch research report on the US dollar at the firm's Web site, http://www.ml.com/research/2004/pdf/retl/44700801.pdf. The Merrill Lynch FX forecasting model is based on a methodology called the *fundamental equilibrium exchange rate (FEER)*.[2]

Note that the theory of the UIRP condition says that the condition will result because of trading by informed FX forecasters. But FX participants in the real world are often tempted to use the UIRP equation to form their expectations, basically extracting the forecast reflected in the financial markets. If all FX market participants did this, then the UIRP condition would be empty, since the condition is based on the presumption that market participants form forecasts on fundamental economic factors, not by using the UIRP equation itself.

SIEGEL'S PARADOX

Recall that to compute the percentage change in the value of a currency, you use FX rates expressed with the currency in the denominator. That is, the percentage change in the spot FX value of the pound over the period from time 0 to time N is $X_N^{\$/£}/X_0^{\$/£} - 1$. For example, if the spot FX value of the pound at time 0 is $X_0^{\$/£} = 1.60$ \$/£, and if the spot FX value of the pound appreciates to 2.00 \$/£, the percentage rise in the spot FX value of the pound is $(2.00 \text{ \$/£})/(1.60 \text{ \$/£}) = 0.25$, or 25%.

Can you say the US dollar correspondingly depreciates by 25% relative to the pound? The answer is: approximately, but not exactly. The reason is a mathematical result known as *Siegel's paradox*.[3] Considering the percentage change in the value of the US dollar relative to the pound requires you to use FX rates from the viewpoint of the US dollar as the denominator currency. In this case, the spot FX rate changes from $X_0^{£/\$} = 1/X_0^{\$/£} = 1/(1.60 \text{ \$/£}) = 0.625$ £/\$ to $X_N^{£/\$} = 1/(2.00 \text{ \$/£}) = 0.50$ £/\$. The percentage change in the spot FX value of the US dollar is $(0.50 \text{ £/\$} - 0.625 \text{ £/\$})/(0.625 \text{ £/\$}) = (0.50 \text{ £/\$})/(0.625 \text{ £/\$}) - 1 = -20\%$, a 20% depreciation of the US dollar. Although the pound appreciates by 25% relative to the US dollar, the US dollar depreciates by 20% relative to the pound. Exhibit 4.1 shows an example of Siegel's paradox: here, the percentage change in an FX rate is not equal to minus the percentage change in the reciprocal of the FX rate.

Assume that the spot FX rate for the Swiss franc goes from 1.50 Sf/\$ to 1.25 Sf/\$. (1) Find the percentage change in the FX value of the Swiss franc and state whether the change is an appreciation or a depreciation of the Swiss franc. (2) Find the percentage change in the FX value of the US dollar relative to the Swiss franc and state whether this change is an appreciation or depreciation of the US dollar.

---

[2]See J. Williamson, *Estimating Equilibrium Exchange Rates* (Washington, DC: Institute for International Economics, 1994).
[3]Siegel's paradox was introduced in Jeremy Siegel, "Risk, Interest Rates, and the Forward Exchange," *Quarterly Journal of Economics*, February 1975.

EXHIBIT 4.1   Exchange Rate Changes

Country	Currency	US$/FOREIGN CURRENCY			FOREIGN CURRENCY/US$		
		Nov-02	Nov-03	Change in FC (%)	Nov-02	Nov-03	Change in US$ (%)
Canada	C$	0.63637	0.76061	0.19523 ⇑	1.57141	1.31473	(0.16334) ⇓
European Monetary Union	€	1.00100	1.16450	0.16334 ⇑	0.99900	0.85874	(0.14040) ⇓
Japan	¥	0.00822	0.00916	0.11466 ⇑	121.63083	109.11908	(0.10287) ⇓
United Kingdom	£	1.57040	1.68380	0.07221 ⇑	0.63678	0.59389	(0.06735) ⇓
Australia	A$	0.56126	0.71372	0.27164 ⇑	1.78171	1.40111	(0.21361) ⇓
Switzerland	Sf	0.68197	0.74511	0.09258 ⇑	1.46634	1.34208	(0.08474) ⇓
New Zealand	NZ$	0.49749	0.62439	0.25508 ⇑	2.01009	1.60156	(0.20324) ⇓

Source: www.fx.sauder.ubc.ca.

In Exhibit 4.1 the percentage change in an FX rate is not equal to minus the percentage change in the reciprocal of the FX rate. This is an examle of Siegel's paradox.

Answers: (1) The FX quotes, in conventional European terms, must be reciprocated to find the percentage change in the FX value of the Swiss franc. Performing this reciprocation directly in the percentage change expression, we have [1/(1.25 Sf/$)]/[1/(1.50 Sf/$)] − 1 = 0.20, or a 20% appreciation in the FX value of the Swiss franc (relative to the US dollar). (2) From the point of view of the Swiss franc as the pricing currency, the FX rate has changed from 1.50 Sf/$ to 1.25 Sf/$. The percentage change in the FX value of the US dollar is (1.25 Sf/$)/(1.50 Sf/$) − 1 = −0.1667, or minus 16.67%. Thus, the FX value of the US dollar depreciated by 16.67% relative to the Swiss franc, while we know in the first half of the example that the FX value of the Swiss franc appreciated by 20% relative to the US dollar.

We can apply an equation that accurately relates the percentage FX changes from two different currency perspectives. The equation with the US dollar/euro FX rate as the representative currencies is:

$$(1 + x^{\$/\euro})(1 + x^{\euro/\$}) = 1 \qquad (4.3)$$

Equation (4.3) can also be restated as $1 + x^{\$/\euro} = 1/(1 + x^{\euro/\$})$, or equivalently $1 + x^{\euro/\$} = 1/(1 + x^{\$/\euro})$.

Apply equation (4.3) to verify the answers to the preceding problem, where the FX value of the Swiss franc appreciated by 20% and the FX value of the US dollar depreciated by 16.67%.
Answer: $(1 + x^{\$/Sf})(1 + x^{Sf/\$}) = (1 + 0.20)(1 − 0.1667) = 1$.

While equation (4.3) is valid for percentage changes over any horizon, it is common to regard $x^{\$/\euro}$ as an *annualized* percentage change.

*SIEGEL'S PARADOX AND FORWARD VS EXPECTED FX RATES

The real power of Siegel's paradox is that it can show that informational efficiency in the FX market cannot be stated as $E(X_1^{\$/€}) = F_1^{\$/€}$. Siegel's paradox implies that even though $X_1^{\$/€}$ will always be equal to $1/X_1^{€/\$}$, the expected future FX spot rate, $E(X_1^{\$/€})$, cannot be equal to $1/E(X_1^{€/\$})$. That is, if 1.20 $/€ is the expected spot FX value of the euro a year from now, the expected spot FX value of the US dollar *cannot be* $1/(1.20\ \$/€) = 0.833\ €/\$$, even though it is true that if the spot FX value of the euro will be 1.20 $/€ a year from now, then the spot FX value of the US dollar a year from now will be $1/(1.20\ \$/€) = 0.833\ €/\$$.

To see this point, assume there are two equally likely possible outcomes for the future spot FX rate for a year from now: 0.80 $/€ ($\equiv$ 1.25 €/$) and 1.60 $/€ ($\equiv$ 0.625 €/$).

Probability	0.50	0.50
$X_1^{\$/€}$	0.80 $/€	1.60 $/€
$X_1^{€/\$}$	1.25 €/$	0.625 €/$

The expected spot FX value of the euro a year from now is thus 0.50(0.80 $/€) + 0.50(1.60 $/€) = 1.20 $/€. That is, the euro is expected to appreciate in FX value by 20% over the next year, since 1.20/1 − 1 = 0.20, or 20%. At the same time, the expected spot FX value of the US dollar for a year from now is 0.50(1.25 €/$) + 0.50(0.625 €/$) = 0.9375 €/$. The US dollar is expected to depreciate by 6.25% over the next year, since (0.9375 − 1)/1 = −0.0625, or −6.25%.

You see that $1/E(X_1^{\$/€}) = 1/(1.20\ \$/€) = 0.8333\ €/\$$ is not equal to $E(X_1^{€/\$})$, which we computed directly to be 0.9375 €/$. Also, $E(x^{\$/€}) \neq -E(x^{€/\$})$, since 20% ≠ −(−6.25%). Moreover, while equation (4.3) always holds for any given FX change, it does not mathematically apply for expectations of those changes. That is, $[1 + E(x^{\$/€})][1 + E(x^{€/\$})] \neq 1$. In our example, (1.20)(1 − 0.0625) = 1.125, not 1.

Taken together, all these mathematical surprises are implications of *Siegel's paradox*. In the example, Siegel's paradox is that even though the expected FX value of the euro is 1.20 $/€, the *expected* FX value of the US dollar is not 1/1.20 $/€ = 0.833 €/$, since the expected FX value of the US dollar is 0.9375 €/$. It is also paradoxical in the manner identified by Siegel that the FX value of the euro (relative to the US dollar) is expected to appreciate by 20%, while at the same time the FX value of the US dollar (relative to the euro) is expected to depreciate by 6.25%.

Assume that the spot FX value of the euro is currently 0.90 $/€. A year from now, there is a 50% chance that the spot FX value of the euro will be 0.75 $/€ and a 50% chance that the spot FX value will be 1.10 $/€. (1) What is the expected spot FX value of the euro a year from now and the expected percentage change in the FX value of the euro between now and a year from now? (2) What is the expected spot FX value of the US dollar a year from now and the expected percentage change in the FX value of the US dollar?

Answers: (1) $E(X_1^{\$/€}) = 0.50(0.75\ \$/€) + 0.50(1.10\ \$/€) = 0.925\ \$/€;\ E(x^{\$/€}) = (0.925\ \$/€)/(0.90\ \$/€)$ $- 1 = 0.0277,\ or\ 2.77\%.$ *(2)* $E(X_1^{€/\$}) = 0.50[1/(0.75\ \$/€)] + 0.50[1/(1.10\ \$/€)] = 1.121\ €/\$;$ *Since* $X_0^{\$/€} = 0.90\ \$/€,$ *and thus* $X_0^{€/\$} = 1.111\ €/\$,\ E(x^{€/\$}) = (1.121\ €/\$)/(1.111\ €/\$) - 1 = 0.009 = 0.9\%.$ *Note that Siegel's paradox in this case is that the euro is expected to appreciate relative to the US dollar (by 2.77%) and the US dollar is expected to appreciate relative to the euro (by 0.9%).*

Assume that the current one-year forward FX rate in the market is 1.6605 Sf/$. A person with Swiss francs can buy one US dollar for 1.6605 Swiss francs, for delivery a year from now. Alternatively, we can say that a person with US dollars can buy Swiss francs forward, and pay 1/(1.6605 Sf/$) = 0.6022 $/Sf, or 0.6022 US dollars per Swiss franc. That is, we can always say that $F_N^{\$/Sf} = 1/F_N^{Sf/\$}$; forward FX rates mathematically reciprocate just like spot FX rates.

Given Siegel's paradox, which reveals that expectations do not reciprocate, we see an immediate problem with the economic theory that forward FX rates are equal to expected spot rates. Suppose that the forward FX rate *is* equal to the expected spot FX rate from the direction of dollars to Swiss francs. In that case, the forward FX rate expressed in Sf/$ *cannot* equal the expected FX rate expressed in Sf/$. Since $F_N^{\$/Sf} = 1/F_N^{Sf/\$}$, but $E(X_N^{\$/Sf}) \neq 1/E(X_N^{Sf/\$})$, the forward FX rate *cannot* be equal to the expected spot FX rate from both currency directions. Since the choice of currency direction viewpoint is arbitrary, Siegel's paradox is a problem for the theory that forward FX rates represent expected spot FX rates.

A common way of dealing with Siegel's paradox in global finance models is to use the approximation: $x^{\$/€} \approx -x^{€/\$} + \sigma_€^2$, where $\sigma_€$ is the FX volatility of the euro, or standard deviation of $x^{\$/€}$. The concept of FX volatility was introduced in Chapter 1. Exhibit 4.2 shows estimated FX volatilities for 2000 and 2003. (Exhibit 4.2 is the same as Exhibit 1.4.) Applying the approximation to expected FX changes, we get equation (4.4):[4]

$$E(x^{\$/€}) \approx -E(x^{€/\$}) + \sigma_€^2 \tag{4.4}$$

For a numerical example of equation (4.4), assume that the expected (annualized) rate of change in the $/€ FX rate is 3.75%. Also assume that the (annualized) volatility of such changes, $\sigma_€$, is 11%, or 0.11. Using equation (4.4), we have $E(x^{€/\$}) \approx -0.0375 + 0.11^2$ $= -0.0254,$ or -2.54%.

In summary, if the FX volatility is 11%, and if the FX value of the euro is expected to appreciate by 3.75% per year relative to the US dollar, the FX value of the US dollar is expected to decline annually by about 2.54% relative to the euro (approximately). Equation (4.4) can be stated in the other currency direction, $E(x^{€/\$}) \approx -E(x^{\$/€}) + \sigma_€^2.$

Expected future FX rates may be found using the following formulas: $E(X_N^{\$/€}) = X_0^{\$/€}[1 + E(x^{\$/€})]^N$ *and* $E(X_N^{€/\$}) = X_0^{€/\$}[1 + E(x^{€/\$})]^N.$ As an example, assume that the spot FX

---

[4]Equation (4.4) may be found in B. Solnik, "Currency Hedging and Siegel's Paradox: On Black's Universal Hedging Rule," *Review of International Economics*, June 1993, 180–187. In this model the volatility of $x^{\$/€}$ is assumed to be equal to the volatility of $x^{€/\$}.$

rate today is $X_0^{\$/€} = 1.125$ \$/€, which is equivalently $1/(1.125 \text{ \$/€}) = 0.889$ €/\$. Assume that the expected annual percentage FX changes are $E(x^{\$/€}) = 2.60\%$ and $E(x^{€/\$}) = -1.50\%$. For a one-year horizon, the expected \$/€ FX rate, $E(X_1^{\$/€})$, is $(1.125 \text{ \$/€})[1.026] = 1.154$ \$/€; the expected €/\$ FX rate is $E(X_1^{€/\$}) = (0.889 \text{ €/\$})(1 - 0.015) = 0.876$ €/\$. Note that 0.876 €/\$ is not equal to $1/(1.154 \text{ \$/€})$. Thus, we see Siegel's paradox: $E(X_1^{\$/€})$ is not equal to $1/E(X_1^{€/\$})$.

Assume a spot FX rate today of $X^{\$/£} = 1.60$ \$/£. Also assume that the annualized expected percentage change in the FX value of the pound is -4% for the next six months, and that the annualized volatility of pound is 12%. Use equation (4.4) to find the annualized expected percentage change in the FX value of the US dollar. What are, for the six-month horizon, the expected future \$/£ FX rate and the expected future £/\$ FX rate?

Answers: From equation (4.4): $E(x^{£/\$}) = -(-0.04) + 0.0144 = 0.0544$, *or 5.44%,* $E(X_{0.50}^{\$/£}) = (1.60 \text{ \$/£})(1 - 0.04)^{0.50} = 1.57$ \$/£; *the expected £/\$ FX rate is* $E(X_{0.50}^{£/\$}) = (0.625 \text{ £/\$})(1.0544)^{0.50} = 0.642$ £/\$.

SUMMARY

We discussed two parity conditions for FX and interest rates. The covered interest rate parity condition is a no-arbitrage condition. Since the arbitrage transactions that enforce the CIRP condition are relatively easy and inexpensive for the highly liquid currencies of developed countries, it is not surprising that the CIRP condition is empirically reliable in these cases. In less liquid currency situations, deviations from the CIRP condition might sometimes be found.

The uncovered interest rate parity condition is a theory that actual forward FX rates reflect informed predictions of future FX spot rates. The economic activity that would enforce the UIRP condition is not easy at all. Indeed it is not easy to even measure whether the UIRP theory does or does not hold. Many economists argue that real-world data do not fit the UIRP theory.

Despite this, the UIRP condition helps identify two factors that affect FX rates: the interest rate differential and interest rate changes. We covered two workhorse theories of how interest rate changes affect FX rates, the asset market theory and the Fisher theory. These two theories are differentiated from each other by the role of inflation. We also saw how real-world situations can often be more complex than the simple theories might suggest.

Finally, you learned about a mathematical effect known as Siegel's paradox. At the basic level, Siegel's paradox is that the percentage change in the FX value of one currency in an exchange rate is not simply equal to the negative of the percentage change in the FX value of the other currency. In the UIRP theory, Siegel's paradox implies that if the forward FX rate is equal to the expected spot FX rate in one currency direction, the equality cannot hold from the other currency direction.

EXHIBIT 4.2   FX Volatility Estimates

Country	CURRENCY		VOLATILITY (%)	
	Code	Name	9/1/2000	9/1/2003
G8/Eurozone				
Australia	AUD	Dollars	9.50	9.67
Canada	CAD	Dollars	4.73	7.66
Euroland	EUR	Euro	10.42	9.03
Japan	JPY	Yen	11.62	8.82
Russia	RUB	Roubles	6.02	1.84
United Kingdom	GBP	Pounds	7.29	7.97
Europe (Non-Euro)				
Czech Republic	CZK	Koruny	10.65	10.04
Denmark	DKK	Kroner	10.39	9.01
Iceland	ISK	Kronur	7.08	9.49
Norway	NOK	Krone	8.59	10.20
Poland	PLN	Zlotych	11.25	9.90
Sweden	SEK	Kronor	8.98	9.15
Switzerland	CHF	Francs	10.28	10.10
Latin America				
Argentina	ARS	Pesos	0.39	15.92
Brazil	BRL	Real	9.21	21.45
Chile	CLP	Pesos	6.47	7.98
Colombia	COP	Pesos	7.81	8.46
Mexico	MXN	Pesos	9.01	10.25
Peru	PEN	Nuevos soles	4.50	3.47
Venezuela	VEB	Bolivares	1.45	25.96
Asia/Africa				
China	CNY	Yuan renmibi	0.06	0.18
Hong Kong	HKD	Dollars	0.14	0.05
India	INR	Rupees	2.01	1.50
Indonesia	IDR	Rupiahs	22.78	8.00
South Korea	KRW	Won	5.26	7.31
Singapore	SGD	Dollars	3.86	4.54
South Africa	ZAR	Rand	8.01	17.83

Source: Used with permission from Justin Pettit and Igor Sokolovsky, "FX Policy Revisited: Strategy & Tactics," Union Bank of Switzerland (UBS) Strategic Advisory Group, October 2003: http://papers.ssrn.com/sol3/papers.cfm?abstract_id=463106.

GLOSSARY

Asset market theory: Changes in interest rates are not the result of changes in expected inflation rates and thus result in changes in current spot FX rates.

Carry trade: See Currency carry trade.

CIRP condition: covered interest rate parity condition: The no-arbitrage relationship between the spot FX rate, the forward FX rate, and the interest rate differential.

Covered interest arbitrage: Simultaneous transactions in the spot FX market, the forward FX market, and the eurocurrency market that exploit price and rate misalignments.

Currency carry trade: Borrowing in a low interest rate currency and investing the exchanged proceeds in a high interest rate currency deposit. This is a common speculative trade based on the belief that the high interest rate currency will not depreciate by as much as would be the case in equilibrium if the UIRP condition holds.

Equilibrium: A condition that holds, or else there will be pressure for the variables in the condition to change until it does hold. Once achieved, the equilibrium condition would tend to change only because of a change in one of the variables.

Fisher open equation: See UIRP condition.

Fisher theory: Changes in interest rates reflect changes in anticipated inflation rates and therefore result in changes in expected future FX rates.

Forward premium puzzle: The tendency for the FX value of a currency to rise if it has the higher interest rate, contrary to the prediction of the UIRP condition.

Fundamental equilibrium exchange rate (FEER): A methodology for forecasting FX rate based on fundamental economic variables.

International Fisher equation: See UIRP condition.

Siegel's paradox: The mathematical result, and its implications, that the percentage change in the FX value of currency A relative to currency B is not equal to the negative of the percentage change in the FX value of currency B relative to currency A.

UIRP condition: uncovered interest rate parity condition: The theoretical economic relationship between the spot FX rate, the expected future FX rate, and the interest rate differential. Also known as the *international Fisher equation or the Fisher open equation.*

DISCUSSION QUESTIONS

1. Compare and contrast the covered interest rate parity (CIRP) condition with the uncovered interest rate parity (UIRP) condition.
2. Assume that the international law of one price holds initially in the goods market and that the UIRP condition holds. Explain why a short-run increase in the interest rate for a currency, other things equal, can cause the currency to be overvalued from the perspective of the goods market. Use this reasoning to explain why countries with high economic growth may be subject to trade deficits.

3. Explain the difference in the reaction of the FX market to (1) an interest rate change driven by a change in inflation expectation and (2) an interest rate change driven by increased asset returns but no inflation change.

PROBLEMS

1. Assume that the one-year rate of interest is 7% in Canadian dollars and 5% in US dollars, and the actual spot FX rate is 1.25 C$/$. Find the one-year forward FX rate if the CIRP condition holds.
2. Suppose the quoted actual one-year forward FX rate is 1.26 C$/$. Given the information in Problem 1, determine a covered interest rate arbitrage strategy, and find the amount of time-0 arbitrage profits, in US dollars, for an actual forward FX contract *amount* of $1050.
3. The annualized six-month interest rate in US dollars is 7% and in yen is 2%. The spot FX rate is 104 ¥/$. What is the six-month forward FX rate if there are no covered interest arbitrage opportunities?
4. The one-year interest rate in US dollars is 4% and in pounds is 6%. Informed FX market participants expect the spot FX rate to be 1.84 $/£ a year from now. What is the spot FX rate now if the UIRP condition holds?
5. Assume one-year interest rates for the US dollar and the euro of 3 and 5%, respectively. Find the one-year expected percentage change in the FX value of the euro, assuming that the UIRP condition holds. With the approximate UIRP condition in equation (4.2c), find the linear approximation to the one-year expected percentage change in the FX value of the euro.
6. Assume that the spot FX rate for the British pound is 1.60 $/£, the one-year US dollar interest rate is currently 8%, and the one-year sterling interest rate is currently 5%. Assume that the one-year US dollar interest rate suddenly rises to 10%, and all else stays the same. Use the UIRP condition to determine the new spot FX rate for the pound if the increase in the US interest rate is (a) driven by the expectation of higher US inflation and (b) driven by higher US short-term asset returns.
7. If the spot yen/dollar FX rate changes from 125.00 ¥/$ at time 0 to 133.33 ¥/$ at time 1, what is the percentage change in the spot FX value of the yen (relative to the US dollar)?
8. The time-0 FX rate between the Swiss franc and the US dollar is 1.50 Sf/$. The time-1 FX rate is 1.75 Sf/$. What is the percentage change in the spot FX value of the Swiss franc (relative to the US dollar)? What is the percentage change in the spot FX value of the US dollar (relative to the Swiss franc)?
9. *Assume that the spot FX rate for the euro is currently 0.90 $/€. There is a 50% chance that the spot FX rate for a year from now will be 0.625 $/€ and a 50% chance that it will be 1.250 $/€. What is the expected spot FX rate for a year from now. What is the expected percentage change in the spot FX value of the euro? What is the expected spot FX value of the US dollar and the expected percentage change in the spot FX value of the US dollar?
*10. Assume that the expected percentage change in the FX value of the euro is 3%. You estimate that the volatility in the $/€ rate, expressed as the standard deviation of the percentage changes, is 12%. What is the approximate expected percentage change in the FX value of the US dollar, using the linear approximation in equation (4.4)?
*11. Assume that the spot FX rate today is $X_0^{¥/\$} = 125$ ¥/$, which is also 0.008 $/¥. Also assume that the expected percentage change in the FX value of the US dollar is −2% (per year) for the next 2 years, and that the FX volatility of the yen (the annualized standard deviation of percentage FX changes) is 10%. Find the approximate expected percentage change in the FX value of the yen (per year) using the approximation in equation (4.4). Then find, for the two-year horizon, the expected future $/¥ FX rate and the expected future ¥/$ FX rate.

ANSWERS TO PROBLEMS

1. 1.274 C\$/\$

2. \$10.84

3. 101.54 ¥/\$ = 104 ¥/\$$(1.02/1.07)^{0.50}$

4. You want to find $X_0^{\$/£}$ such that $E(X_1^{*\$/£}) = 1.84$ \$/£ $= X_0^{\$/£}[(1 + r^\$)/(1 + r^£)] = X_0^{\$/£}[(1.04)/(1.06)]$. Thus, $X_0^{\$/£} = 1.875$ \$/£.

5. $E(x_1^{*\$/€}) = (1 + r^\$)/(1 + r^€) - 1 = 1.03/1.05 - 1 = -0.019$, or -1.9%. Approximately, $E(x_1^{*\$/€}) = r^\$ - r^€ = 0.03 - 0.05 = -0.02$, or -2%.

6. (a) 1.60 \$/£; (b) 1.571 \$/£

7. The yen depreciates by 6.25%.

8. $x^{\$/Sf} = -0.1428$, or -14.28%.; $x^{Sf/\$} = 0.1667$, or 16.67%.

9. $E(X_1^{\$/€}) = 0.9375$ \$/€; $E(x^{\$/€}) = 4.167\%$; $E(X_1^{€/\$}) = 1.20$ €/\$; $E(x^{€/\$}) = 8\%$.

10. 1.56%

11. From equation (4.4), $E(x^{\$/¥}) = -(-0.02) + 0.01 = 0.03$, or 3% per year. $E(X_2^{\$/¥}) = (0.008$ \$/¥$)(1.03)^2 = 0.00849$ \$/¥. The expected ¥/\$ FX rate *is* $E(X_2^{¥/\$}) = (125$ ¥/\$$)(1 - 0.02)^2 = 120.05$ ¥/\$.

LONG-TERM FOREIGN EXCHANGE EXPOSURE

Future FX rates are uncertain, which creates financial risk for firms that conduct international business, and even for many firms that do not conduct business abroad. How a firm measures and manages its risk exposure to foreign exchange variability is a central issue in global financial management.

The four chapters of Part II delve into long-term foreign exchange exposure, defined as the variability in the firm's anticipated future cash flow stream caused by unexpected FX changes. Long-term FX exposure is more complex than FX transaction exposure of a specific receivable or payable. If managers are to hedge or otherwise manage a firm's risk due to FX changes, there must be some quantitative measure of long-term FX exposure.

Chapter 5 introduces the main idea by closely examining the forces that create long-term FX exposure of a firm's operating cash flows. To some extent, this FX exposure can be managed by having operating costs with FX exposures that match the FX exposures of the revenues.

The long-term FX exposure of operating cash flows can also be managed financially, with debt denominated in foreign currency and with currency swap positions. After a discussion of the pros and cons of financial hedging of long-term FX exposure, Chapter 6 considers how a firm's debt level and debt denominations affect the FX exposure of the firm's equity value. Chapter 7 discusses the details of how currency swaps work and how they may be used in managing long-term FX exposure.

Chapter 8 looks at long-term FX exposure from the economic perspective of a firm that maximizes profits. Chapter 8 also shows the idea of competitive FX exposure by applying the profit maximization idea with two firms from different countries that compete internationally.

CHAPTER 5

FOREIGN EXCHANGE OPERATING EXPOSURE

Foreign exchange operating exposure, or *FX operating exposure*, is the long-term FX exposure of a firm's anticipated *operating profit* stream (or operating cash flow stream). The main components of FX operating exposure are *FX revenue exposure* and *FX cost exposure*. These are the long-term FX exposures of a firm's anticipated revenue and cost steams.

This chapter covers the sources of FX operating exposure and explains how it is measured. This exposure is "real," whether or not it is reflected in reported financial statements.

The chapter also presents the idea of operational hedging, which is having operating costs with an FX exposure that offsets the FX exposure of the revenues.

FX OPERATING EXPOSURE

To explain FX operating exposure, we will first look at a European firm's FX operating exposure to the US dollar. Then we'll look at the same firm as if it were owned by a US multinational and examine the FX operating exposure to the euro.

Suppose our example company, Euro Pipe Fittings (EPF), produces aluminum pipe fittings at a plant outside Dublin, Ireland. In addition to local wages and marketing

EXHIBIT 5.1a   EPF Operating Cash Flow Statement (euros): $X^{\$/\text{€}} = 1$ \$/€

Revenues ($R^{\text{€}}$)	€600
Production expense	240
Aluminum	120 ($120 at 1 $/€)
Depreciation	40
EBIT	€200
Taxes	40
EBIAT	€160
Add depreciation	40
After-tax operating cash flow ($O^{\text{€}}$)	€200

expenses, production at the Irish facility requires purchases of raw aluminum. Sales are predominantly to German construction companies.[1] This year, EPF is expected to sell 600 fittings at €1 per fitting, generating revenues in euros ($R^{\text{€}}$) of €600. Production and marketing expenses amount to €0.40 per fitting, or €240. Each fitting requires one pound of aluminum. Aluminum is priced in US dollars, and the price is currently $0.20 per pound. Let us assume the spot FX rate is currently 1 $/€, so the aluminum for 600 fittings will cost $120, or €120 at the current spot FX rate.

Before considering taxes, EPF's operating cash flow (in euros) is €600 − 240 − 120 = €240. Let us assume a tax rate of 20%. This tax rate is the effective tax rate after the company has exploited opportunities in the tax codes to reduce taxes. Assume also that EPF has depreciation expense of €40. Therefore, earnings before interest and taxes (EBIT) €240 − 40 = €200, and taxes are 0.20(€200) = €40. Earnings before interest after taxes (EBIAT) = €160. Adding depreciation back to EBIAT, EPF's expected after-tax operating cash flow in euros, denoted $O^{\text{€}}$, is €160 + 40 = €200.

EPF's projected cash flow statement, given a current spot FX rate of 1 $/€, is shown in Exhibit 5.1a.

What happens to EPF's projected cash flow if the spot FX rate changes from 1 $/€ to 0.80 $/€? While FX changes may have an impact on a company's revenues, as we discuss later, for now we assume that EPF's revenues (in euros) do not change when the spot FX rate changes.[2] That is, EPF still expects to sell 600 fittings at €1 per fitting. Production expense and depreciation also do not change, but the cost in euros of the aluminum, which is fixed in US dollars at $120, is now (1.25 €/$)($120) = €150.

EPF's projected cash flow statement, given the new spot FX rate of 0.80 $/€, is shown in Exhibit 5.1b.

---

[1]This hypothetical scenario is adapted from Stephen Godfrey and Ramon Espinosa, "Value at Risk and Corporate Valuation," *Journal of Applied Corporate Finance*, Winter 1998, 108–115.
[2]Later in this chapter, we look at changes in revenues due to changes in selling prices in response to changes in FX rates. In Chapter 8, we cover simultaneous changes in sales price and sales volume.

EXHIBIT 5.1b   EPF Operating Cash Flow Statement: (euros) $X^{\$/€} = 0.80$ \$/€

Revenues ($R^€$)	€600
Production expense	240
Aluminum	150 ($120 at 0.80 $/€)
Depreciation	40
EBIT	€170
Taxes	34
EBIAT	€136
Add depreciation	40
After-tax operating cash flow ($O^€$)	€176

As we see in Exhibit 5.1b, when the spot FX value of the euro drops to 0.80 \$/€, EPF's after-tax operating cash flow would drop from €200 to €176. EPF thus has a short *FX operating exposure* to a foreign currency, the US dollar. When the US dollar appreciates (as is the case when the FX value of the euro declines to 0.80 \$/€), EPF's operating cash flow declines because the cost of aluminum increases.

Although we are now thinking in terms of a stream of ongoing operating cash flows, EPF's FX operating exposure is similar in principle to the FX transaction exposure you learned about in earlier chapters. In this simple case, EPF could hedge a single year's FX operating exposure to the US dollar by going long a euro-denominated forward FX contract on US dollars with an amount of $A^€$ equal to its aluminum costs in euros, €120.

Real-world companies are not as simple as EPF. For this reason, it will be useful to measure a company's overall FX operating exposure as an elasticity: the percentage change in after-tax operating cash flow, given the percentage change in the FX value of the foreign currency. Since the foreign currency for EPF is the US dollar and the home currency is the euro, EPF's FX operating exposure to the US dollar is $o^€/x^{€/\$}$, where $o^€ = \%\Delta O^€ = (O_1^€ - O_0^€)/O_0^€$ and $x^{€/\$}$ has already been defined to be $\%\Delta X^{€/\$} = (X_1^{€/\$} - X_0^{€/\$})/X_0^{€/\$}$.

We denote FX operating exposure $\xi_{O\$}^€$. We use the symbol ξ to denote FX exposure in general. As usual, the superscript denotes the pricing currency, so for $\xi_{O\$}^€$ the € superscript indicates that the cash flow is measured in euros. The \$ subscript indicates that it is changes in the FX value of the US dollar that causes the FX exposure. That is, the US dollar is the currency to which the firm's cash flows (when viewed in euros) are exposed. The O subscript indicates that the exposure is operating exposure. Other symbols will be used to denote other types of FX exposure.

In the EPF example, the FX change represents a 20% depreciation of the euro and a 25% appreciation of the US dollar, from 1 €/\$ to 1.25 €/\$. The operating cash flow (in euros) drops by 12% (from €200 to €176) when the US dollar appreciates by 25%, so EPF's FX operating exposure to the US dollar, $\xi_{O\$}^€$, is $o^€/x^{€/\$} = -0.12/0.25 = -0.48$. EPF's FX operating exposure to the US dollar, −0.48, indicates that operating cash flow will fall by 0.48% for a 1.00% rise in the FX value of the US dollar.

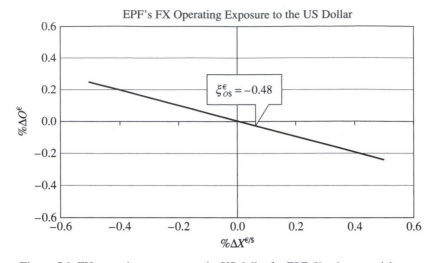

Figure 5.1 FX operating exposure to the US dollar for EPF: *X*-axis, potential percentage changes in the FX value of the US dollar, both positive and negative; *Y*-axis, percentage changes in EPF's euro operating cash flow. The slope of the line, −0.48, is the firm's FX operating exposure to the US dollar.

EPF's operating cash flow (in euros) drops when the US dollar rises because EPF imports of raw materials (aluminum) whose cost in euros rises when the FX value of the US dollar rises.

Figure 5.1 shows EPF's FX operating exposure to the US dollar graphically.

Assume that the cost of a pound of aluminum is $0.25 instead of $0.20. Assume a 25% rise in the FX value of the US dollar as the spot FX rate changes from 1 $/€ to 0.80 $/€. Find EPF's FX operating exposure to the US dollar and explain the difference between the answer and the example in the text.

Answers: The total cost of aluminum for 600 fittings is now $150. At 1 $/€, EPF's initial EBIT in euros will be €600 − 240 − 150 − 40 = €170. EBIAT will be €170(1 − 0.20) = €136, and after-tax operating cash flow will be €136 + 40 = €176. At 0.80 $/€, EPF's EBIT in euros will be €600 − 240 − 187.50 − 40 = €132.50. EBIAT will be €132.50(1 − 0.20) = €106, and after-tax operating cash flow will be €106 + 40 = €146. The percentage change in after-tax operating cash flow is €146/€176 − 1 = −0.17, or −17%, in response to a 25% rise in the FX value of the US dollar. This represents FX operating exposure of −0.68. EPF's operating cash flow is more negatively exposed to the US dollar because the aluminum, whose cost in euros changes with the spot FX rate, is a larger proportion of operating costs.

FX CHANGES AND OPERATING PROFITS: APRIL 2001

A weak euro cost Eastman Kodak Co. millions of dollars in the first quarter. It's not taking the same risk again.

The world's largest photography company, which generates about a quarter of its revenue in Europe, this month joined a list of major US firms hedging to protect themselves against the plunging currency.

"It's becoming the in thing these days," said Bob Brust, chief financial officer of Rochester, New York-based Kodak. "I would have never guessed the euro would be down where it is."

Merck & Co., Johnson & Johnson, and Minnesota Mining and Manufacturing Co. are among other companies that have hedged euro exposure, according to their most recent filings.

Kodak is also not alone in reporting revenue declines caused by the sagging euro, which touched a record low today and has lost 22 percent of its value against the dollar since its debut last year.

Procter & Gamble Co. said the weak euro contributed to a 2 percent sales decline in the January–March quarter, and DuPont Co. said the currency was the primary reason for a 10 percent drop in revenue from Europe in dollar terms.

Gerber Scientific Inc., a South Windsor, Connecticut maker of automated manufacturing systems, will cut jobs and warned profit will drop in the quarter ending April 30, partly because of the euro.

In Kodak's case, a euro worth about 95.5 cents, its level on March 31, would cut earnings 22 cents a share for the full year, the company said.

The euro's 9.5 percent slide this year came after firms such as Goldman, Sachs & Co. and Deutsche Bank AG predicted in December the currency would rise to about $1.10 or $1.12 in the first quarter.

Instead, the euro sank to its weakest levels yet, touching as low as 90.33 US cents and 96.505 yen this week. It started out last year at $1.17 per euro and 133 yen, amid optimism that even had some analysts suggesting it would supplant the dollar as the currency of choice on world financial markets.

The euro has been pummeled as growth in the 11-nation single currency region failed to pick up as quickly as some investors and analysts had expected.

"We take a long-term view," said Alan Resnick, treasurer at Bausch & Lomb Inc., the Rochester, New York maker of eye care products. "At some point the euro is going to turn around."

While the euro's decline can reduce the company's revenue in dollar terms, that is offset to some degree by lower manufacturing costs in Europe created by the drop, Resnick said.

Source: Bloomberg, April 28, 2001.

EXHIBIT 5.2a EPF Operating Cash Flow Statement ($): $X^{\$/\euro} = 1$ $/€

Revenues ($R^\$$)	$600 (€600 at 1 $/€)
Production expense	240 (€240 at 1 $/€)
Aluminum	120
Depreciation	40 (€40 at 1 $/€)
EBIT	$200
Taxes	40
EBIAT	$160
Add depreciation	40
After-tax operating cash flow ($O^\$$)	$200

EXHIBIT 5.2b EPF Operating Cash Flow Statement ($): $X^{\$/\euro} = 0.80$ $/€

Revenues ($R^\$$)	$480.0 (€600 at 0.80 $/€)
Production expense	192.0 (€240 at 0.80 $/€)
Aluminum	120.0
Depreciation	32.0 (€40 at 0.80 $/€)
EBIT	$136.0
Taxes	27.2
EBIAT	$108.8
Add depreciation	32.0
After-tax operating cash flow ($O^\$$)	$140.8

FX OPERATING EXPOSURE OF A FOREIGN SUBSIDIARY

Let us now assume a US firm owns Euro Pipe Fittings. In US dollars, the revenues, production costs, and depreciation change with changes in the FX rate, but the cost of the aluminum does not. The US owner of EPF cares about EPF's financial results in US dollars.

If owned by a US firm, EPF would be subject to income tax in both Europe and the United States, but credit would be given by the United States for taxes paid in Europe. This system means that EPF's tax rate would be the higher of the effective US tax rate and the effective European tax rate. For simplicity, we assume the effective tax rate stays the same if EPF has US owners, 20%.[3]

EPF's initial cash flow statement in US dollars is shown in Exhibit 5.2a for a spot FX rate of 1 $/€. Exhibit 5.2b shows EPF's cash flow statement in US dollars when the spot FX rate changes to 0.80 $/€.

---

[3]A detailed analysis of the tax rules is beyond our scope at present. For more information on tax rules in global business, see Chapters 10 and 11 in M. Scholes, M. Wolfson, M. Erickson, E. Maydew, and T. Shevlin, *Taxes and Business Strategy*, 2nd ed. (Upper Saddle Kiver, NJ: Prentice Hall, 2002).

What is the FX operating exposure to the euro, denoted $\xi_{O\epsilon}^{\$}$, for the US owner of EPF? The euro is the currency to which the operating cash flow, measured in US dollars, is exposed. Thus, $\xi_{O\epsilon}^{\$}$ is defined as the percentage change in the firm's expected US dollar operating cash flow level, $\%\Delta O^{\$}$, given the percentage change in the spot FX value of the euro, $x^{\$/\epsilon}$. Letting $o^{\$}$ denote $\%\Delta O^{\$}$, the elasticity definition of FX operating exposure, from the point of view of US dollars, is shown in equation (5.1).

FX Operating Exposure

$$\xi_{O\epsilon}^{\$} = o^{\$}/x^{\$/\epsilon} \tag{5.1}$$

From Exhibits 5.2a and 5.2b, we see that EPF's operating cash flow in US dollars drops from \$200 to \$140.80, a change of \$140.80/\$200 − 1 = −0.296, or minus 29.6%, when the euro drops by 20% in FX value. Thus, $\xi_{O\epsilon}^{\$} = -0.296/(-0.20) = 1.48$.

In US dollars, EPF's FX operating exposure to the euro is positive. When the euro appreciates, EPF's revenue in US dollars rises and causes operating cash flow to rise.

Note that even if EPF's cash flow were reinvested in its own growth and not repatriated to the United States, the parent still has the same FX operating exposure as if the cash flow were actually converted to US dollars. The reason is the FX changes affect the intrinsic value of EPF's operating cash flows in US dollars, that is, the value that the parent could get by selling EPF as an entity. This point should become clearer in the next chapter.

Figure 5.2 shows the idea of EPF's long FX operating cash flow to the euro, when the cash flows are viewed in US dollars.

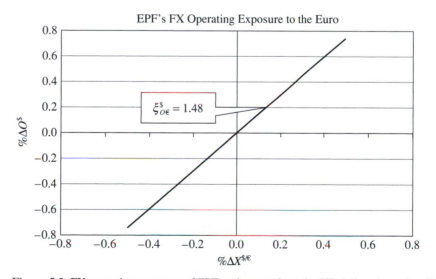

Figure 5.2 FX operating exposure of EPF to the euro from the US dollar viewpoint: X-axis, potential percentage changes in the FX value of the euro, both positive and negative; Y-axis, percentage changes in EPF's operating cash flow in US dollars. The slope of the line, 1.48, is the firm's FX operating exposure to the euro when the financial results are viewed in US dollars.

As shown in Figures 5.1 and 5.2, EPF's FX operating exposure is linear; that is, it is the same for any percentage change in the FX value of the euro. The FX operating exposure is linear for EPF, since sales volume and production of pipe fittings are assumed to be unaffected by FX changes. The next example verifies this linearity by showing that the FX operating exposure to the euro is 1.48 for a different change in the FX value of the euro.

Assume the FX value of the euro rises by 10% from 1 \$/€ to 1.10 \$/€. Find EPF's new projected after-tax operating cash flow in US dollars. Demonstrate that the FX operating exposure to the euro is 1.48.

Answer: EPF's new EBIT in US dollars will be \$660 – 264 – 120 – 44 = \$232. EBIAT will be \$232(1 – 0.20) = \$185.60, and after-tax operating cash flow will be \$185.60 + 44 = \$229.60. The percentage increase in after-tax operating cash flow is \$229.60/\$200 – 1 = 0.148, or 14.8%, in response to a 10% rise in the FX value of the euro. This represents FX operating exposure of 1.48.

In US dollars, EPF's FX operating exposure to the euro is 1.48, while in euros, the same company's FX operating exposure to the US dollar is –0.48. The fact that these two exposure measures sum to 1 is not a coincidence. Equation (5.2) states the relationship:

$$\xi^\$_{O\epsilon} + \xi^\epsilon_{O\$} = 1 \tag{5.2}$$

We have looked at the same company from two currency perspectives, the euro and the US dollar. This should help us see that the currency perspective is not dependent on where the firm is located.

The next example problem extends an earlier problem and demonstrates equation (5.2).

Assume that the cost of a pound of aluminum is \$0.25 instead of \$0.20. Assume a 20% drop in the FX value of the euro as the spot FX rate changes from 1 \$/€ to 0.80 \$/€. Find EPF's FX operating exposure to the euro and show that this FX operating exposure to the euro and the FX operating exposure to the US dollar sum to 1.

Answers: The total cost of aluminum is now \$150. At 1 \$/€, EPF's initial EBIT in US dollars will be \$600 – 240 – 150 – 40 = \$170. EBIAT will be \$170(1 – 0.20) = \$136, and after-tax operating cash flow will be \$136 + 40 = \$176. At 0.80 \$/€, EPF's EBIT in US dollars will be \$480 – 192 – 150 – 32 = \$106. EBIAT will be \$106(1 – 0.20) = \$84.80, and after-tax operating cash flow will be \$84.80 + 32 = \$116.80. The percentage change in after-tax operating cash flow is €116.80/€176 – 1 = –0.336, or –33.6%, in response to a 20% drop in the FX value of the euro. This represents FX operating exposure of 1.68. We found earlier that EPF's FX operating exposure to the US dollar is –0.68, and thus the two FX operating exposures sum to 1.

FX REVENUE AND COST EXPOSURES AND FX PASS-THROUGH

FX revenue exposure and FX cost exposure are the main components of FX operating exposure, and are defined similarly as elasticities (i.e., as percentage change sensitivities). *FX revenue exposure* is the elasticity of a firm's anticipated revenue to FX changes, viewed from the perspective of the firm's base currency. *FX cost exposure* is the elasticity of a firm's anticipated costs to FX changes. If $R^\$$ represents the level of a firm's revenues measured in US dollars, a US firm's FX revenue exposure to the euro would be denoted $\xi_{R\text{€}}^\$$ and would be computed as $\%\Delta R^\$/x^{\$/\text{€}}$. Letting $C^\$$ represent the level of a firm's operating costs measured in US dollars, a US firm's FX cost exposure to the euro would be denoted $\xi_{C\text{€}}^\$$ and would be computed as $\%\Delta C^\$/x^{\$/\text{€}}$.

From the euro perspective in the Euro Pipe Fittings example, the FX revenue exposure (to the US dollar) is 0. That is, FX rate changes do not affect EPF's revenues in euros. Similarly, the FX cost exposure to the US dollar is zero for the production costs and depreciation. For the aluminum, the FX cost exposure to the US dollar is 1. This FX cost exposure is an example of pure *FX conversion exposure*. If the US dollar appreciates by 25%, the cost of the aluminum in euros increases by 25%, since the cost of the aluminum is stable in US dollars.

When the US dollar is assumed to be the base currency in the EPF example, the FX revenue exposure to the euro is 1. This is another example of pure FX conversion exposure. Since the revenues in euros are stable, the revenues in US dollars decline by 20% when the FX value of the euro drops by 20%. In US dollars, EPF's production/ marketing costs and depreciation also have an FX cost exposure to the euro of 1, while the cost of aluminum has an FX cost exposure of 0, since the cost of the aluminum is stable in US dollars.

A firm's FX cost exposure often depends on the international locations of its own operations and those of its suppliers and potential suppliers. If a US firm imports raw materials whose cost is stable in euros, that portion of the firm's costs will have an FX cost exposure to the euro of $\xi_{C\text{€}}^\$ = 1$. A US importer of raw materials from Europe, on the other hand, would have FX cost exposure to the euro of 0, if the materials have a cost that is stable in US dollars.

In our EPF scenarios, there is no change in selling price or sales volume when the FX rate changes, which is why the revenues in euros are stable. In fact, firms typically do experience changes in selling price or sales volume when FX rates change. The influence of FX rate changes on a product's local currency selling price is referred to as *FX pass-through*. We look first at the impact of FX rate changes on selling price alone, without considering any impact on sales volume.

Our example is the system of measuring FX pass-through that Dow Chemical Corporation uses to assess the FX exposure of each of its products sold in Europe. Dow's point of view is its home currency, US dollars. The euro is the currency to which Dow's European revenues are exposed. The more changes in the FX value of the euro are passed through to Dow's European customers, in the form of changes in a product's local price in euros (with no assumed impact on sales volume), the lower is the product's price stability in euros, and the lower is the FX exposure of Dow's revenues (measured in US dollars) to the euro.

Dow's marketing managers are asked to use a price stability rating of 0 to 100 to rate the stability of the local currency prices of each European product. A stability rating of 100 means a product's price in euros is 100% stable; it is expected to be unaffected by changes in the FX rate, and Dow cannot or does not pass through FX changes to the customer. Thus Dow bears 100% of the exposure to FX changes. Because all the FX risk is retained by the seller, not passed through to the buyer, Dow's FX revenue exposure in US dollars to changes in the FX value of the euro is 1 for products with a stability rating of 100.

A price stability rating of 0 implies that the product's price in euros has zero stability when the FX rate changes. Zero stability in local price is good for Dow, since FX changes are entirely passed through to European customers in the product's local price in euros, so Dow's revenues (in US dollars) are not exposed to changes in the FX value of the euro. For example, when the spot FX value of the euro rises, the euro price of a product rated 0 is dropped (and vice versa for drops in the euro), in precisely the right amount to leave Dow's revenues unaffected when viewed in US dollars.

Thus a rating of 0 implies that 0% of the euro price is stable, so 0% of US dollar revenues is exposed to FX changes. The 0 rating represents full pass-through and corresponds to an FX revenue exposure of 0. Full pass-through may be possible for a product for which Dow has no competition or for a product having relatively price-inelastic demand. Full pass-through is basically indexing the product's price in local currency to FX changes.

Of course, most Dow products had a stability rating between 0 and 100. A Dow stability rating of 60 means that 60% of the foreign currency price is stable and not subject to the pass-through of FX changes, while 40% of any FX change is passed through in the form of a partially offsetting change in local euro product prices.

Dow rates magnesium 0, implying that a change in the FX value of euro leads to immediate changes in prices quoted in euros. Caustic soda, by contrast was rated 60, implying less responsiveness of local prices to FX changes. And propylene glycol and agricultural products were rated 80 and 90 respectively, suggesting that FX changes have little effect on local prices.

Figure 5.3 shows FX revenue exposures for two firms. Firm A, with a relatively low FX pass-through, has the higher FX revenue exposure of 0.80. Firm B, with a relatively high FX pass-through, has the lower FX revenue exposure of 0.20.[4]

---

(1) What would be the stability rating of the EPF's revenues (in euros)? (2) If the stability rating of the EPF's revenues (in euros) is 75, what is the FX revenue exposure to the euro, given a US dollar perspective, and what percentage of FX changes are passed through?

Answers: (1) 100. (2) 0.75; 25%.

---

[4]The Dow system is described in John J. Pringle, "Managing Foreign Exchange Exposure," *Journal of Applied Corporate Finance*, Winter 1991, 73–82.

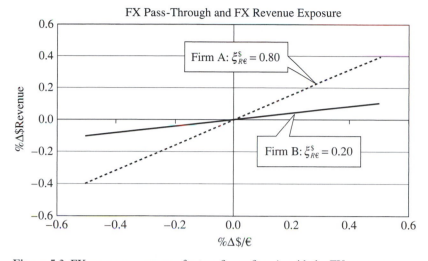

Figure 5.3 FX revenue exposures for two firms: firm A, with the FX revenue exposure of 0.80, has a relatively low FX pass-through; firm B, with the FX revenue exposure of 0.20, has a relatively high FX pass-through.

FX pass-through is related to the concept of a product's *currency of determination* in a given market, which is the currency in which a product's price is (most) stable in that market. Many basic commodities have a single currency of determination throughout the world. The currency of determination of metals is generally the US dollar in all markets, as we have seen with aluminum. At one time, Swedish paper companies were so dominant that the Swedish krona was the currency of determination for paper. For consumer products, the currency of determination is often the local currency in which it is sold. For example, the currency of determination of the Euro Pipe Fittings' products is the local currency in which they are sold, since their prices are held fixed in euros.

In many cases, the currency of determination is ambiguous. If a Dow product in France has a stability rating of 60, then 40% of the FX change is passed through. In this case, the product's price is determined by both currencies, but the euro is the stronger determinant.

The next example shows how a US parent of a foreign subsidiary can have a negative FX operating exposure to the subsidiary country's currency.

DDM Ltd. is the British subsidiary of a US parent firm. The currency of determination of DDM's products is mainly, but not entirely, the British pound. DDM's British pound revenues have a stability rating of 60. Assume that revenues are £1000 and operating costs are £750. Ignore taxes and depreciation. Assume that the currency of determination of the operating costs is the pound. (1) What is the US parent's FX operating exposure to the pound? (2) What would be the FX operating exposure to the pound if the price stability rating were 75 instead of 60? Although the answer does not depend on the spot FX rate, it may help to assume a spot FX rate of 1.60 $/£.

Answers: To answer the questions, do a what-if analysis of how a change in the FX value of the pound affects the operating cash flow in US dollars. The US dollar cash flow is initially $1600 − 1200 = $400.

1. If the FX revenue exposure is 0.60, a 20% drop in the FX value of the pound means that DDM's revenues, when converted to US dollars, are 12% lower than initially. Thus, the revenues in US dollars drop by $192 to $1408. From the US dollar perspective, operating costs drop by 20%, or $240, to $960. Thus the new operating cash flow level after the drop in the FX value of the pound is $448. The percentage change in the operating cash flow is $448/$400 − 1 = 0.12, or 12%. Thus, the parent's FX operating exposure to the pound is 0.12/−0.20 = −0.60.

2. If the FX revenue exposure is 0.75, a 20% drop in the FX value of the pound means that DDM's revenues, when converted to US dollars, are 15% lower, dropping by $240 to $1360. From the US dollar perspective, operating costs drop by 20%, or $240, to $960. Thus the new operating cash flow level after the drop in the FX value of the pound is $400, the same as before. Thus, the US parent's FX operating exposure to the pound is 0.

A firm's FX cost exposure for an imported product is the reciprocal of the exporter's FX revenue exposure for the same product. You can see this in an illustration based on the US firm Caterpillar and the Canadian tractor distributor, Finning. Caterpillar sells tractors to Finning, and Finning then sells them in Canada. If the US dollar appreciates relative to the Canadian dollar, Caterpillar would pass through some but not all of its FX revenue exposure to the Canadian dollar by raising the prices of tractors sold to Finning. If Caterpillar raises its prices to pass through 40% of any FX change, then 40% of the FX risk is transferred to Finning, and Caterpillar's revenues from Finning would have an FX revenue exposure of 0.60 to the Canadian dollar.[5]

In terms of pass-through only, an exporter's FX revenue exposure to the importer's currency and the importer's FX cost exposure to the exporter's currency must sum to 1, much the same idea as in equation (5.2). From its perspective in Canadian dollars, Finning would have an FX cost exposure of 0.40 to changes in the FX value of the US dollar relative to the Canadian dollar. From its perspective of US dollars, Caterpillar has an FX revenue exposure of 1 − 0.40 = 0.60 to changes in the FX value of the Canadian dollar.

The currency (or currencies) of determination of a given product may be different in different markets. For example, if a US firm has no foreign competitor in the US, but its exports are sold into a foreign market where there is a dominant firm, the currency of determination could be the US dollar in the US and the overseas currency in the foreign market.

---

[5]A description of the Caterpillar–Finning pass-through relationship is found in Gregory J. Millman, *The Floating Battlefield: Corporate Strategies in the Currency Wars* (New York: AMACOM, The American Management Association, 1990).

EXHIBIT 5.3   Dow Chemical-Europe FX Ratings

Product	Rating	FX Revenue Exposure to Euro ($)
Magnesium	0	0
Caustic soda	60	0.60
Propylene glycol	80	0.80
Agricultural	90	0.90

Input (cost)	Rating	FX Cost Exposure to Euro ($)
Feedstocks	0	0
Fuel and gas	0	0
Other raw materials	50	0.50
Electric power	100	1
Local inputs	100	1

The Dow Chemical rating system may also be used for major cost components. For example, feedstocks, which consist of petroleum derivatives, are viewed as completely sensitive to FX changes and thus have a rating of 0 (an FX cost exposure of 0 from the US dollar perspective). Other raw materials were given a rating of 50 as a group. Electric power and local inputs and services are given ratings of 100 (FX cost exposure of 1), while fuel and gas costs are entirely sensitive to FX changes (FX cost exposure of 0).

OPERATIONAL HEDGING AND OPERATING LEVERAGE

Suppose the US parent of EPF relocates the fittings production from Ireland to the United States, and the firm is renamed XPF. XPF is a US firm that makes the fittings in the US and again exports them to Germany. As with EPF, XPF's revenues in euros are not affected by FX changes, but all of its operating expenses, not just the cost of aluminum, are stable in US dollars. Thus XPF's FX revenue exposure to the euro is $\xi_{R\epsilon}^{\$} = 1$, and since all operating costs are fixed relative to changes in the FX value of the euro, the firm's FX operating cost exposure to the euro is $\xi_{C\epsilon}^{\$} = 0$. If the euro depreciates in FX value by 20% relative to the US dollar, the firm's revenue stream from the US dollar perspective will drop by 20% to a level of $480, but costs will remain the same (except taxes).

Assume that XPF's production/marketing cost is $0.40 per fitting, for a total cost of $240 for 600 fittings. Assume that depreciation expense is $40. Thus XPF's anticipated after-tax operating cash flow in US dollars at a spot FX rate of 1 $/€ is $200 [= ($600 − 240 − 120 − 40)(1 − 0.20) + $40]. If the spot FX value of the euro drops to 0.80 $/€, the anticipated revenues in US dollars are only (0.80 $/€)(€600) = $480, and the after-tax operating cash flow in US dollars is $104 [= ($480 − 240 − 120 − 40)(1 − 0.20) + $40].

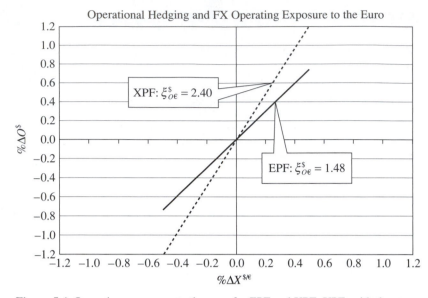

Figure 5.4 Operating exposures to the euro for EPF and XPF: XPF, with the steeper slope of 2.40, does no operational hedging; EPF, with the lower FX operating exposure of 1.48, employs some operational hedging.

The after-tax operating cash flow changes by $\$104/\$200 - 1 = -0.48$, or -48%, in response to the 20% depreciation of the euro. The firm's FX operating exposure to the euro, $\xi^\$_{C\epsilon}$, is thus $-0.48/-0.20 = 2.40$.

XPF's FX operating exposure to the euro (2.40) is higher than EPF's (1.48) because some of EPF's costs are stable in euros, so when viewed in US dollars they are exposed to changes in the FX value of the euro. Since EPF's FX cost exposure matches its FX revenue exposure, EPF's FX operating exposure to the euro is lower than XPF's, whose costs are entirely fixed in US dollars and do not match the changes in revenues in US dollars.

By producing in the Eurozone and thus fixing some costs in the same currency as the revenues (euros), the US owner of EPF is said to be using *operational hedging*. Both EPF and XPF have a higher FX operating exposure to the euro than the FX revenue exposure (which is 1), but XPF has more fixed costs (relative to FX changes), so XPF has more FX operating exposure.

Figure 5.4 shows FX operating exposures to the euro for EPF and XPF. XPF, with the steeper slope of 2.40, does no operational hedging. EPF, with the lower FX operating exposure of 1.48, employs some operational hedging.

The impact of fixed costs is an application of *operating leverage*, a common financial concept in which a firm with more fixed costs relative to operating cash flow will have a higher sensitivity of operating cash flows to unexpected changes in revenues. In the case of FX rate changes, XPF has higher operating leverage than EPF from the US dollar point of view.

THEORETICAL ESTIMATION OF FX OPERATING EXPOSURE

Ignoring depreciation and taxes, and if there is no impact of FX changes on volume of sales and production, there is a relatively simple relationship between FX operating exposure and its main components.

Let G denote the reciprocal of the operating cash flow margin. The operating cash flow margin is $O^\$/R^\$$, so $G = R^\$/O^\$$. For example, if the operating cash flow margin is 0.25, then $G = 4$. The FX exposure relationship is shown in equation (5.3):

$$\xi_{O\epsilon}^\$ = \xi_{R\epsilon}^\$(G) - \xi_{C\epsilon}^\$(G - 1) \tag{5.3}$$

In words, equation (5.3) says that the starting point for FX operating exposure is FX revenue exposure, $\xi_{R\epsilon}^\$$, magnified by G. This term is the operating leverage magnification of FX revenue exposure if all the firm's costs were fixed with respect to changes in the FX value of the foreign currency. The lower the operating profit margin, the more the $\xi_{R\epsilon}^\$$ is magnified. The remaining term, $-\xi_{C\epsilon}^\$(G - 1)$, reflects magnified FX cost exposure. Since $G - 1 = R^\$/O^\$ - O^\$/O^\$ = (R^\$ - O^\$)/O^\$$, and since $R^\$ - O^\$ = C^\$$, the magnification factor $G - 1$ is equal to $C^\$/O^\$$. The higher the ratio of costs to operating cash flow, $C^\$/O^\$$, the larger will be magnification of $\xi_{C\epsilon}^\$$. If the FX cost exposure $\xi_{C\epsilon}^\$ > 0$, the $\xi_{C\epsilon}^\$(G - 1)$ term reflects operational hedging.

We can demonstrate equation (5.3) with the DDM Ltd. example. In US dollars, DDM's FX cost exposure to the pound is 1, since the costs are stable in pounds when the FX value of the pound changes. Operating cash flow is $400 and revenue is $1600. So $G = 4$ and $G - 1 = 3$. When the stability rating is 60 and thus $\xi_{R\pounds}^\$ = 0.60$, equation (5.3) tells us that FX operating exposure to the pound is $\xi_{O\pounds}^\$ = 0.60(4) - 1(3) = -0.60$, as we already found. When the stability rating is 75 and thus $\xi_{R\pounds}^\$ = 0.75$, equation (5.3) tells us that FX operating exposure to the pound is $\xi_{O\pounds}^\$ = 0.75(4) - 1(3) = 0$, as we already found.

Carrier-Europe is a subsidiary of the US multinational United Technologies Corporation (UTC) selling air conditioners in the Eurozone (see box, "Operational Hedging at United Technologies Corporation"). Assume that the price of the air conditioners is stable in euros when the FX rate fluctuates, and the same is true for the 70% of Carrier-Europe's operating costs that are incurred in the Eurozone. The other 30% of operating costs are the compressor costs, which are assumed to be stable in US dollars. Assume that Carrier-Europe has an operating profit margin, $O^\$/R^\$$, of 25%. Approximate Carrier-Europe's FX operating exposure to the euro using equation (5.3).

Answer: Since 70% of operating costs have FX conversion exposure to the euro, $\xi_{C\epsilon}^\$ = 0.70$. Since the operating profit margin, $O^\$/R^\$ = 25\%$, $G = 4$, which implies that $G - 1 = 3$. $\xi_{O\epsilon}^\$ = 1(4) - 0.70(3) = 1.90$.

In the case of Euro Pipe Fittings, where taxes and depreciation are not ignored, we can see that equation (5.3) provides an approximation. From the euro point of view, the FX

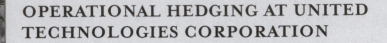

OPERATIONAL HEDGING AT UNITED TECHNOLOGIES CORPORATION

To further see the effects of operational hedging, consider a scenario based on the Carrier Company (air conditioners), a division of United Technologies Corporation (UTC). Let us focus on Carrier's European subsidiary, which sells air conditioners. The price of the air conditioners in Europe is stable in euros.

Carrier can choose where to source compressors, which account for about 30% of the cost of producing an air conditioner. One alternative is to produce the compressors in the United States; the other choice is Ireland. Ireland is part of the Eurozone, so the cost of making a compressor in Ireland is assumed to be stable in euros. Assume that all other inputs, especially labor, in the production of air conditioners by Carrier-Europe are acquired in Europe and have unit costs that are stable in euros.

If Carrier-Europe gets compressors from Ireland, then the entire cost of producing an air conditioner for the European market is stable in euros. From the US dollar point of view, UTC would be making maximal use of euro costs to operationally hedge the FX revenue exposure to the euro. If Carrier chooses to get compressors from the United States, then the cost of producing an air conditioner for the European market is 70% stable in euros and 30% stable in US dollars. From the US dollar point of view of UTC, the FX operating exposure would be higher.

Clearly, UTC's FX operating exposure from Carrier-Europe depends on where the compressors are sourced. If they are sourced in Europe, UTC's FX operating exposure to the euro (from the US dollar point of view) is lower, as more operational hedging is used. Of course, there are other considerations in the decision on where to source the compressors, such as price and quality. Our focus here is only on FX exposure considerations.

revenue exposure to the US dollar is $\xi_{R\$}^{\euro} = 0$. EPF's production costs are €240 and have an FX cost exposure of 0, and aluminum costs are €120 and have an FX cost exposure of 1. Since aluminum costs are one-third of the total costs (excluding depreciation and taxes), EPF's overall FX cost exposure, $\xi_{C\euro}^{\$}$, is 0.333. Since operating cash flow is $200 and revenue is $600, $G = 3$. Using equation (5.3), we get an FX operating exposure of $0(G) - 0.333(2) = -0.67$. The actual FX operating exposure found earlier is -0.48.[6]

Various scenarios in the chapter have shown that a firm's FX operating exposure depends on its business, its location, its competition, and so forth. Some firms have FX operating exposures that are positive and some are negative. An exporter with little ability to pass through FX changes in its overseas product prices and does little operational hedging is likely to have a high FX operating exposure. FX operating exposure is lower

---

[6]The actual equation for EPF's FX operating exposure is $\xi_{OS}^{\euro} = [\xi_{R\euro}^{\$} + (\xi_{R\euro}^{\$} - \xi_{C\euro}^{\$})(C^{\$}/O^{\$})](1 - t) + t(\xi_{d\euro}^{\$})(d^{\$}/O^{\$})$, where $\xi_{d\euro}^{\$}$ is the FX exposure of depreciation (in US dollars) to the euro, t is the tax rate, and $d^{\$}$ is the amount of depreciation terms of US dollars.

EXHIBIT 5.4 Summary of FX Operating Exposure Scenarios

1.	*High positive ($\xi_{O\epsilon}^{\$} > 1$)*	Exporter with low pass-through and little operational hedging
2.	*Low positive ($0 < \xi_{O\epsilon}^{\$} < 1$)*	Exporter with some pass-through or operational hedging
3.	*Low negative ($-1 < \xi_{O\epsilon}^{\$} < 0$)*	Importer with low pass-through and little operational hedging
4.	*High negative ($\xi_{O\epsilon}^{\$} < -1$)*	Parent of foreign subsidiary like case 1 exporting to parent's country

to the extent that FX changes can be passed-through and to the extent that operational hedging can be used.

An importer may have a negative FX operating exposure. If a US firm owns a foreign company that exports to the United States and has a positive FX operating exposure greater than 1, the US firm will have a negative FX operating exposure to the foreign currency. Exhibit 5.4 summarizes some of the scenarios.

REGRESSION ESTIMATION OF FX EXPOSURE BY VULCAN MATERIALS

In some of our hypothetical examples, a foreign subsidiary does not necessarily pose a positive FX operating exposure to its parent. An example of a real company is the US firm Vulcan Materials.

Vulcan used regression to estimate the FX operating exposure of its UK subsidiary to the British pound, from the parent's US dollar point of view. To the surprise of the managers, the estimated FX operating exposure was practically 0.

In analyzing the regression result, Vulcan managers realized that the UK subsidiary's sales pose no FX revenue exposure to the pound from the US dollar perspective. Vulcan UK sells metals like aluminum whose prices in British pounds are indexed to the $/£ FX rate so that the price is essentially stable when viewed from the perspective of US dollars. That is, Vulcan UK keeps the prices of its products stable in US dollars; it fully alters the prices in pounds to offset changes in the $/£ FX rate, with no impact on sales volume. Thus from the US dollar point of view, the sales of Vulcan UK have no FX revenue exposure to the pound, even though the subsidiary's revenues in pounds are volatile.

Moreover, the market price for the raw materials (scrap metal) is also relatively stable in US dollars. Since the scrap metal accounts for about 80% of operating costs, Vulcan UK's operating costs in pounds also largely adjust with changes in the $/£ FX rate. Since both the revenues and costs of Vulcan UK are relatively stable when viewed in US dollars, the approximate FX operating exposure to the pound is 0, even though the subsidiary sources sales and production totally in the United Kingdom.

The Vulcan Materials case is described in C. Kent Garner and Alan C. Shapiro, "A Practical Method of Assessing Foreign Exchange Risk," *Midland Corporate Finance Journal*, Fall 1984, 6–17.

*REGRESSION ESTIMATION OF FX EXPOSURE

FX exposures involve both theory and estimation with actual data. Regression analysis is one way a firm might estimate its overall FX operating exposure. Although a firm's FX exposures are likely to fluctuate over time, regression analysis may still be useful in estimating FX exposures. Regression analysis assumes that FX exposure is linear, as it is in the Euro Pipe Fittings examples given earlier. When FX exposure is not linear, the nonlinearity is ignored.

Table 5.1 shows some empirically estimated FX operating exposures to the yen, the pound, and the German mark (as a proxy for the euro). For example, Merck's FX operating exposure to the yen of 2.711 means that a 1% increase in the FX value of the yen leads to a 2.711% increase in operating profits.

The standard error (SE) is an estimate of the standard deviation of the FX operating exposure estimate. The relatively low standard error of 1.243 suggests that we can have some confidence in Merck's yen exposure estimate of 2.711. The FX operating exposures in the Table 5.1 show high estimated FX exposures for GE; estimates are relatively unreliable, however, judging from the high standard errors. For example, GE's estimated FX operating exposure to the yen is 3.292 with a standard error of 2.830. Because of the relatively high standard error, GE's estimated FX operating exposure to the yen is not significant in a statistical sense. [More sophisticated statistical methods are possible than the simple ordinary least-squares regression used here, which was just to convey the basic idea.]

Table 5.3 at the end of the chapter shows the basic quarterly data for the FX operating exposure estimates in Table 5.1. The currency columns show quarterly historical percentage changes, while the columns for the three firms show the actual quarterly operating income and the computed percentage changes.

Table 5.2 shows some estimated FX revenue exposures for Gillette, Merck, and GE to the yen, the pound, and the German mark (again as a proxy for the euro). GE's estimated

TABLE 5.1 Regression Estimates of FX Operating Exposures

	GILLETTE		MERCK		GE	
	$\xi_O^\$$	SE	$\xi_O^\$$	SE	$\xi_O^\$$	SE
Yen	**−0.306**	0.697	**2.711**	1.243	**3.292**	2.830
Pound	**1.208**	0.926	**−0.192**	1.900	**4.978**	3.817
Mark	**0.476**	0.858	**0.169**	1.628	**2.530**	3.530

TABLE 5.2 Regression Estimates of FX Revenue Exposures

	GILLETTE		MERCK		GE	
	$\xi_R^\$$	SE	$\xi_R^\$$	SE	$\xi_R^\$$	SE
Yen	**−0.234**	0.759	**0.079**	0.141	**1.245**	0.442
Pound	**1.561**	0.998	**0.211**	0.188	**1.348**	0.622
Mark	**0.516**	0.934	**0.111**	0.173	**1.111**	0.573

TABLE 5.3 Data for Table 5.1*

	Yen	Pound	Mark	GILLETTE Operating Income	Change (%)	MERCK Operating Income	Change (%)	GE Operating Income	Change (%)
Dec-89	0.010	0.016	0.122	172,000		552,300		718,000	
Mar-90	−0.063	0.018	0.019	206,600	0.201	602,700	0.091	1,396,000	0.944
Jun-90	−0.003	0.053	0.013	172,800	−0.164	696,800	0.156	1,621,000	0.161
Sep-90	0.110	0.099	0.072	188,100	0.089	673,800	−0.033	3,208,000	0.979
Dec-90	0.034	0.023	0.048	205,200	0.091	678,100	0.006	−748,000	−1.233
Mar-91	−0.025	−0.052	−0.071	220,700	0.076	720,500	0.063	1,515,000	−3.025
Jun-91	−0.017	−0.094	−0.096	201,300	−0.088	814,300	0.130	1,668,000	0.101
Sep-91	0.041	0.047	0.053	208,300	0.035	790,400	−0.029	3,379,000	1.026
Dec-91	0.049	0.058	0.083	231,300	0.110	784,500	−0.007	−911,000	−1.270
Mar-92	−0.036	−0.057	−0.059	248,500	0.074	816,700	0.041	1,570,000	−2.723
Jun-92	0.047	0.076	0.057	222,100	−0.106	931,700	0.141	1,639,000	0.044
Sep-92	0.035	−0.005	0.084	236,600	0.065	892,800	−0.042	1,639,000	0.000
Dec-92	−0.012	−0.160	−0.083	259,900	0.098	850,300	−0.048	679,000	−0.586
Mar-93	0.060	−0.058	−0.039	262,400	0.010	890,300	0.047	1,467,000	1.161
Jun-93	0.089	0.032	−0.005	244,200	−0.069	987,400	0.109	812,000	−0.446
Sep-93	0.017	0.011	0.020	266,800	0.093	1,006,400	0.019	1,783,000	1.196
Dec-93	−0.039	−0.022	−0.052	313,900	0.177	1,029,800	0.023	1,929,000	0.082
Mar-94	0.046	0.000	0.012	297,100	−0.054	1,036,500	0.007	1,549,000	−0.197
Jun-94	0.025	0.023	0.039	293,000	−0.014	1,245,700	0.202	2,285,000	0.475
Sep-94	0.038	0.026	0.050	297,700	0.016	1,211,000	−0.028	1,971,000	−0.137
Dec-94	−0.014	−0.005	−0.014	338,900	0.138	1,105,800	−0.087	7,975,000	3.046
Mar-95	0.107	0.027	0.118	329,100	−0.029	857,900	−0.224	2,121,000	−0.734
Jun-95	0.069	−0.003	0.003	321,900	−0.022	1,210,400	0.411	2,636,000	0.243
Sep-95	−0.158	−0.022	−0.040	338,100	0.050	1,213,200	0.002	2,433,000	−0.077
Dec-95	−0.013	−0.012	0.014	382,200	0.130	1,314,100	0.083	2,751,000	0.131
Mar-96	−0.039	−0.009	−0.025	374,600	−0.020	1,133,500	−0.137	2,378,000	−0.136
Jun-96	−0.028	0.009	−0.033	369,400	−0.014	1,331,100	0.174	2,896,000	0.218
Sep-96	−0.009	0.011	0.013	394,700	0.068	1,346,400	0.011	2,765,000	−0.045
Dec-96	−0.036	0.067	−0.029	910,600	1.307	1,369,900	0.017	3,036,000	0.098
Mar-97	−0.072	−0.033	−0.084	466,000	−0.488	1,352,300	−0.013	4,386,000	0.445
Jun-97	0.074	0.022	−0.019	517,500	0.111	1,524,300	0.127	5,167,000	0.178
Sep-97	−0.055	−0.027	−0.033	575,100	0.111	1,463,600	−0.040	4,866,000	−0.058
Dec-97	−0.068	0.036	0.004	765,400	0.331	1,523,500	0.041	3,084,000	−0.366
Mar-98	0.005	0.001	−0.026	434,000	−0.433	1,439,600	−0.055	5,016,000	0.626
Jun-98	−0.080	−0.007	0.019	595,000	0.371	1,587,200	0.103	5,819,000	0.160
Sep-98	0.044	0.019	0.055	575,000	−0.034	717,100	−0.548	5,670,000	−0.026
Dec-98	0.149	−0.007	0.017	720,000	0.252	2,896,400	3.039	6,341,000	0.118
Mar-99	−0.020	−0.030	−0.071	447,000	−0.379	1,786,400	−0.383	8,077,000	0.274
Jun-99	−0.010	−0.016	−0.047	492,000	0.101	1,980,900	0.109	1,553,000	−0.808
Sep-99	0.129	0.019	0.012	590,000	0.199	1,990,000	0.005	6,277,000	3.042

*Actual quarterly operating income from the three firms ($\times 10^3$) from Primark Disclosure Quarterly 10K Spreadsheets.

FX revenue exposure to the yen, for example, is 1.245 with a standard error of 0.442. The relatively low standard error suggests that the estimate of 1.245 is significant in a statistical sense. The FX revenue exposure estimates are mixed for Gillette, but are relatively unreliable, judging from the standard errors. Table 5.4 shows the basic quarterly data from which the FX revenue exposure estimates are made.

TABLE 5.4 Data for Table 5.2*

	Yen	Pound	Mark	GILLETTE Revenue	GILLETTE Change (%)	MERCK Revenue	MERCK Change (%)	GE Revenue	GE Change (%)
Dec-89	0.010	0.016	0.122	1,052,000		1,761,100		18,944,000	
Mar-90	−0.063	0.018	0.019	1,047,200	−0.005	1,758,400	−0.002	12,599,000	−0.335
Jun-90	−0.003	0.053	0.013	1,029,000	−0.017	1,899,300	0.080	14,352,000	0.139
Sep-90	0.110	0.099	0.072	1,026,300	−0.003	1,914,300	0.008	14,050,000	−0.021
Dec-90	0.034	0.023	0.048	1,242,100	0.210	2,099,500	0.097	16,661,000	0.186
Mar-91	−0.025	−0.052	−0.071	1,114,700	−0.103	2,048,900	−0.024	13,333,000	−0.200
Jun-91	−0.017	−0.094	−0.096	1,088,800	−0.023	2,122,400	0.036	14,774,000	0.108
Sep-91	0.041	0.047	0.053	1,138,000	0.045	2,117,400	−0.002	14,578,000	−0.013
Dec-91	0.049	0.058	0.083	1,342,400	0.180	2,314,000	0.093	16,694,000	0.145
Mar-92	−0.036	−0.057	−0.059	1,206,800	−0.101	2,223,400	−0.039	13,525,000	−0.190
Jun-92	0.047	0.076	0.057	1,198,900	−0.007	2,373,700	0.068	15,188,000	0.123
Sep-92	0.035	−0.005	0.084	1,249,200	0.042	2,464,300	0.038	15,450,000	0.017
Dec-92	−0.012	−0.160	−0.083	1,507,900	0.207	2,601,100	0.056	12,111,000	−0.216
Mar-93	0.060	−0.058	−0.039	1,216,600	−0.193	2,379,600	−0.085	12,700,000	0.049
Jun-93	0.089	0.032	−0.005	1,237,300	0.017	2,573,600	0.082	14,566,000	0.147
Sep-93	0.017	0.011	0.020	1,339,700	0.083	2,544,100	−0.011	14,669,000	0.007
Dec-93	−0.039	−0.022	−0.052	1,617,200	0.207	3,000,900	0.180	17,892,000	0.220
Mar-94	0.046	0.000	0.012	1,361,100	−0.158	3,514,300	0.171	14,182,000	−0.207
Jun-94	0.025	0.023	0.039	1,406,500	0.033	3,792,000	0.079	16,196,000	0.142
Sep-94	0.038	0.026	0.050	1,503,400	0.069	3,792,000	0.000	16,153,000	−0.003
Dec-94	−0.014	−0.005	−0.014	1,799,200	0.197	3,871,500	0.021	13,578,000	−0.159
Mar-95	0.107	0.027	0.118	1,536,000	−0.146	3,817,300	−0.014	15,126,000	0.114
Jun-95	0.069	−0.003	0.003	1,601,000	0.042	4,135,700	0.083	17,809,000	0.177
Sep-95	−0.158	−0.022	−0.040	1,669,800	0.043	4,171,100	0.009	17,341,000	−0.026
Dec-95	−0.013	−0.012	0.014	1,987,900	0.191	4,557,000	0.093	19,752,000	0.139
Mar-96	−0.039	−0.009	−0.025	1,676,900	−0.156	4,530,400	−0.006	17,098,000	−0.134
Jun-96	−0.028	0.009	−0.033	1,745,700	0.041	4,908,800	0.084	19,066,000	0.115
Sep-96	−0.009	0.011	0.013	1,803,300	0.033	4,983,400	0.015	20,021,000	0.050
Dec-96	−0.036	0.067	−0.029	4,471,800	1.480	5,406,100	0.085	22,994,000	0.148
Mar-97	−0.072	−0.033	−0.084	2,180,000	−0.513	5,567,900	0.030	19,998,000	−0.130
Jun-97	0.074	0.022	−0.019	2,285,200	0.048	5,909,200	0.061	21,860,000	0.093
Sep-97	−0.055	−0.027	−0.033	2,436,700	0.066	5,927,700	0.003	21,806,000	−0.002
Dec-97	−0.068	0.036	0.004	3,160,100	0.297	6,232,100	0.051	24,876,000	0.141
Mar-98	0.005	0.001	−0.026	2,025,000	−0.359	6,058,800	−0.028	22,459,000	−0.097
Jun-98	−0.080	−0.007	0.019	2,325,000	0.148	6,470,400	0.068	24,928,000	0.110
Sep-98	0.044	0.019	0.055	2,531,000	0.089	6,838,300	0.057	23,978,000	−0.038
Dec-98	0.149	−0.007	0.017	3,175,000	0.254	7,530,700	0.101	28,455,000	0.187
Mar-99	−0.020	−0.030	−0.071	1,939,000	−0.389	7,536,700	0.001	24,062,000	−0.154
Jun-99	−0.010	−0.016	−0.047	2,414,000	0.245	8,018,200	0.064	15,857,000	−0.341
Sep-99	0.129	0.019	0.012	2,509,000	0.039	8,195,700	0.022	27,112,000	0.710

*Actual quarterly operating income from the three firms ($\times 10^3$) from Primark Disclosure Quarterly 10K Spreadsheets.

SUMMARY

This chapter has described how to measure a firm's FX operating exposure and has described its potential sources in terms of revenues and costs.

You saw that an entity's financial results may be viewed from the perspective of any currency, regardless of where the entity operates. There is a relationship between an entity's FX operating exposure to the euro from the US dollar perspective and its FX operating exposure to the US dollar from the euro perspective.

Operational hedging reduces FX operating exposure by matching costs and revenues exposed to the same currency. Locating production in a country with the same currency to which revenues are exposed is one form of operational hedging.

Various scenarios showed that a firm's FX operating exposure depends on its business, its location, its competition, and so forth. Some firms have FX operating exposures that are positive and some are negative. An exporter that has little ability to pass through FX changes in its overseas product prices and does no operational hedging is likely to have a high FX operating exposure. FX operating exposure is lower to the extent that FX changes can be passed through and to the extent that operational hedging can be used.

An importer may have a negative FX operating exposure. If a US firm owns a foreign company that exports to the United States and has a positive FX operating exposure greater than 1, the US firm will have a negative FX operating exposure to the foreign currency.

The estimation of FX exposure by regression analysis of data was also discussed. This technique may be useful when a firm is relatively complex to analyze with theory.

GLOSSARY

Currency of determination: The currency in which prices of goods are effectively set.

FX conversion exposure: The FX exposure of converting given foreign currency cash flows to a base currency equivalent.

FX cost exposure: The variability in a firm's ongoing operating costs caused by uncertain FX rate changes.

FX operating exposure: A type of long-term FX exposure that focuses on the variability in a firm's ongoing operating cash flow stream caused by uncertain FX rate changes.

FX pass-through: The change in an exporter's local currency price in response to an FX rate change, such that some or all of the FX change is passed along to the local customers.

FX revenue exposure: The variability in a firm's ongoing revenues caused by uncertain FX changes.

Long-term FX exposure: The variability in a firm's value, or in its ongoing cash flows, caused by the effects of uncertain FX rate changes.

Operating leverage: The principle that a higher level of fixed costs makes operating income more sensitive to fluctuations in revenues.

Operational hedging: The arranging of a firm's FX cost exposure to match the currency of its FX revenue exposure.

DISCUSSION QUESTIONS

1. Explain why an exporter may have a positive (long) FX operating exposure to a currency and why an importer may have a negative (short) FX operating exposure.

2. Explain why an exporter may not have a positive FX operating exposure to a currency and why an importer may not have a negative FX operating exposure.

3. Suppose an overseas subsidiary of a US multinational reinvests all cash flows in its own growth, rather than repatriating any to the parent. Does the parent still have FX operating exposure? Discuss.

4. Explain how an overseas subsidiary may *not* expose its parent to any FX operating exposure. *Hint*: Use the DDM example or the Vulcan box in the chapter.

5. The chief executive of Cisco Systems Inc., the number-one maker of Internet networking equipment, said in the year 2001 that Cisco did not have the euro worries that hurt other US companies doing business overseas. "We do most of our business in US dollars over there. It actually has a slight positive effect in terms of expenses. The euro is a non-factor in terms of our exposure versus what other companies do." Discuss this comment in light of the chapter material. Include a discussion of whether Cisco is maintaining stable product prices in US dollars. If so, is there an alternative product, with price set in euros, that European buyers can turn to as Cisco's products become more expensive in terms of euros? Even if Cisco has no competitor and maintains set prices in US dollars, is demand so inelastic that sales volume does not drop in the face of the higher prices in euros?

PROBLEMS

1. Consider a US company with operating cash flow measured in US dollars of $500 per year, given a current spot FX rate of 0.60 $/A$. The company has an FX operating exposure to the Australian dollar of $\xi^\$_{OA\$} = 0.60$. If the Australian dollar appreciates in value by 20% (relative to the US dollar), what is the firm's new expected US dollar operating cash flow level?

2. Assume a firm's home currency is British pounds. Let the current spot FX rate be 1.50 $/£ and the expected revenues be £500 per year. Assume that if the FX value of the pound changes to 1.80 $/£, the expected revenues in pounds would change to £750 per year. Show the correct symbol for, and compute the company's FX revenue exposure to the US dollar?

3. LZX Ltd. is a UK firm that exports products to the United States. LZX's FX operating exposure to the US dollar is 1.70. If a US multinational acquired LZX, what would be the multinational's FX operating exposure to the pound from the LZX operation?

4. DDM Ltd. is the British subsidiary of a US parent firm. The currency of determination of DDM's products is mainly, but not entirely, the British pound. DDM's British pound revenues have a stability rating of 80. Assume that revenues are £1000 and operating costs are £750. Ignore taxes and depreciation. Assume that the currency of determination of the operating costs is the pound. (a) What is the US parent's FX operating exposure to the pound? (b) From the pound perspective, what is DDM's FX operating exposure to the US dollar? To facilitate a what-if analysis, assume a spot FX rate of 1.60 $/£.

5. PXE Company is a US firm that exports products to the United Kingdom. The FX revenue exposure to the pound is 1. Ignoring taxes and depreciation, PXE has revenues of $800, costs of $600, and operating cash flow of $200. Eighty percent of PXE's operating costs are stable in US dollars. The other 20% have an FX cost exposure to the pound of 1. Use equation (5.3) to approximate PXE's FX operating exposure to the pound. What would be the FX operating exposure if all the costs are stable in US dollars?

Questions 6 through 10 are based on the following information. Euro Pipe Fittings (EPF) produces aluminum pipe fittings in Ireland for sale in Germany. At the current spot FX rate of 1 \$/€, the company expects to sell 500 fittings at €1 per fitting. Each fitting requires a pound of aluminum, and aluminum costs \$0.30 per pound. Other than aluminum, each fitting costs €0.40 to produce. The tax rate is 0.30. Assume that depreciation is €50. Thus at the current spot FX rate of 1 \$/€, EPF's pro forma after-tax operating cash flow statement is as follows:

EPF's After-Tax Operating Cash Flow Statement

Revenues	€500
Production costs	200
Aluminum	150
Depreciation	50
EBIT	€100
Taxes	30
EBIAT	€ 70
Add depreciation	50
After-tax operating cash flow	€120

EPF is a wholly owned subsidiary of an American firm, ABC. The management of ABC wants a what-if scenario of EPF's cash flow from the point of view of US dollars. EPF's managers tell ABC that if the spot FX value of the euro falls to 0.80 \$/€, EPF would cut back production to 300 fittings and raise the price to €1.25 per fitting.

6. From the US dollar point of view, what is EPF's FX revenue exposure to changes in the FX value of the euro?

7. From the US dollar point of view, what is EPF's FX operating exposure to changes in the FX value of the euro?

8. Explain EPF's reason for raising price and cutting production if the euro drops in FX value.

9. If EPF's financial results are viewed from the euro perspective, what is FX operating exposure to the US dollar?

10. Explain the impact on the FX operating exposure if ABC decides EPF should produce the pipe fittings in the United States, with a fixed per-fitting production cost in US dollars.

ANSWERS TO PROBLEMS

1. \$560

2. $\xi^£_{R\$} = -3$

3. −0.70

4. (a) The US dollar cash flow is initially \$1600 − 1200 = \$400. Since the FX revenue exposure is 0.80, a 20% drop in the FX value of the pound means that DDM's revenues, when converted to US dollars, are 16% lower than initially. Thus, the revenues in US dollars drop by \$256 to \$1344. From the US dollar perspective, operating costs drop by 20%, or \$240, to \$960. Thus the new operating cash flow level after the drop in the FX value of the pound is \$384. Thus, the operating cash flow in US dollars changes by \$384/\$400 − 1 = −0.04, or minus 4%. The parent's FX operating exposure to the pound is −0.04/−0.20 = 0.20. (b) From the pound perspective, the FX operating exposure to the US dollar is 0.80.

5. Answer: $\xi^\$_{O£} = 1(4) − 0.20(3) = 3.40$; $\xi^\$_{O£} = 4$

6. New euro revenues will be 300(€1.25) = €375. New US dollar revenues will be 0.80 \$/€(€375) = \$300. $\%\Delta R^\$ = 300/500 − 1 = −0.40$. $\xi^\$_{R€} = −0.40/−0.20 = 2$.

7. New euro operating cash flows will be ($€375 - 120 - 112.50 - 50)(1 - 0.30) + €50 = €114.75$. New US dollar operating cash flow will be $0.80 \$/€(€114.75) = \$91.80$. $\%\Delta O^\$ = \$91.80/\$120 - 1 = -0.235$. $\xi^\$_{O€} = -0.235/-0.20 = 1.175$.

8. If the FX value of the euro drops, and the FX value of the US dollar rises, aluminum is relatively more expensive in euros, making fittings less profitable and reducing overall profits. EPF might cut back production and raise prices.

9. -0.175

10. ABC's FX operating exposure to the euro would rise due as a result of the reduction of operational hedging.

CHAPTER 6

Debt and Foreign Exchange Exposure

In this chapter and the next, we cover how and why managers use financial hedging to go beyond operational hedging of FX exposure. We also show how managers need to consider the ultimate impact of FX changes on the firm's stock value and on net cash flow—that is from the viewpoint of the firm's shareholders.

This chapter introduces the idea using financial hedging to mitigate the uncertainty in net cash flows and equity value. The chapter discusses using debt denominated in foreign currencies in financial hedging. Operational hedging and foreign currency debt are considered to be forms of *natural hedging* (i.e., hedging without using derivatives).

Measured in the firm's base currency, interest payments on foreign currency debt fluctuate in the same direction as the operating cash flows, dampening the FX exposure of net cash flows. But any debt, whatever the currency, also creates *financial leverage*, in which fixed interest cost causes an increase in the volatility of net cash flow. In short, financial leverage gives FX operating exposure a greater impact on the firm's bottom line. This chapter shows how we need to keep the financial leverage effect in mind when analyzing the use of foreign currency denominated debt in hedging FX exposure.

By discounting future cash flows, we can think in terms of the intrinsic value of a firm and of its debt and equity. When a firm has a positive FX operating exposure, fluctuations in the value of foreign currency debt tend to reduce the FX exposure of the firm's intrinsic stock value. Again, we will need to keep financial leverage in mind when we analyze the use of foreign currency debt in financial hedging of FX exposure.

US firms increased their foreign currency denominated debt from around $1 billion in 1982 to about $62 billion in 1998. There may be reasons for this increase other than the wish to hedge FX exposure. The interest expense on debt is tax deductible in the United States and in many other countries. For this reason, a multinational may want the legal issuer of its debt to be one of its foreign subsidiaries in a high-tax country. This way, the maximum benefit of the tax deduction can be obtained. Another reason for having an overseas subsidiary issue debt in local currency is that it is sometimes easier and cheaper for the subsidiary to access local borrowing markets than for the multinational parent. But the hedging of FX exposure appears to be the main reason for issuing foreign currency debt.[1]

For hedging purposes, there is no theoretical reason for a multinational parent to care whether it issues foreign currency debt directly, or does so indirectly through an overseas subsidiary. For this reason, we do not draw a distinction in this text between a parent's debt and a foreign subsidiary's debt; that detail would only complicate the analysis with no benefit.

SHOULD FIRMS MANAGE FX EXPOSURE?

Before we delve into how foreign currency debt is used to hedge FX exposure, we discuss pros and cons of the following question. Should firms hedge FX exposure?

Some firms choose not to hedge FX operating exposure because in the theory of perfect financial markets, FX hedging does not affect the *current* stock value, even though hedging does affect the *volatility* of future stock values. But many firms realize that real-world markets are not perfect. These firms believe that Wall Street wants stability in dividends and reported earnings growth rates, and thus that stabilizing the cash flow stream has a desirable impact on the current stock value.

Other firms tend not to hedge FX exposure because the managers think some shareholders want the FX exposure and do not want the managers to hedge. And, any other shareholders who don't want the FX exposure are free to manage it using their own financial hedging. So under this theory, the firm is better off not hedging. In reality though, shareholders often cannot hedge FX exposure on their own even if they want to, because the FX exposure is too complex for them to understand. And providing shareholders with information on FX exposures would be expensive and might reveal strategic information to competitors.

---

[1]See S. Kedia and A. Mozumdar, "Foreign CurrencyDenominated Debt: An Empirical Examination," *Journal of Business*, October 2003, 521–546, and M. Keloharju and M. Niskanen, "Why Do Firms Raise Foreign Currency Denominated Debt? Evidence from Finland," *European Financial Management*, No. 4, 2001, 481–496. Another role of foreign currency debt is in synthetic base currency debt designed to lower financial costs, similar to the PERLs example of Chapter 3. Synthetic debt structures are covered in the next chapter.

Some firms don't hedge because they think the impact of FX changes will even out over the long run. Sometimes this reason is given when actually the managers do not want to run the risk of hedging at the wrong time, especially if the hedging involves derivatives like forward FX contracts. But many firms do not have this view and have embraced the idea of *strategic hedging*. For example, FX swings could cause sudden shortfalls of cash from operations that might undermine a company's ability to follow through on capital investment plans. Many firms practice strategic hedging to avoid the consequences of FX changes on their competitive position. For example, Merck's corporate strategy at one time did not allow it to weather the ups and downs of FX changes in the short run. Merck needed a minimum cash flow stream in US dollars to support research and development to stay competitive with other pharmaceutical firms, and thus did not want FX operating exposure. Stabilizing a firm's stock value may be viewed as a form of strategic hedging as well, reducing the likelihood that a firm will have to obtain outside financing on short notice at inopportune times.

So, while reasons can be found not to hedge FX risk, the many firms that do hedge also have reasons. And FX risk management is now a critical task at many corporations. Jeffrey Wallace of Greenwich Treasury Associates released an excellent report on the trends and practices in managing FX exposure by multinational companies in 1999: "Group of 31 Report: Core Principles for Managing Multinational FX Risk," available at http://www.phoenixhecht.com/PDF/G31Report.pdf.

For many firms, there are limits to which operational hedging can be used. For example, Merck concluded that operational hedging by producing overseas was not viable, given the company's need to centralize research and development efforts in the United States. For other firms, like a mining company, there may be no way to do operational hedging. Even firms that can employ the maximum operational hedging, matching all costs to the currency of the revenue exposure, will have FX operating exposure in the cash flows left after costs have been subtracted from revenues.

So firms manage FX operating exposure by using financial hedging in addition to or instead of operational hedging. Some firms use financial hedging of FX exposures remaining after all possible (or reasonable) strategies for operational hedging have been implemented. Other firms use financial hedging of FX exposures as an alternative to operational hedging, sometimes when operational hedging is too permanent and financial hedging is more flexible. Still other firms use financial hedging as an intermediate-term measure while more strategic operational hedging solutions are being developed.

As we have said, the basic purpose of financial hedging of FX exposure is to eliminate uncertainty in net cash flow and stock value. After a hedge has been put on, it theoretically should not matter to the hedger what the future spot FX rate actually turns out to be. But we're all human and susceptible to 20–20 hindsight: If you hedge a positive FX operating exposure, and the currency depreciates, you enjoy making the right call. But if the currency appreciates, you regret the decision to hedge. If you decide to hedge, you need to avoid this type of thinking.[2]

---

[2]Some of the ideas in this section are discussed in G. Dufey and S. L. Srinivasulu, "The Case for Corporate Management of Foreign Exchange Risk," *Financial Management*, Winter 1983, 54–62. Merck's case is described in J. Lewent and J. Kearney, "Identifying, Measuring, and Hedging

EUROPEAN AUTO MAKERS: JANUARY 2004

BMW's risk management department is responsible for protecting the company, which reaps one-quarter of its $53 billion in annual sales in the United States, from the vagaries of trans-Atlantic exchange rates. At a time when the dollar is plumbing record lows against the euro, that job has become almost as crucial to BMW's financial stability as the popularity of its cars. "Our owners and employees prefer to see smooth operating results," said Joachim Herr, the youthful head of the department. "It's our job to help the company deliver those results."

European carmakers have been hit especially hard by the rising euro, because they pay for parts and labor in euros to build cars they export to the United States, where customers pay in dollars. As the dollar weakens, manufacturers that have not hedged will get fewer and fewer euros' worth of revenue for each dollar sale. There are two ways they can respond: they can raise the dollar prices of their cars in the United States to compensate for the weaker exchange rate, or they can absorb the difference in the form of lower profits. Neither choice is attractive.

Porsche tried the first approach in the early 1990's, the last time the dollar swooned. Customers fled, and Porsche nearly wiped out its American franchise. Today, Porsche has hedged all its exposure to the dollar through July 2007. That means it can keep its prices steady in the United States without absorbing a huge blow to its euro profits. Among German exporters, Porsche's strategy is by far the most conservative. BMW said it had hedged two-thirds of its exposure for this year and one-third for 2005. Volkswagen, after its heavy losses, stepped up its hedging last fall, to 70 percent of its exposure from 30 percent before.

Auto executives talk a lot about "natural" hedging—ways to offset the risks of an unfavorable exchange rate without resorting to exotic financial instruments. The simplest way is to build assembly plants in the United States, as BMW and Mercedes-Benz have done. BMW produces nearly 160,000 cars a year in Spartanburg, S.C., and 100,000 of them are exported, mostly to Europe. BMW pays dollars for the parts and labor that go into those cars, and sells them for euros or other currencies like British

Currency Risk at Merck," *Journal of Applied Corporate Finance*, Winter 1990, 19–28. A good exposition of strategic hedging is in A. Mello and J. Parsons, "Strategic Hedging," *Journal of Applied Corporate Finance*, Fall 1999, 43–54. Also see K. Froot, D. Scharfstein, and J. Stein, "A Framework for Risk Management," *Journal of Applied Corporate Finance,* Fall 1994, 22–32. For useful discussions of operational hedging versus financial hedging, see R. Aggarwal and L. Soenen, "Managing Persistent Real Changes in Currency Values: The Role of Multinational Operating Strategies," *Columbia Journal of World Business*, Fall 1989, 60–67. See G. Allyannis, J. Ihrig, and J. Weston, "Exchange-Rate Hedging: Financial vs. Operating Strategies," *American Economic Review Papers & Proceedings*, 91(2) 2001, 391–395, at http://faculty.darden.virginia.edu/allayannisy/finalAEA%20-%20ihrig.pdf.

pounds or Swiss francs, so a weak dollar makes the vehicles much more profitable for the company. The remaining 60,000 cars from Spartanburg are sold in the United States. BMW's total sales volume in the United States is about 277,000 cars, which means that 217,000 are made in Europe and shipped to America; those cars become less profitable as the dollar weakens. Together, the gains and losses tend to smooth out BMW's overall results, however the exchange rate behaves. DaimlerChrysler plans to expand production at its Mercedes plant in Tuscaloosa, Ala., in part to take advantage of the weak dollar. Daimler as a whole is less vulnerable to exchange rates than other European manufacturers because of its Chrysler Group, which makes and sells most of its cars in the United States. Production decisions, of course, are driven by more than just exchange rates, so for German companies, currency trades are still the most common method of dealing with oscillating dollars and euros.

Source: *New York Times*, January 14, 2004.

DEBT DENOMINATED IN FOREIGN CURRENCIES: EUROBONDS

Opportunities to obtain capital have grown as financial markets have developed, liberalized, and integrated. Governments have long raised funds via *foreign bonds*, which are bonds issued in a foreign country and denominated in the currency of that country. In the 1960s, investment bankers began to see that portfolio investors have the appetite to diversify using bonds from other countries and denominated in currencies *other than* their natural currency. Companies now raise capital in multiple countries and in many currencies.

A *eurobond* is a bond issued outside the country of the bond's currency denomination, *not* a bond denominated in euros. The first eurobond was denominated in US dollars and issued in 1962 by the Italian highway authority, Autostrada. Investors in England, Belgium, Germany, and the Netherlands purchased it. Following its issue, the bonds were listed on the London Stock Exchange. If Autostrada had issued bonds denominated in US dollars in the United States, the bonds would technically have been classified as foreign bonds, not eurobonds. Foreign bonds in the United States must be registered with the US Securities and Exchange Commission (SEC).

Since the 1960s, US dollar-denominated eurobonds of non–US issuers have appealed to many investors outside the United States who believed their currencies were likely to depreciate relative to the US dollar. Investors who feared devaluations and appropriations in their own countries have often kept wealth in more stable countries, especially in private numbered accounts in Swiss banks. US dollar-denominated eurobonds became an ideal portfolio investment for Swiss banks to make for their anonymous clients.[3]

---

[3]A readable and interesting account of the evolution of the global bond market is in Roy C. Smith, *The Global Bankers* (New York: E. P. Dutton, 1989).

EXHIBIT 6.1 McDonald's 10-Year Global Bonds: London, March 2, 2000

Amount: 15 billion yen
Type: Global
Coupon: 2%, payable semiannually
Issue price: 99.927
Reoffer price: 99.927
Reoffer yield: 2.008%, semiannually
Spread: 22 basis points more than governments
Maturity: March 9, 2010

Source: Bloomberg.

The eurobond model gradually evolved into a global bond market. Operating independently of clear regulatory authority, the global bond market has been free to develop innovations that have propelled the globalization of the financial markets. While we say it is unregulated, this market operates under standards set by a voluntary organization called the *Association of International Bond Dealers*, or *AIBD*. Sometimes you hear the term *euromarket* to used refer to the international financial market, a tradition since the first eurobonds.

An example of a foreign currency debt issue is the McDonald's yen bonds floated in 2000 for ¥15 billion (about $125 million); see Exhibit 6.1. Note that although the 10-year bond is denominated in yen, McDonald's could exchange the bond issue proceeds from yen into another currency in the current spot FX market. In other words, the liability does not have to be denominated in the currency of the country where the proceeds of the issue will be put to use.

Note also that the interest rate on the McDonald's bond issue is low, 2%, whereas the interest rate on 10-year US dollar bonds was around 6.50% at the time. Does this mean McDonald's got a cut-rate deal by issuing bonds in yen rather than in US dollars? The answer is no, not necessarily. An interest rate in yen cannot be directly compared to an interest rate in US dollars. They are apples and oranges, because making promised future interest and principal payments in yen is not the same as making promised future interest and principal payments in US dollars.

DEBT AND FX NET CASH FLOW EXPOSURE

We first look at the impact of debt, including foreign currency debt, on *net cash flow* (*NCF*). For simplicity, we define net cash flow as operating cash flow minus interest on debt, ignoring taxes. Thus, $N^\$ = O^\$ - I^\$$, where $I^\$$ is the interest expense expressed in the base currency, assumed here to be US dollars. In terms of US dollars, *FX net cash flow exposure* is defined with the usual elasticity notion, the percentage change in net cash flow in US dollars, $n^\$ = \%\Delta N^\$$, divided by the percentage change in the FX value of the foreign currency. FX NCF exposure measures the sensitivity in percentage terms of the firm's net cash flow, measured in US dollars, to FX changes. The notation for a US firm's FX NCF exposure to the pound is $\xi^\$_{N\pounds}$. $\xi^\$_{N\pounds} = n^\$/x^{\$/\pounds}$.

When a firm's FX operating exposure is positive (> 0), it will have more FX NCF exposure for higher levels of base currency debt. This is the financial leverage effect of debt. The firm will also have less FX NCF exposure if some debt is denominated in the exposure currency than it would with the same amount of base currency debt, because the foreign currency debt is a financial hedge of the firm's FX operating exposure.

You can see all this in two cases involving a hypothetical US firm, ITX Corporation. Say ITX initially has an expected operating cash flow stream of $1000 per year. Assume that the firm's FX operating exposure to the pound is $\xi_{O£}^{\$} = 1$. If the pound depreciates by 20% (relative to the US dollar), ITX's operating cash flow will drop by 20% to $800. Similarly, if the pound appreciates by 20%, operating cash flow will increase by 20% to $1200.

Suppose in the first case that ITX has issued $7500 in US dollar-denominated debt with a coupon interest rate of 5%. The debt interest expense is $0.05($7500$) = 375 per year, and $N^{\$}$ is expected to be $1000 - 375 = 625 as long as the FX rate does not change. If the pound depreciates by 20%, ITX's NCF will drop to $800 - 375 = 425. Correspondingly, if the pound appreciates by 20%, ITX's $N^{\$}$ will increase to $1200 - 375 = 825. The situation is shown as Case I in Exhibit 6.2.

You can see that on a percentage basis, the volatility in net cash flow is greater than the volatility in operating cash flow. Indeed, ITX's $N^{\$}$ changes by $425/$625 - 1 = -0.32$, or -32% when the FX value of the pound (and the operating cash flow) drops by 20%. The FX NCF exposure to the pound, $\xi_{N£}^{\$}$, is thus $-0.32/-0.20 = 1.60$, exceeding the FX operating exposure of 1. This is the financial leverage effect of the base currency debt.

In the second case shown in Exhibit 6.2, ITX has £5000 in pound-denominated debt instead of $7500 of US dollar debt. Assume the time-0 spot FX rate is $X_0^{\$/£} = 1.50$ $/£, and thus that the £5000 of pound debt is the same value as the $7500 of US dollar debt assumed in Case I. Thus in US dollars, ITX has the same amount of debt in both Case I and Case II,

EXHIBIT 6.2 ITX Corporation Net Cash Flow ($); FX Operating Exposure = 1

	Case I: $7500 Debt	Case II: £5000 Debt
$X^{\$/£} = 1.50$ $/£		
Operating cash flow ($O^{\$}$)	$1000	$1000
Interest expense ($I^{\$}$)	375	375
Net cash flow ($N^{\$}$)	$625	$625
$X^{\$/£} = 1.20$ $/£		
Operating cash flow ($O^{\$}$)	$800	$800
Interest expense ($I^{\$}$)	375	300
Net cash flow ($N^{\$}$)	$425	$500
$X^{\$/£} = 1.80$ $/£		
Operating cash flow ($O^{\$}$)	$1200	$1200
Interest expense ($I^{\$}$)	375	450
Net cash flow ($N^{\$}$)	$825	$750

$7500. Assume that the pound debt has a coupon interest rate of 5%. Thus the firm's debt interest is $0.05(£5000) = £250$. This interest expense in US dollars is $I^\$ = £250(1.50 \text{ \$/£})$ $= \$375$, and $N^\$$ will be $\$1000 - 375 = \$625$, the same as in Case I before any FX change.

Now if the pound depreciates by 20% to 1.20 \$/£, ITX's interest payment, measured in US dollars, will be $I^\$ = £250(1.20 \text{ \$/£}) = \$300$. Accordingly, $N^\$$ will drop to $\$800 - 300$ $= \$500$, a change of $\$500/\$625 - 1 = -0.20$, or -20%. Correspondingly, if the FX value of the pound appreciates by 20% to 1.80 \$/£, ITX's interest payment will be $I^\$ = £250$ $(1.80 \text{ \$/£}) = \$450$, and $N^\$$ will rise to $\$1200 - 450 = \$750$, a rise of 20%. With its pound debt, the firm's FX NCF exposure to the pound is only 1, which is the same as the firm's FX operating exposure.

Thus you see that the FX hedging effect of the pound debt results in a lower FX NCF exposure (1) than if an equivalent amount of US dollar debt is used (1.60). Note that the pound debt does not eliminate the firm's FX NCF exposure, or even reduce it below the level of the firm's FX operating exposure. The reason is that the pound debt has a financial leverage effect in addition to its FX hedging effect.

The higher the FX operating exposure, the more pronounced is the financial leverage effect of foreign currency debt relative to the FX hedging effect. Whether a firm's FX net cash flow exposure is greater than, equal to, or less than FX operating exposure when foreign currency debt is used depends on the firm's FX operating exposure. In the special case where the FX operating exposure is 1, the FX hedging effect of pound debt exactly offsets its financial leverage effect. The net result is that the firm's FX NCF exposure is equal to the FX operating exposure, 1. We saw this case in the ITX example.

If a firm's FX operating exposure is greater than 1, the financial leverage effect of foreign currency denominated debt will be stronger than the FX hedging effect, and the result is that the firm's FX NCF exposure will be greater than its FX operating exposure (although less than if debt is not denominated in the FX exposure currency). The following example demonstrates this point.

Suppose ITX's FX operating exposure is 1.50 instead of 1. What would be the company's FX NCF exposure in Case I (US dollar debt) and Case II (pound debt)?

Answers: If $\xi_{O\pounds}^\$ = 1.50$, then a 20% appreciation in the pound implies that the operating cash flow increases by 30% and the new operating cash flow is $1300. For Case I, where US dollar debt is used ($7500 at 5% interest), the new $N^\$ = \$1300 - 375 = \$925$. Thus the FX NCF exposure is $(\$925/\$625 - 1)/(0.20) = 2.40$. (You can verify that the same FX NCF exposure is computed if you use the 20% depreciation scenario.) For Case II, where pound debt is used (£5000 at 5% interest), the FX NCF exposure should be less, due to the FX hedging effect of the pound debt. A 20% appreciation of the FX value of the pound results in an interest payment (as in the text example) of $N^\$ = \$450$. Thus the new $N^\$$ is $\$1300 - 450 = \$850$, and the FX NCF exposure is $(\$850/\$625 - 1)/(0.20) = 1.80$. The FX NCF exposure of 1.80 is lower than in the Case I scenario (2.40), but higher than the firm's assumed FX operating exposure (1.50). The financial leverage effect of the pound debt magnifies the FX operating exposure, but the overall FX NCF exposure is not as great as with the equivalent amount of US dollar debt. The reason is that in this case the FX hedging effect of the pound debt only partially offsets the financial leverage effect when the FX operating exposure is greater than 1.

EXHIBIT 6.3 Summary of ITX Corporation Examples

	FX NET CASH FLOW EXPOSURE	
FX Operating Exposure	*$-Debt*	*£-Debt*
$\xi_{O£}^{\$} = 1$	$\xi_{N£}^{\$} = 1.60$	$\xi_{N£}^{\$} = 1$
$\xi_{O£}^{\$} = 1.50$	$\xi_{N£}^{\$} = 2.40$	$\xi_{N£}^{\$} = 1.80$
$\xi_{O£}^{\$} = 0.50$	$\xi_{N£}^{\$} = 0.80$	$\xi_{N£}^{\$} = 0.20$

If a firm's FX operating exposure is less than 1 but still positive, the financial leverage effect is weaker, and the firm's FX NCF exposure will be lower than its FX operating exposure. Problem 1 at the end of the chapter asks you to demonstrate the details of the case of $\xi_{O£}^{\$} = 0.50$. For the same debt assumptions used earlier, $\xi_{N£}^{\$}$ is only 0.20 with the sterling debt, but is 0.80 with the US dollar debt.

Exhibit 6.3 helps generalize the relationships between FX NCF exposure, FX operating exposure, and use of the two types of debt by summarizing the findings of the ITX examples.

FX VALUE EXPOSURE

The *intrinsic value of a firm's operations (intrinsic V_O)* is defined as the present value of the firm's expected future after-tax operating cash flow stream, using the firm's *cost of capital* as the discount rate. We will go into more detail on the cost of capital later in the text. For now, we can think of this cost in terms of a circular definition: the capitalization (discount) rate applied to a firm's expected operating cash flows to determine the intrinsic value of the firm's operations.

We will simplify the analysis at this stage by assuming that the future cash flow stream is a perpetuity, that is, an infinite stream of equal cash flows. A perpetuity is useful to study because it has the convenient mathematical property that the present value is simply the annual cash flow divided by the discount rate. For example, say a firm's expected after-tax operating cash flow stream is $1 million per year into perpetuity. If the firm's cost of capital in US dollars, $k^{\$}$, is 10%, the intrinsic value of the firm's operations in US dollars, denoted $V_O^{\$}$, is $1 million/0.10 = $10 million.

FX changes cause changes in the intrinsic value of the firm's operations through their impact on the expected stream of the firm's future after-tax operating cash flows. A firm's cost of capital does not change as the FX rate changes. But this does not imply that the firm's cost of capital is independent of its FX operating exposure, as you will see in Chapter 10, when we go into more detail on the cost of capital.

For simplicity, we will assume that when FX rates change, our expectation of the level of the future operating cash flow stream changes by the same percentage as the change in the current operating cash flow. Because of this assumption and because the cost of capital does not change as the FX rate changes, the intrinsic value of the firm's operations changes by the same percentage as the operating cash flow, given an FX change. Thus a firm's *FX value exposure* to the pound, denoted $\xi_{V£}^{\$}$, the elasticity of a firm's intrinsic $V_O^{\$}$ to changes in the FX value of the pound, is equal to its FX operating exposure, as in equation (6.1).

$$\xi_{V\pounds}^{\$} = \xi_{O\pounds}^{\$} \tag{6.1}$$

The equality between FX value exposure and FX operating exposure does not depend on our simplifying assumption of a level perpetual expected cash flow stream. For example, equation (6.1) holds if the cash flow stream is expected to grow. We continue to use perpetuities for convenience.

Suppose a US firm currently has an expected operating cash flow stream of $1000 per year into perpetuity and has a cost of capital of 10%. Thus the intrinsic value of the firm's operations is $10,000. Assume further that the firm's FX operating exposure to the British pound, $\xi_{O\pounds}^{\$}$, is 1.20. Next assume the pound depreciates by 15%. Because of its FX operating exposure, the firm's current operating cash flow (in US dollars) will change by $1.20(-0.15) = -0.18$, or it will decline by 18%, and thus will be $0.82(\$1000) = \$820$. Given that the expected future operating cash flow stream also declines by 18%, the new expected future cash flow stream will be a perpetuity of $820. Given that the firm's cost of capital is 10%, unaffected by the FX change, the new intrinsic $V_O^{\$}$ is $820/0.10 = \$8200$. The percentage change in the firm's $V_O^{\$}$ is $\$8200/\$10,000 - 1 = -0.18$, or -18%, the same as the percentage change in the operating cash flow stream.

Suppose a US firm currently has an expected perpetual operating cash flow stream of $100 per year, a cost of capital of 10%, and thus an intrinsic value of operations of $1000. Assume further that the firm's FX operating exposure to the British pound, $\xi_{O\pounds}^{\$}$, is 0.90. Next assume the pound appreciates by 10%. Find the FX value exposure and the new intrinsic value of the firm's operations.

Answers: The FX value exposure equals the FX operating exposure, 0.90. The expected future operating cash flow stream will change by 0.90(10%) = 9%, and will thus be a perpetuity of $100(1.09) = $109 per year after the FX rate change. Given that the firm's cost of capital is 10%, its new intrinsic $V_O^{\$}$ is $109/0.10 = $1090. The percentage change in the firm's intrinsic $V_O^{\$}$ is $1090/$1000 − 1 = 0.09, or 9%, the same as in the expected operating cash flow stream.

As another example, consider again the Euro Pipe Fittings (EPF) firm. From a euro viewpoint, EPF's FX operating exposure to the US dollar, $\xi_{O\$}^{\euro}$, is -0.48. So, if the US dollar appreciates by 25% (from 1 €/$ to 1.25 €/$), EPF's current operating cash flow (in euros) drops by 12% (from €200 to €176), since $-0.48(25\%) = -12\%$. EPF's FX value exposure is also -0.48, using equation (6.1). Thus the firm's expected future operating cash flow and intrinsic value of operations (in euros) will also change by -12%. EPF's expected operating cash flow stream (in euros) drops by 12% and the firm's intrinsic $V_O^{\euro}$ drops by 12%, when the US dollar appreciates by 25%. That is, EPF's FX value exposure to the US dollar is $-0.12/0.25 = -0.48$.

There is an identity that should be familiar to anyone who has learned basic accounting, although the concept for us is in terms of intrinsic values, not book values: *the intrinsic value of a firm equals the value of debt plus the intrinsic value of equity*. Let $D^{\$}$ represent the value in US dollars of all the firm's debt, in whatever denominations, and let $S^{\$}$ represent the intrinsic value in US dollars of all the shares of the firm's stock, or equity. In symbols, the intrinsic value of the firm, denoted $V^{\$}$, is equal to $D^{\$} + S^{\$}$.

Note that the intrinsic value of the firm is distinct from the intrinsic value of the firm's equity. The intrinsic value of the firm is what the firm is worth as a whole, as if it had no debt. Also keep in mind that the actual price of a firm's stock in the stock market may differ from the intrinsic value. The intrinsic value of a share of equity refers to the price a share of the firm's stock *should be* selling for if it is correctly valued.

We can also say that $S^\$ = V^\$ - D^\$$, that the firm's intrinsic equity value is the shareholders' residual value, after the value of the debt has been subtracted. From this, we see that FX changes affect equity value because of effects on the value of the firm and on the value of the debt.

$$V^\$ = D^\$ + S^\$$$
$$S^\$ = V^\$ - D^\$$$

Unless stated otherwise, we assume that the intrinsic value of a firm and the intrinsic value of its operations are the same, that is, $V_O^\$ = V^\$$. Sometimes $V^\$$ can be higher than $V_O^\$$ if the firm has financial assets in addition to the assets necessary to produce the operating cash flows.

How do FX changes affect the value of a firm's debt? The answer depends on the currency denomination of the debt. If debt is denominated in the firm's base currency, an FX change will not affect the value of the debt. If debt is denominated in a foreign currency, there will be an impact of the FX change on the value of the debt in US dollars.

The impact of FX changes on the US dollar value of foreign currency debt is one-for-one, that is, a pure FX conversion effect. Assume that a firm currently has £625,000 in pound-denominated debt, and the spot FX rate is 1.60 $/£. Thus the value of the debt in US dollars is £625,000(1.60 $/£) = $1 million. Assume that the pound appreciates by 20% to 1.92 $/£. The value of the firm's £-debt in US dollars increases by 20% to $1 million(1.20) = $1.20 million. By itself, the $200,000 increase in the value of the pound debt is a loss to the shareholders. Of course, if the debt is serving as a hedge, the stockholders will also gain from an increase in the value of the firm.

APPLIED MATERIALS USE OF YEN DEBT

The US semiconductor firm Applied Materials (AMAT) reported roughly $50 million worth of long-term Japanese yen debt on its consolidated financial statement at fiscal year-end (October) 1998. AMAT uses yen debt as a hedge of the long-term FX exposure to yen from its Japanese business.

Between October 1998 and 1999, the spot FX rate changed from 134.48 ¥/$ to 106.88 ¥/$, an appreciation of the yen of 26%. Assuming that the value of AMAT's ¥-debt remained constant in yen during that time, the value of AMAT's ¥-debt in US dollars would be 26% higher in 1999 than a year earlier. Thus the value of AMAT's ¥-debt in US dollars would be $50 million(1.26) = $63 million in 1999. Other things equal, the $13 million additional value of the ¥-debt represents a loss of $13 million in the intrinsic value of AMAT's equity unless the debt is hedging the intrinsic value of the firm's operations.

FX EQUITY EXPOSURE

A firm's *FX equity exposure* is defined to be the elasticity of the firm's intrinsic stock value to FX changes, viewed from the perspective of the firm's base currency. We use the subscript "*S*" for "stock" in FX equity exposure notation. Thus, a US firm's FX equity exposure to the euro is denoted $\xi_{S\epsilon}^{\$}$ and is computed as $\%\Delta S^{\$}/x^{\$/\epsilon}$.

Three elements determine a firm's FX equity exposure to a currency: (1) the firm's FX value exposure, (2) the financial leverage (i.e., the ratio of firm's debt value to the firm's intrinsic value), and (3) the relative amount of debt denominated in the FX operating exposure currency.

For example, assume that the US firm XYZ Company has an FX operating exposure and (thus FX value exposure) of 1.20 to the euro, the intrinsic value of the firm in US dollars is $V^{\$} = \$2000$, and its overall debt value in US dollars is $D^{\$} = \$600$. Thus, the intrinsic equity (stock) value of the company is currently $S^{\$} = \$2000 - 600 = \$1400$.

Assume a 5% drop in the spot FX value of the euro. This FX change will reduce the intrinsic value of the firm by 6%, owing to the FX value exposure of 1.20. Since the firm's intrinsic value drops by 6%, it drops to $0.94(\$2000) = \$1880$ when the euro drops by 5% in spot FX value. We compare two cases. In the first, XYX has no debt denominated in euros; all debt is denominated in US dollars. In the second, half of XYZ's $600 of debt is euro-denominated debt.

For the first case, the spot FX change has no impact on the firm's debt value in US dollars, since XYZ's $600 in debt is denominated entirely in US dollars. Since the US dollar value of the debt stays at $600, the new intrinsic value of XYZ's stock must be $1880 - 600 = $1280. Exhibit 6.4 shows value balance sheets for XYZ Company before and after the 5% drop in the FX value of the euro for this case, in which all of XYZ's debt is US dollar debt.

EXHIBIT 6.4 XYZ Company Intrinsic Value Balance Sheet: *All Debt Is US Dollar Debt*

TIME 0

Assets	Liabilities & Equity
	$ 600 $-debt
$2000 $V_O^{\$}$	$1400 equity
$2000 $V^{\$}$	$2000

AFTER EURO DROPS BY 5% (TIME 1)

Assets	Liabilities & Equity
	$ 600 $-debt
$1880 $V_O^{\$}$	$1280 equity
$1880 $V^{\$}$	$1880

EXHIBIT 6.5 XYZ Company Intrinsic Value Balance Sheet:
Euro Debt and US Dollar Debt

TIME 0

Assets	Liabilities & Equity
	$ 300 €-debt
	$ 300 $-debt
$2000 $V_O^\$$	$1400 equity
$2000 $V^\$$	$2000

AFTER EURO DROPS BY 5% (TIME 1)

Assets	Liabilities & Equity
	$ 285 €-debt
	$ 300 $-debt
$1880 $V_O^\$$	$1295 equity
$1880 $V^\$$	$1880

The percentage change in XYZ's intrinsic stock value is $1280/$1400 − 1 = −0.0857, or an 8.57% decline. In short, a 5% drop in the FX value of the euro has resulted in a 6% decline in the firm's intrinsic value and an 8.57% decline in the intrinsic equity value. The 8.57% decline in the equity value is a result of (1) the drop in the value of the firm, (2) the firm's financial leverage, and (3) the fact that the debt value does not change with the FX change because none of the debt is denominated in the FX operating exposure currency, the euro.

Because XYZ's intrinsic stock value drops by 8.57% when the euro drops in FX value by 5%, the firm's FX equity exposure to the euro, $\xi_{S\epsilon}^\$$, is −0.0857/−0.05 = 1.71. This example shows how financial leverage magnifies the effect of an FX change. In this case, the firm's FX value exposure is 1.20, but the FX equity exposure is higher, 1.71.

Now let's assume instead that at time 0 half of XYZ's debt, $300, is debt denominated in euros. Its overall debt ratio (in intrinsic value terms) is still $D^\$/V^\$ = $600/$2000 = 0.30$, while the ratio of euro debt to the intrinsic value of the firm is $D_\epsilon^\$/V^\$ = $300/$2000 = 0.15$. Assume again a 5% drop in the FX value of the euro. As before, this causes the intrinsic value of the firm to drop by 6% to $1880, owing to its FX operating exposure of 1.20. The value of the euro debt, in US dollars, will drop by 5%, to $285, while the value of the rest of the debt stays at $300 because it is denominated in US dollars. Now the new intrinsic value of net worth is $1880 − 285 − 300 = $1295. This case is shown in Exhibit 6.5.

The percentage change in the firm's intrinsic stock value is $1295/$1400 − 1 = −0.075, or −7.5%. The firm's FX equity exposure is thus −0.075/−0.05 = 1.50. Thus you see that if XYZ uses some euro debt instead of some of its US dollar debt, its FX equity exposure of 1.50 is lower than with no euro debt, 1.71.

Figure 6.1 shows XYZ's FX equity exposure for two cases in which the debt-to-value ratio is 30%. XYZ's FX value exposure is 1.20. When 50% of XYZ's debt is euro debt, the FX equity exposure is lower, 1.50, than for the case of no euro debt, 1.71.

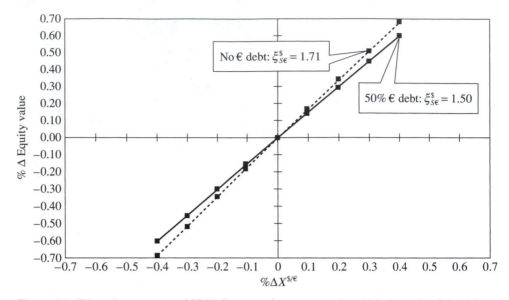

Figure 6.1 FX equity exposure of XYZ Company for two cases in which the ratio of the debt to intrinsic value is 30% and the firm's. FX value exposure is 1.20. When 50% of XYZ's debt is euro debt, the FX equity exposure is lower (1.50), than it is for the case of no euro debt (1.71).

To show all this in an equation, let $D_{€}^{\$}$ denote the value, measured in US dollars, of the firm's euro-denominated debt; $D^{\$}$ denotes the value of all the firm's debt, measured in US dollars regardless of currency denomination. The relationship for FX equity exposure as a function of FX operating exposure and capital structure is shown in equation (6.2):

$$\xi_{S€}^{\$} = \frac{\xi_{O€}^{\$} - D_{€}^{\$}/V^{\$}}{1 - D^{\$}/V^{\$}} \tag{6.2}$$

Equation (6.2) shows how both the FX hedging and financial leverage effects come into play. First, the FX hedging effect of any debt in the exposure currency (here, the euro) is seen in the numerator. The negative sign on the $D_{€}^{\$}/V^{\$}$ term implies that more euro debt will tend to reduce the firm's FX equity exposure to the euro than if non-euro debt is used. Second, the financial leverage effect of all debt, denominated in euros or otherwise, is seen in the denominator. There is a greater FX equity exposure for higher ratios of debt to intrinsic value, representing the opposite direction of the FX hedging effect.

We can demonstrate equation (6.2) using the XYZ Company example. XYZ currently has an intrinsic value of $V^{\$} = \$2000$ and has debt financing with a value of $D^{\$} = \$600$. Thus the firm's equity value is $S^{\$} = \$1400$. The firm's overall debt ratio (in economic terms) is $D^{\$}/V^{\$} = \$600/\$2000 = 0.30$. If all of XYZ's debt is US dollar debt, then $D_{€}^{\$}/V^{\$} = 0$. From equation (6.2), we have that $\xi_{S€}^{\$} = (1.20 - 0)/(1 - 0.30) = 1.71$, as we already have demonstrated. If half of XYZ's $600 in debt is euro debt, then $D_{€}^{\$}/V^{\$} = 0.15$ and $D^{\$}/V^{\$} = 0.30$, and the FX equity exposure of 1.50 (found earlier) is also consistent with equation (6.2): $\xi_{S€}^{\$} = (1.20 - 0.15)/(1 - 0.30) = 1.50$.

ABC Company currently has $V^\$ = \$5000$, $D^\$ = \$3000$, and thus $S^\$ = \$2000$. Assume that ABC has an FX operating exposure of 1.60 to the euro. Assume that $2000 of the firm's $3000 in debt is euro-denominated debt and the rest is US dollar debt. Assume that the euro drops in FX value by 10%. Find the new intrinsic value of ABC's equity, and the FX equity exposure directly. Then use equation (6.2) to verify the FX equity exposure.

Answers: ABC's FX value exposure is 1.60. Thus the intrinsic value of the firm will fall by 1.60(10%), or 16%, to $4200, when the euro drops in FX value by 10%. The value of the euro debt (in US dollars) will drop by 10% to $1800, while the value of the other debt stays at $1000. The new intrinsic equity value will be $4200 − 1800 − 1000 = \$1400. The percentage change in the firm's intrinsic stock value is $1400/$2000 − 1 = −0.30, or −30%. The FX equity exposure is thus −0.30/−0.10 = 3. Since $D_\epsilon^\$/V^\$ = 0.40$ and $D^\$/V^\$ = 0.60$, the FX equity exposure of 3 is consistent with equation (6.2): $\xi_{S\epsilon}^\$ = (1.60 − 0.40)/(1 − 0.60) = 3$.

Note that when all a company's financing is in the form of equity, its FX equity exposure is the same as its FX value exposure, because the value of the firm and its equity would be the same, given an all-equity capital structure.

HEDGING FX VALUE EXPOSURE WITH FOREIGN CURRENCY DEBT

If a firm's FX operating exposure to the euro is positive, you can see from equation (6.2) that setting the ratio of €-debt to intrinsic value ($D_\epsilon^\$/V^\$$) equal to the FX operating exposure ($D_\epsilon^\$/V^\$ = \xi_{O\epsilon}^\$$) will make the FX equity exposure 0. Thus in this case it is possible to completely hedge FX operating exposure solely with euro debt. If a company has an FX operating exposure of 0.20 to the euro, for example, and it has euro-denominated debt in the amount of 20% of the intrinsic value of the firm, the company in theory has zero FX equity exposure to the euro.

ABC Company has currently has $V^\$ = \$5000$, $D^\$ = \$3000$, and thus $S^\$ = \$2000$. Assume an FX operating exposure of 0.30 to the euro. How much of ABC's debt should be euro debt to eliminate the firm's FX equity exposure to the euro?

Answer: Setting $D_\epsilon^\$/V^\$ = \xi_{O\epsilon}^\$ \Rightarrow D_\epsilon^\$ = \xi_{O\epsilon}^\$ V^\$ = 0.30(\$5000) = \$1500$.

FX operating exposure to a currency may be relatively low, say 0.20 for a company with a relatively small proportion of its business in an overseas market. But other companies have higher FX operating exposures. A company with an FX operating exposure of 0.80 could in principle eliminate its FX equity exposure by having foreign currency debt in the amount of 80% of the firm's intrinsic value. Then again, it may be unreasonable for a company to set its ratio of debt to intrinsic value equal to an FX operating exposure as high as 0.80. And when a company's FX operating exposure is greater than 1, it makes no sense to consider a debt level higher than the intrinsic value of the firm. Thus there is a limitation to hedging FX exposure with foreign currency debt.

The ultimate influence of foreign currency debt on a firm's FX equity exposure depends on the way the leverage and hedging effects interact, which depends in turn on the extent of the firm's FX operating exposure (FX value exposure). One might think FX equity exposure would generally be lower if a company uses more exposure currency debt in its capital structure in place of equity, and if the FX operating exposure is positive. But this idea is correct only if the FX operating exposure is less than 1. When FX operating exposure is greater than 1, FX equity exposure is always higher than FX value exposure, and the more foreign currency debt employed in place of equity, the higher the firm's FX equity exposure. When the FX operating exposure is greater than 1, the financial leverage effect dominates the FX hedging effect. The relationship between FX equity exposure and FX value exposure is similar to what we found between FX NCF exposure and FX operating exposure.

To illustrate these points, let's extend the euro debt case of the XYZ Company where the FX equity exposure is 1.50 when the firm starts with $300 euro debt. Assume that at time 0 (before any FX change), XYZ issues an additional $400 in euro debt and uses the proceeds to repurchase equity, thinking that this additional euro debt will reduce the firm's FX equity exposure to the euro. This debt-for-equity swap would bring XYZ's total debt level, measured in US dollars, up to $1000 ($700 of euro debt and $300 of the original US dollar debt) and the equity level down to $1000 (from $1400). The operations of the firm, its expected operating cash flows, and its FX operating exposure to the euro are all unchanged by this purely financial transaction, and the total intrinsic value of XYZ remains at $2000 until the FX value of the euro changes. Thus the firm's new overall debt ratio (in intrinsic value terms) is $D^\$/V^\$ = \$1000/\$2000 = 0.50$, while the new ratio of euro debt to intrinsic value is $D_{\mathring{e}}^\$/V^\$ = \$700/\$2000 = 0.35$.

As before, when the FX value of the euro drops by 5%, the intrinsic value of XYZ drops by 6%, owing to XYZ's FX value exposure of 1.20, to 0.94($2000) = $1880. Now the value of the euro debt in US dollars drops by 5%, from $700 to $665, while the value of the US dollar debt stays at $300. The new intrinsic stock value is $1880 − 665 − 300 = $915. The percentage change in intrinsic stock value is thus $915/$1000 − 1 = −0.085, or an 8.5% reduction. The FX equity exposure is thus −0.085/−0.05 = 1.70. Since $D_{\mathring{e}}^\$/V^\$ = $700/$2000 = 0.35$, and $D^\$/V^\$ = $1000/$2000 = 0.50$, the FX equity exposure of 1.70 is consistent with equation (6.2): $\xi_{S\mathring{e}}^\$ = (1.20 - 0.35)/(1 - 0.50) = 1.70$. This scenario is shown in Exhibit 6.6.

Thus, by increasing its level of euro debt in place of equity, the firm actually *increases* its FX equity exposure to the euro from 1.50 to 1.70. The reason again is that the impact of the higher financial leverage dominates the impact of the euro debt's FX hedging effect when the firm's FX operating exposure is greater than 1. This comparison is depicted in Figure 6.2.

EXHIBIT 6.6 XYZ Company Intrinsic Value Balance Sheet: *Higher Euro Debt and Higher Total Debt*

TIME 0

Assets	Liabilities & Equity
	$ 700 €-debt
	$ 300 $-debt
$2000 $V_O^\$$	$1000 equity
$2000 $V^\$$	$2000

AFTER EURO DROPS BY 5% (TIME 1)

Assets	Liabilities & Equity
	$ 665 €-debt
	$ 300 $-debt
$1880 $V_O^\$$	$ 915 equity
$1880 $V^\$$	$1880

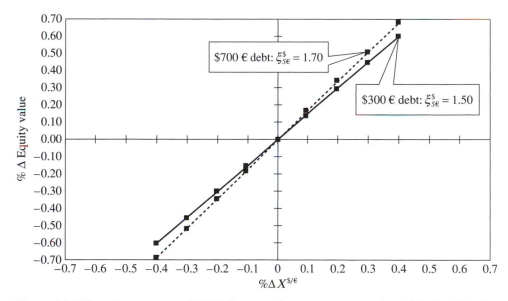

Figure 6.2 FX equity exposure of XYZ Company for two more cases in which the FX value exposure is 1.20. With $700 of euro debt (and $300 in US dollar debt), the FX equity exposure is higher (1.70), than with $300 of euro debt (and $300 in US dollar debt) (1.50).

ABC Company has has $V^\$ = \$5000$, $D^\$ = \$3000$, and thus $S^\$ = \$2000$. Assume that ABC's FX operating exposure to the euro is 1.60. (1) If all of ABC's debt is euro debt, what is ABC's FX equity exposure to the euro? (2) What is the FX equity exposure if ABC issues another $1000 in euro debt and uses the proceeds to repurchase $1000 of the firm's equity?

Answers: (1) $\xi_{S\epsilon}^\$ = (\xi_{O\epsilon}^\$ - D_\epsilon^\$)/(1 - D^\$/V^\$) = (1.60 - 0.60)/(1 - 0.60) = 2.50$; (2) $\xi_{S\epsilon}^\$ = (1.60 - 0.80)/(1 - 0.80) = 4$.

Thus we see that when FX operating exposure is greater than 1, foreign currency debt cannot be used to eliminate FX equity exposure. We will address this problem in the next chapter.

If a company's FX operating exposure is negative, having debt denominated in that currency does not hedge the FX exposure and in fact will exacerbate it. For example, assume that a firm has a natural short FX operating exposure of -1.25 to the yen. Assume that the firm's debt is denominated in yen, and the ratio of debt to intrinsic value is 0.25. The firm's FX equity exposure to the yen, from equation (6.2), is $(-1.25 - 0.25)/(1 - 0.25)$ $= -2$. Thus, a classic importer (with a negative FX operating exposure) cannot use foreign currency denominated debt to manage its FX exposure problem. We'll show how to address this problem in the next chapter.

If a firm's FX operating exposure is 0, then the use of foreign currency debt will create a negative FX equity exposure, which may be calculated using equation (6.2), substituting 0 for $\xi_{O\epsilon}^\$$. For example, assume that $\xi_{O\epsilon}^\$ = 0$, and a firm has euro debt financing such that the ratio of euro debt to intrinsic value is 0.25 (with no other debt). The firm's FX equity exposure to the euro will be $\xi_{S\epsilon}^\$ = (0 - 0.25)/(1 - 0.25) = -0.333$.

FX NET CASH FLOW EXPOSURE VERSUS FX EQUITY EXPOSURE

While foreign currency debt will dampen both FX net cash flow exposure and FX equity exposure at the same time when FX operating exposure exceeds 0, the two exposures will generally be different for a given level of debt. To see this point, let's revisit the ITX example. This time, assume that ITX has an FX operating exposure of 0.75. The expected operating cash flow is a level perpetuity of $1000 per year and the cost of capital is 10%. So the intrinsic value of ITX's operations is $10,000.

Assume ITX has $7500 in British pound debt with a coupon interest rate of 5%. The debt interest expense in US dollars is $375 per year, and $N^\$$ is expected to be $1000 - 375$ $= \$625$, as long as the FX rate does not change. If the pound depreciates by 20%, the interest expense in US dollars will be $300, and NCF will drop to $850 - 300 = \$550$, a change of $\$550/\$625 - 1 = -0.12$, or -12%. The FX NCF exposure to the pound, $\xi_{N\pounds}^\$$, is 0.60. The FX equity exposure, using equation (6.2), is $(0.75 - 0.75)/(1 - 0.75) = 0$.

The use of the pound debt makes both FX NCF exposure and FX equity exposure lower than if US dollar debt is used, as we already know. But there is not a precise amount of pound debt that will make both FX NCF exposure and FX equity exposure equal to zero simultaneously. Firms may have to choose which is more important, reducing FX NCF exposure or reducing FX equity exposure.[4]

There is another issue involving FX NCF exposure and FX equity exposure when the exposures stem from a foreign subsidiary that reinvests its cash flows and does not repatriate them to the parent. Say the intrinsic value of the parent's investment in the subsidiary fluctuates with FX rates, so there is an FX value exposure, but no cash is flowing to the parent. We know that the fluctuations in value get reflected in the parent's intrinsic equity values, so the parent wants to hedge the FX value exposure with foreign currency debt. If the parent issues the debt though, it will have to make foreign currency debt service payments without actually having operating cash inflows in that currency. Note that an exporter may have a similar FX value exposure and a similar hedging strategy of using foreign currency debt. However, the cash flows are not being retained abroad, so that the same problem does not arise as in the case of hedging FX value exposure of an investment in a foreign subsidiary that reinvests cash flows.

One solution to the problem when a subsidiary is involved is for the parent to re-lend the amount it borrows to its foreign subsidiary through an intercompany loan. This way, the parent receives foreign currency cash flows from the subsidiary's debt service payments. The parent can in turn use these payments to service its debt. While the subsidiary would be reinvesting less of its own cash flows, the same thing basically would happen if the hedging were accomplished by the subsidiary issuing the foreign currency debt on its own.

An intercompany loan is often used as a way for an overseas subsidiary to repatriate cash flows to a parent. If a subsidiary is worth $1000, the parent could capitalize the subsidiary with a loan of $600 and equity of $400, rather than equity worth $1000. Either way, the parent owns the subsidiary's cash flows. Having cash flows repatriated as debt service on an intercompany loan often has tax advantages to repatriation as dividends on equity. A parent cannot take this tactic too far, however, or the Internal Revenue Service will construe the intercompany debt for what it is: a form of equity with favorable tax consequences. The limit is reportedly a debt ratio of 4 to 1.

DEBT MATURITY

We have not said anything yet about the impact of debt maturity. The reason is that debt maturity is in principle not an issue in FX exposure management. To show this point, let us compare the use of perpetual foreign currency debt (no maturity) with a perpetual strategy of rolling over one-year foreign currency debt. For this comparison, the annual interest rate is assumed to be constant and 5% for debt of any maturity.

Assume first that a US firm issues €1000 of perpetual euro-denominated debt with a 5% coupon interest payment. Assume a spot FX rate at the issue time (time 0) of 1 $/€, so

---

[4]The reason that FX NCF exposure differs from FX equity exposure has to do with the impact of financial leverage on the risk and valuation of the equity, which affects FX equity exposure but not FX NCF exposure.

the debt's US dollar value is $1000. Now assume at time 1 that the spot FX rate is 1.20 $/€. The firm must lay out $60 to pay the €50 in interest, and the firm's euro debt now has a value of $1200 in US dollars.

What if instead the firm issues €1000 of one-year euro-denominated debt with a 5% coupon interest payment? Again we assume a spot FX rate at time 0 of 1 $/€, so the debt's US dollar value is $1000 when the debt is issued. Now assume at time 1 that the spot FX rate is 1.20 $/€. The firm again must lay out $60 to pay the €50 in interest. Now the firm must also lay out $1200 to pay off the debt's principal. Assume the firm can roll over the obligation, by again borrowing €1000 in one-year euro debt at 5%. The proceeds of the time-1 borrowing will be $1200, exactly the amount needed to retire the prior one-year debt issued at time 0. Going forward, the firm has euro debt with a value in US dollars of $1200.

We can extend the reasoning through time. In both cases, the firm's net outflow in each period is the €50 in interest expense. In effect, debt maturity is not an issue in FX exposure management.

THE BRITISH POUND DEBT OF VULCAN MATERIALS

Consider Vulcan Materials, whose UK subsidiary did not actually expose its US parent to any appreciable changes in the FX value of the pound. Before a regression analysis revealed the FX operating exposure to the pound was ≈0 (see Chapter 5), Vulcan considered denominating debt in British pounds. The reason would be to hedge the FX exposure to the pound that the parent mistakenly perceived was posed by its British subsidiary. Had it issued the sterling-denominated debt, the firm would actually have created a negative FX equity exposure to the pound.

The Vulcan Materials case is described in C. Kent Garner and Alan C. Shapiro, "A Practical Method of Assessing Foreign Exchange Risk," *Midland Corporate Finance Journal*, Fall 1984, 6–17.

ESTIMATION OF FX EQUITY EXPOSURE

While we have looked at the theory of FX equity exposure, some real-world firms may have a hard time in assessing the FX exposures of the intrinsic value of their firm value or equity. Can a firm estimate its FX equity exposure with actual stock returns? This would assume implicitly that stock prices reflect intrinsic stock values. How sensitive actual stock price changes are to FX changes depends on whether investors recognize how FX changes affect the intrinsic value of the firm's equity.

An analyst typically estimates an empirical FX equity exposure by regressing a time series of a firm's stock returns against percentage changes in the spot FX price of a currency. For Gillette, Merck, and GE, Exhibit 6.7 shows estimated FX equity exposures

EXHIBIT 6.7 Empirical Estimates of FX Equity Exposure

	GILLETTE		MERCK		GE		S&P 500 INDEX (US)	
	92–99	99–04	92–99	99–04	92–99	99–04	92–99	99–04
Yen	**0.207**	**0.207**	**−0.298**	**−0.018**	**0.112**	**0.785**	**0.21**	**0.018**
SE	0.261	0.388	0.248	0.464	0.197	0.409	0.14	0.252
Pound	**0.022**	**0.364**	**0.653**	**0.500**	**0.285**	**−0.197**	**0.82**	**−0.057**
SE	0.359	0.498	0.336	0.593	0.268	0.540	0.33	0.323
Euro	**0.369**	**0.463**	**0.132**	**−0.007**	**−0.250**	**−0.364**	**0.18**	**−0.048**
SE	0.339	0.353	0.325	0.427	0.255	0.385	0.28	0.231

Source: Author's estimates using the method of Interactive Exercise 6.1; monthly data from 1992 to May 2004.

to the yen, the pound, and the euro, along with the associated standard errors. (The German mark was used as a proxy for the euro prior to 1999.) FX equity exposure estimates are computed by regressing monthly stock returns on monthly percentage FX changes using data for two periods: 1992 to 1999 and 1999 to May 2004. In the right-most columns, Exhibit 6.7 also shows estimated FX exposures for the US equity market as a whole.

The standard error represents the estimated standard deviation of the FX equity exposure estimate and provides a guide to statistical significance. Merck's estimated FX equity exposure to the pound in 1992–1999, 0.653, is reasonably significant, since the standard error is relatively low, 0.336. So we have some confidence when we say that a 10% rise in the FX value of the pound would have resulted in a 6.53% rise in Merck's stock price on average. Many of the estimated FX equity exposures in Exhibit 6.7 have relatively large standard errors, and so we have less confidence in their statistical significance. Actually, there are more sophisticated methods for estimating FX equity exposure than used for Exhibit 6.7; the purpose here is just to convey the basic idea of estimating FX equity exposure.

You should also be aware that FX equity exposure estimates from time series data like these must be taken with a grain of salt. A firm's FX exposure applies to a given operating and financial structure at a given time, but time series observations may come a period when a firm's operating structure or capital structure are changing. Still, FX equity return exposures estimated this way might be useful.

You may want to use returns for periods longer than one month, because empirical research suggests that equity prices do not respond to FX changes as quickly as they should in an efficient market. This is possibly owing to investors' inability to rapidly grasp the complex implications of FX changes. Similarly, estimated FX exposures are higher the longer the horizon for the returns used in the estimation process.[5]

---

[5]See E. Bartov and G. Bodner, "Firm Valuation, Earnings Expectations, and the Exchange-Rate Exposure Effect," *Journal of Finance*, December 1994, 1755–1786, and E. Chow, W. Lee, and M. Solt, "The Exchange-Rate Risk Exposure of Asset Returns," *Journal of Business*, January 1997, 105–123.

INTERACTIVE EXERCISE 6.1

Estimate the FX Equity Exposure for a Company in US Dollars

Historical prices of equities of individual companies in US dollars (adjusted for dividends and splits) are available for free download at http://biz.yahoo.com/r/. Click "Historical Quotes" under "Research Tools." Indicate the time period (e.g., January 1, 1999, through June 1, 2004), the interval (e.g., "monthly"), and the ticker symbol. The last column of the page that appears is the "adjusted (for dividends and splits) close," which is what you want and what you get when you scroll down and click on "Download to Spreadsheet." Open the file in Excel. Save it as an Excel workbook. The data you want (adjusted prices) are in column E, but first reverse the order. There is a shortcut for this on the toolbar, or you can go to "data," then "sort," and then sort by "date" "ascending." You can then convert the values in column E into a time series of rates of return.

The FX data may be downloaded from the Federal Reserve Bank of St. Louis: http://research.stlouisfed.org/fred2/categories/15. Click on the exchange rate for which you want to download monthly FX rates. You can choose to get the FX rates in an Excel file. The FX rates should be reciprocated if in European terms. Then make a column of time series of the percentage changes in the FX price of the foreign currency.

Next you need to copy/paste (you may have to use "paste special" and "values") the two return series onto a common spreadsheet. Once you have a column of individual stock returns and a column FX percentage changes, consistently aligned by date on the same spreadsheet, you are ready to compute an estimated FX equity exposure. Go to "tools," then "data analysis." [If "data analysis" does not show when you pull down the "tools" menu, choose "add-in," and check the "analysis pack." Then the "data analysis" will be a "tools" option.] Choose "regression" and "OK." For "y range," put in the stock return range; for "x range", put in the FX percentage change range. Then hit "OK." The "X-variable coefficient" will be the estimate of the stock's estimated FX equity exposure, in US dollars.

You may find the following Web site helpful: http://business.fullerton.edu/mstohs/Regression%20in%20EXCEL.htm.

UNLEVERING ESTIMATED FX EQUITY EXPOSURE

We can often estimate a firm's FX equity exposure with observable equity return data. But we do not have data on the value of the firm to directly estimate the firm's FX operating exposure with market information. So we can use a procedure to estimate a firm's FX operating exposure from its estimated FX equity exposure. The procedure is to use equation (6.2) in reverse, and it is called *unlevering* the estimated FX equity exposure.

Suppose a US firm is estimated to have an FX equity exposure of 0.80 to the euro. Assume that the firm has a capital structure that is 20% euro-denominated debt, 25% US dollar debt, and the rest (55%) equity. Assuming that these ratios are the same for intrinsic values, the ratio of total debt to value, $D^\$/V^\$$, is 0.45. Then equation (6.2) may be applied in reverse to unlever the estimated FX equity exposure in order to estimate the firm's FX operating exposure: $\xi_{O\epsilon}^\$ = \xi_{S\epsilon}^\$(1 - D^\$/V^\$) + D_\epsilon^\$/V^\$ = 0.80(1 - 0.45) + 0.20 = 0.64$. You can double-check using equation (6.2) directly: $\xi_{S\epsilon}^\$ = (0.64 - 0.20)/(1 - 0.45) = 0.80$.[6]

ABC Company currently has $V^\$ = \$5000$, $D^\$ = \$2000$, and thus $S^\$ = \$3000$. Assume an estimated FX equity exposure of 0.30 to the euro. Assume that $1500 of the firm's debt is euro debt, and the rest is US dollar debt. Use equation (6.2) to find the estimated FX operating exposure.

Answer: $0.30 = (\xi_{O\epsilon}^\$ - 0.30)/(1 - 0.40) \Rightarrow \xi_{O\epsilon}^\$ = 0.48$.

SUMMARY

This chapter introduced FX exposure from the viewpoint of a firm's equity investors. We covered the use of foreign currency debt in financial hedging of FX exposure.

First, we looked at how the use of foreign currency debt affects FX net cash flow exposure. Then we formulated a simple model of FX equity exposure in terms of FX operating exposure and the proportionate use of debt financing in the exposed currency and in total.

We addressed how and whether a firm can use foreign currency debt to hedge an FX operating exposure. We found that using foreign currency debt to hedge is somewhat complex because it involves a financial leverage effect in addition to the FX hedging effect.

When the FX operating exposure is less than 1, the financial leverage effect is less pronounced, and foreign currency debt is often an effective way to financially hedge a long FX operating exposure. When the FX operating exposure is greater than 1, the financial leverage effect may dominate the FX hedging effect and create problems when managers try to use foreign currency debt for hedging. Using foreign currency debt is similarly not a reasonable way to eliminate FX equity exposure when a firm's FX operating exposure is negative.

When foreign currency debt is not effective in financial hedging of FX exposure, perhaps currency swaps can be, as we learn in the next chapter.

---

[6]Even if we considered taxes, there does not need to be a tax term in the levering/unlevering equation (6.2). Theory that justifies this approach is found in Merton Miller, "Debt and Taxes" *Journal of Finance*, May 1977, 261–275, and James Miles and Russell Ezzell, "The Weighted Average Cost of Capital, Perfect Capital Markets, and Project Life: A Clarification," *Journal of Financial and Quantitative Analysis*, September 1980, 719–730.

GLOSSARY

Cost of capital: The capitalization (discount) rate applied to a firm's expected operating cash flows, to determine the intrinsic value of the firm.

Eurobond: An international debt obligation offered to investors in countries outside the country of the issuer and in a currency, or currencies, other than the investor's base currency.

Euromarket: Refers to the international financial market, a tradition since the first eurobonds.

Foreign bond: A bond issued in the country and currency of the investor and traded in a local, and locally regulated, bond market.

FX equity exposure: The variability in a firm's equity value caused by uncertain FX rate changes.

FX NCF exposure: The variability in a firm's net cash flow caused by uncertain FX rate changes.

FX value exposure: The variability in the value of a firm caused by uncertain FX rate changes.

Financial leverage: The impact of a company's borrowing on the volatility of residual earnings and equity values.

Natural hedging: Hedging without using financial derivatives.

Strategic hedging: Hedging that helps a company avoid the derailment of a strategic plan.

Value of a firm's operations: The present value of a company's expected future stream of operating cash flows; the total value of all a firm's capital, debt plus equity, as opposed to the value of the firm's equity alone.

DISCUSSION QUESTIONS

1. What are some of the reasons corporations might be able to do a better job at managing FX exposure than their investors?
2. Give some examples of cases in which financial hedging is useful instead of operational hedging or in addition to operational hedging.
3. Would issuing foreign currency debt be an effective risk management tool for a company with a negative FX operating exposure? Explain.
4. Discuss the idea that a company's FX net cash flow exposure is not equal to its FX equity exposure. Which of the two exposures do you think is the more important to hedge? Do you think a parent should hedge the FX value exposure of a foreign subsidiary that reinvests its cash flows rather than repatriating them to the parent?

PROBLEMS

1. Use the ITX example in the text. Assume that ITX's FX operating exposure to the pound is 0.50. Find the FX net cash flow exposure for Cases I and II.
2. Assume that a US firm's FX operating exposure to the euro is 1.60, and financing (other than equity) is exclusively US dollar debt financing, with a ratio of debt to intrinsic value of 40%. What is the firm's FX value exposure to the euro? What is the firm's FX equity exposure to the euro?

3. (a) Assume that a firm's FX operating exposure to the euro is 1.60, and 40% of the financing is euro-denominated debt. If all other financing is equity, what is the firm's FX equity exposure? (b) What if 70% of the firm's financing is euro debt, and the rest of the financing is equity?

4. Assume that a US company has FX operating exposure to the pound of 0.40. What amount of pound debt should the firm use if the intrinsic value of the firm is currently $2.50 million and it wants to eliminate its FX equity exposure to the pound?

5. Assume that ABC Company currently has $V^\$ = \$10$ million, $D^\$ = \$4$ million, and thus $S^\$ = \$6$ million. Assume an FX operating exposure of 1.25 to the euro. Assume that $3 million of the firm's debt is euro debt and the rest is US dollar debt. Now the FX value of the euro drops by 10%. Find the new intrinsic equity value and the FX equity exposure directly. Then use equation (6.2) to verify the FX equity exposure.

6. Assume that ABC Company currently has $V^\$ = \$10$ million, $D^\$ = \$4$ million, and thus $S^\$ = \$6$ million. Say $3 million of the firm's debt is euro-denominated debt and the rest is US dollar debt. ABC's FX equity exposure to the euro is estimated to be 0.50. Find ABC's estimated FX operating exposure.

7. Use the ITX example in the text but assume that ITX uses $5000 in debt rather than $7500. The interest rate on the debt is 5% regardless of whether the debt is in US dollars (Case I) or pounds (Case II). Assume that ITX's FX operating exposure to the pound is 0.50. Find the FX net cash flow exposure for Cases I and II. Assume the operating cash flow is an expected level perpetuity of $1000 per year and the cost of capital is 10%. Find the FX NCF exposure and FX equity exposure for Cases I and II. Explain why the FX NCF exposure is not equal to the FX equity exposure.

ANSWERS TO PROBLEMS

1. 0.80; 0.20
2. 1.60; 2.67
3. (a) 2; (b) 3
4. $1 million
5. The intrinsic value of the firm will fall by 12.5% to $8.75 million. The value of the euro-denominated debt in US dollars will drop by 10% to $2.70 million, while the value of the other debt stays at $1 million. The new intrinsic equity value would be $8.75 million − 2.70 million − 1 million = $5.05 million. The percentage change in intrinsic equity value is $5.05 million /$6 million − 1 = −0.158, or −15.8%. The FX equity exposure is −0.158/−0.10 = 1.58. Since $D_\epsilon^\$/V^\$ = 0.30$ and $D^\$/V^\$ = 0.40$, the FX equity exposure of 1.58 is consistent with equation (6.2): $\xi_{S\epsilon}^\$ = (1.25 − 0.30)/(1 − 0.40) = 1.58$.
6. Since $0.50 = (\xi_{O\epsilon}^\$ − 0.30)/(1 − 0.40)$, $\xi_{O\epsilon}^\$ = 0.60$.
7. Case I: ITX has $5000 in US dollar-denominated debt. The debt interest expense is $250 per year, and $N^\$$ is expected to be $1000 − 250 = $750 as long as the FX rate does not change. If the pound depreciates by 20%, ITX's NCF will drop to $900 − 250 = $650, a change of $650/$750 − 1 = −0.133, or −13.3%. The FX NCF exposure to the pound, $\xi_{N\pounds}^\$$, is 0.667. The FX equity exposure, from equation (6.2), is $(0.50)/(1 − 0.50) = 1$.

    Case II: ITX has $5000 in pound debt. The debt interest expense is $250 per year, and $N^\$$ is expected to be $1000 − 250 = $750 as long as the FX rate does not change. If pound depreciates by 20%, NCF will drop to $900 − 200 = $700, a change of $700/$750 − 1 = −0.0667, or −6.67%. The FX NCF exposure to the pound, $\xi_{N\pounds}^\$$, is 0.333. The FX equity exposure, from equation (6.2), is $(0.50 − 0.50)/(1 − 0.50) = 0$.

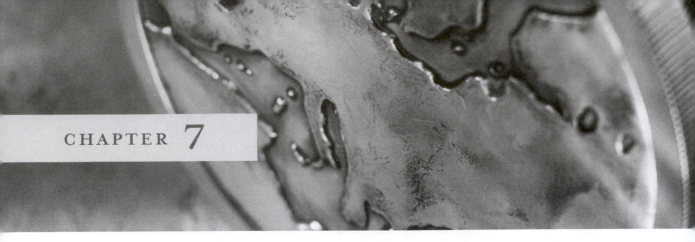

CHAPTER 7

CURRENCY SWAPS

The advent of swaps, as much as anything else, helped transform the world's segmented capital markets into a single, truly integrated, international capital market.

—John F. Marshall and Kenneth R. Kapner (1993)

A *currency swap* is a contract to exchange two streams of future cash flows in different currencies. Currency swaps were designed to circumvent capital controls imposed by governments and to make borrowing more efficient in global markets. We will see that currency swaps are used to convert debt denominated in one currency into synthetic debt denominated in another currency. Synthetic debt created in this way sometimes allows a segment of the capital market to be tapped that would otherwise not be accessible with debt actually denominated in that currency.

When synthetic debt in a currency is created, we think of it as actual debt in that currency when performing analyses of hedging FX exposure. For example, when Fannie Mae issues yen debt but converts it into synthetic US dollar debt by a currency swap, we think of Fannie Mae as having US dollar debt for analytical purposes, even though Fannie Mae nominally has yen debt.

By themselves, currency swap positions are also useful in managing FX operating exposure in situations where foreign currency debt does not work. A firm with a negative FX operating exposure, or a positive FX operating exposure too high to be managed solely by foreign currency denominated debt, might use currency swaps in its FX financial hedging strategies.

WORLD BANK–IBM SWAP

The first currency swap seems to have been a 1982 transaction between the World Bank and IBM. Its details are instructive. The World Bank wanted to raise additional capital and to denominate the liabilities in Swiss francs because of a low interest rate in that currency. The US market, though, was more receptive to World Bank bonds than the Swiss market, since the World Bank had already saturated the Swiss market for its bonds, and US investors regarded World Bank bonds as having much less credit risk than Swiss investors did. And the US investors wanted bonds denominated in US dollars. IBM had financed before by issuing some Swiss franc debt, but had since developed the view that the Swiss franc was going to appreciate relative to the US dollar. It wanted to replace its Swiss franc debt with US dollar debt.

A major global bank observed that both parties could benefit if they made a private deal, which it termed a currency swap. The swap let IBM receive cash flows of Swiss francs from the World Bank, and the World Bank to receive US dollars from IBM. The World Bank could then go ahead and borrow from US investors in the favorable US market, planning to use its US dollar receipts from the currency swap to make the US dollar bond payments. This way, the Swiss franc swap payments to IBM represented the net liability for the World Bank. Similarly, IBM could use the Swiss francs received from the World Bank to meet its Swiss franc debt obligations, while its US dollar payments to the World Bank represented its new effective liability in US dollars.

IBM's motivation was clear. IBM had issued Swiss franc bonds but subsequently wanted to change that liability into a US dollar liability, as it feared an appreciation of the Swiss franc. IBM used the currency swap as an expeditious way to convert Swiss franc debt into US dollar debt, without having to retire its Swiss franc debt and reissue new US dollar debt. This stratagem saved both money and time.

The World Bank, on the other hand, used the currency swap in a capital-raising strategy. You might ask why the World Bank didn't simply issue Swiss franc bonds in the first place, if it wanted its liabilities to be denominated in Swiss francs. The answer is that the currency swap allowed the World Bank to get a lower effective Swiss franc interest rate than it could have had by issuing Swiss franc bonds directly. There was more appetite for World Bank bonds among US investors than among Swiss investors, and US investors thought the World Bank to be a better credit risk than Swiss investors thought. But the US investors wanted bonds denominated in US dollars, so the World Bank took advantage of the financing opportunity in the US market. It achieved its preferred liability denomination of Swiss francs through the swap deal. Figure 7.1 shows the basic structure of the World Bank–IBM currency swap.

We describe the positions in currency swaps like positions in forward FX contracts. Since IBM received Swiss francs and paid US dollars, it had a long Swiss franc position in the swap and a short US dollar position. The World Bank, which paid Swiss francs and received US dollars, had a short Swiss franc position and a long US dollar position.

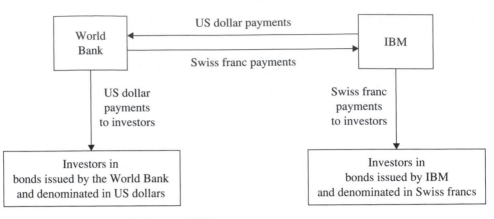

Figure 7.1 World Bank–IBM swap (1982).

FIXED-FOR-FIXED CURRENCY SWAPS

The basic (plain vanilla) currency swap is a *fixed-for-fixed* swap. In this case, the cash flows are based upon straight, or bullet, coupon bonds in two currencies. The swap stipulates the time until maturity, the two coupon rates, and the *notional principal* of the swap. For example, consider two five-year *straight bonds*, one denominated in US dollars and the other in Swiss francs, which make annual coupon interest payments, where a straight bond has no features other than promised coupon interest and principal repayment. Assume that the coupon rate of the five-year US dollar bond is 6%, and the coupon rate of the five-year Swiss franc bond is 4%. Assuming a principal of $1000 for the US dollar bond, the coupon interest payments are 0.06($1000) = $60 per year. At maturity, at the same time as the final interest payment, the $1000 in principal payment must also be repaid.

Now consider the equivalent amount of principal in Swiss francs. Given an assumed time 0 spot FX rate of 1.60 Sf/$, $1000(1.60 Sf/$) = Sf 1600. Thus, the Swiss franc bond makes coupon interest payments of 0.04(Sf 1600) = Sf 64 per year and then also repays the principal of Sf 1600 at the same time as the last coupon payment.

Any two counterparties can agree to exchange the cash flows based "notionally" on these two bonds, whether the counterparties actually own the bonds or not. Counterparty U would agree to receive (from counterparty S) the Swiss franc cash flows of Sf 64 annually for five years, plus Sf 1600 at maturity. Counterparty S would agree to receive (from counterparty U) the US dollar cash flows of $60 annually for five years, plus $1000 at maturity.

If the coupon rates on the underlying bonds are the same as the market yields for the two bonds, the swap is an *at-market swap*. That is, if 6% is the current market yield on five-year on US dollar bonds and 4% is the current market yield on five-year Swiss franc bonds, then the principal of each bond is equal to the present value of its future cash flows. Thus the present values of the swapped cash flows are equivalent at time 0. The two parties are simply exchanging future cash flows worth Sf 1600 today for future cash flows worth $1000 today, which is fair at the assumed current spot FX rate of 1.60 Sf/$. In an at-market swap, no time-0 payment is necessary, because the present values of the underlying notional bonds are equivalent, given the current spot FX rate. Many currency swaps originate as at-market swaps.

You enter into a five-year fixed-for-fixed currency swap to receive a cash flow stream in British pounds and to pay cash flow stream in US dollars. The swap is an at-market swap based on a notional principal of $1 million. What are the cash flows of the swap if the five-year market yields are 5.50% for US dollars and 9.00% for British pounds and the spot FX rate is currently 1.50 $/£?

Answer: The cash flow stream you would pay consists of interest payments of 0.055($1 million) = $55,000 per year for five years, plus a final principal payment of $1 million. The cash flow stream you would receive is based on a sterling-denominated bond with a principal amount equal to the pound equivalent of $1 million, given the spot FX rate of 1.50 $/£. Thus, the principal on the sterling bond is $1 million/(1.50 $/£) = £666,667. At a coupon interest rate of 9%, the sterling cash flow receipts consist of interest components of 0.09(£666,667) = £60,000 per year for five years and a principal component of £666,667 at year 5.

REVIEW OF BOND VALUATION

The value of a bond is the present value of the future interest and principal payments. The definition of yield-to-maturity is the (annualized) interest rate that discounts the promised future bond payments back to the bond's present value. Let us find the value of a *straight bond* (or bullet bond, i.e., with no features other than promised coupon interest and principal repayment) denominated in Swiss francs. The bond has a face value of Sf 100, four years to maturity, and a 5% annual coupon interest rate; the yield to maturity is 7%. The cash flows for the bond are annual interest payments of Sf 5 at the end of each of the next four years plus a principal repayment of Sf 100 at the end of the fourth year. The present value of those cash flows, given a yield to maturity of 7%, is Sf $5/1.07$ + Sf $5/1.07^2$ + Sf $5/1.07^3$ + Sf $105/1.07^4$ = Sf 93.23. For simplicity, the valuation here is for the instant in time after the most recent coupon interest payment. The value might thus be called the "ex-interest" value of the bond.

If the face value had been Sf 1000, the present value of the bond would be Sf 932.30, and if the face value had been Sf 10,000, the present value would be Sf 9323. Rather than specify a principal amount or face value, one can simply quote, as the bond market does, on the basis of percentage of face value. Thus, the value of the four-year, 5% coupon, Swiss franc bond with a 7% yield to maturity is simply quoted as 93.23, with the understanding that this value is a percentage of its face value, which is in Swiss francs.

(continued)

A *par bond's* present value is equal to its face value. A bond is thus a par bond if the yield to maturity is equal to the coupon rate. Many coupon bonds are par bonds, or close to it, when they are issued. If the yield to maturity is greater than the coupon rate, the market value of the bond is less than the face value; in this case, the bond is called a *discount bond*. If the yield to maturity is less than the coupon rate, the value of the bond is greater than the face value; in this case, the bond is called a *premium bond*.

Example swap rates for at-market swaps, taken from a web site now closed to the public, are shown for September 2, 2000 in Table 7.1. DKK is the Danish krone, and SEK is the Swedish krona.

Let's assume that the swap rates in Table 7.1 are current and that you want an at-market five-year currency swap to pay yen and receive US dollars. You would pay yen at the coupon rate of 1.41% on the swap's notional yen principal, and receive US dollars at the rate of 6.87% on the equivalent notional principal in US dollars, at the current spot FX rate.

TABLE 7.1 Swap Rates: September 2, 2000

	SWAP RATES					
	USD	EUR	JPY	CHF	DKK	SEK
2Y	6.84	5.41	0.70	3.885	5.94	5.117
3Y	6.85	5.48	0.93	3.930		5.387
4Y	6.86	5.54	1.17	3.965	5.94	5.600
5Y	6.87	5.60	1.41	4.000	5.96	5.722
7Y	6.90	5.70	1.81	4.095	5.98	5.875
10Y	6.96	5.79	2.20	4.230	6.01	6.008

Source: www.cfoweb.com.

PARALLEL LOANS AND BACK-TO-BACK LOANS

Currency swaps evolved from *parallel loans*, which were devised years ago to get around cross-border capital controls. British law forbade British companies to use capital from their country for overseas investment. The law was intended to encourage the use of British capital in domestic investment and thus to help create jobs at home. There was no law, however, to prevent a British company from lending British pounds to the local UK subsidiary of a US firm. And the US parent could lend the equivalent amount in US dollars to the US subsidiary of the British parent.

While the UK subsidiary of the US parent made pound-denominated interest and principal payments to the British parent, the US subsidiary of the British parent would make US dollar interest and principal payments to the US parent. The US subsidiary of the

British parent would receive the financing it needed, circumventing Britain's capital export controls. Moreover, the US parent could effectively repatriate earnings of its UK subsidiary to the US without paying repatriation taxes to the host government. Parallel loans not only got around capital controls, but were also a way to avoid foreign tax on the repatriated returns of overseas investments.

It isn't much of a leap to see that even if companies in different countries do not need new capital, they can arrange hypothetical loans to each other's subsidiaries and thus accomplish the exchange of future cash flow streams. Suppose the US subsidiary of a Japanese parent is generating US dollars, and the Japanese subsidiary of a US parent is generating yen. The Japanese parent's US subsidiary books a US dollar loan on its balance sheet, payable to the US parent, and then in the future makes US dollar interest and principal payments to the US parent. At the same time, the US parent's Japanese subsidiary books a yen loan on its balance sheet, payable to the Japanese parent, and then makes future yen interest and principal payments to the Japanese parent. No principal amounts are actually exchanged. This type of an arrangement is called a *back-to-back loan*.

Exhibit 7.1 shows balance sheets representing both parallel loan and back-to-back loan arrangements. The spot FX rate is assumed to be 2 $/£. The US subsidiary of the UK parent owes $3000 to the US parent and the UK subsidiary of the US parent owes the equivalent amount in pounds, £1500, to the UK parent.

While parallel loans and back-to-back loans allow firms to avoid cross-border capital controls and repatriation taxes, they have some drawbacks. First, parallel and back-to-back loans are shown on reported balance sheets, so they result in higher debt ratios, a key factor in credit ratings. Second, different legal provisions in different countries make it very difficult to link the loans legally. If one party defaults on its loan, the laws in the other

EXHIBIT 7.1 Parallel Loans or Back-to-Back Loans: Balance Sheets for Parents and Subsidiaries

UK SUBSIDIARY OF US PARENT		US PARENT
Assets	Debt & Equity	Assets
£2500	£1500 debt to UK parent	$ 3000 loan to UK parent's US subsidiary
_____	£1000 equity of US parent	$ 2000 equity investment in UK subsidiary
£2500	£2500	$ 5000 other assets
		$10,000 total

US SUBSIDIARY OF UK PARENT		UK PARENT
Assets	Debt & Equity	Assets
$4000	$3000 debt to US parent	£1500 loan to US parent's UK subsidiary
_____	$1000 equity of UK parent	£ 500 equity investment in US subsidiary
$4000	$4000	£4000 other assets
		£6000 total

country would still require the other party to pay off the loan on its side of the agreement. Third, each side had to make full payment of the cash flow; that is, there is no difference check settlement.

Enter global financial intermediaries to serve as brokers. The various companies would no longer have to search for suitable partners. The global banks were able to take the key step to structure the deals as legal swaps of cash flow streams instead of mutual loans, and thus to cancel the three drawbacks: (1) Swap positions were off balance sheet, and not figured into debt ratio computations. (2) The cash flows could legally be viewed as offsetting legs of a single transaction, which solved the legal problems. In the process, global banks began to serve as swaps dealers, meaning that each counterparty viewed its deal as only with the bank. A bankruptcy by one company would be the bank's problem, not the other company's problem. (3) Structuring currency swaps as instruments whose periodic exchanges can be settled with one-way difference checks, like forward FX contracts, relieved the counterparties from exchange of the full amounts of funds at each exchange time. This feature in turn reduced the counterparty risk of default.

SWAP-DRIVEN FINANCING

As we saw, the difference in credit risk perceptions of US and European investors was a prime driver of the IBM–World Bank currency swap. Europeans often see a strong international company like IBM as having lower credit risk than a supranational agency like the World Bank. US investors, on the other hand, typically have the opposite perception. US investors might require a company like General Electric to pay a higher US dollar interest rate than the World Bank, while Swiss investors might require the World Bank to pay a higher Swiss franc interest rate than General Electric. Then, if the World Bank prefers a Swiss franc liability, while General Electric prefers a US dollar liability, a currency swap can help each organization overcome these asymmetric market perceptions.

Assume that GE would have to pay an 8% interest rate on US dollar bonds, while the World Bank would have to pay only 7%, because of the bank's perceived better credit rating among US investors. Assume that the World Bank would have to pay a 6% interest rate on Swiss franc par bonds while GE would have to pay only 5%, because of the US company's perceived better credit rating among Swiss investors.

For their preferred liability denominations without a currency swap, GE would pay 8% on US dollar bonds, and the World Bank would pay 6% on Swiss franc bonds. If GE issues Swiss franc bonds at 5%, and the World Bank issues US dollar bonds at 7%, however, and the two organizations engage in a currency swap of 7% US dollars for 5% Swiss francs, each ends up with lower effective financing costs in their preferred currencies. The 5% incoming Swiss francs from the swap would cover GE's actual 5% Swiss franc liability, and GE would effectively be paying US dollar interest at the rate of 7%, lower than the 8% it would have to pay on actual US dollar bonds. The World Bank's 7% US dollar liability would be covered by the currency swap receipts, and the net effective liability would be 5% Swiss francs, again a lower rate than the 6% it would have to pay on actual Swiss franc bonds.

Although currency swaps often involve no initial exchange of principal amounts, this may occur when two bond issuers enter a swap. When an organization issues securities to raise capital and simultaneously originates a swap as an integral part of the deal, we call the arrangement *swap-driven financing*.

FANNIE MAE'S FX DISCOUNT NOTES, APRIL 2003

In April 2003, US-based Fannie Mae needed to expand its sources for capital as it expected the demand for mortgage capital in the United States to double over the next decade. Fannie Mae introduced its FX Discount Notes, a multi-currency debt issuance vehicle. These notes help Fannie Mae support mortgage demand. The notes enable international investors to execute transactions during their domestic trading hours and in a currency of their choice.

Fannie Mae will issue predominantly in the euro, British pound, Swiss franc and Japanese yen, in addition to other currencies as warranted by investor demand. The company will swap these foreign currency borrowings into US dollars to help finance its mortgage portfolio, which is US dollar denominated.

Source: http://housing-bubble.com/news/fannie-foreign-currency-110303.html.

In the GE example, GE issues synthetic US dollar bonds through (1) an actual issue of Swiss franc bonds and (2) a long Swiss franc position in a currency swap. A company can create what we call *synthetic base currency debt* as follows:

Synthetic Base Currency Debt

1. Company has actual foreign currency debt.
2. Company takes long swap position in foreign currency.

A short swap position in the foreign currency combined with US dollar debt effectively creates *synthetic foreign currency debt*:

Synthetic Foreign Currency Debt

1. Company has actual base currency debt.
2. Company takes short swap position in foreign currency.

Companies that really want to have foreign currency debt may sometimes find it more advantageous to issue base currency debt, and then swap to create the foreign currency debt synthetically. For example, US companies have sometimes found foreign investors reluctant to accept the risk of a corporate takeover, so it is less expensive to issue synthetic foreign currency debt by combining a swap position with actual US dollar debt issued to US investors. Another example is found in Disney's synthetic yen financing, described in the accompanying box.

DISNEY'S SYNTHETIC YEN FINANCING

In the 1990s, a French utility company with a AAA credit rating wanted to borrow in European Currency Units (ECUs), a basket of European currencies that was a precursor to the euro, but had already borrowed too much from the European market in the sense that its cost of borrowing would be slightly higher than the typical AAA credit.

Disney had a positive FX operating exposure to the yen and wanted therefore to borrow in yen to hedge. But as a company with a single-A credit rating, Disney was not welcome in the Japanese market by the Japanese central bank. Hence, Disney could only borrow from a Japanese bank rather than issue yen-denominated bonds, and at an interest rate higher than a typical company with a single-A credit rating would borrow in Japan.

On the other hand, the French utility was welcome in Japan and would get a fair rate, and Disney was very welcome in Europe and would get a fair rate there. So, each company had a comparative advantage in the other market. This is an interesting point. Even though the French utility could get a better rate than Disney in each market (because it was a AAA-rated company), Disney had the comparative advantage in Europe.

So it was beneficial to both companies to let the French utility borrow in Japan, and let Disney borrow in Europe then swap and share the saving between themselves (and throw a bone to the swap bank who bore the risk the French company was facing —namely swapping with a single-A firm.) The French company did not get much out of the savings. It seems Disney was able to receive most of the benefit.

Source: C. Kester and W. Allen, "Walt Disney Co.'s Yen Financing," Harvard Business School.

SETTLEMENT OF SWAP COMPONENTS WITH DIFFERENCE CHECKS

Although the idea behind a swap is to exchange cash flow streams, the settlement of swap cash flows is often accomplished by means of difference checks. Let's look again at the five-year fixed-for-fixed currency swap of 6% US dollars for 4% Swiss francs for a notional principal of $1000. At the time-0 spot FX rate of 1.60 Sf/$, the currency swap is effectively an exchange of $60 for Sf 64 each year for five years, and then a final exchange of $1000 for Sf 1600 at year 5. The long Swiss franc position has contracted to pay the $60 and receive Sf 64 each year for five years, and to pay $1000 and receive Sf 1600 at year 5.

In fact, each swap cash flow is typically settled by a difference check based the actual spot FX rate. If the spot FX rate has moved to 2 Sf/$ as of the time of the first coupon component, the Sf 64 coupon interest at time 1 would be worth Sf 64/(2 Sf/$) = $32. The long Swiss franc position is scheduled to pay \$60, but the US dollar value of the Sf 64 to be received is now \$32. The scheduled payment may thus be settled simply by a difference payment of \$60 − 32 = \$28, from the counterparty that is long Swiss francs to the counterparty that is short Swiss francs.

A difference check in a currency swap works in a fashion similar to a forward FX contract. The forward FX rate is replaced by an *FX conversion rate* for a component swap payment. There are generally two different FX conversion rates in a fixed-for-fixed swap: one for interest components, and one for the principal component.

The FX conversion rate for the interest components is the spot FX rate times the ratio of the coupon interest rates. The FX conversion rate for the interest components, $C_I^{\text{Sf}/\$}$, is shown in equation (7.1a).

FX Conversion Rate for Interest Component

$$C_I^{\text{Sf}/\$} = X_0^{\text{Sf}/\$}(r^{\text{Sf}}/r^\$) \qquad (7.1a)$$

The FX conversion rate for the principal component, $C_P^{\text{Sf}/\$}$, is simply the spot FX rate at the time the swap originated as shown in equation (7.1b).

FX Conversion Rate for Principal Component

$$C_P^{\text{Sf}/\$} = X_0^{\text{Sf}/\$} \qquad (7.1b)$$

In the US dollar–Swiss franc swap example, the FX conversion rate for the interest components is $C_I^{\text{Sf}/\$}$ = (1.60 Sf/\$)(0.04/0.06) = 1.0667 Sf/\$. [The numerator coupon interest rate should be consistent with the numerator currency.] The FX conversion rate for the principal payment is simply the spot FX rate at time 0, $C_P^{\text{Sf}/\$}$ = 1.60 Sf/\$.

Settlement using a difference check reveals that a swap exchange is essentially a forward FX contract. The FX conversion rate is the forward FX rate; the *size* (Z) is the foreign currency component, and the *amount* (A) is the pricing currency component. Indeed, the difference check at time N from the point of view of the long foreign currency position may be computed using equation (7.2), which is the same as equation (3.1) for forward FX contracts, but using the FX conversion rate (in direct terms from the US dollar point of view) in the place of the forward FX rate:

$$D_{\text{Sf}}^\$ = Z^{\text{Sf}}(X_N^{\$/\text{Sf}} - C^{\$/\text{Sf}}) \qquad (7.2)$$

In the US-Swiss fixed-for-fixed currency swap example, the contract *size* (Z^{Sf}) for the interest component at time 1 is Sf 64, and FX conversion rate is 1.0667 Sf/\$. Thus if the spot FX rate at the time of settling the interest component is 2 Sf/\$, equation (7.2) indicates the long Swiss franc position should receive a difference check settlement of Sf 64[1/(2 Sf/\$) − 1/(1.0667 Sf/\$)] = Sf 64(0.50 \$/Sf − 0.9375 \$/Sf) = −\$28, where the negative sign implies that the long Swiss franc position must pay \$28 to the counterparty that is long US dollars. The remaining interest components are settled similarly using the spot FX rates at the time of the payment.

The difference check settlement for the principal component uses the spot FX rate at the time the swap originated as the FX conversion rate in equation (7.2). The contract *size* (Z^{Sf}) for the principal is the swap's notional principal in foreign currency. Assume that the spot FX rate at the time of principal component settlement is 2.50 Sf/\$. The counterparty short Swiss francs owes Sf 1600, which is equivalent to Sf 1600/(2.50 Sf/\$) = \$640. Since the long position in Swiss francs owes a notional principal of $1000, the counterparty long in Swiss francs must send a difference check for $360 to settle the principal component at maturity. According to equation (7.2), the long position in Swiss francs is entitled to Sf 1600[1/(2.50 Sf/$) − 1/(1.60 Sf/$)] = Sf 1600(0.40 $/Sf − 0.625 $/Sf) = −$360. Since the sign is negative, the long position in Swiss francs settles with a difference check for $360 sent to the short position in Swiss francs.

Because you can view each component of a fixed-for-fixed currency swap as a forward FX contract, you can interpret the swap as a portfolio of forward FX contracts. The forward FX rates in the portfolio of forwards that constitute the swap, however, are the swap contract's FX conversion rates, not the market's forward FX rates for the individual horizons.

Consider a six-year fixed-for-fixed currency swap of 5% US dollars for 7% Japanese yen on notional principal of $1 million. Assume that the spot FX rate when the swap originates is 140 ¥/$. Find the difference check settlement on the interest component if the spot FX value of the yen depreciates to 160 ¥/$ at time 1. Find the difference check settlement on the principal component at time 6 if the spot FX rate then is 160 ¥/$.

Answers: The notional principal in yen is $1 million (140 ¥/$) = ¥140 million. The notional US dollar interest is 0.05($1 million) = $50,000, while the notional yen interest is 0.07(¥140 million) = ¥9.80 million. The FX conversion rate for the interest components is thus ¥9.80 million/$50,000 = 196 ¥/$. At 160 ¥/$, the interest component settles (from the viewpoint of the long position on yen) at ¥9.8 million [1/(160 ¥/$) − 1/(196 ¥/$)] = $11,250. At time 6, the settlement of the principal component (from the viewpoint of the long position on yen) is ¥140 million [1/(160 ¥/$) − 1/(140 ¥/$)] = −$125,000. Thus, the long position on yen would receive $11,250 from the short position in yen to settle the interest component at time 1, while the short position in yen would receive $125,000 [or equivalently $125,000(160 ¥/$) = ¥20 million] from the long position in yen to settle the principal at time 6.

MARK-TO-MARKET VALUATION OF CURRENCY SWAPS

Like other financial instruments, currency swap positions have a mark-to-market value that fluctuates. A swap position's MTM value fluctuates continuously with changes in interest rates in the two currencies and with changes in the spot FX rate. The MTM value of an at-market swap at time 0 is zero.

To find the MTM value of a currency swap position, we take the present value of the future inflows and subtract the present value of the future outflows, using the spot FX rate to compare the present values in a common currency. Look at the long Swiss franc position of a fixed-for-fixed currency swap as a combination of owning a coupon bond in Swiss francs and issuing a coupon bond in US dollars. Thus the MTM value of the long

Swiss franc position, denoted $M_{Sf}^\$$, may be viewed as the swap's one-sided value of the notional Swiss franc bond, $W_{Sf}^\$$, minus the one-sided value of the notional US dollar bond, $W_\$^\$$, as shown in equation (7.3). [The use of W to denote one-sided swap value was an arbitrary choice from letters not being used to denote other variables.]

MTM Value of Currency Swap Position

$$M_{Sf}^\$ = W_{Sf}^\$ - W_\$^\$ \tag{7.3}$$

What would be the MTM value just after the second interest settlement of the long Swiss franc position in a five-year, $1000, 6% US dollar for 4% Swiss franc currency swap that originated as an at-market swap when the spot FX rate was 1.60 Sf/$? To answer this question, you would need to know two things at the time immediately after the second interest component: (1) the spot FX rate and (2) the market yields of both currencies for a horizon equal to the remaining life of the swap. In this case, since the second interest component has just been settled, the swap has three years left.

To focus only on the influence of the FX rate change, let us assume that after the time-2 coupon interest component settlement, the market yields on three-year coupon bonds are 6% in US dollars and 4% in Swiss francs, the same as the original coupon rates of the swap. Thus, with three years left, the present value of the US dollar payments of $60 for three more years, plus the principal payment of $1000, given the 6% market yield, is $1000 (= $60/1.06 + $60/1.06^2 + $1060/1.06^3). This is the one-sided value of the US dollar bond, $W_\$^\$$. (Another look at the box "Review of Bond Valuation", at the beginning of the chapter, may be helpful here.)

Similarly, the present value of the payments of Sf 64 for three years plus the Sf 1600 principal payment at the 4% yield is Sf 64/1.04 + Sf 64/1.04^2 + Sf (64 + 1600)/1.04^3 = Sf 1600. If the spot FX rate is 1.60 Sf/$ at time 2, the one-sided value in US dollars of the Swiss franc bond, $W_{Sf}^\$$, is $1000.

Thus at a spot FX rate at time 2 of 1.60 Sf/$, the long Swiss franc swap position's MTM value is $M_{Sf}^\$ = W_{Sf}^\$ - W_\$^\$ = \$1000 - 1000 = 0$, since the present values of the two sides of the underlying cash flows, $1000 and Sf 1600, balance each other at that spot FX rate. If the spot FX rate at time 2 is 1.25 Sf/$, however, the Sf 1600 present value of the future Swiss franc cash flows would be equivalent to a US dollar value of Sf 1600/ (1.25 Sf/$) = $1280. Thus the long Swiss franc position owns a future cash flow stream of Swiss francs (equivalent to a Swiss franc bond) that has a one-sided value of $W_{Sf}^\$ = \$1280$, but owes a cash flow stream in US dollars (equivalent to a US dollar bond) with a present value of $W_\$^\$ = \$1000$. The MTM value of the swap, from the viewpoint of the long Swiss franc position, is thus $1280 − 1000 = $280.

The MTM value for the short Swiss franc position is the negative of the MTM value for the long Swiss franc position. In the last example, the MTM value of the short Swiss franc position is −$280.

In the second case, the Swiss franc has appreciated from the time the swap was originated, from 1.60 Sf/$ to 1.25 Sf/$, and the long position on Swiss francs has thus gained overall economic value in the amount of $280. Now, if the holder of the long position on Swiss francs wants to liquidate in the open market, essentially finding a third party to assume the long position, the third party would have to pay $280 to take over the long swap position.

In the US dollar–Swiss franc example, what is the MTM value of the long Swiss franc swap position after the second interest component payment, if the spot FX rate is 2 Sf/\$, but all else remains the same? What is the MTM value of the short Swiss franc position?

Answers: After the second interest component settlement, the present value of the remaining Swiss franc cash flows is Sf 1600, which is equivalent to Sf 1600/(2 Sf/\$) = \$800. Thus, the MTM value of the swap from the viewpoint of the long position on Swiss francs is \$800 − 1000 = −\$200. The counterparty that is currently long on Swiss francs would have to pay \$200 to be able to turn the swap position over to a third party, given the assumed spot FX rate of 2 Sf/\$ and the time-2 US dollar and Swiss franc interest rates. In this case, the Swiss franc has depreciated since the swap originated, and the swap's long position on Swiss francs declines by \$200 in value because of the depreciation. The short Swiss franc position's MTM value is \$200.

OFF-MARKET SWAPS

Any two parties can agree at time 0 to exchange cash flow streams that do *not* have the same present value, given the current spot FX rate. In this case, the recipient of the cash flow stream with the higher present value must make some time-0 balancing payment to the party receiving the cash flow stream with the lower present value. The time-0 balancing payment would equalize the present value of the exchange.

This is called an *off-market swap*; it requires a time-0 payment to balance the present values. Assume that the time-0 spot FX rate is 1.60 \$/£. Suppose you want to make the future payments on a five-year, 5.50% coupon, US dollar par bond, and to receive payments on a five-year, 10% coupon, sterling bond. Assume the market yield to maturity on five-year, 10% coupon sterling bonds is 9%, not 10%. Would you, with the long position on sterling, pay or receive a time-0 payment, and for how much?

For a notional principal of \$1000, the sterling notional principal is £625, because the time-0 spot FX rate is assumed to be 1.60 \$/£. The 10% sterling coupon rate means that you'll receive 0.10(£625) = £62.50 per year for five years, in addition to the principal repayment of £625 at year 5. Thus, the present value of the underlying sterling bond payments is £62.50/1.09 + £62.50/1.09^2 + £62.50/1.09^3 + £62.50/1.09^4 + £62.50/1.09^5 + £625/1.09^5 = £649.30, which is equivalent to a US dollar value of £649.30(1.60 \$/£) = \$1039. The present value of the US dollar cash flows you'd be paying is \$1000, while the present value of the sterling cash flows you'd be receiving is equivalent to \$1039. Thus, you should make a time-0 payment of \$1039 − 1000 = \$39.

Now in the same example, what is the off-market time-0 swap payment necessary to be paid to you (or by you), if you have the long sterling position and want a coupon payment of 8%, all else the same?

Answer: The 8% sterling coupon rate means that you'll receive 0.08(£625) = £50 per year for five years, in addition to the principal repayment of £625 at year 5. The present value of the underlying sterling bond payments is £50/1.09 + £50/1.09² + £50/1.09³ + £50/1.09⁴ + £50/1.09⁵ + £625/1.09⁵ = £601, which is equivalent to a US dollar value of £601(1.60 $/£) = $962. Now the present value of the US dollar cash flows you'd be paying is $1000, while the present value of the sterling cash flows you'd be receiving is equivalent to $962. Thus, since you are willing to accept future receipts at a below-market coupon rate, you should receive a time-0 payment of $1000 − 962 = $38.

CURRENCY SWAPS AND FX EQUITY EXPOSURE

Just like foreign currency debt, currency swaps will have an impact on a firm's FX equity exposure. When a firm combines a currency swap position with debt to engineer synthetic debt in a different currency, we regard the synthetic debt as the real debt for purposes of applying equation (6.2) to compute FX equity exposure. Equation (6.2) is $\xi_{S\epsilon}^{\$} = (\xi_{O\epsilon}^{\$} - D_{\epsilon}^{\$}/V^{\$})/(1 - D^{\$}/V^{\$})$. In other cases, a firm may use a currency swap on its own, not to create synthetic debt. We call these *naked currency swap positions*. We can adapt equation (6.2) into equation (7.4) when a firm has a naked currency swap position.

$$\xi_{S\epsilon}^{\$} = \frac{\xi_{O\epsilon}^{\$} - L_{\epsilon}^{\$}/V^{\$}}{1 - D^{\$}/V^{\$}} \tag{7.4}$$

Equation (7.4) is identical to equation (6.2) except that the term $L_{\epsilon}^{\$}$ replaces $D_{\epsilon}^{\$}$. The $L_{\epsilon}^{\$}$ represents the net value of all the firm's euro-denominated liabilities, including both actual euro debt and the one-sided values of the euro currency swap positions. To determine $L_{\epsilon}^{\$}$, the one-sided values of short euro currency swap positions would be added to any actual euro debt, while the one-sided values of long euro swap positions would be subtracted.

For example, if a firm has actual euro debt with a value of $20 million and a short euro position in a currency swap with a one-sided value of $15 million, then $L_{\epsilon}^{\$}$ = $35 million. If a firm has actual euro debt with a value of $20 million and a long euro position in a currency swap with a one-sided value of $15 million, then $L_{\epsilon}^{\$}$ = $5 million.

While $L_{\epsilon}^{\$}/V^{\$}$, the ratio of euro liabilities to value in the numerator of equation (7.4), must be the ratio of net euro liabilities (actual debt and swap positions) to the firm's intrinsic value, the debt-to-value ratio in the denominator, $D^{\$}/V^{\$}$, should be the ratio of only the *actual* debt to the firm's intrinsic value, as it measures the firm's financial leverage.

Assume that XYZ Company has an intrinsic value of $2000, $200 of actual euro debt, $200 of actual non-euro debt, and thus an intrinsic equity value of $1600. In addition, assume that it has a naked short currency swap position on euros with notional principal of $1000. Assume that the swap currently has no MTM value. Assume that XYZ has an FX operating exposure to the euro of 2. Use equation (7.4) to find XYZ's FX equity exposure.

EXHIBIT 7.2 XYZ Company Intrinsic Value Balance Sheets, Including Off–Balance Sheet Short Euro Currency Swap Position

TIME 0

	Assets	Liabilities & Equity
(Off)	$1000 (long \$, $W_\$^\$$)	$1000 (short €, $W_€^\$$)
		$ 200 €-debt
		$ 200 \$-debt
	$2000 $V_O^\$$	$1600 equity
	$2000 $V^\$$	$2000

AFTER EURO DROPS BY 5% (TIME 1)

	Assets	Liabilities & Equity
(Off)	$1000 (long \$, $W_\$^\$$)	$ 950 (short €, $W_€^\$$)
	$ 50 (gain on swap, $M_€^\$$)	$ 190 €-debt
		$ 200 \$-debt
	$1800 $V_O^\$$	$1460 equity
	$1850 $V^\$$	$1850

Since the currency swap has no MTM value at time 0, the value in US dollars of the euro liability side of the swap is $1000. Thus, $L_€^\$/V^\$ = (\$200 + \$1000)/\$2000 = \$1200/\$2000 = 0.60$, and we have that $\xi_{S€}^\$ = (2 - 0.60)/(1 - 0.20) = 1.75$. If the FX value of the euro falls by 5%, the intrinsic value of the firm falls to $1800, by virtue of the FX operating exposure of 2. The value of the actual euro debt (in US dollars) falls to $190, while the value of the actual US dollar debt stays at $200. Before considering the swap position, the new intrinsic equity value would be $1410. The euro side of the swap position will have a new value of $950, when the euro drops in FX value by 5%. The currency swap position is short euros, so there is an MTM gain of $1000 − 950 = $50. With this gain, the new intrinsic value of XYZ's equity is $1410 + 50 = $1460. The FX equity exposure computed directly is $(\$1460/\$1600 - 1)/-0.05 = 1.75$, which reconciles with the one found by using equation (7.4).

It might help you to visualize what is going on in the example to see the two intrinsic balance sheets before and after the FX rate change in Exhibit 7.2. The one-sided values of the currency swap are shown above the dashed line, as off-balance sheet. The one-sided value of the long US dollar side is shown on the asset side, while the one-sided value of the short euro side is shown on the liability side. We put the MTM value of the swap below the dashed line onto the intrinsic balance sheet, with net MTM gains shown as an asset and net MTM losses as a liability. There is no MTM value on the time-0 balance sheet, since the swap originated as an at-market swap.

ABC Company currently has $V^\$ = \$5000$, $D^\$ = \$3000$, and thus $S^\$ = \$2000$. Assume an FX operating exposure of 1.40 to the euro. Let us say that $2000 of the firm's debt is euro debt and the rest is US dollar debt. ABC also has a long euro position in a currency swap with notional principal of $1000. The swap is currently an at-market swap. What is ABC's FX equity exposure from equation (7.4)? Assume that the euro drops by 10% in FX value. Find ABC's new intrinsic equity value and show the FX equity exposure directly.

Answers: The net amount of euro liabilities is $L_\epsilon^\$ = \$2000 - 1000 = \$1000$. Thus $L^\$/V^\$ = \$1000/\$5000 = 0.20$. $D^\$/V^\$ = \$3000/\$5000 = 0.60$. Thus we have that $\xi_{S\epsilon}^\$ = (1.40 - 0.20)/(1 - 0.60) = 3$. If the FX value of the euro falls by 10%, the intrinsic value of the firm falls by 14% to $4300, by virtue of the FX operating exposure of 1.40. The value of the actual euro debt (in US dollars) falls to $1800, while the value of the actual US dollar debt stays at $1000. Before considering the currency swap position, the new intrinsic equity value would be $1500. The euro side of the currency swap position will have a new value of $900, when the euro drops in FX value by 10%. Since the currency swap position is long euros, there is an MTM loss on the currency swap position: $900 − 1000 = −$100. With this loss, the new intrinsic value of ABC's equity is $1500 − 100 = $1400. We see that the FX equity exposure computed directly is ($1400/$2000 − 1)/−0.10 = 3. This reconciles with the FX equity exposure found using equation (7.4).

MANAGING FX EXPOSURE WITH CURRENCY SWAPS

A firm may have a long FX operating exposure that is too great to hedge through actual foreign currency denominated debt. It may then want to consider supplementing actual foreign currency debt with a naked short currency swap position.

To see how a currency swap works to hedge FX equity exposure in this case, let us return to the XYZ Company and assume now that XYZ puts on a $3800 (notional principal) short euro position in a currency swap. Before any FX change, the intrinsic value of XYZ is $2000, and the on–balance sheet capital structure consists of $200 of euro debt, $200 of non-euro debt, and $1600 of equity. In addition, there is now the off–balance sheet short euro currency swap position. If the FX value of the euro falls by 5%, the intrinsic value of the firm falls to $1800 by virtue of its FX operating exposure of 2. The US dollar value of the actual euro debt falls to $190, while the value of the US dollar debt stays the same at $200. Before considering the currency swap position, the new intrinsic equity value would be $1410, as before.

The currency swap position is short euros, so the position will have a gain of 5% of the value (in US dollars) of the euro debt side of the swap, when the euro drops in value by 5%. The gain on the currency swap position is thus 0.05($3800) = $190. With this gain, the intrinsic value of XYZ's equity is $1410 + 190 = $1600 after the 5% drop in the FX value of the euro, exactly the intrinsic equity value prior to FX change. In this scenario, the $200 actual euro debt level ($D_\epsilon^\$$) and the $3800 short currency swap position combine to hedge the firm's FX operating exposure (of 2) to the euro, so that the firm's FX equity exposure is zero, all things considered.

The key is to make the *total* amount of euro liabilities, $L_\epsilon^\$$ (including both the actual euro debt and the off–balance sheet short euro position of the currency swap), equal to the FX operating exposure times the intrinsic value of the firm, $\xi_{O\epsilon}^\$ V^\$$. In this case, $\xi_{O\epsilon}^\$ = 2$ and $V^\$ = \$2000$; thus the total euro liability level in US dollar terms, including the actual euro debt level and the short swap position's notional principal, should be $L_\epsilon^\$ = \xi_{O\epsilon}^\$ V^\$ = 2(\$2000) = \$4000$. Since XYZ already had $200 in actual euro debt, the hedge is completed by the $3800 short currency swap position on euros.

ABC Company currently has $V^\$ = \$5000$, $D^\$ = \$3000$, and thus $S^\$ = \$2000$. Assume an FX operating exposure of 1.60 to the euro. Let us say that $2000 of the firm's debt is euro debt, and the rest is US dollar debt. Determine the notional principal of a currency swap position that will eliminate ABC's FX equity exposure. Assume that the euro drops by 10% in FX value. Show how the intrinsic equity value stays at $2000.

Answers: The total amount of euro liabilities should be $L_\epsilon^\$ = \xi_{O\epsilon}^\$ V^\$ = 1.60(\$5000) = \$8000$. Since the firm already has $2000 in actual euro debt, the (at-market) currency swap should have a notional principal of $6000. Because of the FX operating exposure of 1.60, the intrinsic value of the firm will fall by 16%, from $5000 to $4200, when the euro drops by 10% in FX value. The US dollar value of the actual euro debt will drop by 10% to $1800, while the value of the other actual debt stays at $1000. The new intrinsic equity value for the firm would be $4200 − 1800 − 1000 = $1400 before considering the currency swap gain or loss. The swap has a gain of $600, since the swap position is short on $6000 worth of euros, and the euro depreciates in FX value by 10%. Thus this $600 gain on the swap position would bring the firm's intrinsic equity value back to $2000.

A firm with a negative FX operating exposure can manage this exposure with a long position on the foreign currency in a currency swap. The notional principal should be equal to the absolute value of $\xi_{O\epsilon}^\$ V^\$$. For example, assume that Fly By Night's firm value is £100 million and its FX operating exposure to the US dollar is −1.25. Then Fly By Night could hedge its FX exposure, eliminating the FX equity exposure, via a long currency swap position on the US dollar with a notional principal of £125 million.

DEF Company currently has $V^\$ = \$5$ million, $D^\$ = \$3$ million, and thus $S^\$ = \$2$ million. Assume an FX operating exposure of −1.60 to the euro. All the firm's actual debt is US dollar debt. Determine the currency swap position that will eliminate DEF's FX equity exposure.

Answers: The total amount of euro liabilities should be $L_\epsilon^\$ = \xi_{O\epsilon}^\$ V^\$ = -1.60(\$5 \text{ million}) = -\$8 \text{ million}$. To have a "negative liability" of $8 million in euros, the firm should take a naked long currency swap position on euros with a notional principal of $8 million. The intrinsic value balance sheets for DEF (Exhibit 7.3) illustrate how the FX equity exposure is zero.

EXHIBIT 7.3 DEF Company Intrinsic Value Balance Sheets with Off–Balance Sheet Long Euro Swap Position

TIME 0

	Assets	Liabilities & Equity
(Off)	\$8 million (long €, $W_€^\$$)	\$8 million (short \$, $W_\$^\$$)
	$\underline{\text{\$5 million } V_O^\$}$	\$2 million \$-debt \$3 million equity
	\$5 million $V^\$$	$\underline{}$ \$5 million

AFTER EURO DROPS BY 10% (TIME 1)

	Assets	Liabilities & Equity
(Off)	\$7.20 million (long €, $W_€^\$$)	\$8 million (short \$, $W_\$^\$$)
	$\underline{\text{\$5.80 million } V_O^\$}$	\$0.80 million (MTM loss, $-M_€^\$$) \$2 million \$-debt \$3 million equity
	\$5.80 million $V^\$$	$\underline{}$ \$5.80 million

As a long-term multiperiod instrument, the currency swap is a better hedging device for FX operating exposure than a single, short-horizon derivative, such as a forward FX contract. One reason is that the entire settlement on the derivative may have to be in cash, and cash might not be available. For example, suppose XYZ Company, discussed earlier in connection with currency swaps and FX exposure, tries to hedge its FX operating exposure with a one-year forward FX contract in the amount of \$3800 instead of the currency swap. If a drop in the FX value of the euro causes the intrinsic value of the firm to fall, the company is not in trouble because it has an offsetting gain in the forward FX contract. But if an appreciation of the FX value of the euro causes the intrinsic value of the firm to rise, the company has an offsetting loss in the forward FX contract. While the economic gain on the firm's value offsets the economic loss on the forward FX contract, the gain in the intrinsic firm value is not a cash inflow, in principle, however, the company will need cash at time 1 to settle its loss on the forward FX contract.

It is possible that the cash settlement may be avoided by "rolling" the forward FX contract, but two problems still exist. One is that cash deposits, or margins, are often required, and these margins will be raised as the unrealized losses in forward FX contracts mount. Such margin increases will be a cash drain for the hedging firm, even if the forward FX contracts do not have to be fully settled in cash. The other problem is the appearance of the unrealized losses on the firm's books, which may create its own problems. Currency swap positions accomplish FX hedging without affecting the firm's balance sheet at the time the swap originates. As the FX value of the euro changes, though, The MTM gains/losses will affect the balance sheet, since they affect the intrinsic equity value in the manner described.

We have been using FX value exposure as a convenient way to summarize the FX exposure of the firm's stream of future cash flows. A currency swap position may be viewed as hedging the impact of FX changes on the intrinsic value of the firm or on its future cash flows. If one wants to take the view that a currency swap is hedging cash flows, then the principal component presents a bit of a problem. Market innovation has solved this problem through a derivative called an *amortizing swap*, in which the swap cash flows are based on a level annuity instead of a fixed coupon bond.

*UNLEVERING ESTIMATED FX EQUITY EXPOSURE

Suppose a US firm is estimated to have an FX equity exposure of 0.80 to the euro. Assume that the firm has a capital structure that is 20% actual euro debt, 25% actual US dollar debt, and the rest equity (55%). Thus the ratio of total debt to intrinsic value, $D^\$/V^\$$, is 0.45. Assume also that the firm has a naked short euro currency swap position with a one-sided value equal to the value of the actual euro debt. Then we can apply equation (7.4) "in reverse" to unlever the estimated FX equity exposure and to estimate the firm's FX operating exposure: $\xi_{Oe}^\$ = \xi_{Se}^\$(1 - D^\$/V^\$) + L_e^\$/V^\$ = 0.80(1 - 0.45) + 0.40 = 0.84$. Double-check using equation (7.4) directly: $\xi_{Se}^\$ = (0.84 - 0.40)/(1 - 0.45) = 0.80$.

ABC Company currently has $V^\$ = \$5000$, $D^\$ = \$2000$, and thus $S^\$ = \$3000$. Assume an estimated FX equity exposure of 0.30 to the euro. Let us say that $1500 of the firm's actual debt is euro debt and the rest is US dollar debt. What is the estimated FX operating exposure from equation (7.4) if ABC also has a $2000 short euro currency swap position?

Answer: $0.30 = (\xi_{Oe}^\$ - 0.70)/(1 - 0.40) \Rightarrow \xi_{Oe}^\$ = 0.88$.

---

*CURRENCY SWAPS AND TAX ARBITRAGE

In 1985, New Zealand dollar (NZ$) investments seemed very attractive to global investors because of both the currency's stability compared with the US dollar and the high coupon rates available on NZ$ debt. Yet two withholding taxes discouraged foreign investors. The first was a 15% tax on interest paid to resident holders of domestic New Zealand bonds and a 15% withholding tax on interest disbursements to foreign holders of domestic New Zealand bonds. The second tax was a withholding tax issuing corporations from New Zealand paid on interest to offshore eurobond borrowers in NZ$, but not in other currencies.

The first tax meant that both domestic and foreign holders of domestically issued NZ$ bonds would require a higher coupon interest rate than they would on NZ$ eurobonds issued by non–New Zealand organizations, which could not be subject to the withholding tax. The second tax meant that New Zealand borrowers would have to pay a higher effective interest rate on NZ$ eurobonds than non–New Zealand borrowers.

Suppose the New Zealand Roadworks Authority (NZRA) sought NZ$ debt financing. If NZRA issued NZ$ bonds in the domestic New Zealand market, but to nonresident investors, it would have to pay a high coupon to compensate the investors for the first tax; if the agency issued NZ$ eurobonds, it would have to pay the second tax. Enter Nippon Products, Inc., which actually wants US dollar debt financing for a subsidiary in the United States. If Nippon Products issues NZ$ eurobonds to non–New Zealand residents, it avoids taxes 1 and 2.

Assume that NZRA would have to pay 12% on domestic NZ$ bonds and an even higher effective interest rate on offshore NZ$ eurobonds, after accounting for taxes. Assume that Nippon Products would have to pay only a 10% interest rate on NZ$ eurobonds. And either organization could tap the eurodollar bond market at an interest rate of 8%. Rather than NZRA paying 12% on NZ$ debt and Nippon Products paying 8% on US dollar debt, NZRA could issue the US dollar debt at 8%, while Nippon Products issued the NZ$ eurobonds at 10%.

NZRA and Nippon Products could do a currency swap of 8% US dollars for 11% NZ$, with NZRA receiving US dollars and Nippon Products receiving the NZ dollars. NZRA would pay 8% on its actual US dollar debt, receive 8% dollars from the swap to offset the US dollar liability, and then pay 11% in NZ$ on the swap. In this way, NZRA effectively reduces its cost of NZ$ financing from 12% to 11%.

Nippon Products pays 10% on its actual NZ$ eurobonds, but receives NZ$ at 11% from the swap to more than offset the actual liability. Since Nippon Products pays 8% US dollars on the currency swap, it comes out better than if it paid 8% on actual eurodollar bonds, because it has the excess NZ dollars, which it can exchange into yen, US dollars, or whatever. Each organization has been able to reduce its financing costs over what they would be without the swap. The currency swap enables swap-driven financing to the benefit of both.

Source: Adapted from Michael Bowe, *Eurobonds* (Homewood, IL: Dow Jones-Irwin, 1988).

SUMMARY

Currency swaps are in widespread use in global financial management. Currency swaps are used to expand firms' financing alternatives, letting them hedge FX exposure when they seek low-cost financing in foreign currencies. There is no question that currency swaps have played a significant role in globalizing the world's financial markets.

Through currency swaps and other similar market innovations, corporate financial managers have learned that the choice of market, the type of instrument, and the currency in which debt is raised can all be totally independent of the type of liability a firm ultimately wants to assume. One important use of currency swaps is in creating synthetic debt in another currency by covering the FX risk of debt issued in markets offering opportunities for favorable financing costs.

Currency swaps, like forward FX contracts, may be viewed to represent physical delivery of cash flows on some underlying financial instruments. A fixed-for-fixed currency swap is essentially an exchange of fixed coupon bond payments in one currency for those of another currency. Like forward FX contracts, currency swaps often involve settlement with difference checks. In fact, a fixed-for-fixed currency swap is really nothing more than a package of off-market forward FX positions of various maturities and payment sizes (since the principal payment is much larger than the interest payments). The mark-to-market value of a currency swap is found by valuing the underlying financial instruments represented in the swap.

Another important use of currency swaps is the hedging of long-term FX operating exposures that are either negative or too large to be managed with foreign currency debt.

GLOSSARY

Amortizing swap: A type of swap in which the cash flows are based on a level annuity instead of a fixed coupon bond.

At-market swap: A swap with a present value of zero that involves no time-0 cash flow to initiate a position.

Back-to-back loan: A precursor to currency swaps. Back-to-back loans call for payments by a parent company in country A to the subsidiary of a parent in country B, and vice versa, even though the loan proceeds cancel out and thus are not exchanged.

Currency swap: A contract to exchange two streams of future cash flows in different currencies.

FX conversion rate: The rate to use as the forward FX rate for an underlying payment of a currency swap.

Fixed-for-fixed currency swap: An exchange of cash flows calculated as the exchange of fixed-coupon bond payments in one currency for those in another currency.

Fixed-for-floating currency swap: Also called a cross-currency swap. An exchange of cash flows calculated as the exchange of fixed coupon bond payments in one currency for floating-rate payments in another currency.

Naked currency swap position: Use of a currency swap on its own instead of to create synthetic debt.

Notional principal: The presumable amount of bond principal upon which a swap's payment amounts are based.

Off-market swap: A swap with present value of not zero that involves an immediate cash flow to initiate a position.

Par bond: A coupon bond whose market value is equal to its face value and whose yield to maturity is thus exactly equal to the coupon rate.

Parallel loan: A precursor to currency swaps: a loan by a parent company in country A to the subsidiary of a parent firm in country B, and vice versa.

Premium bond: A coupon bond whose market value is greater than its face value and whose yield to maturity is thus lower than the coupon rate.

Straight bond: Also called bullet bonds or coupon bonds. A bond that makes interest and principal payments at a set coupon rate in a single currency and has no call provisions or other innovative features.

Swap-driven financing: The use of swaps as a planned part of a financing strategy.

Synthetic base currency debt: Actual foreign currency debt combined with a long foreign currency swap position.

Synthetic foreign currency debt: Actual base currency debt combined with a short foreign currency swap position.

PROBLEMS

1. You enter into a three-year, fixed-for-fixed currency swap, so that the cash flow stream you are receiving is in Japanese yen and the cash flow stream you are paying is in US dollars. The swap has a notional principal of $1 million. What are the cash flows upon which the currency swap is based, if the swap is an at-market swap and the three-year par coupon rates are 5% for US dollars and 2% for yen, and the spot FX rate is currently 112.50 ¥/$?

2. Consider the same swap as in Problem 1, a three-year, fixed-for-fixed currency swap of 5% US dollars for 2% Japanese yen. The spot FX rate was 112.50 ¥/$ when the swap originated. The notional principal is $1 million. What is the FX conversion rate for the interest component settlements? Find the difference check settlement if the yen depreciates to 120 ¥/$ at time 1 (the time of the first payment), and state which counterparty gets the check.

3. What would be the settlement of principal at maturity of the swap in Problem 2 if the spot FX rate at that time is 120 ¥/$?

4. Consider a six-year, fixed-for-fixed currency swap of 5% US dollars for 8% British pounds at the current spot exchange rate of 1.60 $/£, on notional principal of $1 million. What are the two final difference checks, interest and principal, if the spot FX rate is 1.80 $/£ at that time. State the direction of each check.

5. What is the MTM value, after three payments, of the long yen position in a six-year, $1 million, 5% fixed US dollar versus 2% fixed yen currency swap that originated as an at-market swap when the spot FX rate was 110 ¥/$? Assume a spot FX rate of 120 ¥/$ at time 3, and market yields on three-year coupon bonds of 2% in yen and 5% in US dollars at time 3.

6. DZD Company currently has $V^\$ = \$5$ million, $D^\$ = \$3$ million, and thus $S^\$ = \$2$ million. Assume an FX operating exposure of 1.60 to the euro. Let us say that $2 million of the firm's actual debt is euro debt and the rest is US dollar debt. DZD also has a naked short currency swap position on euros with a notional principal of $2 million. Find DZD's FX equity exposure directly by using a 10% depreciation of the FX value of the euro, and reconcile the answer by means of equation (7.4).

7. ABC Company currently has $V^\$ = \$10$ million, $D^\$ = \$4$ million, and thus $S^\$ = \$6$ million. Assume an FX operating exposure of 1.25 to the euro. Assume that $3 million of the firm's actual debt is euro debt and the rest is US dollar debt. Determine the notional principal of a

currency swap position that will eliminate ABC's FX equity exposure. Assume that the FX value of the euro rises by 10%. Show how the intrinsic equity value stays at $6 million.

8. *ABC Company currently has $V^\$ = \$10$ million, $D^\$ = \$4$ million, and thus $S^\$ = \$6$ million. Let us say that all $4 million of the firm's debt is US dollar debt. Assume also that ABC has a long position on euros in a currency swap with a value of $2 million. Assume that ABC's FX equity exposure to the euro is estimated to be 0.50. Find ABC's estimated FX operating exposure.

ANSWERS TO PROBLEMS

1. You would be receiving ¥2.25 million per year for three years and a principal payment of ¥112.50 million at year 3. You would pay $50,000 per year for three years and then a payment of $1 million.

2. The FX conversion rate is 45 ¥/$. The short position on yen gets $31,250.

3. The net payment to the short position on yen is $62,500.

4. The long position on pounds receives $40,000 to settle the interest component. The principal on the swap at maturity is settled with a difference check of $125,000 to the long position on pounds.

5. The swap has an MTM value in US dollars of −$83,333.

6. DZD's intrinsic value will fall by 16% to $4.20 million. The US dollar value of the actual euro debt will drop by 10% to $1.80 million, while the US dollar value of the other actual debt stays at $1 million. The new intrinsic equity value for the firm would be $4.20 million − 1.80 million − 1 million = $1.40 million before considering the currency swap MTM gain or loss. The swap has a gain of $200,000, since the swap position is short on $2 million worth of euros, and the euro depreciates in FX value by 10%. Thus the new intrinsic equity value is $1.60 million. The firm's FX equity exposure to the euro is ($1.60 million/$2 million − 1)/(−0.10) = 2. To use equation (7.4), the total amount of euro liabilities (actual plus off balance sheet) is $4 million, and the ratio of euro liabilities to the intrinsic value of the firm is $4 million/$5 million = 0.80. Thus the firm's FX equity exposure to the euro is (1.60 − 0.80)/(1 − 0.60) = 2.

7. The total amount of ABC's euro liabilities should be 1.25($10 million) = $12.5 million. Since the firm already has $3 million in actual euro debt, the swap should have a notional principal of $9.50 million. The intrinsic value of the firm will rise by 12.5% to $11.25 million. The US dollar value of the actual euro debt will rise by 10% to $3.30 million, while the value of the other debt stays at $1 million. The firm's new intrinsic equity value would be $11.25 million − 3.30 million − 1 million = $6.95 million before considering the swap gain or loss. The swap has a loss of $950,000, since the swap position is short $9.50 million worth of euros, and the euro appreciates by 10%. Thus the intrinsic equity value remains at $6 million.

8. $\xi_{O\epsilon}^\$ = \xi_{S\epsilon}^\$(1 - D^\$/V^\$) + L_\epsilon^\$/V^\$ = 0.50(1 - 0.40) - 0.20 = 0.10$. Note that the long swap position on euros results in a negative value for $L_\epsilon^\$/V^\$$.

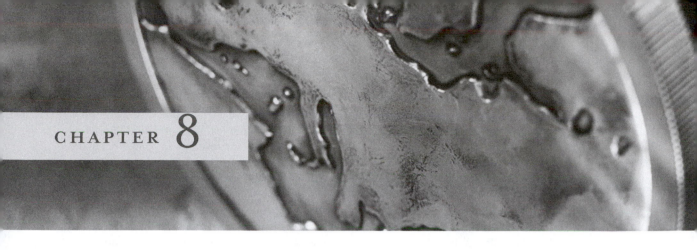

CHAPTER 8

ECONOMIC FOREIGN EXCHANGE EXPOSURE

You saw in Chapter 5 that changes in FX rates can affect prices, revenues, costs, and operating cash flows. These FX operating exposure effects are basic aspects of *economic FX exposure*. Another consideration is the impact of FX changes on the volume of output and sales. This chapter explores these impacts.

One form of economic FX exposure that involves changes in sales volume is *indirect FX exposure*. Consider the Canadian tractor distributor, Finning. Finning's customers often sell their products in the United States, and when the US dollar appreciates, Finning's customers have higher revenues in Canadian dollars, and buy more tractors from Finning. Finning has an indirect FX revenue exposure to the US dollar.

Similarly, a company with only domestic suppliers could have indirect FX cost exposure, since the prices of the raw materials could be indirectly linked to FX rates, particularly if the domestic suppliers pass along their own FX cost exposures. For example, when paper prices were significantly related to the FX value of the Swedish krona, a firm that used a great deal of paper products could have operating costs exposed to the Swedish krona, even if the supplier was a US paper company.

Another form of economic FX exposure involving sales volume changes is *wealth FX exposure*, where sales volume responds to wealth effects of FX changes. Consider the case of the now-defunct Laker Airways, a UK firm whose base currency was British pounds. Laker Air specialized in flying British vacationers to the United States at a time when the pound was relatively strong in the sense of having good overseas purchasing power. When the US dollar underwent a prolonged appreciation relative to the pound, however, the expenses incurred in the United States rose for British tourists, discouraging them from flying across the Atlantic. Thus Laker's revenues dropped. The revenues in pounds declined as the foreign currency (the US dollar) appreciated, so the firm's FX revenue exposure to the US dollar was negative. American Airlines has also experienced negative (or short) FX revenue exposure to foreign currencies under similar conditions.

Similarly, when the US dollar appreciates, the revenues of tourist attractions in the United States tend to decline, as more US tourists go abroad rather than vacation in the United States. When the US dollar depreciates, revenues tend to increase, as more US tourists spend their vacations in their own country.

We see from these examples that even a company with only domestic customers could have an FX revenue exposure. And a firm with purely domestic production and with no imports of raw materials might have an FX cost exposure.

ECONOMICS OF FOREIGN EXCHANGE, PRICE, AND VOLUME

When the spot FX value of a foreign currency changes, firms frequently make changes to both sales price and volume simultaneously. For example, a US exporter may want to cut back on production and raise prices when the US dollar rises, since revenues have declined in US dollars. We can see this in the following profit maximization scenario, given a particular demand function for the exporter's products.

Consider Monopolist Widgets, Inc. (MWI), a US firm that exports widgets to the Eurozone. MWI is assumed to produce the widgets in the United States at a cost of $1400 per widget and to have no competitors in the Eurozone market; that is, MWI is in fact a monopolist. Assume that MWI faces the demand curve (relationship between product price and quantity sold): $p^{\epsilon} = \epsilon 2900 - Q$, where p^{ϵ} is the price of a widget in euros, and Q is the volume of widgets sold.

Thus MWI's widget revenues in euros are $R^{\epsilon} = p^{\epsilon}Q = (\epsilon 2900 - Q)Q$. If more widgets are sold, revenues will increase; but to sell more widgets, price must be lowered, reducing revenues on all other units sold when price is lowered across the board. Sometimes the net result of increased sales but lower prices is lower total revenue. This leads us to think in terms of *marginal revenue*, or the change in revenue for an additional unit sold, given the new price for all units necessary to sell all the units. Up to a point, the marginal revenue from selling additional units will exceed the increase in the cost of production. The optimal output occurs when the marginal revenue equals the marginal cost of additional production.

Using calculus, you find MWI's marginal revenue function by taking the first derivative of total revenue with respect to output, Q. MWI's marginal revenue in euros is $MR^{\epsilon} = \epsilon 2900 - 2Q$. Figure 8.1 shows the demand curve and the marginal revenue function. [The demand curve is actually a straight line, as shown in Figure 8.1, but economists use the term "demand curve."]

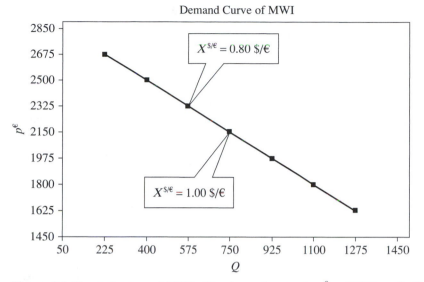

Figure 8.1 Demand curve of MWI: The demand curve is $p^€ = €2900 - Q$. Two points are highlighted: (1) If $X^{\$/€} = 1$ \$/€, $Q = 750$ and $p^€ = €2150$. (2) If $X^{\$/€} = 0.80$ \$/€, $Q = 575$ and $p^€ = €2325$.

Looking at the situation from MWI's perspective in US dollars, marginal revenue expressed depends on the spot FX rate, $MR^\$ = X^{\$/€}(€2900 - 2Q)$. By setting the marginal revenue in US dollars equal to the assumed marginal cost in US dollars, \$1400, we can solve for MWI's optimal output decision Q, given any assumed spot FX rate.

For example, if $X^{\$/€} = 1$ \$/€, then setting 1 \$/€(€2900 - 2Q) equal to \$1400, and solving for Q, we get a Q of 750 widgets. Using the demand function, $p^€ = €2900 - Q$, we can find that if MWI produces 750 widgets, it will set a price per widget in euros of $p^€ = €2150$. The firm's revenue in euros, $R^€$, is thus €2150(750) = €1,613,000. MWI's revenue in US dollars, $R^\$$, is 1 \$/€(€1,613,000) = \$1,613,000.

What if the FX value of the euro depreciates to 0.80 \$/€? Then, setting the new marginal revenue in US dollars equal to the marginal cost of \$1400, $MR^\$ = 0.80$ \$/€(€2900 - 2Q) = \$1400, gives a solution for Q of only 575 widgets. The euro's FX value is lower, and in response MWI reduces its US production of widgets exported to Euroland from 750 to 575. Along with the lower production, MWI raises the price charged for a widget in euros. Using the demand curve, $p^€ = €2900 - Q$, we find that MWI will now set a price in euros of $p^€ = €2325$. At this price of €2325, and with a sales volume of 575, the firm's revenue in euros, $R^€$, will be €2325(575) = €1,337,000. MWI's revenue in US dollars, $R^\$$, will be 0.80 \$/€(€1,337,000) = \$1,070,000.

Note that the same solutions result if MWI performs the optimization analysis from the perspective of euros rather than US dollars. When the FX rate is different, the marginal cost in euros is different, not the marginal revenue function; but the same solutions obtain. Setting marginal revenue in euros €2900 - 2Q equal to marginal cost in euros at 1 \$/€, €1400, the optimal output is 750, and setting marginal revenue in euros €2900 - 2Q equal

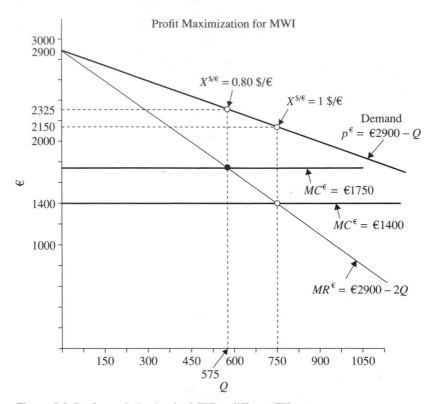

Figure 8.2 Profit maximization by MWI at different FX rates.

to marginal cost in euros at 0.80 $/€, $1400(1 $/€) = €1750, the optimal output is 575. Figure 8.2 summarizes the two analyses in euros graphically.

We see from this scenario that if the FX value of the euro drops by 20%, from 1 $/€ to 0.80 $/€, the widget price response is from €2150 to €2325, an increase of about 8%. Thus, only about 40% of the FX change was passed through in the form of a price adjustment in local currency. In addition, MWI will sell a lower volume at the higher price, 575 widgets, down from 750.

What is MWI's FX revenue exposure to the euro, $\xi_{Re}^{\$}$? The euro depreciates by 20% from 1 $/€ to 0.80 $/€; in response, MWI's US dollar revenues change by a percentage equal to $1,070,000/$1,613,000 − 1 = −0.34$, or −34%. Thus using the definition of $\%\Delta R^{\$}/x^{\$/€}$, the FX exposure of MWI's US dollar revenues to the euro, $\xi_{Re}^{\$}$, is $−0.34/−0.20 = 1.70$. Thus, if the euro drops in FX value by 20%, the firm's revenues in US dollars drop by 1.70(20%), or by 34%. The decline in the FX value of the euro has a double impact: MWI's euro revenues drop as a result of the economic impact of the price/volume interaction, and the revenues in US dollars drop all the more owing to the added effect of FX conversion exposure.

Because the demand curve is assumed in this example to be linear, the FX revenue exposure here is nonlinear, meaning that for a change in the FX value of the euro other than 20%, the computed FX revenue exposure would be different from 1.70. In our second example, presented next, MWI's FX revenue exposure is estimated to be 1.56 with a different what-if assumption for the FX rate change: a 25% appreciation of the euro. The arc average of these two estimates, about 1.62, seems like a reasonable answer if you want to boil MWI's estimated FX revenue exposure to the euro down to a one-number approximation. You can get a constant FX revenue exposure with a nonlinear demand curve, but this may not be worth the effort given that rough approximations are the best one can do in this kind of analysis.

Find MWI's FX revenue exposure to the euro when the spot FX rate begins at 1 \$/€ and the euro appreciates to 1.25 \$/€.

Answer: If the FX value of the euro is 1.25 \$/€, then setting $MR^\$ = 1.25 \$/€(€2900 - 2Q) = \$1400$ gives a solution for Q of 890 widgets. The euro's FX value is higher, and in response MWI increases its production of widgets sold in Euroland. With the higher production the price charged for a widget in euros will be lower. Using the demand function $p^€ = €2900 - Q$, we find that $p^€ = €2010$. The firm's revenues in euros, $R^€$, will be €2010(890) = €1,789,000. MWI's revenue in US dollars, $R^\$$, will be 1.25 \$/€(€1,789,000) = \$2,236,000. The euro has appreciated by 25%. In response, MWI's US dollar revenue has changed by \$2,236,000/\$1,613,000 − 1 = 0.39, or 39%. MWI's FX revenue exposure to the euro is 0.39/0.25 = 1.56.

A firm's economic FX exposure depends on the nature of its demand curve, which may not be explicitly known to managers of complex firms in the real world. In general, if a product's demand function is relatively inelastic, the firm can pass through FX changes without a relatively significant impact on sales volume; the currency of determination is more closely related to the exporter's currency; and the exporter's FX revenue exposure will be low. If an exporter faces a relatively elastic demand curve, however, the customers' local currency plays a greater role in determining the product price, and an exporter's economic FX exposure will be higher.

The economic FX exposure would be absent if MWI moves its production to Euroland. In this case, there would be no economic impact of FX changes on the optimal output and price of widgets. If the cost of producing a widget were €1400 in Euroland, regardless of the FX rate, then MWI would find it optimal to produce 750 widgets and sell them for €2150 per widget, regardless of the \$/€ FX rate. That is, the currency of determination of widgets sold in Euroland would be unambiguously the euro, since all production and purchasing of widgets takes place in euros. The firm's revenues in euros would be stable, €1,613,000, relative to FX changes. The firm's US dollar revenues would be $X^{\$/€}(€1,613,000)$, so it would have only FX conversion exposure. Then, if the FX value of the euro depreciates by 10%, MWI's US dollar revenues would decline by 10%. The firm's revenues would have an FX conversion exposure, $\xi_{R€}^\$$, of 1.

In many cases, an exporter will partially produce a product in one country and then finish it in the sales country. The next example uses this case.

> **MWI produces widget components in the US, for an operating cost of $840 per widget, and finishes the widgets in Euroland, for €560 per widget. What is MWI's FX revenue exposure for a 20% decline in the FX value of the euro, from 1 $/€ to 0.80 $/€?**
>
> *Answer: At a spot FX value of 1 $/€, the operating cost of producing a widget is $1400; MWI's Q will be 750; the widget price will be €2150; and MWI's revenues in US dollars will be $1,613,000. If the FX value of the euro drops to 0.80 $/€, the total cost of producing a widget (in US dollars) is $840 + €560(0.80 $/€) = $840 + 448 = $1288. Since production costs are neither totally in the United States nor totally in the Eurozone, we might expect MWI's FX revenue exposure to be somewhere between 1.70 and 1.00 for the 20% drop in the value of the euro. Setting $MR^\$ = 0.80 \, \$/€(€2900 - 2Q) = \$1288$, and solving for Q, results in Q = 645. Thus the widget price is $p^€ = €2900 - 645 = €2255$, and MWI's revenues in US dollars will be 0.80 $/€(€2255)(645) = $1,164,000, representing a percentage change of $1,164,000/$1,613,000 - 1 = -0.28. Thus the FX revenue exposure to the euro is -0.28/-0.20 = 1.40.*

If MWI moves its production to the Eurozone, there would be two effects on FX operating exposure (other than the obvious impact on shipping costs, which is ignored here). You know that the economic incentive to adjust production and price as the FX rate changes would no longer be present. In this case, MWI's FX revenue exposure to the euro would fall from about 1.62 to a pure FX conversion exposure of 1. You also now know that MWI would be using operational hedging, by fixing production costs in euros, eliminating the operating leverage of production costs (per widget) that are fixed in US dollars.

We want to examine the overall impact of production location on FX operating exposure. When it produces in the United States, if the spot FX rate is 1 $/€, then MWI produces 750 widgets and receives revenues measured in US dollars of about $1,613,000. At the production cost per widget of $1400, the total cost of producing widgets is $1400(750) = $1,050,000, and the firm's operating cash flow in US dollars is thus $1,613,000 − 1,050,000 = $563,000. If the spot FX rate is 0.80 $/€, MWI Company produces 575 widgets and receives US dollar revenues of about $1,070,000. Since the total cost of producing 575 widgets is $1400(575) = $805,000, the operating cash flow (at an FX rate of 0.80 $/€) is $1,070,000 − 805,000 = $265,000.

With the change in the spot FX rate, the firm's operating cash flow in US dollars drops from $563,000 to $265,000, a percentage change of $265,000/$563,000 − 1 = −0.53, or −53%. Since the operating cash flow level drops by 53% as the FX value of the euro depreciates by 20% (from 1 $/€ to 0.80 $/€), MWI's FX operating exposure to the euro is $\xi^\$_{O€} = -0.53/-0.20 = 2.65$. Since production is in the United States, MWI's FX revenue exposure of 1.62 is magnified by an operating leverage effect, as production costs (per widget) are fixed in US dollars while the revenue (per widget) varies with the FX rate. Thus MWI's FX operating exposure is 2.65 if it produces in the United States.

With production in the Eurozone, If the spot FX rate is 1 $/€, MWI produces 750 widgets and has euro operating profit of €563,000, which is $563,000 in US dollars. If the spot FX rate is 0.80 $/€, MWI still produces 750 widgets and has euro operating profit of €563,000, but this amount is worth only $450,000 in US dollars. So, if the spot FX rate changes from 1 $/€ to 0.80 $/€, the firm's operating cash flow in US dollars drops from $563,000 to $450,000, a percentage decline of $450,000/$563,000 − 1 = −0.20, or −20%. Since the operating cash flow level drops by 20% as the FX value of the euro depreciates by 20% (from 1 $/€ to 0.80 $/€), MWI's FX operating exposure to the euro is $\xi_{O\epsilon}^{\$} = -0.20/-0.20 = 1$, when production is in the Eurozone. When it combines the effects of (1) eliminating the economic FX revenue exposure and (2) the operational hedging of fixing widget costs in euros, MWI reduces its FX operating exposure from about 2.65 to 1 by moving its production entirely to the Eurozone.

Another example shows MWI's FX operating exposure assuming it uses operational hedging in a partial manner, if MWI produces components in the United States and assembles them into widgets in the Eurozone. This example extends the preceding example.

Suppose MWI's widget assembly plant is located in the Eurozone, with an assembly cost of €560 per widget. The rest of the cost of producing a widget ($840) is fixed in US dollars, since the Eurozone plant sources widget component parts from the United States. Recall from the earlier example that at a spot FX rate of 1 $/€, MWI produces 750 widgets, and sells them at €2150, for revenues in US dollars of $1,613,000. At a spot FX rate of 0.80 $/€, MWI produces 645 widgets and sells them for €2255, for revenues in US dollars of $1,164,000. What is MWI's FX operating exposure to the euro from the perspective of US dollars?

Answer: MWI's operating cash flow is $563,000 if the spot FX rate is 1 $/€, as found in the text. If the spot FX rate is 0.80 $/€, operating costs in US dollars are 645[$840 + 0.80 $/€($560)] = $831,000. The operating cash flow is $1,164,000 − 831,000 = $333,000. The percentage change in operating cash flow is thus $333,000/$563,000 − 1 = −0.41. MWI's FX operating exposure is thus −0.41/−0.20 = 2.05, given the 20% decline in the FX value of the euro from 1 $/€ to 0.80 $/€. This FX operating exposure (2.05) is greater than if all production is in the Eurozone (1.00), but less than if all production is in the United States (2.65).

*COMPOUND FX REVENUE EXPOSURE

Compound FX revenue exposure is a form of economic FX exposure. We illustrate compound FX revenue exposure using a hypothetical Australian mining company, called Koala Mining Company (KMC). Assume that the firm sells products with a US dollar currency of determination and has sales *only* in Euroland, so that 100% of the revenues are subject to the economic FX exposure to the $/€ FX rate.

For simplicity, assume initially that the spot FX rates are 1 $/A$ and 1 $/€. Thus, the initial FX rate between Australian dollars and euros is 1 A$/€. Assume that under the initial FX conditions, KMC expects to ship 1000 tons to Euroland per year. Assume that the going price in the international metal markets (with a US dollar currency of determination) is $1000 per ton. This US dollar price means that the Europeans pay €1000 per ton at the assumed time-0 spot FX rate of $X_0^{\$/\epsilon} = 1$ $/€. Since KMC expects to receive $1000/ton, the original expectation for the future revenue stream in US dollars is $R_0^{\$} = \$1$ million per year, and the expected Australian dollar revenue stream is $R_0^{A\$} = \$1$ million/$(1 \ \$/A\$) =$ A\$1 million per year.

Now suppose the FX market experiences a unilateral change in the spot FX value of the US dollar relative to the other two currencies. Both the euro and the Australian dollar depreciate by 20% relative to the US dollar. The new FX rates are $X_1^{\$/A\$} = 0.80 \ \$/A\$$; $X_1^{\$/\euro} = 0.80 \ \$/\euro$; and $X_1^{A\$/\euro}$ remains the same at 1 A\$/\euro. Given a stable US dollar price of \$1000 per ton, the new sales price in euros to Europeans is $(\$1000/\text{ton})/(0.80 \ \$/\euro) =$ €1250/ton, a pass-through resulting from the change in the \$/\euro FX rate.

Assume from the demand curve that the price increase in euros causes the expected demand in Euroland to fall to 880 tons from the original demand of 1000 tons. Thus, KMC's new expected revenues in US dollars are lower, $R_1^{\$} = (\$1000/\text{ton})(880 \text{ tons}) = \$880,000$ per year. The firm's revenues, in US dollars, drop by 12% (from \$1 million to \$880,000) in response to a 20% depreciation of the euro relative to the US dollar, an FX exposure of the US dollar revenues to the euro of $\xi_{R\euro}^{\$} = 0.12/0.20 = 0.60$. Assume 0.60 is the FX revenue exposure of KMC's US dollar revenues to the euro for any change in the \$/\euro FX rate.

At $X_1^{\$/A\$} = 0.80 \ \$/A\$$, the new expected Australian dollar revenue level is \$880,000/ $(0.80 \ \$/A\$) = $ A\$1.1 million. The 10% increase in the expected Australian dollar revenues, from A\$1.0 million to A\$1.1 million, is due to the combined, indeed compounded, impact of two exposures. The first is the economic FX exposure of the US dollar revenues to the \$/\euro FX rate. The second is the FX conversion exposure to the A\$/\$.

What if, instead, there is a unilateral change in the spot FX value of the Australian dollar, relative to all other currencies, in the form of a 20% depreciation to 0.80 \$/A\$ and 1.25 A\$/\euro, so the \$/\euro FX rate remains the same at 1 \$/\euro? This implies a 25% appreciation of both the euro and the US dollar relative to the Australian dollar. If this unilateral change in the FX value of the Australian dollar occurs, the expected revenues in US dollars would be unchanged, since the stability of the \$/\euro FX rate would imply no wealth changes by the Europeans. The FX conversion exposure of the A\$ revenues to the US dollar, however, would imply that the new expected A\$ revenues would be \$1 million/$(0.80 \ \$/A\$) =$ A\$1.25 million, an increase of 25%.

KMC's FX exposure *cannot* be measured simply in terms of changes in the A\$/\euro FX rate. In the case of a unilateral US dollar move, you saw that the expected A\$ revenues change even though the A\$/\euro FX rate did not change. Thus, KMC's FX exposure problem cannot be described as an FX exposure of its A\$ revenues to the A\$/\euro FX rate. Instead, KMC's FX exposure problem must be measured in terms of *two* FX rates: the \$/\euro FX rate and the A\$/\$ FX rate.

This FX exposure is a *compound FX revenue exposure*; that is, the firm's revenues are exposed to changes in the \$/\euro FX rate when the revenues are viewed in US dollars, and that exposure is compounded into the FX conversion exposure of the revenues to the A\$/\$ FX rate when the revenues are viewed in Australian dollars. Using the notation for the percentage change in the FX value of the euro in terms of US dollars, $x^{\$/\euro}$, the percentage change in KMC's Australian dollar revenues can be written in the compound formulation in equation (8.1).

$$\%\Delta R^{A\$} = [1 + \xi_{R\euro}^{\$}(x^{\$/\euro})][1 + \xi_{R\$}^{A\$}(x^{A\$/\$})] - 1 \tag{8.1}$$

In the KMC example, $\xi_{R\euro}^{\$}$ is 0.60 and $\xi_{R\$}^{A\$}$ is 1. What happens when the US dollar FX move is unilateral (i.e., when the euro depreciates by 20% relative to the US dollar and the

Exhibit 8.1 KMC Scenarios of Compound FX Exposure: $\xi_{R\epsilon}^{\$} = 0.60$; $\xi_{R\$}^{A\$} = 1$; $R_0^{\$} = \$1$ million

1. $x_1^{\$/\epsilon} = -0.20 \quad \Rightarrow \quad R_1^{\$} = \$880,000 \quad \Rightarrow \quad x_1^{A\$/\$} = 0.25 \quad \Rightarrow \quad R_1^{A\$} = A\$1,100,000$
    $[1 + 0.60(-0.20)][1 + 1(0.25)] - 1 = 0.10$

2. $x_1^{\$/\epsilon} = 0 \quad \Rightarrow \quad R_1^{\$} = \$1,000,000 \quad \Rightarrow \quad x_1^{A\$/\$} = 0.25 \quad \Rightarrow \quad R_1^{A\$} = A\$1,250,000$
    $[1 + 0.60(0)][1 + 1(0.25)] - 1 = 0.25$

3. $x_1^{\$/\epsilon} = 0.25 \quad \Rightarrow \quad R_1^{\$} = \$1,150,000 \quad \Rightarrow \quad x_1^{A\$/\$} = -0.05 \quad \Rightarrow \quad R_1^{A\$} = \$1,092,500$
    $[1 + 0.60(0.25)][1 + 1(-0.05)] - 1 = 0.0925$

US dollar appreciates by 25% relative to the Australian dollar)? From equation (8.1), the percentage change in the expected A$ revenues is $[1 + 0.60(-0.20)][1 + 1(0.25)] - 1 = (0.88)(1.25) - 1 = 0.10$, or an increase of 10%, as found earlier.

Next, consider what happens when the Australian dollar move is unilateral (i.e., when the FX value of the euro is unchanged relative to the US dollar and the FX value of the US dollar appreciates by 25% relative to the Australian dollar). From equation (8.1), the percentage change in the A$ revenues is $[1 + 0.60(0)][1 + 1(0.25)] - 1 = (1.00)(1.25) - 1 = 0.25$, or an increase of 25%, as found earlier.

As a third example, assume that the euro rises by 25% relative to the US dollar and the US dollar drops by 5% relative to the Australian dollar. Equation (8.1) tells us that the percentage change in KMC's expected revenues in Australian dollars is $[1 + 0.60(0.25)][1 + 1(-0.05)] - 1 = (1.15)(0.95) - 1 = 0.0925$, or an increase of 9.25%. To verify, the US dollar revenues will be $1.15 million and these will convert to 0.95 A$/$($1.15 million) = A$1.0925 million, a rise of 9.25% from the originally expected level of A$1 million. The three scenarios are summarized in Exhibit 8.1.

Find the percentage change in KMC's expected Australian dollar revenues, assuming (1) that the US dollar revenues have an exposure of 0.40 to the euro; (2) that the euro appreciates by 20% relative to the US dollar; and (3) that the US dollar depreciates by 5% relative to the Australian dollar. Given a time-0 FX rate of 1 A$/$ and an expected future US dollar revenue stream of $1 million per year, find the original expected A$ revenues and the new expected A$ revenues. Show that the percentage change in the expected A$ revenues can be reconciled with the computed value for $\%\Delta R^{A\$}$ from the application of equation (8.1).

Answer: Using the compound FX exposure measurement formulation in equation (8.1), $\%\Delta R^{A\$} = [1 + 0.40(0.20)][1 + 1(-0.05)] - 1 = (1.08)(0.95) - 1 = 0.026$. The percentage change in the expected A$ revenues should be 2.60%. Let us show this result with the fundamental details, given original expected future US dollar revenue stream of $1 million per year. Note first that the new expected future US dollar revenues are 8% higher, given the FX exposure to the euro of 0.40 and given the 20% appreciation of the euro relative to the US dollar. Thus the new US dollar revenues are $1.08 million per year. Given a time-0 FX rate of 1 A$/$ and a 5% depreciation of the US dollar relative to the Australian dollar, the new FX rate is 0.95 A$/$, and the new expected A$ revenues are $1.08 million(0.95 A$/$) = A$1.026 million, 2.60% higher than the original expected revenues of A$1 million.

How can a KMC hedge its compound FX revenue exposure? KMC cannot do operational hedging, since the mines are in Australia, so KMC must rely on financial hedging. Because of the compound FX exposure, KMC needs to hedge twice. First, KMC must take a short euro position in a US dollar–denominated hedging vehicle. As we know from Chapter 7, a currency swap is a good instrument for hedging multiyear cash flow stream. We want a short position on a swap whose interest component *amount* is equal to $\xi_{R\mathfrak{e}}^{\$}(R_0^{\$})$ = 0.60($1 million) = $600,000. At 1 $/€, the *size* of the swap interest component is €600,000. When the euro drops by 20% from 1 $/€ to 0.80 $/€, the swap difference check will be $120,000 = −€600(0.80 $/€ − 1 $/€). This difference check makes up for the $120,000 drop in KMC's revenues from the Eurozone from $1 million to $880,000. The notional principal will depend on the interest rate. If the swap interest rate in euros is 5%, then the notional principal should be €1.2 million. This hedge will protect the US dollar revenues against the impact of the changing FX value of the euro. To check whether this size works for a different change in the FX value of the euro, take a 10% drop instead of a 20% drop. In this case, KMC's revenues from the Eurozone, in US dollars, will drop by 6%, to $940,000. The difference check on the swap will be −€600,000(0.90 $/€ − 1 $/€) = $60,000, which makes up for the drop in US dollar revenue.

In addition to stabilizing the US dollar revenue at $1 million, KMC needs to hedge its FX conversion exposure to the US dollar. KMC could accomplish this by having US dollar–denominated debt or taking a short US dollar position in a US dollar–Australian dollar currency swap. Since KMC's time-0 revenue expectation is A$1 million, debt interest amount or the swap interest component *amount* should be A$1 million. This position will hedge the FX conversion exposure to changes in the FX value the US dollar (relative to the Australian dollar).

Both hedges are required. It will not work for KMC to take only a short position on euros in a euro–Australian dollar currency swap. The reason is that the component FX revenue exposures are different: the US dollar FX revenue exposure to the euro is 0.60 but the Australian dollar FX revenue exposure to the US dollar is 1.

WESTERN MINING COMPANY

Western Mining Company is an Australian producer of minerals and metals. The firm exports to the United States, Canada, and Europe, and the currency of determination for the products in all three export markets is the US dollar. For many years, the management at Western Mining had believed that from the perspective of its home currency, Australian dollars (A$), the only FX revenue exposure was FX conversion exposure to the US dollar.

Then, when the US dollar appreciated relative to the Australian dollar, Western Mining did not experience the increase in A$ revenues it had expected. The reason, managers discovered, was that the US dollar had also appreciated relative to European currencies (represented now by the euro), and as metals prices increased in Europe in terms of euros, the demand by Europeans declined. Western Mining then became aware of an additional exposure in its revenue stream: the economic exposure of the revenues from European sales to changes in the $/€ FX rate.

Western Mining Company has sales in the United States and Canada besides in Europe. A complete analysis would segment the revenues by market currency. You would analyze the US revenues to entail simple FX conversion exposure to the A$/$ exchange rate, and analyze the European and Canadian portions using an equation for compound FX revenue exposure, like equation (8.1), using the euro and the Canadian dollar as the foreign currencies.

Source: Abstracted from Peter J. Maloney, "Managing Foreign Exchange Exposure: The Case of Western Mining," *Journal of Applied Corporate Finance*, Winter 1990, 29–34.

*COMPETITIVE FX REVENUE EXPOSURE

There may be additional economic effects on FX revenue when a firm doing business in a foreign country competes with a local firm or firms from other countries. This is a form of economic FX exposure called *competitive FX exposure*.

TRACTORS IN CANADA: CATERPILLAR VS KOMATSU

The heavy equipment manufacturers Caterpillar, from the United States, and Komatsu, from Japan, compete against each other around the world. Let's look at the tractor market in Canada. If the Canadian dollar rises unilaterally against the both the US dollar and the yen, we know that tractors will be less expensive to Canadians. Our analysis of a single producer can be extended to reason that the sales of both Caterpillar and Komatsu will rise when the FX value of the Canadian dollar rises unilaterally, and vice versa. In addition, the revenues of both Caterpillar and Komatsu are higher in their home currency when the Canadian dollar rises unilaterally, and vice versa, owing to the FX conversion effect.

What if the Canadian dollar rises relative to the US dollar but not relative to the yen? That is, what if there is a unilateral drop in the FX value of the US dollar relative to the Canadian dollar and the yen? In this case, Caterpillar will want to produce more and see the tractor price lower while Komatsu will cut back production in the face of this pressure toward a less profitable environment for it. The reverse would happen in the case of a unilateral drop in the FX value of the yen. This situation means that Caterpillar's revenues have FX exposure to both the Canadian dollar and the yen and Komatsu's revenues have FX exposure to both the Canadian dollar and the US dollar. These exposures are relatively complex, being both economic and compound.

Competitive FX exposure can be very complex to analyze, as revealed in the box on the tractor competition in Canada between Caterpillar and Komatsu. An example of an even more complex competitive FX exposure scenario is the global automobile industry. In this case, there are major competitors from three currency areas: the United States, Japan, and the Eurozone. The competition is in those areas and elsewhere around the world. While a detailed analysis is complex, the basic idea is that when any one of the three currencies drops in FX value unilaterally relative to the other two, automakers from that country receive a competitive boost.

Competitive FX exposure can take other forms, too. Consider a US firm operating in Germany. Suppose the euro appreciates relative to the US dollar, and as a result more US companies become inclined to compete for business in Germany. The additional competition could result in a reduced market share and lower German sales volume (and maybe in price changes as well). Empirical estimation, as discussed in Chapter 5, may be the best way to estimate FX exposure when a firm's competitive FX exposure is too complex to understand with a theoretical model.

Our example has two firms competing in the same market and is thus called a *duopoly*. A US firm, Duopolist United Overseas, Inc. (DUO), produces widgets for export to the Eurozone. DUO has a local competitor, Local Competitor in Eurozone, SA (LCE). The two competing duopolists have the same capacity for production. The demand curve for the widgets sold in the Eurozone is the same as you saw in the MWI example, but it is industry-wide and involves the widget sales of DUO and LCE, denoted Q_D and Q_E, respectively. The industry demand curve in this competitive scenario is $p^{\text{€}} = \text{€}2900 - Q_D - Q_E$.

Figure 8.3 shows the industry demand curve. Also shown on the demand curve in Figure 8.3 are the two solution points for total industry production and widget price. We'll next show how to find those solution points.

Assume that LCE produces widgets in the Eurozone for €1400 per widget, while DUO produces them in the United States for $1400. LCE's revenues in euros are $R_E^{\text{€}} = p^{\text{€}}Q_E = (\text{€}2900 - Q_D - Q_E)Q_E$, and (by taking the first derivative of the revenues in euros with respect to Q_E), LCE's marginal revenue in euros is $MR_E^{\text{€}} = \text{€}2900 - Q_D - 2Q_E$.

DUO's revenues in euros are $R_D^{\text{€}} = p^{\text{€}}Q_D = (\text{€}2900 - Q_D - Q_E)Q_D$. In US dollars, DUO's revenues are thus $X^{\$/\text{€}}(\text{€}2900 - Q_D - Q_E)Q_D$. DUO's marginal revenue function in US dollars, found by taking the first derivative of US dollar revenues with respect to Q_D, depends on the FX rate, $MR_D^{\$} = X^{\$/\text{€}}(\text{€}2900 - 2Q_D - Q_E)$. Now we need to simultaneously equate marginal revenue and marginal cost for each firm. By setting LCE's $MR_E^{\text{€}}$ equal to its $MC_E^{\text{€}}$ (= €1400), and setting DUO's $MR_D^{\$}$ equal to its $MC_D^{\$}$ (= $1400), we solve simultaneously for the optimal widget output of both firms in the duopoly, Q_D and Q_E.

For example, if $X^{\$/\text{€}} = 1$ \$/€, the firms share the market equally, and both Q_D and Q_E equal 500 widgets. To see this, simultaneously solve the two $MR = MC$ equations for DUO [1 \$/€($\text{€}2900 - 2Q_D - Q_E$) = $1400] and LCE ($\text{€}2900 - Q_D - 2Q_E = \text{€}1400$). Simplify the first equation by dividing through by 1 \$/€. Now the two equations to solve simultaneously are (1) $\text{€}2900 - 2Q_D - Q_E = \text{€}1400$, and (2) $\text{€}2900 - Q_D - 2Q_E = \text{€}1400$. Solve the two equations simultaneously by first multiplying equation (2) by −2 to get $-\text{€}5800 + 2Q_D + 4Q_E = -\text{€}2800$. Then add this new equation to equation (1) to get $-\text{€}2900 + 3Q_E = -\text{€}1400$, from which you solve that $Q_E = 500$. Plug this solution for Q_E into either original simultaneous equation and obtain $Q_D = 500$. Finally, using the demand curve, $p^{\text{€}} = \text{€}2900 - Q_D - Q_E$,

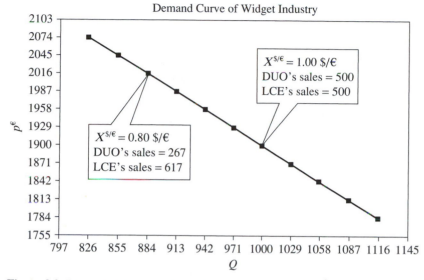

Figure 8.3 Demand curve of widget industry, with Q given by $p^{€} = €2900 - Q_D - Q_E$. Two points on the demand curve are highlighted: (1) If $X^{\$/€} = 1$ \$/€, $Q = 1000$ and $p^{€} = €1900$; DUO's sales are 500 and LCE's sales are 500. (2) If $X^{\$/€} = 0.80$ \$/€, $Q = 884$ and $p^{€} = €2016$; DUO's sales are 267 and LCE's sales are 617.

we find that the widget price in euros will be $p^{€} = €1900$. In total, industry production is 1000 units. Each firm generates revenues in euros of $500(€1900) = €950,000$. DUO's revenue in US dollars is 1 \$/€$(500)(€1900) = \$950,000$.

Figure 8.4 shows the solution to the simultaneous optimization problem for the two firms in diagram form, with the $MR = MC$ analysis set in euros. The marginal revenue function $€2900 - 2Q$ applies for each firm and assumes that the optimal output solution (500) for the other firm has been found. With an industry total output of 1000, the demand curve is used to find that the price is €1900.

If $X^{\$/€} = 0.80$ \$/€, then simultaneous solution of the two $MR = MC$ equations tells you that DUO will produce fewer widgets, $Q_D = 267$, and LCE will produce more widgets, $Q_E = 617$.[1] The total widget production is $267 + 617 = 884$. Using the demand curve, $p^{€} = €2900 - Q_D - Q_E$, we find that the widget price in euros will be higher, $p^{€} = €2016$. DUO's revenue in US dollars is 0.80 \$/€$(267)(€2016) \approx \$430,000$.

What is DUO's FX revenue exposure to the euro, $\xi_{RE}^{\$}$? The FX value of the euro depreciated by 20% from 1 \$/€ to 0.80 \$/€; in response, DUO's US dollar revenue changed

---

[1]Actual computations: Set $€2900 - Q_D - 2Q_E = €1400$ and 0.80 \$/€$(€2900 - 2Q_D - Q_E) = \$1400$. Simplify the two equations to (1) $2900 - Q_D - 2Q_E = 1400$ and (2) $2900 - 2Q_D - Q_E = 1750$. Solve the two simplified equations simultaneously by first multiplying equation (1) by -2 to get $-5800 + 2Q_D + 4Q_E = -2800$, and then adding this new equation to equation (2) to get $-2900 + 3Q_E = -1050$, which simplifies to $Q_E = 617$. Substitution of $Q_E = 617$ into either equation will yield $Q_D = 267$.

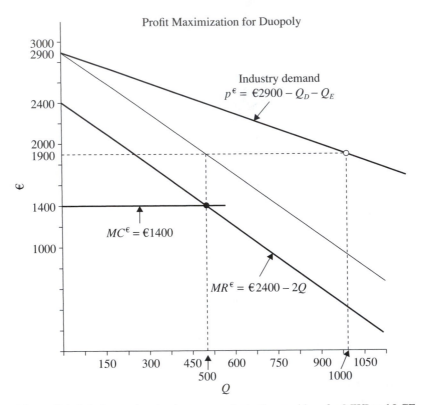

Figure 8.4 Solution to the simultaneous optimization problem for MWI and LCE.

by \$430,000/\$950,000 − 1 = −0.547, or −54.7%. Thus using the definition of $\%\Delta R^{\$}/x^{\$/€}$, the FX exposure of DUO's US dollar revenue to the euro is $\xi^{\$}_{R€} = -0.547/-0.20 = 2.74$.

Again, the linearity of the demand function results in an FX revenue exposure that is nonlinear. Another example shows the FX revenue exposure to be 2.52 if the euro appreciates in value by 25%. On average, we might estimate DUO's FX revenue exposure to the euro at about 2.63.

Find DUO's FX revenue exposure to the euro when the FX rate begins at 1 \$/€ and the FX value of the euro appreciates to 1.25 \$/€.

Answer: If the FX value of the euro is 1.25 \$/€, then simultaneous solution of the two MR = MC equations yields that $Q_D = 686$ widgets and $Q_E = 407$ widgets (actual computations not shown). Using the demand curve, $p^{€} = €2900 - Q_D - Q_E$, we find that $p^{€} = €1807$. DUO's revenue in US dollars is 1.25 \$/€(686)(€1807) ≈ \$1,550,000. The FX value of the euro appreciates by 25%; in response, DUO's US dollar revenue has changed by \$1,550,000/\$950,000 − 1 = 0.63, or 63%. Thus using the definition of $\%\Delta R^{\$}/x^{\$/€}$, the FX exposure of DUO's US dollar revenues to the euro, $\xi^{\$}_{R€}$, is 0.63/0.25 = 2.52.

DUO's FX revenue exposure is about 2.63, and the monopolist MWI's FX revenue exposure is about 1.62. As a result of DUO's competition with the local firm LCE, changes in the FX value of the euro have more impact on DUO than on the monopolist MWI. Thus, other things equal, we would expect an exporter to have greater FX revenue exposure to the local currency if it must compete against local firms. DUO's euro revenues drop substantially when the FX value of the euro falls, owing to the competitive exposure, and the impact of this drop on DUO's revenues in US dollars is compounded by the impact of FX conversion exposure.

If DUO moves its production from the United States to Euroland, the competitive FX exposure to the euro disappears. Now there is no economic impact of FX changes on the optimal output and price of widgets, for either DUO or LCE. If the cost of producing a widget is €1400 in Euroland, both DUO and LCE would find it optimal to produce 500 widgets and sell them for €1900 per widget, whatever the $/€ FX rate. Each firm's revenues in euros would be stable, €950,000. DUO's US dollar revenues would be $X^{\$/€}(€950,000)$. Now if the value of the euro depreciates by 10%, DUO's US dollar revenues would decline by 10%. DUO would have only a pure FX conversion exposure, and $\xi_{R€}^{\$}$ would be 1.

Moving production to Euroland would reduce DUO's FX revenue exposure from about 2.63 to 1. We found earlier that MWI could reduce FX revenue exposure from about 1.62 to 1 by moving production to Euroland. Together, the DUO and MWI examples show that operational hedging produces greater FX exposure-reducing benefits when a local competitor is present. Analysts have argued that Japanese automakers substantially reduced their FX operating exposure by building plants in the United States.[2]

In the DUO/LCE example, the cost of producing widgets is the same in either country (and for either firm) at the FX rate of 1 $/€, since the cost of producing a widget in Euroland is €1400 and the cost of producing a widget in the United States is $1400. At any other FX rate, though, the cost of producing a widget is not the same when viewed in a common currency. If the FX value of the euro is greater than 1 $/€, then producing a widget in Euroland is relatively more expensive than in the United States, giving DUO an economic advantage, and vice versa.

*FX REVENUE EXPOSURE: DOMESTIC FIRM WITH A FOREIGN COMPETITOR

What is the nature of the FX revenue exposure for a domestic company when there is competition from a foreign firm that is exporting a product from its country? We can examine this question by looking at the DUO–LCE competition from the perspective of the Euroland firm, LCE. LCE's home currency is euros, and both sales and costs are

---

[2]Dennis E. Logue, "When Theory Fails: Globalization as a Response to the (Hostile) Market for Foreign Exchange," *Journal of Applied Corporate Finance*, Fall 1995, 39–48.

measured in euros. Still, LCE is exposed to a foreign currency, the US dollar, because its competitor DUO imports widgets produced in the United States into LCE's local Euroland market.

We already know that at an FX rate of 1 $/€, LCE produces 500 widgets and sells them for €1900 per widget for expected revenue of €950,000. At 0.80 $/€ (1.25 €/$ in direct terms from LCE's euro point of view), LCE's output is 617 widgets, and revenues = €2016(617) = €1,244,000. LCE's revenues (in its home currency, euros) rise from €950,000 to €1,244,000 (an increase of 31%), when the FX value of the foreign currency (the US dollar) rises from 1 €/$ to 1.25 €/$ (an appreciation of 25% of the US dollar). Thus LCE's FX revenue exposure to the US dollar is $\xi_{R\$}^{\epsilon} = 0.31/0.25 = 1.24$.

Find LCE's FX revenue exposure to the US dollar when the FX rate begins at 1 $/€ and the spot FX value of the euro appreciates to 1.25 $/€.

Answer: Recall from the preceding problem that if the FX value of the euro is 1.25 $/€, the simultaneous solution of the two MR = MC equations yields that Q_E = 407 widgets and p^{ϵ} = €1807. LCE's revenue in euros is (407)(€1807) ≈ €735,000. The US dollar has depreciated by 20%; in response, LCE's euro revenue has changed by €735,000/€950,000 − 1 = −0.226, or −22.6%. Thus using the definition of $\%\Delta R^{\epsilon}/x^{\epsilon/\$}$, the FX exposure of LCE's euro revenues to the US dollar, $\xi_{R\$}^{\epsilon}$, is −0.226/−0.20 = 1.13.

Note that if DUO decides to move its production to Euroland, fixing DUO's cost of producing widgets in euros, LCE no longer has FX revenue exposure, even though its competitor is technically a US firm. As long as DUO and LCE produce in different countries, the competitive FX exposure scenarios show that neither the euro nor the US dollar is the unambiguous currency of determination for widgets in Euroland.

We haven't factored in the relative power of the competitors, though. If the competitor from a given country has more clout, its currency is more likely to determine product prices.

*FX OPERATING EXPOSURE OF A FOREIGN SUBSIDIARY WITH A FOREIGN COMPETITOR

Look again at LCE, the duopolist local competitor of DUO in Euroland. If DUO produces in the United States and exports to Euroland, LCE will produce 500 widgets, have euro revenues of €950,000, and produce operating profit of €250,000, given an FX rate of 1 $/€. At 0.80 $/€, LCE's output is 617 widgets; its revenues are €2016(617) = €1,244,000, and operating profits are €1,244,000 − 864,000 = €380,000.

LCE's operating profits (in home currency, euros) rise from €250,000 to €380,000 (an increase of 52%), when the value of the foreign currency (the US dollar) rises from 1 €/$

to 1.25 €/$ (an appreciation of 25%). Thus LCE's FX operating exposure to the US dollar is $\xi_{O\$}^{\euro} = 0.52/0.25 = 2.08$. There is an operating leverage effect for LCE, since its revenues have FX exposure to changes in the value of the US dollar (1.24, found earlier), while its cost per widget is fixed in euros.

If LCE is acquired by a US multinational, what would the US parent's FX operating exposure to the euro now be? LCE's operating profits (in US dollars) would be $250,000 if the FX rate is 1 $/€, and (0.80 $/€)€380,000 = $304,000. Thus the operating profit in US dollars rises from $250,000 to $304,000 (an increase of 21.6%), when the FX value of the foreign currency (the euro) drops from 1 $/€ to 0.80 $/€ (a depreciation of 20% of the euro). The US parent's FX operating exposure to the euro would be $\xi_{O\euro}^{\$} = -0.216/-0.20 = -1.08$.

Notice that LCE's US owner has a *negative* FX operating exposure to the euro. The reason is that LCE is a local producer competing with a company that produces in the United States and exports to Euroland (DUO). So, when the FX value of the euro falls, LCE makes more profits in euros, and vice versa. In fact, since the sensitivity of LCE's profits (in euros) to changes in the FX value of the US dollar is 2.08, the change in LCE's profits outweighs the impact (in the opposite direction) of the FX conversion effect of the euro profits into US dollars. When the euro falls in FX value, therefore, the US owner of LCE has higher operating profits in US dollars, and vice versa. This means the US owner of LCE has a negative FX operating exposure to the euro, even with LCE as its overseas subsidiary.

If LCE's foreign competitor, DUO, moves all widget production to Euroland, LCE would produce and sell 500 widgets regardless of the FX rate. As a European firm, LCE in this case would have stable operating profits of €250,000, and no FX operating exposure to the US dollar. A US owner of LCE would now have an FX operating exposure of 1 to the euro. When the FX value of the euro drops by 20%, from 1 $/€ to 0.80 $/€, the operating profits of LCE's US owner would drop by 20% in US dollar terms. In this case, the US owner of LCE will have an FX operating exposure to the euro of 1 if LCE's US competitor produces locally in Euroland, but an FX operating exposure of −1.08 to the euro if the competitor produces in the United States.

SUMMARY

This chapter has described a firm's economic FX exposure and its potential sources. These included indirect FX exposure, wealth FX exposure, price–volume effects, compound FX revenue exposure, and competitive FX exposure. Purely domestic firms can have FX operating exposure owing to indirect FX exposure, wealth FX exposure, or competitive FX exposure.

We examined how FX changes affect the profit-maximizing decisions on output and pricing of an exporter with no competitor. If the FX value of the foreign currency falls, the firm cuts production and raises price, and vice versa.

We also examined how FX changes affect the profit-maximizing decisions on output and pricing of two competitors based in different currency zones. Other things the same, the FX operating exposure is more severe if a firm has a competitor than when it has no competitor.

We showed how overseas subsidiaries may sometimes impose a negative FX exposure on their parent firm, if the subsidiary is competing against a firm producing in the parent's home country.

GLOSSARY

Competitive FX exposure: Economic FX exposure due to the effects of FX changes on a firm's competitive environment and thereby on its revenues and operating cash flows.

Duopoly: Two firms competing against each other in one market.

Compound FX revenue exposure: A form of economic FX exposure attributable to the compounding effect of different FX rates.

Economic FX exposure: The effects of FX changes on a firm's prices, costs, and sales/output volume, and thus on revenues and operating cash flows.

Indirect FX exposure: A form of economic FX revenue exposure attributable to the impact of FX rates on customers or suppliers.

Marginal revenue: The change in revenue for an additional unit sold, given the new price for all units necessary to sell all the units.

Wealth FX exposure: Economic FX exposure in which sales volume changes in response to the wealth effects of FX changes.

DISCUSSION QUESTIONS

1. Describe a scenario of FX exposure due to wealth effects.
2. Describe a scenario of indirect FX exposure.
3. Describe a scenario of compound FX revenue exposure.
4. Describe a scenario of competitive FX exposure.
5. Discuss how a purely domestic company, with no foreign trade or FX transactions, can have an FX operating exposure greater than 1 through (1) indirect FX exposure and (2) competitive FX exposure.
6. Discuss how a multinational's foreign subsidiary, which operates purely as a local domestic company, with no foreign trade or FX transactions, can cause the parent to have an FX operating exposure less than 0 through competitive FX exposure.

PROBLEMS

1. Use the MWI scenario in the text, and find MWI's FX revenue exposure to the euro for an original FX rate of 1 $/€ and a new FX rate of 1.15 $/€.
*2. Assume that your US company generates euro revenues in Euroland, with an FX revenue exposure to the yen of $\xi_{R\yen}^{\euro} = 0.80$, due to Japanese competition in Euroland. From the US dollar perspective, there is also an FX conversion exposure to the euro, $\xi_{R\euro}^{\$} = 1$. If the FX value of the yen does not change relative to the US dollar, and the euro appreciates by 10% (relative to the

US dollar), what is the percentage change in the US dollar level of the company's revenues generated in Euroland? *Note*: The FX value of the euro appreciates by 10% relative to yen, so the FX value of the yen depreciates by 9.1% relative to the euro.

*3. Using the scenario in the chapter, find DUO's FX operating exposure to the euro if the FX value of the euro depreciates by 20% from 1 \$/€ to 0.80 \$/€.

*4. Use the DUO/LCE scenario in the text. Find DUO's FX revenue exposure to the euro when DUO competes with LCE and the FX rate changes from 1 \$/€ to 1.15 \$/€.

*5. Extend Problem 4; find LCE's FX revenue exposure to the US dollar.

*6. Maintain the DUO/LCE scenario, but assume that DUO produces widgets partially in the United States and partially in Euroland. The cost of the components produced in the United States is \$840 per widget. The cost of assembling the components is Euroland is €560 per widget. Find the FX revenue exposure for DUO (to the euro) and LCE (to the US dollar), for a movement of the spot FX rate from 1 \$/€ to 0.80 \$/€.

*7. Suppose that DUO's widget assembly operation is in Euroland, as described in Problem 6. What is DUO's FX operating exposure to the euro from the perspective of US dollars?

*8. Following on from Problems 6 and 7, what would be the FX operating exposure to the euro of a US parent of LCE?

ANSWERS TO PROBLEMS

1. Sales, 841 units; euro revenue, €1.731 million; US dollar revenue, \$1.99 million; $\xi_{R\epsilon}^{\$} = 1.57$.

2. 2%.

3. If $X^{\$/\epsilon} = 1$ \$/€, DUO produces 500 and revenue in US dollars is \$950,000. Costs are \$700,000, and thus operating cash flow is \$250,000. If $X^{\$/\epsilon} = 0.80$ \$/€, DUO produces 267 and revenue in US dollars is \$430,000. Costs are 267(\$1400) = \$373,800. Thus operating cash flow is \$430,000 − 373,800 = \$56,200. DUO's US dollar operating cash flow changes by \$56,200/\$250,000 −1 = −0.775, or −77.5%. Thus using the definition of %$\Delta O^{\$}/x^{\$/\epsilon}$, $\xi_{O\epsilon}^{\$} = 3.88$.

4. Sales, 622 units; euro revenue, €1.143 million; US dollar revenue, \$1.315 million; $\xi_{R\epsilon}^{\$} = 2.56$.

5. Sales, 439 units; euro revenue, €807,000; $\xi_{R\$}^{\epsilon} = −0.15/−0.13 = 1.15$.

6. At 1 \$/€, production, price, and revenues are the same as when production is entirely in the United States. At 0.80 \$/€, DUO produces 360, LCE produces 570, and the price is €1970. So DUO's revenues are \$567,000, while LCE's are €1,123,000. DUO's revenues decline by 40.28%, while LCE's revenues increase by 18.20%. DUO's FX revenue exposure to the euro is 2.014, while LCE's FX revenue exposure to the US dollar is 0.728.

7. At 1 \$/€, production, price, and revenues are the same as when production is entirely in the United States. Both firms have operating cash flow of \$250,000, when measured in US dollars. At 0.80 \$/€, DUO produces 360 units, revenues are \$567,000, costs are 360[\$840 + 0.80\$/€(€560)] = \$464,000, so operating cash flow is \$104,000. Operating cash flow drops by 58.5%, when the euro falls by 20.0%. DUO's FX operating exposure to the euro is 2.93.

8. At 0.80 \$/€, LCE produces 570, revenues are €1,123,000, operating costs are 570(€1400) = €798,000, so operating cash flow is €325,000. Operating cash flow rises by 30%, when the US dollar rises by 25%. LCE's FX operating exposure to the US dollar is 1.20. In US dollars, LCE's operating cash flow rises from \$250,000 to \$260,000, about 4%, when the euro falls by 20%. From the US dollar perspective, LCE's FX operating exposure to the euro is 0.04/−0.20 = −0.20.

PART III

COST OF CAPITAL AND CROSS-BORDER INVESTMENT DECISIONS

Part III covers issues related to the cost of capital, the valuation of overseas assets, and decision making for foreign investments.

Chapter 9 shows how to estimate the weighted average cost of capital (WACC) for a company when it is part of the integrated financial markets. The chapter describes the use of the global capital asset pricing model (global CAPM) in estimating a firm's cost of equity in US dollars.

The traditional uncovered interest rate parity (UIRP) condition (Chapter 4) is used to estimate the cost of foreign currency denominated debt in US dollars. An asterisked section of Chapter 9 shows how to adjust the UIRP for systematic FX risk using the global CAPM.

Chapter 10 shows how to estimate the cost of capital for a company's overseas subsidiaries and projects. The difficulty is that the company's WACC is generally not the correct cost of capital for a project whose risk is different from that of the company as a whole. So we show how to deal with this problem.

In addition to basic techniques that apply to overseas investments in developed countries, Chapter 10 shows adjustments that should be made when the investment is in an emerging market country where there is political risk or liquidity risk. We also show how to convert the cost of capital for a foreign investment from US dollars into its equivalent in the foreign currency.

Chapter 11 is about accounting for FX translation when a company has overseas assets and foreign currency debt. Chapter 11 also covers some accounting rules promulgated in 1998 for hedging FX exposure (SFAS 133).

Chapter 12 deals with decisions for overseas investments entailing acquisitions, relocation of production facilities, and expansions. While a basic net present value (NPV) framework is used, there is the important issue of whether to perform the NPV analysis from the perspective of the home currency or the foreign currency. If the FX rate is correctly valued, this choice is theoretically irrelevant, but a manager must consider the quality of the information available for each currency perspective.

If the FX rate is not correctly valued, causing a manager to forecast that the FX rate is likely to change at a rate different from that implied in the UIRP condition, the NPVs from the home currency perspective and foreign currency perspective are not equal. We delve into the decision implications in this case, including the choice of hedging and financing.

Chapter 12 also reviews some trends and issues in cross-border mergers and acquisitions.

CHAPTER 9

GLOBAL FINANCE AND THE COST OF CAPITAL

A firm's cost of capital is central to its valuation, investment (and divestment) decisions, measures of economic profit, and performance appraisal. This chapter describes how a company can estimate its weighted average cost of capital (WACC) in US dollars.

We introduce the global capital asset pricing model (global CAPM) and show how to use it to estimate the cost of equity in US dollars. The global CAPM is a simple extension of the traditional CAPM that you may have learned in other courses. The global CAPM is logically superior to the traditional CAPM in a world of integrated financial markets and internationally diversified investors. Since financial capital now flows fairly freely throughout the world's financial markets, and since investors worldwide are finding it increasingly simple and convenient to invest internationally, our use of the global CAPM seems justified.

When a US firm with foreign currency denominated debt wants to find its cost of debt, it must convert the known interest cost in the foreign currency into an equivalent measure in US dollars. This procedure requires using an expected rate of change in the FX value of the foreign currency that is consistent with the risk–return relationship in the global financial market. The traditional uncovered interest rate parity (UIRP) condition of Chapter 4 may be used to get a very good estimate. Theoretically, we can improve on the UIRP in a minor way by using the global CAPM to adjust it for systematic risk, which we do in an asterisked section.

RETURNS ON FOREIGN ASSETS

To prepare for our presentation of the global CAPM, we first look at the rate of return of a non–US asset in terms of US dollars. In US dollars, the rate of return on a non–US asset has two components. The first is the asset's rate of return in its own local currency. The second is the change in FX price of that local currency in terms of the US dollar.

For example, the rate of return on a French stock on the Paris Bourse from the point of view of a US owner consists of two components: (1) the local rate of return to French investors in euros and (2) the percentage change in the spot FX price of the euro relative to the US dollar. The two components are combined in a compound fashion.

Let $R_i^\$$ denote the rate of return on asset i from the viewpoint of US dollars. If the asset is denominated in euros, with a local rate of return in euros of $R_i^{€}$, and if $x^{\$/€}$ represents the percentage change in the spot FX price of the euro relative to the US dollar, then we have the following identity for the asset's returns:

Across-Currency Return Identity

$$R_i^\$ = (1 + R_i^{€})(1 + x^{\$/€}) - 1 \tag{9.1a}$$

TABLE 9.1 One-Year Rates of Return, Ending January 2, 2004 (%)

Country	Return in Local Currency	Δ % in FX Price of Foreign Currency	Return in US Dollars
Australia	12.34	34.57	51.18
Austria	33.53	21.36	62.05
Belgium	12.48	21.36	36.50
Canada	25.58	21.89	53.07
Denmark	25.09	21.05	51.41
Finland	−4.07	21.36	16.42
France	14.08	21.36	38.44
Germany	29.67	21.36	57.36
Greece	42.03	21.36	72.36
Hong Kong	39.59	0.44	40.21
Ireland	16.93	21.36	41.90
Italy	13.74	21.36	38.03
Japan	22.96	11.94	37.64
Netherlands	4.29	21.36	26.56
New Zealand	25.69	25.68	57.97
Norway	43.11	5.17	50.51
Portugal	19.49	21.36	45.00
Singapore	37.38	2.46	40.76
Spain	29.43	21.36	57.07
Sweden	32.10	22.34	61.61
Switzerland	20.75	13.06	36.52
United Kingdom	17.71	11.94	31.77
United States	24.57	0.00	24.57

Source: MSCIDATA.com.

Let's examine the Alstom Company, which manufactures power equipment. Assume that Alstom's share price on the Paris Bourse is €50 per share at time 0, when the spot FX rate is 1 $/€, and the share price is €60 per share at time 1, when the spot FX rate is 1.25 $/€. In this case, Alstom's local rate of return in euros is $R_i^{€} = €60/€50 - 1 = 0.20$, or 20%, while the rate of change of the FX price of the euro (relative to the US dollar) is $x^{\$/€} = (1.25 \text{ \$/€})/(1 \text{ \$/€}) - 1 = 0.25$.

From equation (9.1a), we find that the rate of return for a US investor holding Alstom shares is $R_i^{\$} = (1 + 0.20)(1 + 0.25) - 1 = 0.50 = 50\%$. One can verify this answer as follows: starting with $500 at time 0, exchanging this amount into €500 at the spot FX rate of 1 $/€, and then buying 10 shares of Alstom; then at time 1, you liquidate the 10 Alstom shares for 10(€60) = €600, and exchange the €600 into US dollars at the time-1 spot FX rate of 1.25 $/€, receiving €600(1.25 $/€) = $750. In US dollars now, the rate of return is $750/$500 - 1 = 0.50, or 50%.

Note in this example that Alstom's performance on the Paris Bourse was compounded by the appreciation of the euro relative to the dollar. The net effect is a large rate of return for US investors.

Alstom's shares are priced at €50 per share at time 0, when the spot FX rate is 1.10 $/€. The share price is €42 per share at time 1, when the spot FX rate is 0.90 $/€. What is the rate of return on Alstom shares in US dollars?

Answer: Alstom's local rate of return in euros is $R_i^{€} = €42/€50 - 1 = -0.16$, or −16% while the rate of change of the FX price of the euro (relative to the US dollar) is $x^{\$/€} = (0.90 \text{ \$/€})/(1.10 \text{ \$/€}) - 1 = -0.182$. From equation (9.1a), the rate of return for a US investor holding Alstom shares is $R_i^{\$} = (1 - 0.16)(1 - 0.182) - 1 = -0.313 = -31.3\%$. One can verify this answer as follows: starting with $550 at time 0, exchanging this amount into €500 at the spot FX rate of 1.10 $/€, and then buying 10 shares of Alstom; then at time 1, you liquidate the 10 Alstom shares for 10(€42) = €420 and exchange the €420 into US dollars at the time-1 spot FX rate of 0.90 $/€, receiving €420(0.90 $/€) = $378. In US dollars now, the rate of return is $378/$550 - 1 = -0.313, or −31.3%.

Table 9.1 shows equation (9.1a) in action for the stock market indexes of a number of developed market countries.

An asset's across-currency return identity in equation (9.1a) has a linear approximation that will be useful. This approximation is shown in equation (9.1b):

Across-Currency Return Identity
Simple Linear Approximation

$$R_i^{\$} \approx R_i^{€} + x^{\$/€} \tag{9.1b}$$

In the Alstom example, where the local rate of return in euros is 20% and the percentage change in the FX price of the euro is 25%, equation (9.1b) says that Alstom's rate of return in US dollars is 20% + 25% = 45%. Of course, this is an approximation of the true rate of return in US dollars, 50%, found earlier. The approximation in equation (9.1b) is better the smaller the returns and FX changes, and the lower the correlation between the two.[1]

DEPOSITARY RECEIPTS

While US investors can often buy foreign shares directly in foreign equity markets, many foreign shares are conveniently traded in the United States as *American depositary receipts (ADRs)*. A depositary, like Bank of New York, will hold the actual foreign shares in that foreign country, while the US office issues US dollar-denominated receipts that are more easily traded in US markets. Stocks traded on both their home and foreign exchanges are said to be *cross-listed stocks*.

In 1990 there were only 352 non–US stocks traded on the New York Stock Exchange (NYSE) and NASDAQ, but, by the end of 2002, the number exceeded 850. If one includes over-the-counter and private placement issues, there are more than 2300 foreign companies with shares traded in the United States. This situation reflects the US investors' need for international diversification and the desire of foreign companies to access global capital, broaden their shareholder base, and enhance company visibility.

The price of an ADR must obey the international law of one price, or there will be a relatively easy arbitrage between the ADR shares and the actual underlying shares, called the *ordinary shares*. In the Alstom example, if the ordinary Alstom shares are priced in Paris at €60 per share at time 1, when the spot FX rate is 1.25 $/€, the ADRs will be priced in the United States at $75. Otherwise, there would be an easy arbitrage opportunity for traders who have access to both markets. And if the ordinary shares are priced in Paris at €50 per share at time 0, when the spot FX rate is 1 $/€, then the ADRs will be priced at $50 in the United States.

It is difficult to gauge the amount of arbitrage that occurs between ADRs and underlying ordinaries. However, there are a number of vehicles to facilitate the process, including the Bank of New York's DR Converter, which is a proprietary cost analysis model for ADRs versus home-market ordinaries with Web-based access for global investors. Citibank's ADR division has initiated a system to reduce the settlement delays and risks for its customers in ADR issuances and cancellations. The *ADR Cross-Book*

---

[1]The approximation in equation (9.1b) is a special case of the Itô linear approximation:

$$R_i^\$ \approx R_i^\epsilon + x^{\$/\epsilon} + cov(R_i^\epsilon, x^{\$/\epsilon}) \tag{9.1c}$$

In equation (9.1c), the $cov(R_i^\epsilon, x^{\$/\epsilon})$ term is the covariance between the asset's return in euros and the FX changes, reflecting the statistical relationship between the asset's return in euros and FX changes, and is equal to the correlation between R_i^ϵ and $x^{\$/\epsilon}$ (denoted $\rho_{i\epsilon}$) times the volatility of R_i^ϵ (denoted σ_i^ϵ) times the volatility of the euro (σ_ϵ). That is, $cov(R_i^\epsilon, x^{\$/\epsilon}) = \rho_{i\epsilon}\sigma_i^\epsilon\sigma_\epsilon$. There will be correlation between the asset's euro returns and FX changes if the asset has some economic FX exposure. In some cases later in this chapter, zero is the assumed correlation between the asset's euro returns and FX changes, so the covariance term is also zero. In this case, the approximation in equation (9.1c) simplifies to the one in equation (9.1b).

Maximizer of J. P. Morgan's ADR division is the market's first online automated marketplace for ADR traders and brokers to execute ADR–ordinary share exchange transactions.

The amount of US trading in foreign company ADRs varies. For some stocks, trading in the United States represents less than 5% of global trading, while for others the US trading is over 90%. Tomkins, a UK engineering company, has very low trading in the United States, but GlaxoSmithKline, a UK pharmaceutical company, experiences US trading of about 30%. The larger the percentage of trading in the United States, the more the price is determined in the US market instead of the home market, that is, the more the "tail wags the dog." But the no-arbitrage relationship holds regardless of which market price determination takes place.[2]

ADRs often trade in a share ratio different from one-for-one. For example, one ADR for Telefonos de Mexico represents 20 underlying Mexican shares, while one ADR for Diageo (a British company that resulted from the merger of Guinness and Grand Metropolitan in 1997) represents four ordinary UK shares. One ADR for Norsk Hydro represents one underlying Norwegian share.

Table 9.2 lists some large ADRs from J. P. Morgan's Web site: www.adr.com.

An investor in Alstom ADRs would earn a rate of return in US dollars of $75/$50 − 1 = 0.50, or 50%. Ignoring transaction costs, you see there is really no difference whether a US investor holds actual Alstom shares or the ADRs. Either way, the rate of return in US dollars is the same: the ADR returns will reflect both returns on an ordinary share and changes in the spot FX rate.[3]

The ordinary shares for Diageo are denominated in British pounds and traded on the London Stock Exchange (LSE). There are four ADR shares for each ordinary share. If the actual shares are priced at £150 in London and the spot FX rate is 1.60 $/£, what is the no-arbitrage price of a Diageo ADR share in US dollars? What will be the rate of return to a US investor who buys the Diageo ordinary shares now (time 0) and holds until time 1, when the ordinary shares are priced at £165 and the spot FX rate is 1.20 $/£? What is the time-1 price of an ADR share?

Answers: An actual share is worth £150(1.60 $/£) = $240. Since one ordinary share underlies four ADR shares, an ADR share should be priced at $240/4 = $60. The rate of return on Diageo in British pounds is £165/£150 − 1 = 0.10, or 10%. The FX value of the pound changed by (1.20 $/£)/(1.60 $/£) − 1 = −0.25, or −25%. Thus the rate of return in US dollars, using equation (9.1a), is (1.10)(1 − 0.25) − 1 = −0.175, or −17.5%. The new ADR share price at time 1 will be £165(1.20 $/£)/4 = $49.50.

---

[2]A recent study shows that trading for a cross-listed stock tend to be highest in the market where the stock's return has the highest correlation with other stocks in the market. See S. Baruch, A. Karolyi, and M. Lemmon, "Multi-Market Trading and Liquidity: Theory and Evidence," downloadable from http://papers.ssrn.com/sol3/papers.cfm?abstract_id=482502.

[3]See R. Maldonado and A. Saunders, "Foreign Exchange Restrictions and the Law of One Price," *Financial Management*, Spring 1983, 19–23.

TABLE 9.2 American Depositary Receipts, December 31, 2003

Security	INSTITUTIONAL HOLDINGS ($MM)	Price	Volume
BP p.l.c. [BP]	23,596	49.35	2,462,900
Nokia [NOK]	12,401	17.00	8,454,600
Royal Dutch/Shell [RD]	11,658	52.39	1,323,400
Teva Pharmaceuticals [TEVA]	8,795	56.71	1,227,853
Vodafone [VOD]	8,441	25.04	1,785,400
TelMex [TMX]	6,498	33.03	594,300
GlaxoSmithKline [GSK]	6,354	46.62	474,900
AstraZeneca [AZN]	5,756	48.38	454,500
América Móvil [AMX]	5,458	27.34	355,700
Unilever [UN]	4,934	64.90	327,700
Total [TOT]	4,787	92.51	516,900
TSMC [TSM]	4,251	10.24	4,028,700
KT Corporation [KTC]	3,736	19.07	516,500
Novartis [NVS]	3,672	45.89	486,100
Ryanair [RYAAY]	3,604	50.64	274,422
HSBC [HBC]	3,451	78.82	177,800
SAP [SAP]	3,076	41.56	583,100
Sony [SNE]	2,978	34.67	309,800
News Corp. [NWS]	2,851	36.10	758,800
PETROBRAS [PBR]	2,783	29.24	268,000
Grupo Televisa [TV]	2,757	39.86	103,800
CVRD [RIO]	2,636	58.50	137,200
Philips [PHG]	2,466	29.09	351,100
CEMEX [CX]	2,207	26.20	320,600
Diageo [DEO]	2,120	52.86	118,500
Telefonica [TEF]	2,034	44.19	119,500
ASML [ASML]	1,865	20.05	1,909,763
Rio Tinto [RTP]	1,732	111.31	124,200
AmBev [ABV]	1,714	25.51	102,500
ST [STM]	1,610	27.01	812,800
Aventis [AVE]	1,596	66.26	330,600
Matsushita [MC]	1,530	13.94	71,400
Ericsson [ERICY]	1,436	17.70	750,290
Shell T & T [SC]	1,404	45.03	216,600
SK Telecom [SKM]	1,336	18.65	252,400
POSCO [PKX]	1,313	33.97	381,600
FEMSA [FMX]	1,227	36.88	271,700
Repsol [REP]	1,217	19.55	121,500

Source: www.adr.com.

The Alstom and Diageo examples illustrate again that there are two components to the return of a foreign asset in the pricing currency (US dollars): the basic return on Diageo's ordinary shares in London in pounds, and the change in the FX rate. Understanding the basic economic equivalence of ordinary shares and their depositary receipts will help you understand why a common risk–return relationship should apply to all stocks in the global market.

COST OF CAPITAL

As you know from other finance courses, a standard way to express a firm's cost of capital is via the weighted average cost of capital, or WACC: $k_w = w_d k_d(1 - t) + w_s k_s$, where k_d is the (before-tax) cost of debt, k_s is the cost of equity, t is the effective corporate tax rate, and the ws are the weights of each component as a percent of total capital, so the weights sum to 1. For simplicity, the WACC formula is expressed in terms only of two capital sources, debt and equity, but it can easily be expanded to include other sources. The weights should be measured using intrinsic values, not historical book values.

Finance theory teaches us that if we use the WACC to discount the firm's expected future after-tax operating cash flows, the result is the intrinsic value of the firm, as in Chapter 6. To maintain, at a minimum, the current intrinsic value of the firm's equity shares, a new investment that does not change a firm's risk must earn at least the firm's WACC.

A firm's cost of capital is generally a different number expressed in different currencies, even though the numbers are different ways to express the same cost of capital. You must be careful to specify which currency you are using to express the firm's cost of capital. To discount a firm's expected cash flows when viewed in euros, you use the firm's euro cost of capital; to discount the same expected cash flows converted from euros into US dollars using forecasted future FX rates, you use the US dollar cost of capital, and so forth. That a firm has only one cost of capital, but the number is different when expressed in different currencies, is no different from saying that a firm's equity has only one value, but it is a different number when expressed in different currencies. For example, you can express a firm's equity value either as $160 or £100 assuming a spot FX rate of 1.60 $/£. Similarly, a firm's cost of capital might be 10% expressed in US dollars and 8% expressed in pounds. Here in Chapter 9, we focus only on a firm's cost of capital in US dollars. Chapter 10 takes a look at a firm's cost of capital in other currencies.

The cost of any capital component in the WACC should be measured in terms of current market conditions, not at rates in effect in the past when the capital was raised. For example, if debt was issued when the interest rate was 5%, but now the market yield on new debt would be 7%, then the (before-tax) cost of debt is 7% even if the firm is not issuing new debt.

We will return to the weighted average idea, but first we must cover the *cost of equity*. Unlike the cost of debt, the cost of equity is not directly observable. One does not find an item for cost of equity on a firm's profit and loss (P&L) statement or on the stock certificate. Instead, the cost of equity is an *opportunity cost*, the minimum expected rate of return that an equity investor requires as compensation for taking risk and supplying capital. The cost of equity is also called the equity investors' *required rate of return*.

One way to estimate a firm's cost of equity uses a discounted cash flow model of intrinsic stock value, such as the well-known *Gordon model*, $S = D/(k_s - g)$. In the Gordon model, the cash flows are the firm's future dividends, which we assume are expected to grow at a constant rate, g, into perpetuity. With an estimate of g and next year's dividend, D, one can deduce a current estimate of k_s by assuming that the firm's observed current stock price, P, is equal to its intrinsic value, S. That is, $k_s = D/P + g$. You may have learned this method in a previous course.

If P and D are denominated in US dollars, the estimated cost of equity is also in US dollars, and should be denoted $k_s^\$$. The cost of equity for the firm in euros could be found by setting up the same model but denominating D and P in euros. Note that the expected growth rate of a firm's future dividends expressed in euros will not necessarily be equal to the expected growth rate of the *same* future dividends expressed in US dollars, mainly because of the expected rate of change of the FX rate.

THE CAPITAL ASSET PRICING MODEL

In an efficient stock market, it is reasonable to assume that $P = S$, but what if the market is not efficient? One would not want to use an observed stock price to deduce a cost of equity if the price of the stock is known to be different from its intrinsic value. Or, what if the valuation model used to estimate the cost of equity is not correct, perhaps because the model's growth rate assumption is not valid?

For these reasons a second approach to estimate the cost of equity has become standard: a risk–return model, particularly the CAPM. In a 1995 survey of 27 highly regarded companies, the most common model used to estimate the cost of equity was found to be the CAPM. A more comprehensive survey published in 2001 reported that 73.5% of 392 responding companies use the CAPM to estimate the cost of equity.[4]

In the CAPM, asset i's *equilibrium* expected rate of return is $k_i = r_f + \beta_{iM}[RP_M]$, where r_f is the risk-free rate of interest, β_{iM} is the systematic risk (beta) of asset i relative to the market portfolio, and RP_M is the *market risk premium*. An asset's beta measures the risk the asset contributes to a well-diversified portfolio.

The market risk premium, RP_M, is equal to $k_M - r_f$, the minimum rate of return over the risk-free rate that investors (in the aggregate) require as compensation for the risk in the most diversified portfolio possible, the market portfolio. The market risk premium, RP_M, depends not only on how much risk is in the overall market but also on the average investor's degree of risk aversion. Thus RP_M can change as market volatility changes and as investors become more or less averse to risk.

---

[4]The first study is in R. F. Bruner, K. M. Eades, R. S. Harris, and R. C. Higgins, "Best Practices in Estimating the Cost of Capital: Survey and Synthesis," *Financial Practice and Education*, Spring/Summer 1998, 13–28. The second is in J. R. Graham and C. R. Harvey, "The Theory and Practice of Corporate Finance: Evidence from the Field," *Journal of Financial Economics*, May 2001, 187–243. An example of valuation with the CAPM is in Samuel Thompson, "Demystifying the Use of Beta in the Determination of the Cost of Capital and an Illustration of Its Use in Lazard's Valuation of Conrail," at http://papers2.ssrn.com/paper.taf?ABSTRACT_ID=223797.

Sometimes k_M is called the expected return on the market portfolio, but this terminology can be misleading. It is more accurate to say that k_M is the *equilibrium* expected return on the market portfolio, not the actually expected rate of return. Similarly, the equilibrium expected rate of return on stock i, k_i, is not the actual expected stock return; rather, it is the minimum expected return, or required rate of return, that investors must earn to compensate for the risk the stock contributes to their well-diversified portfolios. This is the cost of equity.

As the world's financial markets continue to integrate, especially through electronic systems, we have realized that the CAPM must be interpreted in a global sense. We should think in terms of a common risk–return trade-off for *all* assets in an integrated global financial market, given the common currency chosen to express asset returns. This is a provocative idea. It means that we have to consider all assets, regardless of nationality or whether we choose to express the trade-off in US dollars, in euros, or in any other currency. For example, we think of the required rate of return in US dollars on a euro-denominated bond.

Figure 9.1 shows the idea graphically. You can think of the line as representing the expected rate of return that would be required on an asset in US dollars as compensation for risk. Actual expected returns for assets may plot off the line, but the line shows the relationship between risk and expected return in equilibrium.

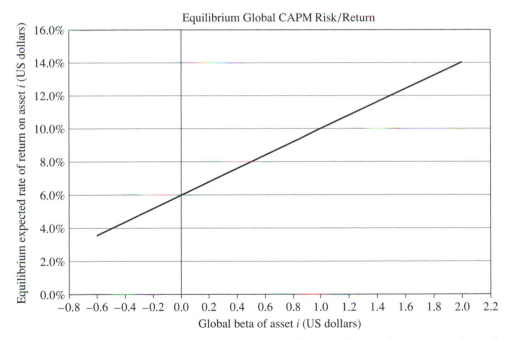

Figure 9.1 The equilibrium risk–return relationship of the global CAPM; the assets are from all countries, but the returns are in US dollars. The risk–return trade-off line intercepts the Y-axis at the US dollar risk-free rate, and the slope is the risk premium in US dollars required on the global market portfolio.

This notion of using one risk–return trade-off for all assets in the world, including foreign equities, bonds, and other assets, requires a conceptual leap because we have traditionally taken a risk–return relationship in US dollars to apply to US assets, or a risk–return relationship in British pounds to apply to UK assets, and so on. In fact, the tradition comes out of an implicit assumption that national financial markets are segmented rather than related to the rest of the world. Today, with a global financial market, we must abandon this traditional notion. These days, we are in a new world, and the most logical risk–return model is the global CAPM applied to all assets.

In the CAPM tradition, the required rate of return on asset i in the global CAPM depends on three factors: a beta, a market risk premium, and a risk-free rate. It is the interpretation of the three factors that distinguishes the global CAPM from the traditional CAPM. Asset i's equilibrium expected rate of return in US dollars, $k_i^\$$, is given in the global CAPM in equation (9.2):

$$k_i^\$ = r_f^\$ + \beta_{iG}^\$(RP_G^\$) \tag{9.2}$$

In the global CAPM, we interpret the market portfolio as the *global market portfolio*, which would theoretically be the portfolio of all risky assets in the world. Even though the global market portfolio includes assets from countries around the world, the rate of return on it is expressed in terms of US dollars for purposes of applying equation (9.2). In other words, we do not simply combine the rates of return on all risky assets from the standpoint of their local currencies. Instead, we must adjust all rates of return to one currency. That is, the global market index should be an *unhedged index* meaning that the FX changes are part of the returns, as in the case of the US dollar returns of Alstom.

Although the Dow Jones World Index is an unhedged global index reported in US dollars in the *Wall Street Journal*, many regard the MSCI World Index as the best global market index. (MSCI stands for Morgan Stanley Capital International.) The MSCI World Index is an unhedged index that can be expressed from the point of view of any currency, inclusive of the impact of FX changes on foreign shares.

In equation (9.2), $RP_G^\$$ represents the *global risk premium* in US dollars, the equilibrium required rate of return on the overall unhedged global market portfolio in US dollars minus the US dollar risk-free rate. Again, this risk premium reflects two factors: (1) the level of risk in the global equity market and (2) the degree to which investors are averse to risk. Thus the global risk premium is likely to change with market conditions. Different sources recommend different estimates for $RP_G^\$$. Based on recent estimates, we will consistently use 4% for $RP_G^\$$ in all our examples.[5]

In CAPM theory, investors hold the market portfolio. Thirty years ago, we said that investors could not possibly hold the entire market portfolio, or even the S&P 500 stock portfolio. But the creation of index funds in the 1970s changed that. We do not know of a global index fund or a world index fund at present, but the emergence of such a fund seems only a matter of time. Already there are *iShares* for many of the MSCI country indexes.

---

[5]See G. Donaldson, M. Kamstra, and L. Kramer, "Stare Down the Barrel and Center the Crosshairs: Targeting the Ex Ante Equity Premium," at http://papers.ssrn.com/sol3/papers.cfm? abstract_id=308743. Note that the global beta of the US market has been about 1 in recent years, so the US equity market risk premium and the global risk premium would be the same.

The iShares are *exchange-traded funds (ETFs)*, which are like mutual funds of baskets of stocks, but ETFs trade continuously. The iShares on MSCI country indexes are like ADRs, but the underlying "stock" is an MSCI country index. There are also iShares on many other stock indexes, including stock indexes for entire regions of the world, so why not one for the MSCI World Index? You can find out more about iShares by a means of a Web search; one site is http://mutualfunds.about.com/cs/etfs/l/blisharelist.htm.

There are versions of international asset pricing models more complex than the global CAPM in equation (9.2). Some of the versions contain extra factors for FX risk. In practice, the marginal benefits of using a more complex model may not justify the additional complexity. That is, the simple global CAPM in equation (9.2) should be sufficient as a model of risk and return to provide a useful estimate a firm's cost of equity.[6]

One worry that some have about the global CAPM is that investors tend to invest more in stocks of their own country than would be advisable given the benefits of international diversification. This tendency is called *home bias*. Researchers are exploring why home bias occurs and debating whether it means that a local CAPM should be applied instead of a global CAPM. Despite the home bias, the global CAPM seems to be a better model of risk and return in integrated financial markets than the local CAPM.

GLOBAL EQUITY BETA AND THE COST OF EQUITY

One factor that determines an asset's required rate of return in US dollars in equation (9.2) is the asset's *global beta* measured in US dollars, denoted $\beta_{iG}^{\$}$. An asset's global beta measures the tendency of its US dollar returns to move systematically with the US dollar returns of an unhedged global market index.

Estimated global equity betas against the MSCI World Index, in US dollars, for selected firms are shown in Table 9.3, along with the estimated traditional local (US) equity betas for comparison. Several estimation periods are shown. For example, with monthly returns from January 1992 through January 2000, IBM's global equity beta in US dollars was estimated to be 0.83. This estimate represents the systematic risk of the firm's equity as viewed by a holder of US dollars in an unhedged, globally diversified equity portfolio.

Let us assume that the US dollar risk-free rate is 6%. With a global risk premium of 4% and IBM's global equity beta in US dollars estimated at 0.83, the US dollar cost of equity for IBM is $k_i^{\$} = 0.06 + 0.83(0.04) = 0.093$, or 9.30%. Sony, with an estimated global beta of 1.66 (in US dollars), would have a cost of equity in US dollars of $0.06 + 1.66(0.04) = 0.126$, or 12.6%.

---

[6]More details on the simple global CAPM by one of the pioneers of international asset pricing theory are in R. Stulz, "Globalization of Capital Markets and the Cost of Capital: The Case of Nestlé," *Journal of Applied Corporate Finance*, Fall 1995, 30–38. A study that supports the use of the simple global CAPM over the more complex international asset pricing models is in D. Ng, "The International CAPM When Expected Returns Are Time-Varying," *Journal of International Money and Finance*, February 2004, 189–230.

TABLE 9.3 Global Betas vs Local US Betas

Company	Period	BETAS (US$)	
		Global	Local
IBM	1992–2000	0.83	1.06
	1993–2000	0.78	1.03
	1994–2000	1.02	1.02
	1995–2000	1.00	1.02
Procter & Gamble	1992–2000	0.70	0.92
	1993–2000	0.73	0.87
	1994–2000	0.88	0.89
	1995–2000	0.84	0.84
Kellogg	1992–2000	0.28	0.49
	1993–2000	0.37	0.57
	1994–2000	0.52	0.56
	1995–2000	0.54	0.62
Coca-Cola	1992–2000	0.77	0.94
	1993–2000	0.78	0.95
	1994–2000	0.96	0.93
	1995–2000	1.02	1.06
Colgate-Palmolive	1992–2000	1.24	1.30
	1993–2000	1.38	1.33
	1994–2000	1.56	1.38
	1995–2000	1.61	1.42
Sony	1992–2000	1.66	0.96
	1993–2000	1.69	1.00
	1994–2000	1.62	1.03
	1995–2000	1.57	1.02
Local US market	1970–2000	0.90	1.00
	1970–1980	1.03	1.00
	1980–1990	0.91	1.00
	1990–2000	0.75	1.00
	1992–2000	0.84	1.00
	1995–2000	0.99	1.00

Source: Author's computations using the method of Interactive Exercise 9.1.

If Colgate-Palmolive's global beta were 1.50, what would be the firm's cost of equity in US dollars, given US dollar risk-free rate of 5.60% and a global risk premium of 4% in US dollars?

Answer: Using equation (9.2), Colgate-Palmolive's estimated cost of equity in US dollars would be 0.056 + 1.50(0.04) = 0.116, or 11.60%.

In general, the global CAPM and the local CAPM will not give the same cost of equity estimates, as shown in the box on Coca-Cola. Since the global beta of the US market index is about 1 (see Table 9.3), the risk premium on the US market should be the same as the global risk premium. [In the early 1990s the US equity markets and those of other countries diverged enough to result, for a time, in a global beta of the US equity market lower than 1. Of course this could happen again, but in 2005 the global beta of the US market appears to be around 1.] Thus the error one would make in using the local US CAPM when the global CAPM is the correct theory will be a function of the extent of difference between a stock's global beta and local beta.

A firm's global beta may be higher or lower than its traditional local beta. For example, IBM's local beta versus the US market was 1.06 over the 1992–2000 period, higher than its global beta of 0.83. On the other hand, for 1994–2000, Colgate-Palmolive's global beta, 1.56, was higher than its local beta with the US market, 1.38.

Sony, a Japanese firm, had ADR returns in US dollars that had a global beta of 1.66 over the 1992–2000 period. Sony's returns in US dollars were more sensitive than IBM's to the global index returns. Using the estimated global beta, Sony will have a higher cost of equity, expressed in US dollars, than IBM. That Sony is headquartered in Japan has no bearing on the fact that a US investor holding a globally diversified portfolio views Sony's risk as its beta relative to the global market index.

Sony's global beta estimates are also higher than its beta estimates versus the national US index. The Sony betas may help one see that a firm with a higher correlation with the global than with the national index is likely to have a higher global beta than local beta. Correspondingly, a firm more correlated with the national index than with the global index may have a higher local beta than global beta.

According to a study of the differences in the cost of equity estimates, measured in US dollars, of the global CAPM and local US CAPM, the average difference in the cost of equity estimates for almost 3000 US stocks, is about 50 basis points.[7] Many analysts may view 50 basis points as insignificant, especially given the imprecision of forecasted cash flows. This may explain why many companies are currently continuing to use the traditional (local US) CAPM in cost of equity estimation for US stocks.

COST OF EQUITY FOR COCA-COLA: GLOBAL CAPM VS LOCAL CAPM

Let us say that we want to use 1993–2000 data in Table 9.3 to estimate the cost of equity for Coca-Cola. Let us assume a risk-free rate in US dollars of 5% and a global risk premium in US dollars of 4%.

(continued)

---

[7]For 70 ADRs from developed markets, the corresponding average difference is 76 basis points. For 48 ADRs from emerging markets, the corresponding average difference is 57 basis points. See D. Mishra and T. O'Brien, "A Comparison of Cost of Equity Estimates of Local and Global CAPMs," *Financial Review*, November 2001, 27–48, at http://papers.ssrn.com/sol3/papers.cfm?abstract_id=261052.

Coke's global beta is estimated to be 0.78. So the cost of equity in US dollars would be estimated to be $0.05 + 0.78(0.04) = 0.0812$, or 8.12%.

Assuming that the global CAPM is the best model of risk and required return, how much error would be made in Coke's cost of equity estimate if one uses the local CAPM instead? Since the global beta of the US market is about 1, it is reasonable to think that the required risk premium on the US market portfolio is the same as on the global market portfolio, 4%. Coke's local beta is estimated to be 0.95. So the cost of equity would be estimated to be $0.05 + 0.95(0.04) = 0.088$, or 8.80%.

If the local CAPM is used, the estimated cost of equity of 8.80% is 68 basis points higher than the cost of equity estimate from the global CAPM.

Right now, there are no easy-to-find published global beta estimates. The only way to obtain a global beta estimate is to use regression analysis, as described in Interactive Exercise 9.1. Of course, the choice of time span affects the estimated beta. And one must use judgment in determining whether the company's operating and financial structures were consistent during the estimation span with conditions expected in the future.[8]

Local betas are readily available, so you might be tempted to think you can calculate a firm's global beta by multiplying its local beta by the global beta of the local US market index. This would not be correct; a global beta is not estimated in this indirect way. You can see this looking at 1992–2000 data from Table 9.3. The directly calculated estimate of the global beta of the local US market is 0.84 (see Table 9.3). Using the indirect method, and recalling that IBM's local US equity beta is 1.06, you would get a global beta estimate for IBM of 0.89 $(= 1.06 \times 0.84)$. This estimate is obviously incorrect, since it is not equal to IBM's global beta calculated directly, 0.83. The indirect approach is invalid whenever the global market index can explain any portion of an asset's returns not explained by the national market index, as is usually the case.

INTERACTIVE EXERCISE 9.1

Estimate the Global Equity Beta for a Company in US Dollars

The MSCI World Index values (in US dollars) from 1970 can be downloaded at no charge at http://www.mscidata.com/. You may have to register, which will take a few minutes.

To download the monthly values of the Developed Market "Gross Index" (i.e., with dividends reinvested) into Excel, first click on the World Index, the first listing on the home page. On the next page change "type" to "Gross Index (DM)," and put in the "span." Then click on "Download to Excel." When you open the file in Excel, save it as an Excel workbook file. You can then convert the MSCI World Index values into rates of return.

---

[8]For a useful exposition of beta estimation, see Aswath Damodaran, "Estimating Risk Parameters." Go to http://www.stern.nyu.edu/~adamodar/, then click "Research & Papers."

Historical prices of equities of individual companies in US dollars (adjusted for dividends and splits) can be downloaded at no change at http://chart.yahoo.com/t. Go to the site and indicate the time period (e.g., January 31, 1992, through January 31, 2003), the interval (e.g., "monthly"), and the ticker symbol. The last column of the page that appears is the "adjusted (for dividends and splits) close," which is what you want and what you get when you scroll down and click on "download spreadsheet format." Open the file in Excel. Save it as an Excel workbook. The data you want (adjusted prices) are in column E, but first reverse the order. There is a shortcut for this on the toolbar, or you can go to "data," then "sort," and then sort by "date" "ascending." You can then convert the values in column E into a time series of returns as done with the MSCI World index.

Next you need to copy/paste (you may have to use "paste special" and "values") the two return series onto a common spreadsheet. Once you have a column of individual stock returns and a column of MSCI World Index returns, consistently aligned by date on the same spreadsheet, you are ready to compute global betas. Go to "tools," then "data analysis." If "data analysis" does not show when you pull down the "tools" menu, choose "add-in," and check the "analysis pack." Then the "data analysis" will be a "tools" option. Choose "regression" and "OK." For "y range," put in the stock return range; for "x range," put in the MSCI World Index range. Then hit "OK." The "X-variable coefficient" will be the estimate of the stock's global equity beta, in US dollars.

You may find the following Web site helpful: http://business.fullerton.edu/mstohs/Regression%20in%20EXCEL.htm.

RISK-FREE RATE

The risk-free rate used in equation (9.2) is for an asset that is risk-free in US dollars. It is *not* some kind of world average of risk-free rates in various currencies. The term "risk-free rate" as used here means the *nominal* interest rate on an asset that has no credit risk.

There has been much debate over whether US firms should use a short-term Treasury bill rate or a long-term Treasury bond rate as the risk-free rate in the CAPM. Indeed, surveys find that companies are split on the issue. The best approach may be to view the proper risk-free rate as dependent on the horizon of the application. For cost of equity estimation, the horizon is long-term.

Rather than use a straight Treasury bond yield, though, an adjustment may be advantageous. Since Treasury bond returns fluctuate with interest rate levels, and since interest rate levels affect the overall economy, it is reasonable to think that Treasury bond returns may be related somewhat to the market portfolio. Indeed, studies have shown the beta of long-term Treasury bonds to be between 0.10 and 0.20, so let's assume a long-term Treasury bond beta of 0.15.[9] Assume further that the current 30-year US Treasury bond rate is 5%.

---

[9] See B. Cornell and K. Green, "Measuring the Investment Performance of Low-Grade Bond Funds," *Journal of Finance*, March 1991, 29–48.

Now what is the long-term risk-free rate? To answer this question, we apply the global CAPM as if the long-term Treasury bond is asset *i*. The required return on the asset is observable, 0.05. Put this return on the left-hand side of equation (9.2). On the right-hand side, plug in the bond's global beta of 0.15 and an assumed global risk premium of 0.04. We see from equation (9.2) that the required rate of return of 0.05 equals the risk-free rate plus 0.15(0.04), or 0.006. Thus the long-term US dollar risk-free rate is about 60 basis points lower than the long-term US Treasury bond rate. If the long-term T-bond rate is 5%, then the long-term risk-free rate is 0.050 − 0.006 = 0.044, or 4.40%; if the long-term T-bond rate is 4%, then the long-term risk-free rate is 0.040 − 0.006 = 0.034, or 3.40%.

Given a long-term US Treasury bond rate of 6.40%, a global beta of 0.15 for the long-term US Treasury bond, and a global market risk premium of 4% in US dollars, what is the long-term US dollar risk-free rate?

Answer: The long-term US dollar risk-free rate is 0.064 − 0.15(0.04) = 0.058, or 5.80%.

Warning: The analysis in this section of the long-term risk-free rate is not commonly used. Most analysts simply use a US Treasury bond yield as the US dollar risk-free rate for long-term investments.

COST OF DEBT AND THE WACC

Suppose McDonald's has total debt of $100 million; $50 million of it is US dollar debt yielding 8% and $50 million is yen-denominated debt yielding 2% in yen. Does this mean McDonald's overall cost of debt is 0.50(8%) + 0.50(2%) = 5%? No, because US dollar debt is apples while yen-denominated debt is oranges. Yields in different currencies cannot be compared or averaged meaningfully. What we need to know is the cost of yen-denominated debt in US dollars, given that its yield in yen is 2%.

The approximation in equation (9.1b) tells us that the ex post rate of return on yen-denominated debt to a US investor will be approximately equal to the debt's yield in yen plus the percentage change in the FX price of the yen, $x^{\$/¥}$. We are making a reasonable assumption of a zero correlation between the debt's return in yen and FX changes, so that we can use equation (9.1b) rather than equation (9.1c). If the interest rate on the debt is 2% and the yen appreciates by 10%, the total ex post cost of the yen debt is approximately 12% in US dollars. Thus we see that in addition to the yield in yen, the cost of yen debt in US dollars must account for the change in the FX price of the yen.

To figure a firm's cost of debt for investment analysis, you use the ex ante cost of debt. In the same manner that a cost of equity is a required expected rate of return in US dollars, the cost of yen-denominated debt in US dollars involves the required rate of return by investors in US dollars. Since investors will receive the yen debt's yen yield, they also *require* a minimum expected change in the FX value of the yen to make the bond's required return in US dollars consistent with its risk in US dollars.

The required expected change in the FX value of the yen by investors makes the yen debt's US dollar expected return plot on the equilibrium global CAPM line in Figure 9.1. Thus, the required expected change in the FX value of the yen is the equilibrium expected change in the FX value of the yen, $E(x*^{\$/¥})$. As in Chapter 4, the asterisk denotes equilibrium. If the yield on yen-denominated debt is 2% in yen, we need to add to that the equilibrium expected change in the spot FX value of the yen, $E(x*^{\$/¥})$, to find the cost of the debt in US dollars to the firm that issues the debt.

For example, if the equilibrium expected percentage change in the FX value of the yen, $E(x*^{\$/¥})$, is 5%, then the cost of the yen debt in US dollars in this case is 2% + 5% = 7%.

The cost of a firm's debt is generally denoted k_d, but we need to add a pricing currency superscript. The overall cost of all of a firm's debt, measured in US dollars, will be denoted $k_d^{\$}$, and the overall cost of all its debt measured in yen is denoted $k_d^{¥}$. We use another subscript to denote the currency in which a debt is denominated. $k_{\$d}^{\$}$ would denote the cost of US dollar-denominated debt in US dollars, $k_{¥d}^{\$}$ the cost of yen-denominated debt in US dollars, $k_{¥d}^{¥}$ the cost of yen debt in yen, and so forth. The US dollar cost of a firm's yen debt is expressed in equation (9.3):

$$k_{¥d}^{\$} = k_{¥d}^{¥} + E(x*^{\$/¥}) \tag{9.3}$$

The traditional UIRP condition of Chapter 4 provides a way to estimate the expected equilibrium percentage change in the FX value of the yen. In linear approximation form, $E(x*^{\$/¥}) = r_f^{\$} - r_f^{¥}$. If we are thinking about the short run, say, a year, one-year LIBOR (eurocurrency) rates should be good proxies for risk-free rates. If the horizon is longer, one could reasonably use government bond yields as proxies for the risk-free rates. [Even though we adjusted the T-bond yield to get the long-term risk-free rate earlier, it is not worth the effort to do this here; the adjustments for the two interest rates would likely almost cancel each other out.]

Let's say that the risk-free rate in US dollars is 6% and the risk-free rate in yen is 1%. Then with the linear approximation of the traditional UIRP, we estimate $E(x*^{\$/¥})$, to be 5%. Thus if a firm issues yen-denominated debt at a yield of 2%, the cost of the yen-denominated debt in US dollars is 2% + 5% = 7%, from equation (9.3).

To find a firm's overall cost of debt in a given currency, we need to specify all the costs from that currency's point of view. Assume again that half of McDonald's debt is US dollar debt, and the other half is yen debt. If the US dollar cost of US dollar debt is 6.5% and the US dollar cost of yen debt is 7%, McDonald's overall cost of debt is US dollars, $k_d^{\$}$, is 0.50(0.065) + 0.50(0.070) = 0.0675, or 6.75%.

Assume that McDonald's debt represents 35% of the firm's intrinsic value. Assume McDonald's cost of equity in US dollars is 9% and its effective tax rate is 30%.[10] Then McDonald's WACC in US dollars would be $k_w^{\$} = w_d k_d^{\$}(1 - t) + w_s k_s^{\$} = 0.35(1 - 0.30)$ (0.0675) + 0.65(0.09) = 0.075, or 7.5%.

---

[10]A detailed analysis of the tax rules is beyond the scope at present. Moreover, the tax rate does not have a big impact on the WACC. For more information on tax rules in global business, see Chapters 10 and 11 in M. Scholes, M. Wolfson, M. Erickson, E. Maydew, and T. Shevlin, *Taxes and Business Strategy*, 2nd ed. (Upper Saddle River, NJ: Prentice Hall, 2002).

GRANDMET'S WACC (1997)

Grand Metropolitan, PLC, was at one time a multinational company in the food and beverage industry. The company has since merged with Guinness to form Diageo. GrandMet's capital structure consisted 25% US dollar debt, 20% British pound debt, and 55% equity. The effective tax rate was 35%.

In 1997, historical ADR returns in US dollars were used to estimate GrandMet's equity global beta, 1.25. Given a US dollar risk-free rate of 5% and a global risk premium of 4%, GrandMet's estimated cost of equity was 10%.

Say the before-tax cost of the US dollar debt in US dollars was 5.75% and the before-tax cost of the British pound debt in British pounds was 8.25%. Assume that the British pound risk-free rate was 7%. Using the traditional UIRP, the estimate of the equilibrium expected percentage change in the FX value of the pound would be 5% − 7% = −2%. The before-tax cost of the British pound debt in US dollars, from equation (9.3) would be 8.25% − 2% = 6.25%.

GrandMet's WACC in US dollars would be 0.25(1 − 0.35)(5.75%) + 0.20 (1 − 0.35)(6.25%) + 0.55(10%) = 7.25%.

A more detailed example of GrandMet's WACC is in T. O'Brien, "The Global CAPM and a Firm's Cost of Capital in Different Currencies," *Journal of Applied Corporate Finance*, Fall 1999, 73–79.

XYZ Company has 70% US dollar debt with a yield of 7%, and 30% Swiss franc debt with a yield of 5%. The debt percentages are figured using current market values of the debt. XYZ managers have estimated the equilibrium expected percentage change in the FX value of the Swiss franc is 2.60% per year. Assume that XYZ's debt represents 40% of the firm's intrinsic value, the firm's effective tax rate is 25%, and its cost of equity in US dollars is 10%. (a) What is XYZ's cost of the Swiss franc debt in US dollars? (b) What is the overall cost of its debt in US dollars? (c) What is XYZ's WACC in US dollars?

Answers: (a) The US dollar cost of the Swiss franc debt is 0.05 + 0.026 = 0.076, or 7.60%. (b) XYZ's overall cost of debt in US dollars is 0.70(0.070) + 0.30(0.076) = 0.0718, or 7.18%. (c) XYZ's WACC in US dollars would be $k_w^\$ = w_d k_d^\$ (1 - t) + w_s k_s^\$ = 0.40(1 - 0.25)(0.0718) + 0.60(0.10) = 0.082$, or 8.20%.

Note that we do not use managers' actual forecasted percentage change in the FX price of the yen to find the cost of yen debt in US dollars. If the forecasted percentage change in the FX price of the yen is different from the estimated *equilibrium* expected percentage change in the FX value of the yen, then the firm is predicting a windfall gain or loss in US dollars on its yen-denominated debt, but such a gain or loss is not an element in the cost of capital. A firm's cost of capital should reflect the minimum required rate of return as compensation for risk, apart from any projected gain or loss because the FX rate is forecasted to provide a change different from the equilibrium expected change.

There is a similar issue with using financial engineering to exploit a market inefficiency in financing. For example, ABC may be able to use a currency swap to obtain a lower interest rate, by taking creative advantage of some inefficiency such as a difference in credit perceptions of issuers and investors. Although the company might end up with a lower effective interest rate in US dollars on synthetic US dollar debt than actual US dollar debt, ABC should look at this as a windfall profit from a special situation that would not be available all the time. ABC should still view the cost of its debt as the market yield for actual US dollar debt, which is the opportunity cost of raising new US dollar debt.

In a market where there are no inefficiencies and all securities are properly priced, the cost of actual US dollar debt and synthetic US dollar debt through a swap should be the same. Suppose your firm's US dollar cost of US dollar debt is 6.50%. If you issue yen debt and then take a long yen position in a currency swap, you are effectively swapping the yen debt into synthetic US dollar debt. The interest rates built into the swap will force the cost of synthetic US dollar debt to be the same as actual US dollar debt (except possibly for some pocket of market inefficiency). After you take the swap position, the debt effectively becomes US dollar debt, even if it is synthetic. If you take no swap position, and you thus maintain the yen-denominated debt, the cost of the debt, measured in US dollars, is 7%, not 6.50%. That is, the cost of yen debt, measured in US dollars, is not the same as the cost of US dollar-denominated debt (synthetic or not), as we know.

So why would a firm have any yen debt at all, if the cost of yen debt in US dollars is higher than the cost of US dollar debt? We discussed the use of foreign currency debt in hedging long-term FX exposure Chapter 6. But there is more that we can say after we look at systematic FX risk.

SYSTEMATIC FX RISK

We can think of the FX rate for a currency as having a beta like any other asset. Since equity values of individual stocks are sensitive to changes in FX rates, it makes sense that a covariance exists between stocks on the whole (i.e., the market) and FX rates.[11]

This covariance is measured by the beta of the FX rate. We denote the beta of percentage exchange rate changes, $x^{\$/€}$, as $\beta_€^\$$, and call it the euro's *FX global beta*. The FX global beta of the euro is the beta of the percentage changes in the FX value of the euro versus the global market index, where the US dollar is the pricing currency.

Some rudimentary FX global beta estimates are shown in Table 9.4. These estimates were made with the simple regression approach in Interactive Exercise 9.2 and are only to

---

[11]Empirical evidence supports this. See B. Francis and D. Hunter, "The Role of Currency Risk in Industry Cost of Capital," Working Paper, University of South Florida, 2004.

TABLE 9.4 FX Global Beta Estimates

Currency	May 1999– March 2004	November 1995– October 2000
Australian dollar	0.21	0.34
Euro (mark)	−0.02	0.05
Japanese yen	0.10	0.30
Swedish krona	0.07	0.10
Swiss franc	−0.043	−0.14
UK pound	0.04	0.10

Source: Author's computations using the method in Interactive Exercise 9.2.

convey the idea. As you can see in Table 9.4, estimates of FX global betas with actual FX data will change some over time. The changes occur for statistical reasons as well as because of changes in the economic structure of a particular country compared with the rest of the world and other changes in market conditions. More accurate estimates would have to be based on market factors and would require advanced econometric techniques. We'll use FX global betas in the next section and in Chapter 10.

INTERACTIVE EXERCISE 9.2

Estimate the FX Global Beta for a Currency

The MSCI World Index returns in US dollars, as in Interactive Exercise 9.1, should be used (in US dollars) as the X variable again.

The FX data may be downloaded from the Federal Reserve Bank of St. Louis at http://www.stls.frb.org/fred/data/exchange.html.

At the location, click on the exchange rate for which you want to download monthly FX rates. You can choose to get the FX rates in an Excel file. The FX rates should be reciprocated if in European terms. Then make a column of time series of the percentage changes in the FX price of the foreign currency, and copy the column. Paste ("paste special", "values") the FX percentage changes into the worksheet with the MSCI World Index returns. You are ready to do "tools," "data analysis," and then "regression" to get estimates of the FX global beta.

---

*RISK-ADJUSTED UNCOVERED INTEREST RATE PARITY

We can use the global CAPM to improve the traditional uncovered interest rate parity (UIRP) condition by adding a risk premium for systematic FX risk. This improvement in the UIRP will result in a modest improvement in estimates of the equilibrium expected rate of change in FX values.

We start with the cost of debt in US dollars on a risk-free euro asset, denoted $k_{\mathpalette\@\relax f}^{\$}$. Denoting the cost of risk-free euro debt in euros as $r_{f}^{\euro}$, the application of equation (9.3) results in $k_{\mathpalette\@\relax f}^{\$} = r_{f}^{\euro} + E(x*^{\$/\euro})$. But we can also look at the US dollar required rate of return on the risk-free euro asset using the global CAPM. Since the only uncertainty in the US dollar return on a risk-free euro asset is FX uncertainty, a risk-free euro asset has a global beta in US dollars that is equal to the global beta of $x^{\$/\euro}$, $\beta_{\euro}^{\$}$.

We can apply the global CAPM in equation (9.2) to estimate a US dollar investor's *required* return on a risk-free euro asset, as compensation for the (global) systematic risk of the euro: $k_{\mathpalette\@\relax f}^{\$} = r_{f}^{\$} + \beta_{\euro}^{\$}[RP_{G}^{\$}]$. What we are saying is that the required rate of return on the risk-free euro asset must be consistent with its global beta; that is, the asset must plot on the risk–return line of the global CAPM in Figure 9.1, like all assets. Assuming $r_{f}^{\$} = 6\%$, $RP_{G}^{\$} = 4\%$, and $\beta_{\euro}^{\$} = 0.20$, the US dollar *required* rate of return on a risk-free euro asset would be $0.06 + 0.20(0.04) = 0.068$, or 6.80%. The risk-free euro asset's required rate of return in US dollars is 6.80%, in equilibrium. Thus we can also say that the US dollar cost of risk-free euro debt is 6.80%.

We did not specify the euro risk-free rate, $r_{f}^{\euro}$, to find the cost of risk-free euro debt in US dollars using the global CAPM. A currency's own risk-free rate, such as on a government security, is observable just like the US dollar risk-free rate. Let us assume that we observe $r_{f}^{\euro} = 3\%$. Let us use this rate, after setting the linear approximation of the expected equilibrium US dollar return on the risk-free euro asset, $r_{f}^{\euro} + E(x*^{\$/\euro})$, equal to the equilibrium required rate of return of 6.80% found using the global CAPM. When we plug 0.03 in for $r_{f}^{\euro}$, the equilibrium expected percentage change in the FX value of the euro, $E(x*^{\$/\euro})$, is $0.068 - 0.03 = 0.038$, or 3.80%.

We have equated the definition of the equilibrium expected US dollar return on the risk-free euro asset, $r_{f}^{\euro} + E(x*^{\$/\euro})$ (an application of equation (9.3)), with the asset's required US dollar return, $r_{f}^{\$} + \beta_{\euro}^{\$}[RP_{G}^{\$}]$ (an application of the global CAPM in equation (9.2)). The result is a risk-adjusted UIRP relationship in linear approximation percentage form, expressed in equation (9.4).

Risk-Adjusted UIRP Condition
Percentage Form—Linear Approximation

$$E(x*^{\$/\euro}) = r_{f}^{\$} - r_{f}^{\euro} + \beta_{\euro}^{\$}(RP_{G}^{\$}) \tag{9.4}$$

The risk-adjusted UIRP relationship in equation (9.4) adds the risk premium $\beta_{\euro}^{\$}(RP_{G}^{\$})$ to the traditional linear percentage form of the UIRP, $E(x*^{\$/\euro}) = r_{f}^{\$} - r_{f}^{\euro}$. This lets us adjust the traditional UIRP for the systematic risk of the FX rate (i.e., the FX global beta).

Note that we specify the risk-adjusted UIRP in equation (9.4) only in the direction of the US dollar as the pricing currency, which is expressed in terms of the expected change in the value of the non–US dollar currency. Equation (9.4) cannot be rotated into European terms to find the expected change in the FX value of the US dollar (relative to the foreign currency), the way we can turn around the traditional UIRP condition. The reason has to do with the risk adjustment factor. We will address this problem in Chapter 10.

Assume an FX global beta for yen of $\beta_\yen^\$ = 0.25$. Assume that the yen risk-free interest rate is $r_f^\yen = 0.02$ and the US dollar risk-free rate is $r_f^\$ = 0.055$. (a) For an issuer of risk-free yen debt, use the global CAPM to find the cost of the debt in US dollars. (b) Find the equilibrium expected percentage change in the FX value of the yen, given the global CAPM, and assuming a global risk premium of 4%.

Answers: (a) Using the global CAPM, the US dollar cost of the yen risk-free debt is 0.055 + 0.25(0.04) = 0.065. (b) Using the risk-adjusted UIRP condition in equation (9.4), $E(x^{*\$/\yen}) = r_f^\$ - r_f^\yen + \beta_\yen^\$[RP_G^\$] = 0.055 - 0.02 + 0.25(0.04) = 0.045$, or 4.5%. Since the US dollar cost of the yen risk-free debt (6.50%) is equal to the yen risk-free rate (2%) plus $E(x^{*\$/\yen})$, we can reconcile that 6.50% = 2% + 4.50%.

How much difference in WACC estimation does it make to incorporate systematic FX risk? The answer depends on how big the FX global beta is and how much of the debt is foreign currency debt. Assume an FX global beta for the British pound of 0.10 (see Table 9.4), a risk-free rate in US dollars of 5%, a risk-free rate in British pounds of 7%, and a global risk premium of 4%. Using equation (9.4), the equilibrium expected rate of change in the FX value of the pound would be 5% − 7% + 0.10(4%) = −1.60%, instead of 5% − 7% = −2% with the traditional UIRP condition. This says that when the systematic risk of FX changes are considered, as is the case in the risk-adjusted UIRP condition, investors require a higher return in US dollars on the pound bond than they would when this risk is ignored, as it is in the traditional UIRP condition. The required rate of return in US dollars by investors in GrandMet's pound debt would be 8.25% − 1.60% = 6.65% instead of 8.25% − 2% = 6.25% in the box on GrandMet. The estimated cost of British pound debt in US dollars for GrandMet would be 6.65% if the risk-adjust UIRP condition is used instead of 6.25% with the traditional UIRP condition.

Because the risk adjustment is not very large, and because the pound-denominated debt is only 20% of GrandMet's capital structure, GrandMet's WACC in US dollars would not be much different when the risk-adjusted UIRP condition is used: 0.25(1 − 0.35)(5.75%) + 0.20(1 − 0.35)(6.60%) + 0.55(10%) = 7.29%. The WACC was 7.25% in the GrandMet box, where the traditional UIRP condition was used.

We see now that a firm's cost of its yen debt in US dollars differs from the cost of US dollar debt in US dollars partly because of the portion of the expected equilibrium change of the yen that compensates investors for the systematic risk of the yen. This helps us better understand why a firm has any yen debt at all, if its cost in US dollars is higher than the cost of US dollar debt. The cost of yen debt in US dollars is based on the equilibrium expected change in the FX value of the yen, given the systematic risk of the yen, $\beta_\yen^\$$. If the cost of yen debt in US dollars is higher than the cost of US dollar debt, $\beta_\yen^\$$ must exceed 0. A positive-beta liability means that the firm will have a lower equity beta, all else equal, if it uses yen debt in place of US dollar debt. The higher cost in US dollars of the yen debt will be exactly offset by a lower cost of equity. This explanation is based on Modigliani–Miller (MM) theory: the value of a firm does not depend on the currency denomination of the debt.

SUMMARY

This chapter showed how a firm can estimate its weighted average cost of capital (WACC) in US dollars, given the global finance environment.

We introduced the global CAPM as a tool that helps a firm estimate its cost of equity. The global CAPM gives a more logical estimate of the cost of equity than the traditional local CAPM, at least for stocks traded in open and globally integrated financial markets. The chapter discusses the inputs to the global CAPM: the global risk premium, global betas, and the risk-free rate.

Another challenge in estimating the WACC in global finance is finding the cost of foreign currency debt from the US dollar perspective. We showed how a firm can use the UIRP condition to estimate the cost of foreign currency debt in US dollars.

We also introduced a risk-adjusted version of the UIRP based on the global CAPM as the risk–return model and incorporating the systematic risk of changes in FX rates.

GLOSSARY

American depositary receipts (ADRs): Receipts on foreign-issued shares denominated in US dollars and traded on US markets.

Cost of capital: The discount rate applied to a firm's expected base currency operating cash flows to determine the value of the firm; the minimum expected return a firm must earn on new investment to maintain the intrinsic value of its current shares.

Cost of equity: The expected rate of return that an equity investor requires as compensation for taking risk and supplying capital. The minimum expected rate of return a firm must earn on new *equity* investment to maintain the intrinsic value of its current shares.

Cross-listed stocks: Stocks traded on both their home and foreign exchanges.

Exchange-traded funds (ETFs): Securities that are like mutual funds of baskets of stocks but trade continuously.

FX global beta: The beta of the percentage changes in the FX value of a currency versus the unhedged global market index in US dollars.

Global beta: The beta of an asset's rate of return in US dollars versus the unhedged global market index in US dollars, measuring the tendency of the asset's US dollar returns to move systematically with the US dollar returns of an unhedged global market index.

Global risk premium: The minimum rate of return over the risk-free rate that investors (in the aggregate) require as compensation for the risk in a *globally diversified* portfolio.

Home bias: The tendency of investors to invest more in stocks of their own country than would be advisable given the benefits of international diversification.

iShares: Exchange-traded funds (ETFs) on stock indexes.

Market risk premium: The minimum rate of return over the risk-free rate that investors (in the aggregate) require as compensation for the risk in a well-diversified portfolio.

Ordinary shares: The actual local market shares that underlie depositary receipts traded in another market.

Required rate of return: The expected rate of return required as compensation for investing capital and bearing risk. Also called the equilibrium expected rate of return, and for a firm's stock, the cost of equity.

Unhedged index: Index in which the FX changes are part of the returns on foreign assets.

DISCUSSION QUESTIONS

1. Discuss the pros and cons of using the global CAPM to estimate a firm's cost of equity.
2. Why is the cost of yen debt in US dollars different from the cost of US dollar debt in US dollars?
3. Why would a firm have yen debt if the cost of yen debt in US dollars is higher than the cost of US dollar debt in US dollars?

PROBLEMS

1. Sony's shares are denominated in yen and traded on the Tokyo Stock Exchange. At time 0, the shares are priced at ¥3750 in Tokyo, and the spot FX rate is 110 ¥/$. What is the rate of return to a US investor who buys Sony shares now and holds them until time 1, when the shares are priced at ¥4375 and the spot FX rate is 125 ¥/$?
2. Sony's ADR shares are traded on the New York Stock Exchange. There is one ADR share of Sony for each actual Tokyo share. If the actual shares are priced at ¥3750 in Tokyo, and if the spot FX rate is 110 ¥/$, what is the no-arbitrage price of a Sony ADR share in US dollars? What is the time-1 price of a Sony ADR share when the actual shares are priced at ¥4375 and the spot FX rate is 125 ¥/$?
3. What is the rate of return to a US investor who buys Sony ADRs at time 0 and holds until time 1? Use information from Problem 2.
4. Assume that Coca-Cola's global beta in US dollars in 0.77. Estimate Coke's cost of equity in US dollars, given a long-term US dollar risk-free rate of 6% and a global risk premium of 4% in US dollars.
5. Assume a long-term US Treasury bond rate of 6%, a global beta of 0.15 for the long-term US Treasury bond, and a global risk premium of 4% in US dollars. Estimate the long-term US dollar risk-free rate.
6. Assume that the equilibrium expected percentage change in the FX value of the Swedish krona is 2% per year, 60% of TDX Company's debt is US dollar debt with a yield of 8%, and 40% is Swedish krona debt with a yield of 6.50%. The debt percentages are figured by using current market values of the debt. Assume that TDK's debt represents 20% of the firm's value, the firm's effective tax rate is 30%, and its cost of equity in US dollars is 11%. (a) What is TDK's cost of the krona debt in US dollars? (b) What is the overall cost of its debt in US dollars? (c) What is TDK's WACC in US dollars?
*7. Assume that the FX global beta for the Swiss franc is −0.10 and the Swiss franc risk-free interest rate is 3.50%. Assume a US dollar risk-free rate of $r_f^\$ = 5.40\%$. Find the equilibrium expected percentage change in the FX value of the Swiss franc, given the risk-adjusted UIRP and the global CAPM, for a global risk premium in US dollars of 4%.

ANSWERS TO PROBLEMS

1. The rate of return in yen is ¥4375/¥3750 − 1 = 0.1667, or 16.67%. The value of the yen fell, by (0.008 $/¥)/(0.00909 $/¥) − 1 = −0.12, or −12%. Thus the rate of return in US dollars, from equation (9.1a), is (1.1667)(1 − 0.12) − 1 = 0.0267, or 2.67%.

2. An ADR share is worth ¥3750/(110 ¥/$) = $34.09. The new ADR share price will be ¥4375/(125 ¥/$) = $35.

3. The rate of return on Sony ADRs is $35/$34.09 − 1 = 0.0267, or 2.67%.

4. Using the global CAPM, 0.06 + 0.77(0.04) = 0.091, or 9.1%.

5. The long-term US dollar risk-free rate is 0.060 − 0.15(0.04) = 0.055, or 5.50%.

6. (a) The US dollar cost of TDK's Swedish krona debt is 0.065 + 0.02 = 0.085, or 8.5%.
   (b) TDK's overall cost of debt in US dollars is 0.60(0.08) + 0.40(0.085) = 0.082, or 8.2%.
   (c) TDK's WACC = 0.20(1 − 0.30)(0.082) + (0.80)(0.11) = 0.0995, or 9.95%.

7. $E(x^{*\$/Sf}) = r_f^\$ - r_f^{Sf} + \beta_{Sf}^\$[RP_G^\$] = 0.054 - 0.035 - 0.10(0.04) = 0.015$, or 1.50%.

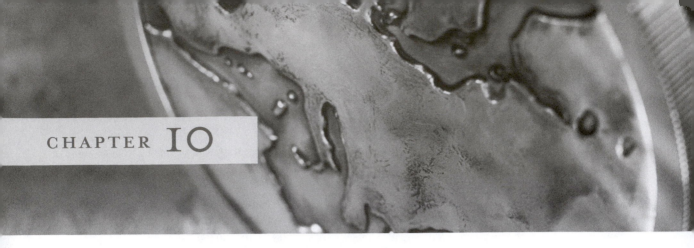

CHAPTER 10

Cost of Capital
for Overseas
Investments

Financial managers in multinational companies need to estimate the cost of capital for overseas investments. And because of different degrees of risk of the various operations, they often want to apply different costs of capital for subsidiaries or divisions in different countries.

As we saw in Chapter 9, the weighted average cost of capital (WACC) is often used to estimate the cost of capital for a firm, because we can observe the financing component costs and weights fairly easily for a firm as a whole. But the WACC approach does not work very well for finding the cost of capital for overseas divisions, since a firm's stake in these divisions does not generally have its own separate financing.

So we have to develop a different approach for the cost of capital for an overseas division. In addition to techniques for finding the cost of capital for a division in a developed country, this chapter also looks at the case of a division in an emerging market country, where there are additional risks to consider.

A multinational company sometimes wants to measure an overseas division's cost of capital from the US dollar perspective, and sometimes from the local foreign currency perspective. For global performance evaluation and overall strategic planning, a US headquarters may use the cost of capital estimate from the US dollar perspective. For decentralized decision making, an overseas subsidiary may want a cost of capital expressed in terms of the local currency that is consistent with the division's cost of capital in terms of US dollars. This chapter shows how to make this conversion.

OPERATING RISK APPROACH

Our approach in this chapter is based on the idea that a multinational corporation can be viewed as a portfolio of subsidiaries. The overall intrinsic value of the multinational is viewed to be the sum of the intrinsic values the subsidiaries would have if they were independent operations. Based on this *value-additivity principle*, each subsidiary's risk contributes to the multinational's overall "portfolio" risk. The cost of capital of an overseas subsidiary is the rate of return that would be required in the global financial market as compensation for risk if the subsidiary were independently owned and traded.[1]

If a division tends to contribute an above-average amount to a multinational's overall "portfolio" risk, its cost of capital should be higher than the multinational's overall cost of capital. If the company's overall cost of capital were used as the division's cost of capital, some investments might be made that do not offer enough reward to compensate for risk. If a division's risk tends to lower the multinational's overall risk, the division's cost of capital should be lower than the multinational's overall cost of capital. Multinational managers who do not recognize this may miss out on profitable foreign expansion opportunities by setting the cost of capital too high for some overseas investments.[2]

This framework suggests that we use a model of risk and return based on the company's *operating risk*. We can think of a company's operating risk as the risk the asset's owners would have if the company were entirely equity financed. In the context of the global CAPM, a company's operating risk is its (global) *operating beta*, which is basically the beta of the company's intrinsic value, as if the company was an all-equity company. You can plug the operating beta into the global CAPM to arrive at the company's cost of capital as an alternative to the WACC.

In principle, the WACC and operating risk approaches should give the same cost of capital estimates. If you know the financing component weights and costs, you can use the WACC approach and do not need to estimate the operating risk. Since we don't know the financing component weights and costs for a subsidiary, we'll use the operating risk approach. We compare of the WACC and operating risk approaches later in the chapter.

---

[1]Researchers are studying the question of whether international diversification creates values that are different from that based on value additivity. There are reports of a premium, as would be expected if synergy is present between the divisions. There are also reports of a *diversification discount*.

[2]This point are made in Justin Pettit, Mack Ferguson, and Robert Gluck, "A Method for Estimating Global Corporate Capital Costs: The Case of Bestfoods," *Journal of Applied Corporate Finance*, Fall 1999, 80–90.

We have noted that an overseas division has an operating risk that may differ from the multinational's overall operating risk. One reason is that the division and the multinational are likely to define their basic relationship with the global economy in different ways. For example, the sales volume or the operating cost of a Japanese division may have a different correlation with the global market from the rest of the multinational. Thus the operating beta of a Japanese division may be different from the operating beta of the firm as a whole, even when both operating betas are measured in US dollars.

Another reason is the difference in FX operating exposures. The FX operating exposure is lower for foreign subsidiaries that produce locally and higher for those that operate more as assembly or distribution businesses.

In addition, an overseas division's operating risk may differ from that of the firm as a whole if the division is in an emerging market country. Because emerging markets tend to be less integrated with the global markets than are developed markets, estimating the cost of capital for an investment in an emerging market country entails considerations besides the investment's operating beta. A given emerging market country may have considerable political risks (expropriation risk, risk of war or civil disturbance, risk of policy changes, etc.).

In this chapter, we first show how to estimate the operating beta and cost of capital for a division in a developed country. In this case, we simply plug the estimated operating beta into the global CAPM to estimate the cost of capital for the division. Then we show adjustments that may be appropriate if the division is in an emerging-market country. After that, we show how the cost of capital in US dollars can be converted into its equivalent in the foreign currency.

ACCOUNTING BETA METHOD

A division's operating beta is difficult to estimate because we have no historic return data for a privately owned division, as we have for an overall firm's equity beta. One way to deal with this problem is the *accounting beta* method. An accounting beta is estimated by regressing a time series of *return on assets* (ROA) observations against the corresponding returns of the global market index. ROA is operating profit divided by the total assets. Although an accounting construction of profit per dollar of assets, ROA is conceptually similar to the rate of return usually used to calculate a beta.

A Japanese division's operating beta is different from the parent's overall operating beta because of fundamental economic differences between the particular operations in Japan and the multinational's other operations in the rest of the world. The accounting beta method suggests that we can capture that difference by looking at the accounting betas.

We first find the division's *accounting beta ratio*, which is the ratio of the division's accounting beta to the overall firm's accounting beta. Then we assume that the accounting beta ratio is equal to the *operating beta ratio*, the ratio of the division's operating beta (the unknown that we want to find) to the multinational's overall operating beta. By knowing the accounting beta ratio and the overall firm's operating beta, we can estimate the division's operating beta.

Suppose the US Global Corporation is the parent of divisions in the United States, Europe, and Japan. Assume that the accounting beta of the US division is 0.40, the accounting beta of the European division is 0.50, the accounting beta of the Japanese division is 0.60, and the accounting beta of Global Corporation as a whole is 0.50. Thus the accounting beta ratios are 0.80, 1.00, and 1.20 for the US, European, and Japanese divisions, respectively. Say we estimate US Global Corporation's overall operating beta to be 0.90. With the accounting beta approach, the operating beta for the US division is 0.90(0.80) = 0.72. The operating beta for the European division is 0.90(1) = 0.90. The operating beta for the Japanese division is 0.90(1.20) = 1.08.

In US dollars, the accounting beta of Special Chemical Company (SCC) as a whole is 0.45 and for its Australian division is 0.90. Assume that the operating beta for SCC is 0.80. What is the estimated operating beta of the Australian division according to the accounting beta method? Assume a US dollar risk-free rate of 5% and a global risk premium of 4%. What is the Australian division's cost of capital in US dollars according to the global CAPM?

Answers: The operating beta of the Australian division is estimated to be 0.80(0.90/0.45) = 1.60. SCC-Australia's estimated cost of capital in US dollars is 0.05 + 1.60(0.04) = 0.114, or 11.4%.

The logic of the accounting beta method is that managers have the information to estimate the accounting betas of a division and the overall firm. That is, they know something about a division's accounting beta from the inside, while the market (in the form of returns) does not reflect this information. The drawback is that we cannot directly use the division's accounting beta with the global CAPM risk–return trade-off equation to estimate the division's cost of capital. The reason is that accounting betas are different from return betas, because market sentiment and other factors enter into returns in the market.[3]

COUNTRY BETA METHOD

An alternative to the accounting beta method is the *country beta method*. This method assumes that a division's operating beta ratio is equal to the ratio of the division's *country beta* to the overall world beta.

A country beta in US dollars, $\beta_C^\$$, may be estimated by regressing the returns of a country's equity index against the returns of the global market index, expressing both index returns in US dollars, as reported in Table 10.1 for a number of developed countries. The (global) country betas in Table 10.1 are calculated with monthly data from the period December 1998 through December 2003 as in Interactive Exercise 10.1.

Since the overall world beta is the average of all country betas and is equal to 1 by definition, the country beta method boils down to estimating a division's operating beta by multiplying the company's overall operating beta times the country beta for the country that the division is in. Say a US multinational with an overall operating beta of 0.50 has a

---

[3]See J. Campbell and J. Mei, "Where Do Betas Come From? Asset Price Dynamics and the Sources of Systematic Risk," *Review of Financial Studies*, Vol. 6, 1993, 567–592.

TABLE 10.1 Country Beta Estimates and Country Risk Premium Estimates*
(US Dollars) in Developed Countries

Country	$\beta_C^\$$	$RP_C^\$$
Australia	0.862	3.4%
Austria	0.476	1.9%
Belgium	0.849	3.4%
Canada	1.122	4.5%
Denmark	0.911	3.6%
Finland	1.757	7.0%
France	1.151	4.6%
Germany	1.477	5.9%
Hong Kong	1.020	4.1%
Ireland	0.864	3.5%
Italy	0.877	3.5%
Japan	0.771	3.1%
Netherlands	1.141	4.6%
New Zealand	0.798	3.2%
Norway	1.098	4.4%
Singapore	1.027	4.1%
Spain	1.041	4.2%
Sweden	1.666	6.7%
United Kingdom	0.835	3.3%
United States	1.030	4.1%
The World Index	1	4.0%

Source: MSCIDATA.com and http://www.stls.frb.org.

*The country risk premiums are based on the country betas and a global risk premium of 4%.

subsidiary in Sweden. If Sweden has an estimated country beta of 1.67 (see Table 10.1), it is likely the Swedish division of the multinational has an operating beta that is higher than the operating beta of the multinational as a whole. Since the Swedish country beta estimate is 1.67 times the world beta (average country beta) of 1, you can reason that the Swedish division's estimated operating beta is 1.67 times the overall operating beta of the multinational, 0.50. Thus, the Swedish division's operating beta is estimated to be 1.67(0.50) = 0.835.

Special Chemical Company (SCC) is a US multinational firm with an estimated overall operating beta relative to the global market index of 1.45. Assume that the country beta of the Australian equity market index in US dollars is 0.862 (Table 10.1). Use the country beta method to estimate the operating beta of SCC's Australian division. Assume that the US dollar risk-free rate is 6% and the global risk premium is 4%. What is the Australian division's estimated cost of capital in US dollars?

Answers: The estimated operating beta of the Australian division is 1.45(0.862) = 1.25. SCC-Australia's cost of capital in US dollars is estimated to be 0.06 + 1.25(0.04) = 0.11, or 11%.

INTERACTIVE EXERCISE 10.1

Estimate a Country Beta

Find the (global) country beta of a country index in US dollars. Registered users can download the MSCI World Index values (in US dollars) from 1970 at no change at http://www.mscidata.com/.

To download into Excel the monthly values of the Developed Market "Gross Index" (i.e., with dividends reinvested), first click on the World Index, the bottom of the first group of listings on the home page. On the next page from the drop-down menus change "market" to "Developed Market", change "type" to "Gross Index (DM)," and put in the "span from Dec 31, 1998 to Dec 31, 2003," and from the drop-down menu for "Index" choose an appropriate index/country. Wait for the graph to appear in the page, and then click on "Download." The data will appear in an Excel file; select and copy the data and paste in the appropriate Excel file. You can then convert the MSCI Index values into rates of returns from January 1999 to December 2003 and save in the file "INDEX RETURN." Next you need to copy/paste (you may have to use "paste special" and "values") the two return series onto a common spreadsheet.

When you have a column of individual country index returns and a column of MSCI World index returns, consistently aligned by date on the same spreadsheet, you are ready to compute the global beta of the country index. Go to "tools," then "data analysis." If "data analysis" does not show when you pull down the "tools" menu, choose "add-in," and check the "analysis pack." Then the "data analysis" will be a "tools" option. Choose "regression" and "OK." For "y range," put in the country index return range; for "x range", put in the MSCI World Index range. Then hit "OK." The country beta estimate is the "X-variable coefficient." The "X-variable coefficient" will be the estimate of the country index's global beta, in US dollars.

EMERGING MARKET INVESTMENTS

For investments in emerging markets, many companies add a premium for *political risk* to the usual premium for global beta. Political risk is a catchall term used to describe the additional risks posed by emerging market investments in terms of illiquidity, civil disruptions, corruption, political intervention, expropriation, imposition of controls on funds, repatriation, irresponsible economic management by the country's leaders, and the like.

We may think of the *political risk premium* for country C, denoted $PR_C^\$$, as a premium above the global CAPM risk premium that global investors require for the political risk of investing in the country's equity index portfolio. Many managers and analysts estimate a country's political risk premium by the country's *sovereign risk premium*, the spread between the yield on a US dollar-denominated sovereign bond issued by the country's government (denoted $r_{sC}^\$$) and the yield on a US Treasury bond. Alternatively, they may use the yield spread between euro-denominated sovereign bonds issued by the country's government and euro-denominated bonds issued by a Eurozone government.

TABLE 10.2 Sovereign Risk and Country Risk Ratings, March 2003

Country	Sovereign Risk Premium	S&P Country Risk Rating	*Institutional Investor* Country Credit Rating
Canada	0.0078	AAA	89.9
Spain	0.0084	AA+	86.1
Italy	0.0086	AA	84.3
Japan	0.0090	AA−	82.0
Hong Kong	0.0093	A+	68.6
Greece	0.0108	A	74.6
Israel	0.0353	A−	56.1
Poland	0.0133	BBB+	60.6
Mexico	0.0203	BBB−	58.5
Egypt	0.0503	BB+	43.8
Russia	0.0401	BB	41.7
Peru	0.0540	BB−	36.3
Brazil	0.1147	B+	36.1
Turkey	0.0919	B−	34.9

Sources: Bloomberg, *Standard & Poor's Global Ratings Handbook*, and *Institutional Investor's 2002 Country Credit Ratings* (March 2003 Issue).

If the emerging market has no sovereign bonds denominated in US dollars or euros, then a political risk premium is often estimated as a function of a *country risk rating*. Country risk ratings may be found is several places, including Standard & Poor's (S&P), the *Institutional Investor* magazine, and *Euromoney* magazine. Table 10.2 shows some sovereign yield spreads, S&P country risk ratings, and *Institutional Investor* ratings for March 2003. Figure 10.1 shows the correlation between the sovereign yield spreads and the *Institutional Investor* ratings for March 2003.

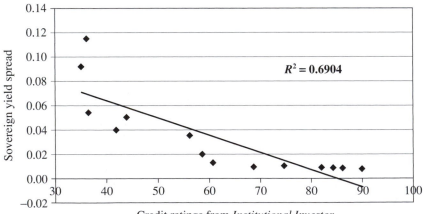

Figure 10.1 Scatter diagram and a line-fitting data points between sovereign yield spread and the country credit ratings from *Institutional Investor* magazine. The *Institutional Investor* ratings explain about 69% of the variation in sovereign yield spread.

There is also a fee-based service called the International Country Risk Guide (ICRG), whose country risk ratings are explained at the Web site http://www.icrgonline.com/. Professor Campbell Harvey of Duke University provides a nice Java tool to graph country risk at the following Web site: http://www.duke.edu/~charvey/applets/CountryRisk/test.html.

Since emerging market governments could be more likely to default than companies in some cases, the sovereign risk premium might overstate the political risk premium of a country's equity index. Still, sovereign risk premiums are in wide use as a proxy measure of political risk premiums.

The *country risk premium* is determined by both the premium for the country index's systematic risk relative to the global index and the political risk premium. Often, the political risk premium of a developed country is assumed to be zero. In this case, the country risk premium is determined only by the index's systematic risk relative to the global index. The estimates of the country risk premiums for some developed market countries where the political risk is assumed to be zero (Table 10.1) are based on the estimated country betas and a global risk premium of 4%. Table 10.2 shows small sovereign risk premiums for selected developed countries (Canada, Spain, Italy, Japan, and Hong Kong.)

If $\beta_C^{\$}$ denotes the (global) country beta of country C, then the required rate of return for an investment into country C's equity index is $k_C^{\$} = r_f^{\$} + \beta_C^{\$}[RP_G^{\$}] + PR_C^{\$}$. For example, assume that a country's global beta is 0.80 and its political risk premium is 5%. If the long-term risk-free rate in US dollars is 3.5% and the global risk premium is 4%, the required rate of return on the country index (in US dollars) is $0.035 + 0.80(0.04) + 0.05 = 0.117$, or 11.7%. The country risk premium would be $0.117 - 0.035 = 0.082$.

Individual emerging market investments, subsidiaries, and divisions, pose different degrees of political risk to global investors. Some emerging market investments may be relatively free of political risk. An example would be a large company with wide access to global capital markets, especially a company whose shares have American depositary receipts (ADRs). Another example might be a tomato processing plant in the stable Korean food market. At the other end of the spectrum are emerging market investments in industries that are highly susceptible to political intervention, like the power and oil industries, or have a relatively high potential for corruption. We denote an emerging market investment's sensitivity to the country's political risk, that is, its *political risk exposure*, as $\Phi_i^{\$}$. The cost of capital for an individual emerging market asset (in US dollars) is given in equation (10.1):

$$k_i^{\$} = r_f^{\$} + \beta_i^{\$}[RP_G^{\$}] + \Phi_i^{\$}[PR_C^{\$}] \qquad (10.1)$$

If an investment has the average political risk of the country, or if the manager has no subjective opinion about the relative political risk exposure of the investment, $\Phi_i^{\$} = 1$. For investments with higher than average political risk exposure, $\Phi_i^{\$}$ should be higher than 1. For investments judged to have half the average political risk exposure of investments in the country, $\Phi_i^{\$} = 0.50$.

For example, assume that a US multinational wants to estimate the cost of capital in US dollars for its subsidiary in Argentina. Assume a yield on long-term US dollar-denominated Argentine sovereign bonds of 9.5% and a yield on long-term US Treasury bonds of 3.5%. Assume that Argentina's political risk premium is equal to its sovereign risk premium, which is 9.5% − 3.5% = 6%. Assume that the subsidiary is in an industry that has about average political risk for Argentina. Assume that the subsidiary's global operating beta is 1.25, the long-term risk-free rate in US dollars is equal to the long-term US Treasury bond yield, 3.5%, and the global risk premium in US dollars is 4%. The Argentine subsidiary's cost of capital in US dollars, from equation (10.1), is $k_i^\$ = 0.035 + 1.25(0.04) + 1(0.06) = 0.145$, or 14.5%.

BRAZILIAN FIRMS EMBRAER AND EMBRATEL

Professor Aswath Damodaran of New York University has suggested two methods to try to measure political risk exposure, $\Phi_i^\$$, for a firm in an emerging market country.* He estimated $\Phi_i^\$$ for two Brazilian firms: Embraer, an aerospace company that manufactures and sells aircraft to many of the world's leading airlines, and Embratel, the large Brazilian telecommunications company.

The first method is the ratio of the firm's local revenues to the local revenues of the average firm of the country. The more revenues come from outside the country, the lower the political risk exposure. The higher the firm's local revenues, the higher the political risk exposure. Embraer derives only about 3% of its revenues locally, while Embratel derives 95% of its revenues locally. Since the average Brazilian firm generates 77% of its revenues locally, the $\Phi_i^\$$ for Embraer would be 3%/77% = 0.04, and the $\Phi_i^\$$ for Embratel would be 95%/77% = 1.23.

The second method is to estimate $\Phi_i^\$$ as the coefficient of a time series of the firm's equity returns (converted to US dollars) against the returns on a Brazilian sovereign bond (converted to US dollars). For Embraer, the estimated $\Phi_i^\$$ was 0.27. For Embratel, it was 2.00.

*For a more complete discussion of these methods, see A. Damodaran, "Measuring Company Exposure to Country Risk: Theory and Practice," *Journal of Applied Finance*, Fall/Winter 2003, 63–75.

Special Chemical Company (SCC) is a US-based multinational firm wanting to estimate the cost of capital in US dollars of its division in Chile. The division is in an industry that has above-average political risk for Chile and thus $\Phi_i^\$$ is estimated to be 1.50. The subsidiary's operating beta is 0.75, the long-term risk-free rate in US dollars is equal to the long-term Treasury bond yield, 3%, and the global risk premium in US dollars is 4%. Assume that the yield on long-term US dollar-denominated Chilean sovereign bonds is 8% and that Chile's political risk premium is equal to its sovereign risk premium. What is the Chilean division's estimated cost of capital in US dollars?

Answer: $k_i^\$ = 0.03 + 0.75(0.04) + 1.50(0.05) = 0.135$, *or 13.5%.*

Under the common assumption that the long-term US Treasury bond yield is equal to the long-term risk-free rate in US dollars, the cost of capital for a company with average political risk for the country ($\Phi_i^\$ = 1$) is $k_i^\$ = r_{sC}^\$ + \beta_i^\$[RP_G^\$]$, where $r_{sC}^\$$ is the yield on country C's US dollar-denominated sovereign debt. So when estimating the required return for a country's index or for an asset with typical political risk, you can use the global CAPM with the country's yield on sovereign US dollar-denominated debt in place of the US dollar risk-free rate term. In the Argentina example, $k_i^\$ = 0.095 + 1.25(0.04) = 0.145$, or 14.5%. This shortcut is often used when an analyst does not know $\Phi_i^\$$ and assumes it to be 1 by default.[4]

COST OF CAPITAL IN FOREIGN CURRENCY

Financial managers often want to express a particular asset's cost of capital in an overseas currency, given that the cost of capital is known in US dollars. A multinational company may have an estimated US dollar cost of capital for a subsidiary that is based upon the subsidiary's operating risk, but it will want to supply the subsidiary's managers with a *consistent* cost of capital in their own local currency, so that they can make local investment decisions.

Consider the Eurozone subsidiary AEM, with an estimated operating beta in US dollars of 1.25. Assume a risk-free rate in US dollars of 5% and a global risk premium in US dollars of 4%. The global CAPM tells us that AEM's cost of capital in US dollars is $0.05 + 1.25(0.04) = 0.10$, or 10%. The US dollar cost of capital, 10%, is the proper capitalization rate for AEM's expected after-tax operating cash flows, as measured in US dollars, if we want to find the firm's intrinsic value in US dollars.

We can also think AEM's future cash flow stream from the point of view of euros (or any other currency). The question is what discount rate should be used to find the present value of the cash flow stream measured in euros. In other words, what is AEM's cost of capital in euros, consistent with its 10% cost of capital in US dollars?

Essentially there are two ways to find an asset's cost of capital in another currency. The first is to use a conversion formula, based on a known cost of capital in US dollars, as we shall do here. The second is the direct use of a risk–return model (asset pricing model)

---

[4]The model for the cost of capital for emerging market investments in equation (10.1) adapts ideas from diverse places in the literature. Like most, we adjust for political risk in the cost of capital (denominator adjustment), but some advocate adjustments to expected cash flows (numerator adjustment) to compensate for political risks. Some helpful sources are M. Zenner and E. Akaydin, "A Practical Approach to the International Valuation and Capital Allocation Puzzle," Salomon Smith Barney, 2002 (unpublished); D. Lessard, "Incorporating Country Risk in the Valuation of Offshore Projects," *Journal of Applied Corporate Finance*, Fall 1996, 52–63; S. Godfrey and R. Espinosa, "A Practical Approach to Calculating Costs of Equity for Investments in Emerging Markets," *Journal of Applied Corporate Finance*, Fall 1996, 80–89; C. Harvey, "The Drivers of Expected Returns in International Markets," *Emerging Markets Quarterly*, Fall 2000, 1–17; and A. Damodaran, "Measuring Company Exposure to Country Risk: Theory and Practice," *Journal of Applied Finance*, Fall/Winter 2003, 63–75.

from the foreign currency point of view. For technical reasons discussed later, it is difficult to use a risk–return model in a foreign currency consistent with a US dollar cost of capital estimated with the global CAPM.

The conversion approach is expressed in equation (10.2), which is derived in the appendix at the end of this chapter:

$$k_i^{\euro} = k_i^{\$} - E(x^{*\$/\euro}) + (1 - \xi_{i\euro}^{\$})\sigma_{\euro}^2 \tag{10.2}$$

In words, equation (10.2) says that to get asset i's cost of capital in euros, $k_i^{\euro}$, we start with the asset's US dollar cost of capital, $k_i^{\$}$. Then we adjust for the equilibrium expected percentage change in the FX value of the euro, relative to the US dollar, $E(x^{*\$/\euro})$. This is the expected rate of FX change that is consistent with the equilibrium risk–return relationship for global investments in a common currency. Next we adjust for the statistical interaction between the asset's returns and FX rate changes. This statistical interaction is the covariance between the asset return in euros and $x^{\$/\euro}$, which can be expressed as $\xi_{i\$}^{\euro}\sigma_{\euro}^2$, where $\xi_{i\$}^{\euro}$ is the asset's FX exposure to the US dollar and $\sigma_{\euro}$ is the volatility of the euro. Since $\xi_{i\$}^{\euro} = 1 - \xi_{i\euro}^{\$}$, as in equation (5.2), and we are converting the asset's cost of capital from the US dollar viewpoint to the euro viewpoint, we use $(1 - \xi_{i\euro}^{\$})\sigma_{\euro}^2$ in equation (10.2).

To convert AEM's 10% US dollar cost of capital into its equivalent in euros using equation (10.2), we need to find the equilibrium expected percentage change in the FX value of the euro, $E(x^{*\$/\euro})$. For this we can use a version of the uncovered interest rate parity (UIRP) condition. Assume that the long-term risk-free rate in US dollars is 5% and the long-term risk-free rate in euros is 3%. Using the linear approximation of the traditional UIRP condition, $E(x^{*\$/\euro}) = r_f^{\$} - r_f^{\euro} = 0.05 - 0.03 = 0.02$, or 2% per year.[5]

To use equation (10.2), we also need to know AEM's FX exposure to the euro, which we'll assume is 0.75. Also, assume the volatility of the euro, $\sigma_{\euro}$, to be 0.10. Then, application of equation (10.2) yields that AEM's euro cost of capital is $k_i^{\euro} = k_i^{\$} - E(x^{*\$/\euro}) + (1 - \xi_{i\euro}^{\$})\sigma_{\euro}^2 = 0.10 - 0.02 + (1 - 0.75)0.10^2 = 0.0825$, or 8.25%.

The result that AEM's cost of capital expressed in euros is 8.25% is based on its cost of capital in US dollars of 10% and given the other assumptions, including AEM's FX exposure to the euro of 0.75. AEM really has only one basic cost of capital that compensates investors for risk, and 10% and 8.25% are equivalent expressions of that cost of capital in two different currencies. While AEM's cost of capital in euros is a lower percentage than in US dollars, the two are equivalent in economic content.

Equation (10.2) reveals the reasons why AEM's cost of capital is lower when represented in euros (8.25%) rather than US dollars (10%). The first reason is the impact of the equilibrium expected percentage change in the FX value of the euro, based on the

---

[5]Using the traditional UIRP condition implies that we are assuming an FX global beta of the euro of zero. You could also use the risk-adjusted UIRP relationship from the global CAPM, equation (9.4), $E(x^{*\$/\euro}) = r_f^{\$} - r_f^{\euro} + \beta_{\euro}^{\$}[RP_G^{\$}]$. Assume that the FX global beta of the euro, $\beta_{\euro}^{\$}$, is 0.125 and the global risk premium (in US dollars) is 4%. The equilibrium expected percentage change in the FX value of the euro, given the risk-adjusted UIRP relationship, is $E(x^{*\$/\euro}) = r_f^{\$} - r_f^{\euro} + \beta_{\euro}^{\$}[RP_G^{\$}]$ = $0.05 - 0.03 + 0.125(0.04) = 0.025$, or 2.5% per year.

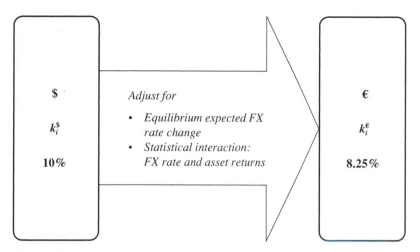

Figure 10.2 Cross-border cost of capital conversion.

risk-free interest rate differential. That is, the risk-free rate in US dollars (5%) is higher than the risk-free rate in euros (3%), so it is reasonable that an asset's cost of capital will be lower when expressed in euros than in US dollars. The second reason is AEM's FX exposure. Because AEM's returns in US dollars are related to changes in the FX value of the euro, we need to adjust for this interaction when we convert AEM's US dollar cost of capital into its equivalent in euros. Figure 10.2 summarizes the process of converting a cost of capital from US dollars to euros.

Suppose the Japanese division of a US multinational has an FX operating exposure of 1.60 to the yen and a cost of capital in US dollars estimated to be 9%. The US dollar risk-free rate is 5%, the yen risk-free rate is 2%, and the volatility of the yen is 0.16. What is the overseas division's estimated cost of capital expressed in yen? To estimate the equilibrium expected rate of change in the FX value of the yen, assume that the linear approximation of the traditional UIRP condition holds.

Answers: First, estimate the equilibrium expected percentage change in the FX value of the yen:
$E(x^{*\$/¥}) = r_f^\$ - r_f^¥ = 0.05 - 0.02 = 0.03$. *Second, use equation (10.2) to find the division's cost of capital in yen:* $0.09 - 0.03 + (1 - 1.60)0.16^2 = 0.0446$, *or 4.46%.*

Equation (10.2) takes on a simplified form in the special case of an asset's returns in euros not being correlated with the FX changes, that is, the FX exposure to the US dollar, $\xi_{i\$}^\epsilon$, is zero. In this case, $k_i^\epsilon = k_i^\$ - E(x^{*\$/\epsilon})$. An example is a firm that has no economic FX exposure in euros, and thus the returns in US dollars have only FX conversion exposure to the euro, $\xi_{i\epsilon}^\$ = 1$. Another example is the special case of converting the cost of debt, which has no FX exposure from the perspective of the debt's currency. Equation (9.3), $k_{¥d}^\$ = k_{¥d}^¥ + E(x^{*\$/¥})$, is an application of this special case.

UNLEVERING EQUITY BETAS: BASIC CASE

Finding divisional operating betas often requires you to have an estimate of the overall firm's operating beta. You saw this need in the accounting beta and country beta methods. This section introduces the idea of estimating the firm's overall operating beta from its equity beta, using a procedure for removing the effects of capital structure. Since a company's equity beta, denoted $\beta_S^\$$, depends on its operating beta, denoted $\beta_O^\$$, and its capital structure, we can back out an operating beta estimate from an equity beta estimate and the capital structure.

In the basic case of a US firm's having its debt denominated entirely in US dollars and no currency swap positions, there is a simple relationship between the firm's equity beta and its operating beta: $\beta_S^\$ = \beta_O^\$/(1 - D^\$/V^\$)$. This relationship should look somewhat familiar to you because it is like equation (6.2) except that we are referring to betas here, not FX exposures. If the operating beta is 0.75 and the ratio of debt to intrinsic value ($D^\$/V^\$$) is 0.50, then the equity beta will be $0.75/(1 - 0.50) = 1.50$, assuming that all the debt is denominated in US dollars and there are no currency swap positions. Looking at this from the other direction, if we estimate an equity beta of 1.20 for a firm that has a debt-to-value ratio of 0.25, then the estimated operating beta would be $1.20(1 - 0.25) = 0.90$. When we estimate an operating beta from an equity beta in this way, we are *unlevering* the equity beta.

> **You estimate an equity beta of 0.90 for a firm that has a debt-to-value ratio of 0.40. If all the firm's debt is denominated in US dollars and the firm has no currency swap positions, what is the firm's estimated operating beta?**
>
> *Answer: 0.90(1 − 0.60) = 0.54.*

WACC AND OPERATING RISK

As we said earlier, the WACC and operating risk approaches should in principle result in the same cost of capital. However, this equivalence is not exact with our basic beta unlevering formula, $\beta_S^\$ = \beta_O^\$/(1 - D^\$/V^\$)$, because for simplicity we've ignored the value of the tax shield on debt interest.

We can show that our operating risk approach gives the same cost of capital as the <u>before-tax</u> WACC: $w_d k_d + w_s k_s$. To see this, assume that a US company has US dollar debt that is 50% of the company's intrinsic value and has an operating beta of 0.75; the company's debt is risk-free and the risk-free rate is 5%. Assume a global risk premium of 4% and a corporate tax rate of 25%. Using the operating risk approach with the global CAPM, the company's cost of capital is $5\% + 0.75(4\%) = 8\%$. The equity beta is $0.75/(1 - 0.50)$ $= 1.50$. We see from the global CAPM that the cost of equity is $5\% + 1.50(4\%) = 11\%$. The WACC is $0.50(5\%)(1 - 0.25) + 0.50(11\%) = 7.375\%$, which is lower than the operating risk cost of capital, 8%. The before-tax WACC, however, is equal to the cost of capital of the operating risk approach, since the before-tax WACC is 0.50(5%) + 0.50(11%) = 8%.

The WACC is lower than the operating risk cost of capital because the WACC considers the impact of the tax deductibility of the interest on debt. This impact is equal to $w_d k_d t$, where t is the corporate tax rate. In our example, $w_d k_d t = 0.50(5\%)(0.25) = 0.625\%$. Users of the operating risk approach may want to adjust the US dollar cost of capital estimated by the operating risk approach by subtracting $w_d k_d t$, if they want to include the tax benefit of the firm's debt in the cost of capital.[6]

*UNLEVERING EQUITY BETAS: GENERAL CASE

In the general case of a firm having debt denominated in foreign currencies or currency swap positions, the relationship between equity beta and operating beta is more complex than in the basic case. This is explained by the need to account to the systematic FX risk that may be in foreign currency denominated liability positions. Equation (10.3) shows this relationship with the operating beta on the left-hand side.

$$\beta_O^{\$} = \beta_S^{\$}(1 - D^{\$}/V^{\$}) + \beta_{\euro}^{\$}(L_{\euro}^{\$}/V^{\$}) + \beta_{\pounds}^{\$}(L_{\pounds}^{\$}/V^{\$}) + \beta_{\yen}^{\$}(L_{\yen}^{\$}/V^{\$}) + \cdots \qquad (10.3)$$

Equation (10.3) first adjusts the estimated equity beta for the overall degree of financial leverage, $D^{\$}/V^{\$}$, the ratio of the actual debt value to the intrinsic value of the firm. (Both are shown measured in US dollars.) Any or all of the actual debt may be denominated in any currencies. Although $D^{\$}$ will include net accumulated mark-to-market gains/losses on swaps that appear on the balance sheet, it does *not* include the notional principal amounts of any off–balance sheet currency swap positions.

The next components of equation (10.3) adjust for any systematic FX risk in foreign currency debt or swap positions. $L_{\euro}^{\$}$ represents the value (in US dollars, at the current FX rate) of all euro-denominated liabilities, including both actual euro debt and the notional value of currency swap positions on euros. As in Chapter 9, $\beta_{\euro}^{\$}$ is FX global beta of the euro. The notation is the same for pounds and yen in the next terms of equation (10.3). Liabilities in other currencies are represented in equation (10.3) by the three elliptical periods $(\cdots)$. If the FX global beta of a currency is positive, the use of foreign currency debt and swap positions reduces the equity beta. We add back in the systematic portion of the liabilities' FX hedging effect to the equity beta to calculate the estimated operating beta.

It may be helpful to think in the other direction and show the impact of capital structure on equity beta, given a firm's operating beta. We assume that the US firm XYZ Company has an operating beta, $\beta_O^{\$}$, of 0.90. If XYZ has no swap positions and only US

---

[6]A precise equivalence between the operating risk and WACC approaches can be shown in the Miller theory (M. Miller, "Debt and Taxes," *Journal of Finance*, May 1977, 261–275). In the Miller theory, the risk-free rate used in the CAPM is $r_f^{\$}(1 - t)$, which is $5\%(1 - 0.25) = 3.75\%$ in our example. The cost of capital with the operating risk approach is $3.75\% + 0.75(4\%) = 6.75\%$. The cost of equity is $3.75\% + 1.50(4\%) = 9.75\%$. The WACC is the same as the operating risk cost of capital: $0.50(5\%)(1 - 0.25) + 0.50(9.75\%) = 6.75\%$.

dollar debt representing 40% of the firm's intrinsic value, the firm's equity beta would be $0.90/(1 − 0.40) = 1.50$. Now assume that XYZ has only actual euro-denominated debt, again representing 40% of the firm's value, and has no other debt or currency swap positions, and the FX global beta of the euro ($\beta_\epsilon^\$$) is 0.10. We can rearrange equation (10.3) to find that XYZ's equity beta would be $[0.90 − 0.10(0.40)]/(1 − 0.40) = 1.433$. Finally, assume instead that XYZ is levered with actual euro-denominated debt representing 20% of the firm's value and has a short currency swap position on euros with an one-sided value representing 10% of the firm's overall intrinsic value (in US dollars). Now $L_\epsilon^\$$ is 0.30, while $D^\$/V^\$$ is only 0.20. If the FX global beta of the euro ($\beta_\epsilon^\$$) is 0.10, XYZ's equity beta would be $[0.90 − 0.10(0.30)]/(1 − 0.20) = 1.0875$.

XYZ Company's estimated equity beta (in US dollars) is 1.35. XYZ's equity has an intrinsic value of \$1400. In addition, XYZ has US dollar debt with a value of \$200 and euro-denominated debt with a value in US dollars (at the current spot FX rate) of \$400. XYZ also has a short currency swap position on pounds, with a notional one-sided value (not MTM) in US dollars (at the current spot FX rate) of \$200. Assume that the FX global beta of the euro is 0.10 and the FX global beta of the pound is 0.15. What is XYZ's estimated operating beta (in US dollars)?

Answer: Note that the total intrinsic value of XYZ (\$2000) is equal to the value of all of the actual debt (\$600) and the intrinsic value of the equity (\$1400). The value of the actual debt, \$600, is 30% of XYZ's total intrinsic value. Thus $D^\$/V^\$ = 0.30$. The euro debt with a value of \$400 has an FX global beta of 0.10. The sterling liabilities (notional swap value) are \$200, which is 10% of the firm's intrinsic value, and the FX global beta of the pound is 0.15. Thus, using equation (10.3), $\beta_O^\$ = 1.35(1 − 0.30) + 0.10(0.20) + 0.15(0.10) = 0.98$.

---

*PURE PLAY PROXY METHOD

An alternative to the accounting beta and country beta methods for estimating divisional operating betas is based on the proxy approach, using information for other overseas companies. If we are lucky, there may be a *pure play proxy* firm, which is a company that operates in the country of the multinational's overseas division, is in a similar line of business, and has observable equity returns with which to estimate an equity beta. Then we could use the pure play as a proxy for the division.

To estimate the equity beta of the pure play from the US dollar perspective, we convert the local currency returns of the pure play into US dollars. A Eurozone firm's equity returns can be converted into US dollar terms by using the across-currency return identity $(1 + R_i^\$) = (1 + R_i^\epsilon)(1 + x^{\$/\epsilon})$ [equation (9.1a)]. The next step is to estimate the global equity beta of the pure play by regressing its equity returns, measured in US dollars, against the returns of the global market index in US dollars. The pure play's operating beta, measured in US dollars, is then estimated by making the capital structure adjustments called for in equation (10.3). Figure 10.3 summarizes this approach.

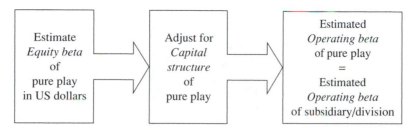

Figure 10.3 Pure play proxy method.

Let's say UVC is a division of a US multinational operating in France. There is a pure play company called FPF, which operates locally in France. Let us assume FPF's stock is listed on the Paris Bourse, so share prices are available in euros. Let us further assume that, after the conversion of FPF's stock returns into US dollars, we estimate FPF's equity beta versus the global market index, in US dollars, to be 0.90. Thus 0.90 would be the global beta of FPF's American depositary receipts, if these ADRs exist.

But 0.90 is not the final estimate of the global beta of UVC, because we must use equation (10.3) to unlever FPF's estimated equity beta to get its estimated operating beta. Assume that FPF has euro-denominated debt representing 45% of the firm's value. Assume further that the FX global beta of the euro is 0.10. Given that FPF's equity beta (in US dollars) is estimated to be 0.90, the proxy's estimated operating beta (in US dollars) can be found using equation (10.3): $\beta_O^\$ = 0.90(1 - 0.45) + 0.10(0.45) = 0.54$.

A US-based multinational wants to estimate the cost of capital for its Japanese division. There is a pure play proxy firm in Japan whose ADR has a global equity beta in US dollars of 1.20. Assume that the foreign proxy firm is financed with yen-denominated debt representing 30% of the firm's intrinsic value, and the rest of its capital is equity. Assume that the FX global beta of the yen is 0.20. Show how the US multinational should use the pure play information to estimate the operating beta of the overseas division in US dollars. If the US dollar risk-free rate is 5% and the global risk premium in US dollars is 4%, what is the overseas division's estimated cost of capital expressed in US dollars?

Answers: Unlever the US dollar equity beta of the overseas pure play to get its estimated operating beta, using equation (10.3): 1.20(1 − 0.30) + 0.20(0.30) = 0.90. The estimated cost of capital of the overseas subsidiary, in US dollars, is 0.05 + 0.90(0.04) = 0.086, or 8.6%.

---

*FX EXPOSURE AND BETA

We know that companies with different operational hedging strategies may have different FX operating exposures. One firm may produce entirely locally, while a second may import some raw materials or finished goods. Even if both companies were to sell the same product in the same market, their FX operating exposures would be different.

Assume that a company has FX exposure to changes in the FX value of a currency, and the currency has systematic risk relative to the global market portfolio. Then one of the determinants of the firm's operating beta is its FX exposure to the currency, and differences in FX operating exposure imply differences in operating beta. We'd like to develop an analytical connection between FX exposure and beta to help in subsequent applications.[7]

Let us differentiate the FX exposures to the euro of two assets i and j using the notation $\xi_{i\epsilon}^{\$}$ and $\xi_{j\epsilon}^{\$}$. If the only reason that assets i and j have different betas is that they have different FX exposures to the euro, we can use equation (10.4):

$$\beta_j^{\$} = \beta_i^{\$} + \beta_\epsilon^{\$}(\xi_{j\epsilon}^{\$} - \xi_{i\epsilon}^{\$}) \tag{10.4}$$

Equation (10.4) says that the difference between the global beta for asset i and asset j is equal to the FX global beta of the euro times the difference between the FX exposures of assets i and j to the euro. (Equation (10.4) is derived in the appendix to this chapter.)

To illustrate this, we assume that if the US widget exporter, MWI, Inc., were to relocate a production facility from the US to the Eurozone, the company's FX operating exposure to the euro would drop from 1.20 to 0.40, because of the operational hedging of producing in the overseas country. Now we want to know what impact the relocation would have on MWI's operating beta. Because MWI still sells the same widgets in the same market, the Eurozone, its operating beta would change with the facility relocation largely because the FX operating exposure to the euro would drop from 1.20 to 0.40.

MWI's new operating beta depends on the systematic risk of the euro, that is, the FX global beta of the euro, $\beta_\epsilon^{\$}$. We can characterize MWI producing in the United States as asset i, and MWI producing in the Eurozone as asset j, and use equation (10.4) to examine the impact of the relocation of its production on AEM's operating beta. Let us assume that the FX global beta of the euro, the systematic risk of the $\$/\epsilon$ FX rate, is 0.10. To apply equation (10.4), assume that MWI's operating beta before the plant relocation is $\beta_i^{\$} = 1.25$. Since MWI's FX operating exposure to the euro before the move (asset i) is $\xi_{i\epsilon}^{\$} = 1.20$, and after the move (asset j) is $\xi_{j\epsilon}^{\$} = 0.40$, then according to equation (10.4), MWI's new operating beta will be $\beta_j^{\$} = 1.25 + 0.10(0.40 - 1.20) = 1.17$ after the relocation of production to the Eurozone. That is, by moving its production to the Eurozone, MWI will lower its operating beta (from 1.25 to 1.17) because the euro has systematic risk ($\beta_\epsilon^{\$} = 0.10$) and because MWI is reducing its FX operating exposure to the euro.

If the risk-free rate in US dollars, $r_f^{\$}$, is 5%, and if the global risk premium in US dollars, $RP_G^{\$}$, is 4%, the company's current cost of capital is $k_i^{\$} = r_f^{\$} + \beta_i^{\$}(RP_G^{\$})$ $= 0.05 + 1.25(0.04) = 0.10$, or 10%. MWI's pro forma cost of capital, given the decision to relocate the plant to Europe, is $k_j^{\$} = r_f^{\$} + \beta_j^{\$}(RP_G^{\$}) = 0.05 + 1.17(0.04) = 0.0968$, or 9.68%.

MWI reduces its cost of capital (in US dollars) by the plant relocation because it reduces the operating risk (beta) of the operation. A lower cost of capital alone, however, does not necessarily make relocation a good decision. MWI would need to consider the outlay necessary to purchase or build the plant in the Eurozone, how much it could obtain from liquidating its plant in the United States, and changes in its expected cash flow stream.

---

[7]Empirical evidence supports the impact of FX exposure on the cost of capital. See B. Francis and D. Hunter, "The Role of Currency Risk in Industry Cost of Capital," Working Paper, University of South Florida, 2004.

Factors affecting cash flows include the projected cost of producing widgets in the Eurozone compared to the US (now and in the future), taxes, and the forecasted rate of change in the FX value of the euro, $E(x^{\$/€})$. If $E(x^{\$/€}) > 0$, then incurring costs of production that are fixed in euros instead of US dollars will mean that production costs are forecasted to rise in US dollar terms, as the euro is forecasted to appreciate in FX value.

The US firm BBX Company exports widgets to the Eurozone. BBX has an FX operating exposure to the euro of 3.88, which is high because of competitive FX exposure compounded by FX conversion exposure. With its production in the United States, BBX has an operating beta of 1.50. Assume that if BBC relocates its production to the Eurozone, its FX operating exposure to the euro will fall from 3.88 to 1 because of operational hedging. If the euro's FX global beta is 0.12, find BBX's new operating beta if it moves production to the Eurozone. Find BBX's cost of capital before and after the move, if the risk-free rate in US dollars is 5% and the global risk premium in US dollars is 4%.

Answers: Using equation (10.4), BBX's new operating beta is 1.50 + 0.12(1 − 3.88) = 1.154. The old cost of capital is 0.05 + 1.50(0.04) = 0.114, or 11%. The new cost of capital is 0.05 + 1.154(0.04) = 0.0962, or 9.62%.

If a pure play proxy has the same operating structure as the multinational's overseas division, its estimated operating beta (in US dollars), is the proxy for the subsidiary's operating beta. If the subsidiary sources raw materials or parts from the United States it might then have a different FX operating exposure from the pure play because of different operational hedging, and thus a different operating beta. With an estimate of the FX operating exposure of the subsidiary to the local currency, we can make an adjustment for this FX exposure with the help of equation (10.4).

To explore this, assume that UVC's FX exposure to the euro is higher than the pure play FPF's, because UVC imports some of its raw materials from the United States, and FPF does not, so UVC uses less operational hedging than FPF. For simplicity, assume that from the US dollar perspective, UVC's FX operating exposure to the euro is 1.80, while FPF's is 1.

Now we use equation (10.4) to adjust the proxy's estimated operating beta, 0.54, given UVC's FX operating exposure to the euro. Assume the FX global beta of the euro is 0.10. Let FPF be asset i in equation (10.4), while UVC is asset j. The estimated operating beta of UVC should be 0.54 + 0.10(1.80 − 1) = 0.62, after adjusting for different FX operating exposures to the euro for the overseas subsidiary (UVC) and the foreign proxy firm (FPF). Once the multinational parent has estimated UVC's operating beta (in US dollars) to be 0.62, it can use the global CAPM to find the subsidiary's cost of capital in US dollars. For example, assume that the US dollar risk-free rate is 5% and the global risk premium is 4%. Then UVC (the overseas subsidiary) has a cost of capital in US dollars of 0.05 + 0.62(0.04) = 0.0748, or 7.48%.

AGV Company is an Australian subsidiary of a US multinational. AGV imports some raw materials from one of the parent's US divisions. You have estimated AGV's FX operating exposure to the Australian dollar to be 2. KUB is a local pure play proxy for AGV, except that the different production locations imply the different FX exposures. In Australian dollars, KUB has an FX operating exposure to the US dollar of 0.75. You have estimated KUB's operating beta (in US dollars) to be 0.85. Assume the FX global beta of the Australian dollar to be 0.12. What is AGV's estimated operating beta?

Answer: First, convert KUB's FX operating exposure to the US dollar to an FX operating exposure to the Australian dollar via equation (5.2): $\xi_{OA\$}^{\$} = 1 - \xi_{O\$}^{A\$} = 1 - 0.75 = 0.25$. Using equation (10.4), AGV's operating beta is estimated to be $0.85 + 0.12(2 - 0.25) = 1.06$.

*RISK AND RETURN IN NON–US DOLLAR CURRENCIES

Why should we use equation (10.2) to convert an asset's cost of capital, instead of simply applying the global CAPM from the perspective of euros? The answer is a very technical one: when the global CAPM holds for assets in US dollars, $k_i^{\$} = r_f^{\$} + \beta_i^{\$}[RP_G^{\$}]$, the risk–return relation cannot generally take that simple form in any other currency and still provide a consistent cost of capital across currencies. In other words, if we try to use the global CAPM equation expressed in euros, we will get a cost of capital in euros that is *not* consistent with the one in the global CAPM in US dollars. For currencies other than the US dollar, we need to add an additional factor. If the global CAPM holds for assets in US dollars, the consistent risk–return relationship in euros is equation (10.5)[8]:

$$k_i^{\unicode{x20AC}} = r_f^{\unicode{x20AC}} + b_{iG}^{\unicode{x20AC}}[RP_G^{\unicode{x20AC}}] + b_{i\$}^{\unicode{x20AC}}[RP_{\$}^{\unicode{x20AC}}] \tag{10.5}$$

As you can see, the risk–return trade-off in equation (10.5) is more complex than one in US dollars. It has two risk factors instead of one. The first risk factor relates to the global market portfolio: $RP_G^{\unicode{x20AC}}$, the global risk premium expressed in euros, is not necessarily numerically equal to the global risk premium expressed in US dollars, $RP_G^{\$}$, even though the index is the same in either case. The second risk factor is an *FX risk factor* from the *euro perspective*: $RP_{\$}^{\unicode{x20AC}}$ represents a risk premium for the FX risk of holding US dollars, from the euro point of view. That is, $RP_{\$}^{\unicode{x20AC}}$ is the difference between the equilibrium

---

[8]This result is difficult to derive mathematically and is thus not derived here. See S. Ross and M. Walsh, "A Simple Approach to the Pricing of Risky Assets with Uncertain Exchange Rates," in R. Hawkins et al., eds., *Research in International Business and Finance*, Vol. 3 (Greenwich, CT: JAI Press, 1983), pp. 39–54.

expected rate of return, in euros, on the US dollar risk-free asset $r_f^\$ + E(x^{*€/\$})$, and the euro risk-free rate, $r_f^{€}$.[9]

Note that the two systematic risk (b) terms in equation (10.5) must be found via a *bivariate* regression of asset i's returns in euros on the two independent variables. The first variable is the global market returns in euros; the second is the percentage changes in the spot FX price of the US dollar from the euro point of view, $x^{€/\$}$. As bivariate regression coefficients, the b terms are not what we think of as the asset's global beta in euros and FX exposure to the US dollar from the euro perspective. Instead, as bivariate regression coefficients, the b terms take into consideration the interaction between the returns on the global market index (in euros) and the percentage changes in the spot FX price of the US dollar (in euros).

Although it is not easy to see, equations (10.2) and (10.5) give reconciling estimates for the cost of equity in euros because the two equations are mathematically equivalent when we assume the global CAPM in US dollars. Some managers might prefer the idea of using a risk–return relationship in a foreign currency to estimate a foreign currency cost of capital directly, but there is extra work involved to estimate both risk premiums and to compute the bivariate regression coefficients. The conversion method in equation (10.2) is easier to use, given that both the cost of equity in US dollars and the FX exposure to the foreign currency have already been estimated.

SUMMARY

This chapter has discussed one of the most pressing issues in global financial management: estimation of the cost of capital for overseas investments. Several methods were suggested: the accounting beta method, the country beta method, and the pure play method. All these methods rely on the concept of operating risk. In the global CAPM, operating risk is measured by operating beta. The chapter also discussed adjusting the cost of capital for political risk in emerging markets investments.

The chapter shows how to convert an asset's cost of capital from US dollars into another currency. In general, the conversion relies on the UIRP condition, the asset's FX exposure to the currency, and the volatility of the currency. For technical reasons, the conversion approach is easier than using a risk–return relation directly.

---

[9]Note that the equilibrium expected percentage change in the FX value of the US dollar, $E(x^{*€/\$})$, is (approximately) equal to minus the expected percentage change in the FX value of the euro, $E(x^{*\$/€})$, plus $\sigma_{€}^2$. That is, $E(x^{*€/\$}) = -E(x^{*\$/€}) + \sigma_{€}^2$. (See Chapter 4.) This relationship implies that if the FX risk premium for the euro (in US dollars) is positive, the FX risk premium for the US dollar (in euros), $RP_\$^{€}$, is likely to be negative. A negative risk premium for the US dollars was observed by L. Capiello, O. Castren, and J. Jaaskela, "Measuring the Euro Exchange Rate Risk Premium: The Conditional International CAPM Approach," at http://papers.ssrn.com/sol3/delivery.cfm/SSRN_ID391986_code030426600.pdf?abstractid=391986#PaperDownload.

In estimating the cost of capital for an overseas division, it is often necessary to adjust an estimated equity beta for capital structure to find an estimated operating beta. We showed how this unlevering adjustment works.

If an FX rate has systematic risk, then a firm's FX operating exposure affects its operating beta. In this case, a change in FX operating exposure, such as in relocating a plant overseas, will result in a change in the cost of capital.

GLOSSARY

Accounting beta: A beta found based on return on assets (ROA).

Accounting beta ratio: A division's accounting beta divided by the overall firm's accounting beta.

Country risk premium: The minimum rate of return over the risk-free rate that investors (in the aggregate) require as compensation for the risk in a portfolio of stocks representing a country's stock market index, determined by both the premium for the country index's systematic risk relative to the global index and the country's political risk premium.

Country risk rating: A general measure of country risk provided by private investment advisories, like Standard & Poor's, *Institutional Investor*, and *Euromoney*.

Diversification discount: A hypothesis that the value of a globally diversified firm is generally less than sum of the separate intrinsic values of its subsidiaries and divisions.

Operating beta: The beta an asset would have if it were entirely equity financed; for a company, the beta of the firm's intrinsic value.

Operating beta ratio: A division's operating beta divided by the multinational company's overall operating beta.

Operating risk: The risk the owners of an asset would have if it were entirely equity financed.

Political risk: A catchall term used to describe the additional risks posed by emerging market investments in terms of illiquidity, civil disruptions, corruption, political intervention, expropriation, poor economic management by the country's leaders, and the like.

Political risk exposure: An emerging market investment's sensitivity to the country's political risk.

Political risk premium: The premium above the global CAPM risk premium that global investors require for the political risk of investing in a country's equity index portfolio.

Pure play proxy: A company that operates in the country of the multinational's overseas division, is in a similar line of business, and has observable equity returns with which to estimate an equity beta.

Return on assets (ROA): Operating cash flow or profit, divided by total assets.

Sovereign risk: The risk that a country's government will not repay its obligations.

Sovereign risk premium: The long-term yield spread between US dollar-denominated sovereign bonds issued by the country's government and US Treasury bonds.

Unlever: To estimate an operating variable (such as operating beta) by removing the effects of capital structure on an estimated equity variable (such as an equity beta.)

Value-additivity principle: The concept that the overall intrinsic value of a multinational is viewed to be the sum of the intrinsic values the subsidiaries would have if they were independent.

DISCUSSION QUESTIONS

1. Discuss the pros and cons of the various methods covered in the chapter for finding the cost of capital for an overseas subsidiary or division.
2. Discuss the pros and cons of using of the sovereign risk premium as the political risk premium.
3. What types of industry do you think would have high political risk? Low political risk?
4. Explain why a firm's cost of capital expressed in euros is a different number from the same cost expressed in US dollars.

PROBLEMS

1. The US multinational Goodfoods has estimated its overall (global) operating beta to be 0.70. From the US dollar point of view, Goodfoods's New Zealand division has an accounting beta of 0.50, and the accounting beta of Goodfoods as a whole is 0.40. Use the accounting beta method to find the estimated operating beta of Goodfoods's New Zealand division.
2. Continue with Problem 1. Assume that Goodfoods's investment in the New Zealand division has an FX operating exposure to the New Zealand dollar of 1. Assume that the US dollar risk-free rate is 6%, the New Zealand dollar (NZ$) risk-free rate is 6.90%, the volatility of the local currency is 0.07, and the global risk premium in US dollars is 4%. Find the New Zealand division's estimated cost of capital in US dollars. Find the New Zealand division's estimated cost of capital in NZ dollars using the linear approximation of the traditional UIRP condition for the equilibrium percentage change in the FX value of the New Zealand dollar.
3. Goodfoods has estimated its overall (global) operating beta to be 0.70. The global beta of the New Zealand stock index is 1.22. Use the country beta method to find the estimated operating beta of Goodfoods's New Zealand division.
4. Continue with Problem 3. Assume that Goodfoods's investment in the New Zealand division has an FX operating exposure to the New Zealand dollar of 1.20. Assume that the US dollar risk-free rate is 6%, the NZ$ risk-free rate is 6.90%, the volatility of the NZ$ is 0.11, and the global risk premium in US dollars is 4%. Find the New Zealand division's cost of capital in US dollars and in NZ$, using the linear approximation of the traditional UIRP condition for the equilibrium percentage change in the FX value of the NZ$.
5. A US multinational wants to estimate the cost of capital in US dollars for its subsidiary in Bulgaria. Assume that the yield on long-term US dollar-denominated Bulgarian sovereign bonds is 11.5% and the yield on long-term US Treasury bonds is 3.5%. Assume that Bulgaria's political risk premium is equal to its sovereign risk premium. Assume that the subsidiary is in an industry that has about half the average political risk for Bulgaria. Assume that the subsidiary's global operating beta is 1, the long-term risk-free rate in US dollars is 3%, and the global risk premium in US dollars is 4%. What is the Bulgarian subsidiary's cost of capital in US dollars?
*6. XYZ Company's estimated equity beta (in US dollars) is 1.20. XYZ's equity has an intrinsic value of $3000. XYZ also has US dollar debt with a value of $500 and euro-denominated debt with a value in US dollars (at the current spot FX rate) of $500. XYZ has a short currency swap position on euros, with a notional principal in euros that has a one-sided value in US dollars (at the current spot FX rate) of $300. XYZ also has a short currency swap position on pounds, with a notional principal in pounds that has a one-sided value in US dollars (at the current spot FX rate) of $1000. Assume that the FX global beta of the euro is 0.08 and the FX global beta of the pound is 0.20. What is XYZ's estimated operating beta (in US dollars)?

*7. A US multinational's investment in its Australian subsidiary has an FX operating exposure to the Australian dollar of -0.25. A pure play proxy firm in Australia whose equity beta in US dollars is 1.35 has debt denominated in only Australian dollars and a debt-to-value ratio of 0.25. Assume the FX global beta of the Australian dollar is 0.10, and its volatility is 0.09. The multinational wishes to use the pure play to estimate the unobservable operating beta of the division in US dollars. What should that estimated operating beta be? If the US dollar risk-free rate is 6%, the risk-free rate of the Australian dollar is 7%, and the global risk premium in US dollars is 4%, what is the Australian division's cost of capital expressed in US dollars and in Australian dollars, using the linear approximation of the traditional UIRP condition to estimate the equilibrium expected rate of change in the FX value of the Australian dollar?

*8. SCC's Japanese division has an FX operating exposure of 1.42 to the yen, and a cost of capital in US dollars of 0.124. Assume that the US dollar risk-free rate is 6%, the FX global beta of the yen is 0.05, and the global risk premium is 4%. Assume that the risk-free interest rate in yen is 3% and that the volatility of the yen is 0.18. Find the Japanese division's cost of capital in yen by using the risk-adjusted version of the UIRP to estimate the equilibrium expected rate of change in the FX value of the yen.

*9. UVC Company has an operating beta (in US dollars) of 1.35, given that its entire production (components and assembly) is in the United States. If UVC relocates its assembly plant to the Eurozone, keeping only its component production in the US, its FX operating exposure to the euro will fall from 3.88 to 1.80. Assuming that the euro's FX global beta is 0.05, find UVC's new operating beta if it relocates its assembly to the Eurozone. Find UVC's cost of capital (in US dollars) before and after the move, if the risk-free rate in US dollars is 5%, and if the global risk premium in US dollars is 4%. Convert the US dollar cost of capital into euros, assuming that the euro's FX global beta is 0.05, volatility is 0.08, and the risk-free rate in euros is 3%; use the risk-adjusted UIRP to estimate the equilibrium expected rate of change in the FX value of the euro.

*10. PPC Company is a British subsidiary of a US multinational. PPC imports some components from a US division of the multinational. From the US dollar viewpoint, PPC's FX operating exposure to the British pound is 1.50. PPC has a local competitor, CVB Ltd. In British pounds, CVB has an FX operating exposure to the US dollar of 1.25. You have estimated CVB's operating beta (in US dollars) to be 0.85. CVB is a pure play proxy for PPC, except that the different production locations imply the different FX operating exposures. If the FX global beta of the British pound is 0.08, what is PPC's estimated operating beta?

ANSWERS TO PROBLEMS

1. The estimated operating beta of the New Zealand division (in US dollars) is $(0.50/0.40)(0.70) = 0.875$.

2. Goodfoods-New Zealand's cost of capital in US dollars is $0.06 + 0.875(0.04) = 0.095$. The equilibrium expected change in the FX value of the New Zealand dollar is $0.06 - 0.069 = -0.009$. We find Goodfoods-New Zealand's cost of capital in local currency by using equation (10.2): $0.095 - (-0.009) + (1 - 1)0.07^2 = 0.104$, or 10.4%.

3. The estimated operating beta of the New Zealand division is $0.70(1.22) = 0.854$.

4. Goodfoods-New Zealand's cost of capital in US dollars is $0.06 + 0.854(0.04) = 0.094$. The equilibrium expected change in the FX value of the New Zealand dollar is $0.06 - 0.069 = -0.009$. We find Goodfoods-New Zealand's cost of capital in local currency by using equation (10.2): $0.094 - (-0.009) + (1 - 1.20)0.11^2 = 0.10$, or 10%.

5. From equation (10.1), the answer is $k_i^\$ = 0.03 + 1(0.04) + 0.50(0.08) = 0.11$, or 11%.

6. The intrinsic value of XYZ is the total value of the actual debt and equity, $4000. The value of the actual debt, $1000, is 25% of XYZ's intrinsic value. Thus $D^\$/V^\$ = 0.25$. The total value of the euro liabilities is $500 + $300 = $800, which is 20% of the firm's intrinsic value, and the FX global beta of the euro is 0.08. The sterling liabilities (notional swap principal) are $1000, which is 25% of the firm's intrinsic value, and the FX global beta of the pound is 0.20. Thus, $\beta_O^\$ = 1.20(1 - 0.25) + 0.08(0.20) + 0.20(0.25) = 0.966$.

7. Unlever the US dollar equity beta of the overseas pure play to get its estimated operating beta, using equation (10.3): $1.35(1 - 0.25) + 0.10(0.25) = 1.0375$. The cost of capital of the overseas subsidiary, in US dollars, is $0.06 + 1.0375(0.04) = 0.1015$, or 10.15%. The equilibrium expected percentage change in the FX value of the Australian dollar is $0.06 - 0.07 = -0.01$. The division's estimated cost of capital in Australian dollars is $0.1015 - (-0.01) + (1 - (-0.25))(0.0081) = 0.1216$, or 12.16%.

8. The estimated equilibrium expected rate of change in the FX value of the yen is $0.06 - 0.03 + 0.05(0.04) = 0.032$. From equation (10.2), SCC-Japan's cost of capital in yen is $0.124 - 0.032 + (1 - 1.42)0.18^2 = 0.078$, or 7.80%.

9. The new operating beta is $1.35 + 0.05(1.80 - 3.88) = 1.25$. The old cost of capital in US dollars is $0.05 + 1.35(0.04) = 0.104$, or 10.4%. The new cost of capital in US dollars is $0.05 + 1.25(0.04) = 0.10$, or 10%. The equilibrium expected change in the FX value of the euro is $0.05 - 0.03 + 0.05(0.04) = 0.022$. The old cost of capital in euros is $0.104 - 0.022 + (1 - 3.88)0.08^2 = 0.0636$, or 6.36%. The new cost of capital in euros is $0.10 - 0.022 + (1 - 1.80)0.08^2 = 0.073$, or 7.3%.

10. First, convert CVB's FX operating exposure to the US dollar to an FX operating exposure to the British pound via equation (5.2): $\xi_{O\pounds}^\$ = 1 - \xi_{O\$}^\pounds = 1 - 1.25 = -0.25$. From equation (10.4), PPC's operating beta is estimated to be $0.85 + 0.08[1.50 - (-0.25)] = 0.99$.

APPENDIX

Derivation of Equation (10.2)

An asset's across-currency return identity $(1 + R_i^\$) = (1 + R_i^\epsilon)(1 + x^{\$/\epsilon})$ has the linear approximation (Itô) $R_I^\$ \approx R_i^\epsilon + x^{\$/\epsilon} + \text{cov}(R_i^\epsilon, x^{\$/\epsilon})$. Applying expectations to the linear approximation, we have that $E(R_I^\$) \approx E(R_i^\epsilon) + E(x^{\$/\epsilon}) + \text{cov}(R_i^\epsilon, x^{\$/\epsilon})$. Note that $\text{cov}(R_i^\epsilon, x^{\$/\epsilon}) = -\text{cov}(R_i^\$ - x^{\$/\epsilon}, x^{\$/\epsilon}) = \sigma_\epsilon^2 - \text{cov}(R_i^\$, x^{\$/\epsilon})$, and that $\text{cov}(R_i^\$, x^{\$/\epsilon}) = \xi_{i\epsilon}^\$\sigma_\epsilon^2$, where $\xi_{i\epsilon}^\$$ represents the FX exposure of asset i to the euro, and σ_ϵ is the standard deviation of $x^{\$/\epsilon}$, that is, the volatility of the FX value of the euro from the US dollar point of view. Thus we have the mathematical relationship that $E(R_i^\epsilon) \approx E(R_i^\$) - E(x^{\$/\epsilon}) + (1 - \xi_{i\epsilon}^\$)\sigma_\epsilon^2$. Expressed in terms of equilibrium concepts, this relationship is equation (10.2).

Derivation of Equation (10.3)

We start with the notion that the overall firm is a portfolio consisting of liabilities and equity. The beta of the overall firm (the portfolio), as if it were an all-equity firm, is the operating beta, denoted $\beta_O^\$$. The portfolio beta is a weighted average of the betas of the liabilities and the equity.

Liabilities denominated in the home currency (the US dollar here) are assumed to have zero beta. The beta of a liability denominated in a foreign currency is equal to the FX global beta of the currency. The total amount of liability in, say, euros, $L_\epsilon^\$$, consists of the fair value of the actual euro debt positions (including the net MTM gain or loss that has been taken to the balance sheet) and of the currency swap positions on euros.

Letting $(1 - D^\$/V^\$)$ be the weight on the equity beta and $L_\mathrm{€}^\$/V^\$$ be the weight on the euro liabilities, and so forth, equation (10.3) may be seen as a portfolio beta formulation.

Derivation of Equation (10.4)

Start with the linear return–generating model, $R_i^\$ = a_i^\$ + \xi_{i\mathrm{€}}^\$ x^{\$/\mathrm{€}} + \varepsilon_i^\$$, where $\xi_{i\mathrm{€}}^\$$ is asset i's FX exposure to the euro. Take the covariance of both sides of this equation with the return on the global market (in US dollars), $R_G^\$$, to get $\mathrm{cov}(R_i^\$, R_G^\$) = a_i^\$ + \xi_{i\mathrm{€}}^\$ \mathrm{cov}(x^{\$/\mathrm{€}}, R_G^\$) + \mathrm{cov}(\varepsilon_i^\$, R_G^\$)$. Divide both sides by the variance of $R_G^\$$, and note that the definition of a beta is covariance with $R_G^\$$, divided by the variance of $R_G^\$$, to get $\beta_i^\$ = \xi_{i\mathrm{€}}^\$ \beta_\mathrm{€}^\$ + \beta_{\varepsilon i}^\$$. Repeat for asset j to get $\beta_j^\$ = \xi_{j\mathrm{€}}^\$ \beta_\mathrm{€}^\$ + \beta_{\varepsilon j}^\$$. Subtract the second beta equation from the first and note that if assets i and j have different betas only on account of FX exposure, then $\beta_{\varepsilon i}^\$ = \beta_{\varepsilon j}^\$$. The result is equation (10.4).

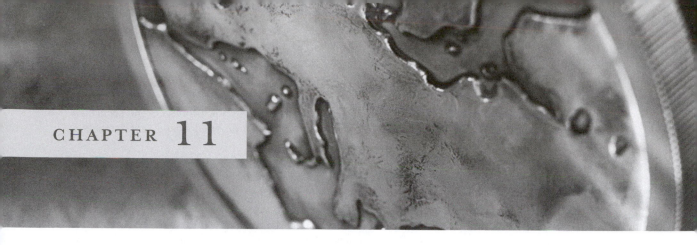

CHAPTER 11

ACCOUNTING
FOR FOREIGN
INVESTMENTS
AND HEDGING

This chapter compares the impact of exchange rate changes on a firm's cash flows and intrinsic equity value with the impact on reported financial statements. The impact of FX changes on reported financial statements is termed *FX accounting exposure*.

We review the rules for the accounting translation of foreign assets and liabilities for US firms. These rules are laid out in Statement of Financial Accounting Standards No. 52 (SFAS 52), *Foreign Currency Translation*, which has been in effect since 1981, and in a series of related subsequent pronouncements under the general framework of SFAS 52. *Translation* is similar to conversion but refers specifically to accounting items, not intrinsic values or cash flows. *FX translation exposure* is a specific aspect of FX accounting exposure that relates to the impact of FX changes on a firm's reporting of foreign assets, liabilities, and income.

We also give an introduction to some relevant aspects of Statement of Financial Accounting Standards No. 133 (SFAS 133), *Accounting for Derivative Instruments and Hedging Activities*, issued in 1998. Its main requirement is that the mark-to-market value of derivatives (e.g., forward contracts, options, swaps) be reflected in reported financial statements. The rules also apply to derivatives embedded in other contracts and securities. The impact of the MTM changes of these derivatives on reported financial statements is another aspect of FX accounting exposure.

Since the accounting rules are very detailed and complex, we cover only main ideas. In particular, we show that although a company may hedge FX exposure with foreign currency debt or a currency swap, the impact of FX changes on reported current earnings might not reflect their impact on net cash flow. And changes in its reported book value of equity may not reflect the true changes in the intrinsic equity value. As you'll see, reported current earnings can be volatile even when net cash flows are stable, and the reported book value of a firm's equity can change even when the intrinsic value is stable, and vice versa.

FX TRANSLATION AND SFAS 52

SFAS 52 deals with two main issues, the restatement of individual accounting items transacted in a foreign currency and the translation of foreign affiliates' financial statements as a precondition for their inclusion in a parent's consolidated statements. There is a parallel standard under the international accounting standards with similar, albeit not identical rules, International Accounting Standard No. 21 (IAS 21).

SFAS 52 requires a US parent to choose a *functional currency* for each overseas affiliate (branch, subsidiary, division, joint venture, etc.). As defined by SFAS 52, the functional currency is the currency of the primary economic environment in which the entity generates and expends cash. In some cases, the functional currency is the US dollar. For example, an affiliate in a less developed country might use cheap labor to assemble parts from the United States and then export the finished products back to the United States. A *maquiladora* in Mexico is typical of such arrangements.

If an entity's functional currency is the US dollar, any asset or liability that is carried on the entity's local currency books at historical cost is translated into US dollars at the historical FX rate at the time the item was recorded. Any asset or liability that is carried on the entity's local currency books at fair value is translated at the current spot FX rate. This method is the called the *temporal method*. Under the temporal method, there is FX accounting exposure only for the fair value accounts, and the gains and losses must be included in the parent's current reported earnings. The economic reasoning behind this treatment is that the US dollar is the primary economic environment in which the entity generates and expends cash, so the impact of FX changes figure directly into the entity's short-run profitability.

SUMMARY OF SFAS NO. 52: FOREIGN CURRENCY TRANSLATION (ISSUED IN DECEMBER 1981)

Application of this Statement will affect financial reporting of most companies operating in foreign countries. The differing operating and economic characteristics of varied types of foreign operations will be distinguished in accounting for them. Adjustments for currency exchange rate changes are excluded from net income for those fluctuations that do not impact cash flows and are included for those that do. The requirements reflect these general conclusions:

The economic effects of an exchange rate change on an operation that is relatively self-contained and integrated within a foreign country relate to the net investment in that operation. Translation adjustments that arise from consolidating that foreign operation do not impact cash flows and are not included in net income.

The economic effects of an exchange rate change on a foreign operation that is an extension of the parent's domestic operations relate to individual assets and liabilities and impact the parent's cash flows directly. Accordingly, the exchange gains and losses in such an operation are included in net income.

Contracts, transactions, or balances that are, in fact, effective hedges of foreign exchange risk will be accounted for as hedges without regard to their form.

More specifically, this Statement replaces FASB Statement No. 8, *Accounting for the Translation of Foreign Currency Transactions and Foreign Currency Financial Statements*, and revises the existing accounting and reporting requirements for translation of foreign currency transactions and foreign currency financial statements. It presents standards for foreign currency translation that are designed to (1) provide information that is generally compatible with the expected economic effects of a rate change on an enterprise's cash flows and equity and (2) reflect in consolidated statements the financial results and relationships as measured in the primary currency in which each entity conducts its business (referred to as its "functional currency").

An entity's functional currency is the currency of the primary economic environment in which that entity operates. The functional currency can be the dollar or a foreign currency depending on the facts. Normally, it will be the currency of the economic environment in which cash is generated and expended by the entity. An entity can be any form of operation, including a subsidiary, division, branch, or joint venture. The Statement provides guidance for this key determination in which management's judgment is essential in assessing the facts.

A currency in a highly inflationary environment (3-year inflation rate of approximately 100 percent or more) is not considered stable enough to serve as a functional currency and the more stable currency of the reporting parent is to be used instead.

(continued)

The functional currency translation approach adopted in this Statement encompasses:

a. Identifying the functional currency of the entity's economic environment
b. Measuring all elements of the financial statements in the functional currency
c. Using the current exchange rate for translation from the functional currency to the reporting currency, if they are different
d. Distinguishing the economic impact of changes in exchange rates on a net investment from the impact of such changes on individual assets and liabilities that are receivable or payable in currencies other than the functional currency

Translation adjustments are an inherent result of the process of translating a foreign entity's financial statements from the functional currency to US dollars. Translation adjustments are *not* included in determining net income for the period but are disclosed and accumulated in a separate component of consolidated equity until sale or until complete or substantially complete liquidation of the net investment in the foreign entity takes place.

Transaction gains and losses are a result of the effect of exchange rate changes on transactions denominated in currencies other than the functional currency (for example, a US company may borrow Swiss francs or a French subsidiary may have a receivable denominated in kroner from a Danish customer). Gains and losses on those foreign currency transactions are generally included in determining net income for the period in which exchange rates change unless the transaction hedges a foreign currency commitment or a net investment in a foreign entity. Intercompany transactions of a long-term investment nature are considered part of a parent's net investment and hence do not give rise to gains or losses.

Source: www.fasb.org.

For most affiliates, especially those in developed economies, the functional currency is the local currency of the country in which the entity operates. The treatment of translation gains and losses in this case is by the so-called *modified closing rate method*. Under this method, all the affiliate's assets and liabilities are translated at the current spot FX rate and the equity is translated at historical rates. This way, the translated values of the affiliate's balance sheet will not equal out. The resulting differences represent FX translation exposure and are booked in a special category of the parent's consolidated equity called the *cumulative translation adjustment (CTA)*, which is part of a broader equity account called *accumulated other comprehensive income (AOCI)*.

As an example, consider the US parent, MRT Company, of a Eurozone subsidiary, DEP LLC. The functional currency of DEP is the euro. The total book value of DEP's assets is assumed to be €3 million. Assume further that DEP has €1 million in euro-denominated debt, and that MRT owns all of DEP's €2 million in equity. Assume a current spot FX rate of 1 $/€ and a historical spot FX rate for DEP's equity of 1.25 $/€. DEP's assets are translated as $3 million, DEP's liabilities as $1 million, and equity as $2.50 million. Also in its equity section, MRT will show a CTA for DEP of −$0.50 million. Looking at the two

EXHIBIT 11.1 FX Translation

TIME-0 BALANCE SHEET TRANSLATION (US$) FOR DEP

Assets	Liabilities & Equity
	$1 million DEP debt
	−$0.50 million AOCI
	$2.50 million common stock
$3.00 million DEP assets	$2 million net investment in DEP
$3 million	$3 million

TIME-1 BALANCE SHEET TRANSLATION (US$) FOR DEP

Assets	Liabilities & Equity
	$0.80 million DEP debt
	−$0.90 million AOCI
	$2.50 million common stock
$2.40 million DEP assets	$1.60 million net investment in DEP
$2.40 million	$2.40 million

equity accounts together, the net book value of MRT's equity entries related to DEP is $2.50 million − 0.50 million = $2 million. We call this the book value of MRT's net investment in DEP. It is equal to the net of DEP's translated assets minus its translated liabilities, $3 million − 1 million = $2 million.

If the spot FX value of the euro depreciates to 0.80 $/€ at the next accounting time (time 1), DEP's assets are translated as $2.40 million, DEP's liabilities as $0.80 million, but equity again as $2.50 million. Now in its equity section, MRT will show a CTA for DEP of −$0.90 million. The book value of MRT's net investment in DEP is now $2.50 million − 0.90 million = $1.60 million. The same answer is found by $2.40 million − 0.80 million = $1.60 million. There is a drop of $0.40 million from the time-0 net investment of $2 million. The $0.40 million drop is the change in the AOCI (CTA) account, that is, an FX translation loss for the period. See Exhibit 11.1.

Like pure FX conversion exposure, FX translation exposure is always one-for-one when translation is at the current spot FX rate. For example, we saw that MRT's net investment in DEP dropped by 20%, from $2 million to $1.60 million, when the euro declined by 20%. Denoting the FX translation exposure (to the euro) of a parent's net investment as $\xi_{T\epsilon}^{\$}$, we have equation (11.1):

$$\xi_{T\epsilon}^{\$} = 1 \tag{11.1}$$

Extending the MRT/DEP example, if the euro appreciates by 10% between time 1 and time 2, from 0.80 $/€ to 0.88 $/€, what is MRT's net investment in DEP at time 2? Show that the FX translation exposure is 1.

Answers: If the spot FX value of the euro appreciates to 0.88 $/€ at time 2, DEP's assets are trans-lated as $2.64 million, liabilities as $0.88 million, but equity again as $2.50 million. Now in its equity section, MRT will show a CTA for DEP of −$0.74 million. The book value of MRT's net investment is now $2.50 million − 0.74 million = $2.64 million − 0.88 million = $1.76 million, a gain of $0.16 million from the time-1 level of $1.60 million. The $0.16 million gain is the change in the AOCI (CTA) account, that is, an FX translation gain for the period. Since the book value of the net investment rises by 10% when the FX value of the euro rises by 10%, we see that the FX translation exposure is 1.

Under SFAS 52, FX translation gains and losses are not included in a parent's current reported earnings when the US dollar is not the functional currency of the affiliate. Basically, the FX translation gains and losses are reserved in the AOCI (CTA) account until the affiliate is liquidated (if ever), at which time the accumulated FX translation gain or loss up to that point will be included in the parent's current reported earnings.

A firm's FX translation changes would ideally represent intrinsic value changes, but often this is not the case. For example, consider a parent's net investment in a subsidiary that has a pure FX conversion exposure (= 1), although the intrinsic value of the net invest-ment does not equal its book value. Although the FX value and FX translation exposures of the parent's net investment are both equal to 1, the US dollar changes in the intrinsic value are not equal to the US dollar changes in the book value.

For example, assume the intrinsic value of DEP's equity at time 0 is €3 million. The intrinsic value of DEP's equity is converted at the spot FX rate into the intrinsic value of MRT's net investment in DEP in US dollars: €3 million(1 $/€) = $3 million at time 0. Since the FX value exposure of MRT's net investment in DEP is assumed to be 1, the time-1 intrinsic value of MRT's net investment in DEP in US dollars is 0.80($3 million) = $2.40 million. We see that the intrinsic value of MRT's net investment in DEP drops by $0.60 million when the euro drops by 20%. This loss in intrinsic investment value is more than the drop in the book value of MRT's net investment, $0.40 million. The reason is that the intrinsic value of MRT's net investment into DEP at time 0, $3 million, is higher than the book value, $2 million.

In principle, intrinsic values form a better basis for managerial decision making than accounting values. But intrinsic values are often hard to measure. Accounting values, while somewhat arbitrary, are important because participants in the financial markets may interpret them as estimates of intrinsic values in the absence of other information. You need to understand the difference. As the chapter goes on, you'll see more comparisons of intrinsic values and accounting values.

A US company may borrow Swiss francs or have a receivable denominated in Danish kroner. Under SFAS 52, the accounting items for these FX transactions are restated each period using the current spot FX rate. The change in the statement value from the prior period is a gain or loss that must be included in determining reported earnings for the period, unless the transaction hedges a foreign currency commitment or a net investment in a foreign entity. Since the accounting rules for FX hedging were extended and clarified under SFAS 133, we cover them next as part of that topic.

HEDGING AND SFAS 133

Managers who want to hedge FX exposure should know how the hedging would be reflected in their firms' financial statements. The US accounting rules for hedging are laid out in SFAS 133, which retains the hedging rules of SFAS 52. There is an international accounting standard that contains rules similar to SFAS 133 called *International Accounting Standard 39 (IAS 39)*. The basic ideas we cover in this chapter on SFAS 133 also generally apply under IAS 39.[1]

In general, SFAS 133 requires that the MTM value of all positions in derivatives appear on the balance sheet and the changes in MTM value be included in the computation of current reported earnings. SFAS 133 also spells out conditions under which a derivative position may qualify for *hedge accounting*: special rules for the treatment of derivatives when hedging to achieve a matching of a derivative's gains and losses with those of the underlying hedged item in reported earnings.

SFAS 133 recognizes three categories of hedges: (1) *fair value hedges*, where the company is hedging the fair value of an asset or liability; (2) *cash flow hedges*, where the company is hedging an anticipated cash flow; and (3) *net investment hedges*, where the company is hedging the net investment (book value) of a foreign asset, a foreign subsidiary, for example.

SUMMARY OF SFAS NO. 133: ACCOUNTING FOR DERIVATIVE INSTRUMENTS AND HEDGING ACTIVITIES (ISSUED 6/98)

This Statement establishes accounting and reporting standards for derivative instruments, including certain derivative instruments embedded in other contracts (collectively referred to as derivatives) and for hedging activities. It requires that an entity recognize all derivatives as either assets or liabilities in the statement of financial position and measure those instruments at fair value. If certain conditions are met, a derivative may be specifically designated as (a) a hedge of the exposure to changes in the fair value of a recognized asset or liability or an unrecognized firm

(continued)

---

[1]SFAS 133 also refers to a Financial Accounting Standards Board (FASB) 800-page compendium, the "Green Book," which includes amendments to SFAS 133 and interpretations and clarifications by the Derivatives Implementation Group (DIG), consisting of derivatives experts of accounting firms. A useful site is http://www.trinity.edu/rjensen/acct5341/speakers/133glosf.htm#0000Begin.

commitment, (b) a hedge of the exposure to variable cash flows of a forecasted transaction, or (c) a hedge of the foreign currency exposure of a net investment in a foreign operation, an unrecognized firm commitment, an available-for-sale security, or a foreign-currency-denominated forecasted transaction.

The accounting for changes in the fair value of a derivative (that is, gains and losses) depends on the intended use of the derivative and the resulting designation.

- For a derivative designated as hedging the exposure to changes in the fair value of a recognized asset or liability or a firm commitment (referred to as a fair value hedge), the gain or loss is recognized in earnings in the period of change together with the offsetting loss or gain on the hedged item attributable to the risk being hedged. The effect of that accounting is to reflect in earnings the extent to which the hedge is not effective in achieving offsetting changes in fair value.

- For a derivative designated as hedging the exposure to variable cash flows of a forecasted transaction (referred to as a cash flow hedge), the effective portion of the derivative's gain or loss is initially reported as a component of other comprehensive income (outside earnings) and subsequently reclassified into earnings when the forecasted transaction affects earnings. The ineffective portion of the gain or loss is reported in earnings immediately.

- For a derivative designated as hedging the foreign currency exposure of a net investment in a foreign operation, the gain or loss is reported in other comprehensive income (outside earnings) as part of the cumulative translation adjustment. The accounting for a fair value hedge described above applies to a derivative designated as a hedge of the foreign currency exposure of an unrecognized firm commitment or an available-for-sale security. Similarly, the accounting for a cash flow hedge described above applies to a derivative designated as a hedge of the foreign currency exposure of a foreign-currency-denominated forecasted transaction.

- For a derivative not designated as a hedging instrument, the gain or loss is recognized in earnings in the period of change.

Under this Statement, an entity that elects to apply hedge accounting is required to establish at the inception of the hedge the method it will use for assessing the effectiveness of the hedging derivative and the measurement approach for determining the ineffective aspect of the hedge. Those methods must be consistent with the entity's approach to managing risk. This Statement applies to all entities. A not-for-profit organization should recognize the change in fair value of all derivatives as a change in net assets in the period of change. In a fair value hedge, the changes in the fair value of the hedged item attributable to the risk being hedged also are recognized. However, because of the format of their statement of financial performance, not-for-profit organizations are not permitted special hedge accounting for derivatives used to hedge forecasted transactions. This Statement does not address how a not-for-profit organization should determine the components of an operating measure if one is presented.

This Statement precludes designating a nonderivative financial instrument as a hedge of an asset, liability, unrecognized firm commitment, or forecasted transaction except that a nonderivative instrument denominated in a foreign currency may be designated as a hedge of the foreign currency exposure of an unrecognized firm commitment denominated in a foreign currency or a net investment in a foreign operation.

This Statement amends FASB Statement No. 52, *Foreign Currency Translation*, to permit special accounting for a hedge of a foreign currency forecasted transaction with a derivative. It supersedes FASB Statements No. 80, *Accounting for Futures Contracts*, No. 105, *Disclosure of Information about Financial Instruments with Off–Balance–Sheet Risk and Financial Instruments with Concentrations of Credit Risk*, and No. 119, *Disclosure about Derivative Financial Instruments and Fair Value of Financial Instruments*. It amends FASB Statement No. 107, *Disclosures about Fair Value of Financial Instruments*, to include in Statement 107 the disclosure provisions about concentrations of credit risk from Statement 105. This Statement also nullifies or modifies the consensuses reached in a number of issues addressed by the Emerging Issues Task Force.

This Statement is effective for all fiscal quarters of fiscal years beginning after June 15, 1999. Initial application of this Statement should be as of the beginning of an entity's fiscal quarter; on that date, hedging relationships must be designated anew and documented pursuant to the provisions of this Statement. Earlier application of all of the provisions of this Statement is encouraged, but it is permitted only as of the beginning of any fiscal quarter that begins after issuance of this Statement. This Statement should not be applied retroactively to financial statements of prior periods.

Source: www.fasb.org.

The simplest case is the fair value hedge, where the risk being hedged is a change in the fair value of an asset or liability that will affect current reported earnings. For example, suppose a US company issues a euro-denominated bond as part of a swap-driven financing, with the company hedging the FX exposure of the bond by taking a long euro position in a currency swap. In this case, the swap position may be regarded as a fair value hedge of FX risk. No special hedge accounting treatment applies in this case, but an example of the accounting treatment is instructive.

The accounting for the euro-denominated bond follows the FX transaction rules of SFAS 52. The US dollar value of the bond is restated each period using the current spot FX rate, and the gains and losses are reported in current earnings. The accounting for the swap follows the rules of SFAS 133. The MTM value the swap position must be shown on the balance sheet, and changes in the MTM value are included in the computation of current reported earnings.

By design of the synthetic US dollar debt, the gain or loss on changes in the value of the bond in US dollars and the MTM gain or loss on the currency swap position tend to offset each other. If the FX value of the euro increases, the fair value of the bond in US dollars increases (a loss for the issuer), while the MTM value of the long euro swap position rises. If the FX value of the euro decreases, the fair value of the bond in US dollars drops (a gain for the issuer), while the MTM value of the swap position drops. For simplicity, our example will show the offset to be exact, although the actual offset may not be exact owing to differences in the credit risk of the counterparties involved, timing differences between the swap payments and debt interest payments, and so forth.

Exhibit 11.2 shows this situation for XYZ Company. SFAS 133 requires that the MTM value of the swap be shown on the balance sheet. The one-sided values of the two notional principal amounts are not shown on the actual balance sheet. Exhibit 11.2 shows them "off." At time 0, the swap is at market (i.e., the one-sided values of the swap are equal), so there is no MTM value on the balance sheet at time 0. When the FX value of the euro drops by 20%, the unrealized MTM loss on the swap position is shown as an unrealized liability on the reported balance sheet in Exhibit 11.2, but the net result is no change

EXHIBIT 11.2 Fair Value Hedge: XYZ Company Reported Balance Sheets for Long Euro Currency Swap Hedging Euro-Denominated Debt

TIME 0

	Assets	Liabilities & Equity
(Off)	$ 200 (long €, $W_\epsilon^\$$)	$ 200 (short $, $W_\$^\$$)
		$ 200 €-debt
	$2000 assets of firm	$1800 equity
	$2000	$2000

IF EURO DROPS BY 20% (TIME 1)

	Assets	Liabilities & Equity
(Off)	$ 160 (long €, $W_\epsilon^\$$)	$ 200 (short $, $W_\$^\$$)
		$160 €-Debt
		$ 40 MTM loss on swap, $M_\epsilon^\$$
		$ 200 total liabilities
	$2000 assets of firm	$1800 equity
	$2000	$2000

IF EURO RISES BY 20% (TIME 1)

	Assets	Liabilities & Equity
(Off)	$ 240 (long €, $W_\epsilon^\$$)	$ 200 (short $, $W_\$^\$$)
	$ 40 MTM gain on swap, $M_\epsilon^\$$	$ 240 €-debt
	$2000 assets of firm	$1800 equity
	$2040	$2040

in total liabilities because the value of the euro debt is also restated. The unrealized gain on the euro bond and the unrealized MTM loss on the swap position go to current reported earnings, but there is no net impact, since the gain and the loss are offsetting. This accounting boils down to being equivalent to the case of the firm that has simply issued debt denominated in US dollars, as it should be for synthetic US dollar debt.

If the euro appreciates by 20% instead of depreciating, euro debt would be restated at $240. The long side of the swap would be worth $240 and the MTM value of the swap would be $40. In this case the MTM value would show as an asset in the form of an unrealized gain. The unrealized loss on the euro bond and the unrealized MTM gain on the swap position go to current reported earnings, but there again is no net impact, since the two amounts are offsetting. This accounting boils down to being equivalent to the case of the firm that has simply issued debt denominated in US dollars, as it should be for synthetic US dollar debt.

Could a foreign currency debt or swap position that a firm uses to hedge FX value exposure qualify as a fair value hedge? This might be difficult for a firm to establish because changes in the intrinsic value of an ongoing operation may be difficult to measure. But if a firm were able to establish a hedge of intrinsic value changes as a fair value hedge under SFAS 133, the accounting treatment would require that the changes in fair (intrinsic) value of the underlying investment be reflected on the firm's balance sheet (not historical book value or translated net investment value). Then the change in the fair (intrinsic) value of the underlying investment must be included in the computation of reported current earnings along with the MTM changes of the hedge instrument.

This period-by-period recognition of the unrealized changes in fair value of the underlying hedged investment is a deviation from normal accounting rules and constitutes hedge accounting in the case of fair value hedges to create a matching of gains and loss. That is, hedge accounting in the case of a fair value hedge involves and acceleration of the recognition as earnings of the changes in value of the hedged investment, while the hedge position is treated as it would be if it were not considered to be a hedge.

CASH FLOW HEDGES

Another type of hedge position in SFAS 133 is a hedge of an anticipated cash flow, that is, a cash flow hedge. In terms of accounting, if a firm gets a hedge position qualified as a cash flow hedge under SFAS 133, the benefit is that the hedge position receives hedge accounting treatment. In the case of cash flow hedges, "hedge accounting treatment" means that the MTM changes on the hedge position are deferred from inclusion in current reported earnings until the underlying cash flow being hedged is included in current earnings.

To qualify as a hedge of an anticipated cash flow under SFAS 133, a hedge position must pass a test for *hedge effectiveness*. If the firm wants the position to qualify as a cash flow hedge, it must file written documentation prior to taking a hedge position. This formal documentation must include (1) identification of the hedging instrument and the hedged item or transaction; (2) the nature of the risk being hedged, including proof of a high probability that the cash flow will occur; (3) the risk management objective or strategy; and (4) an explanation of how hedging effectiveness will be assessed. Hedge effectiveness must be reviewed frequently; if a hedge position no longer passes the test, changes in the MTM value of the position must be immediately and fully recorded in current earnings. A complication is that a hedge position might only partially hedge some underlying risk. In this case, the ineffective portion of the hedge must be measured and included in current reported earnings.

An example of a simple cash flow hedge may be constructed in the context of hedging FX transaction exposure with a forward FX position. Assume you expect to pay €2000 to buy a machine in two years. Although the outlay is planned, it is not a legal obligation, so it is not a liability on your books. Assume that the two-year forward FX rate is $F_2^{\$/€} = 1.25$ \$/€. To hedge the FX transaction exposure, you take a long two-year forward position on euros with a contract size of $Z^{€} = €2000$. The contract amount is $A^{\$} = €2000(1.25 \text{ \$/€}) = \$2500$. After a year has passed, there is one year left until the delivery time. Assume that the spot FX rate is then 1 \$/€, the one-year US dollar interest rate is 5% and the one-year euro interest rate is 3%. The MTM value of the long forward FX position taken a year earlier is 1 \$/€(€2000/1.03) − \$2500/1.05 = −\$439. [This computation follows equation (3–4).]

Regardless of whether the forward FX position qualifies as a cash flow hedge, SFAS 133 requires that the \$439 MTM loss now appear as an unrealized liability on the firm's reported balance sheet, and the firm's reported equity will be lower by \$439 than it otherwise would have been.

If the firm filed the proper documentation at time 0, including evidence that the anticipated cash outflow of €2000 was highly probable, and if that is still the case a year later, then the forward FX position is very likely to qualify as a cash flow hedge under SFAS 133. In such a case, the \$439 MTM loss receives hedge accounting treatment, where the loss does not have to be reported as part of the company's current earnings. Instead, −\$439 is regarded as other comprehensive income and added to the AOCI account in the equity section. The AOCI for the hedge will be reclassified into current earnings when the cash flow being hedged is included in current earnings.

If none of the forward FX position qualifies as a hedge under SFAS 133, the entire MTM loss is included in the computation of current reported earnings. On the balance sheet, the firm's reported equity is still lower by \$439, but this time it is the accumulated retained earnings account that is lower, not the AOCI account.

Exhibit 11.3 shows the changes in the accounts on the company's reported balance sheet when accounting for the forward FX contract. The firm is assumed to have assets and equity of \$50,000 at time 0. The firm's equity consists of \$30,000 of common stock, \$20,000 of accumulated retained earnings, and 0 of AOCI. Assume that reported current earnings would be \$5000 (all cash) at time 1, ignoring the MTM loss. The firm pays no dividends, so the cash earnings are reinvested into the firm's assets. At time 1, the firm has assets of \$55,000, an unrealized liability of \$439, and equity of \$54,561. Under the hedge accounting treatment, the MTM loss is not included in current earnings and is taken to the AOCI account. Without hedge accounting treatment, the MTM loss is included in current earnings and taken to the accumulated retained earnings account. [There are no tax implications because the cash flow and the hedge outcome have not been realized.]

EXHIBIT 11.3 Cash Flow Hedge and Reported Financial Statements

TIME 0

Assets	Liabilities & Equity
	$30,000 common stock
	$20,000 accumulated retained earnings
$50,000 assets of firm	$50,000 equity
$50,000	$50,000

AFTER EURO DROPS BY 20% (TIME 1)

Forward FX Position Qualifies as a Cash Flow Hedge

Assets	Liabilities & Equity
	$439 unrealized MTM loss
	$30,000 common stock
	$25,000 accumulated retained earnings
	−$439 AOCI
$55,000 assets of firm	$54,561 equity
$55,000	$55,000
Reported current earnings: $5000	

Forward FX Position Does NOT Qualify as a Cash Flow Hedge

Assets	Liabilities & Equity
	$439 unrealized MTM loss
	$30,000 common stock
	$24,561 accumulated retained earnings
$55,000 assets of firm	$54,561 equity
$55,000	$55,000
Reported current earnings: $4561	

The reported balance sheets in Exhibit 11.3 do not consider the change in the intrinsic value of the future cash flow being hedged. If changes in the intrinsic value of the anticipated cash flow were also marked to market and reflected in the reported financial statements, these changes would tend to offset those of the forward FX position. In that case, the accounting treatment would be consistent with the economic function of the hedge. Often, however, the changes in the intrinsic value of the underlying hedged item cannot be reflected in the reported balance sheet.

The box on Kashima Oil shows what can happen when the MTM changes on hedging instruments must be included in current earnings but changes in the intrinsic value of the hedged item cannot be.

KASHIMA OIL

Accounting for MTM changes in FX derivative positions, when the FX exposure being hedged is not reported in earnings, produces volatility in earnings for a firm. The effect can create severe problems. An example is Kashima Oil, which refines imported oil for the Japanese market. In the early 1990s, the strong yen meant cheap inputs and high profits. Concerned that the US dollar would appreciate, and thus that the price of oil would rise in yen terms, Kashima took long forward FX positions on the US dollar to hedge its anticipated future oil purchases. Then the US dollar instead continued to depreciate against the yen. While this depreciation was good news in terms of Kashima's anticipated future operating costs and operating cash flows, it was bad news in terms of its forward FX positions.

When the US dollar depreciated, Kashima had unrealized losses of ¥153 billion ($1.50 billion) on the forward FX positions, which dwarfed the company's total current annual pretax profit of ¥12.5 billion. While this was an unrealized accounting loss that did not require cash at that point (but would later), the accounting loss was measured, but the corresponding economic gain on the present value of the anticipated future revenue stream being hedged was not (and could not be) accounted for on paper. The circumstances required the firm to sell ¥100 billion worth of property and securities, and four parent firms and 29 banks had to infuse fresh capital.

If a company's FX exposure is to a foreign currency that does not have liquid trading in hedging instruments, the firm may be able to *cross-hedge* with instruments denominated in a different foreign currency that is highly correlated with the actual currency of the FX exposure. SFAS 133 requires that the company be able to prove the correlation between the actual currency of the exposure and the currency selected as the hedging vehicle, and it is likely that only a portion of the hedge position will pass the effectiveness test.

If a firm wants to use a currency swap position to hedge the FX exposure of foreign currency debt, the firm can generally get the position qualified as a cash flow hedge instead of a fair value hedge if it wants. We can see this in the box containing note 17 to Altria Group's 2002 Financial Statements. The impact on financial statements is generally the same as if the situation were a fair value hedge, although there may be some preferred short-run accounting consequences of one or the other.

Multinationals usually apply cash flow hedge accounting when they hedge the FX exposure of their anticipated (i.e., budgeted) FX cash flows over a relatively short-term planning horizon. Hedge accounting for positions that hedge the long-term FX operating exposure of a stream of future cash flows may be possible under SFAS 133, as long as the cash flows are somewhat predictable. This predictability may be difficult to establish under the SFAS 133 rules, in which case the manager may be able to obtain hedge accounting for the position, or at least part of it, as a net investment hedge, as we cover next.[2]

ALTRIA GROUP: NOTE 17 TO 2002 CONSOLIDATED FINANCIAL STATEMENTS

Altria Group, Inc. operates globally, with manufacturing and sales facilities in various locations around the world, and utilizes certain financial instruments to manage its foreign currency and commodity exposures, which primarily relate to forecasted transactions and debt. Derivative financial instruments are used by Altria Group, Inc., principally to reduce exposures to market risks resulting from fluctuations in foreign exchange rates and commodity prices, by creating offsetting exposures. Altria Group, Inc. is not a party to leveraged derivatives and, by policy, does not use derivative financial instruments for speculative purposes. Financial instruments qualifying for hedge accounting must maintain a specified level of effectiveness between the hedging instrument and the item being hedged, both at inception and throughout the hedged period. Altria Group, Inc. formally documents the nature and relationships between the hedging instruments and hedged items, as well as its risk-management objectives, strategies for undertaking the various hedge transactions and method of assessing hedge effectiveness. Additionally, for hedges of forecasted transactions, the significant characteristics and expected terms of a forecasted transaction must be specifically identified, and it must be probable that each forecasted transaction will occur. If it were deemed probable that the forecasted transaction will not occur, the gain or loss would be recognized in earnings currently.

A substantial portion of Altria Group, Inc.'s derivative financial instruments is effective as hedges under SFAS No. 133. Altria Group, Inc. uses forward foreign exchange contracts and foreign currency options to mitigate its exposure to changes in exchange rates from third-party and intercompany forecasted transactions. The primary currencies to which Altria Group, Inc. is exposed include the Japanese yen, Swiss franc and the euro. At December 31, 2002 and 2001, Altria Group, Inc. had option and forward foreign exchange contracts with aggregate notional amounts of $10.1 billion and $3.7 billion, respectively, which are comprised of contracts for the purchase and

(continued)

---

[2]For additional insights on SFAS 133, see A. Ronner and M. Blok, "Hedging Foreign Currency Exposure: Consequences of FAS 133," *Journal of Applied Finance*, No. 1, 2001, 23–34. Also see J. Wallace, "Derivative Accounting & Hedging Under FAS 133," Greenwich Treasury Advisors, at http://www.greenwichtreasury.com/download/Derivative_Accounting.pdf.

sale of foreign currencies. Included in the foreign currency aggregate notional amounts at December 31, 2002 were $2.6 billion of equal and offsetting foreign currency positions, which do not qualify as hedges and that will not result in any net gain or loss. The effective portion of unrealized gains and losses associated with forward contracts and the value of option contracts is deferred as a component of accumulated other comprehensive losses until the underlying hedged transactions are reported on Altria Group, Inc.'s consolidated statement of earnings.

In addition, Altria Group, Inc. uses foreign currency swaps to mitigate its exposure to changes in exchange rates related to foreign currency denominated debt. These swaps typically convert fixed-rate foreign currency denominated debt to fixed-rate debt denominated in the functional currency of the borrowing entity. A substantial portion of the foreign currency swap agreements are accounted for as cash flow hedges. The unrealized gain (loss) relating to foreign currency swap agreements that do not qualify for hedge accounting treatment under SFAS No. 133 was insignificant as of December 31, 2002 and 2001. At December 31, 2002 and 2001, the notional amounts of foreign currency swap agreements aggregated $2.5 billion and $2.3 billion, respectively. Aggregate maturities of foreign currency swap agreements at December 31, 2002 (in millions) were as follows: 2003 ($142); 2004 ($189); 2006 ($968); and 2008 ($1165).

Altria Group, Inc. also designates certain foreign currency denominated debt as net investment hedges of foreign operations. During the years ended December 31, 2002 and 2001, losses of $163 million, net of income taxes of $88 million, and losses of $18 million, net of income taxes of $10 million, respectively, which represented effective hedges of net investments, were reported as a component of accumulated other comprehensive losses within currency translation adjustments.

Source: Notes to Financial Statements, 2002: http://www.altria.com/annualreport2002/ar2002_07_07_1400.asp.

NET INVESTMENT HEDGES

SFAS 52 permits the MTM gains and losses on positions that hedge the FX translation changes of a parent's net investment in foreign operations to receive the same accounting treatment as the translation changes themselves. SFAS 133 retains this accounting structure under *net investment hedges*. Foreign currency denominated debt and currency swap positions (naked positions or those in synthetic foreign currency debt) are examples of positions that will qualify as net investment hedges.

We think in terms of hedging the FX exposure of the intrinsic value of an investment in a foreign operation to reduce the uncertainty in a firm's equity value. From the point of view of SFAS 52 and SFAS 133, foreign currency debt or currency swap positions will be regarded as net investment hedges only against book value of the net investment in the foreign operation. The excess of a firm's hedge position over the net investment book value does not qualify as a net investment hedge.

The treatment of gains and losses on actual foreign currency denominated debt that does not qualify as a hedge is covered under SFAS 52, while the treatment of MTM gains and losses on currency swap positions that do not qualify as a hedge is covered under SFAS 133. The effect in both cases is the same: the gains and losses on foreign currency debt and currency swap positions that do not qualify as hedges must be reported in current earnings.

For example, suppose MRT wants to hedge 100% of the FX value exposure of its net investment in DEP with euro-denominated debt or a short currency swap position on euros. Given that the intrinsic value of MRT's net investment in DEP is $3 million and has an FX value exposure to the euro equal to 1, we know that $3 million in euro-denominated debt will hedge the FX value exposure to the euro at time 0. For simplicity, we net DEP's translated asset and liability accounts into one account, the net investment in DEP. At time 0, the book value of the net investment in DEP is $2 million. Assume that MRT has $6 million in other assets. Assume MRT has the $3 million in euro-denominated debt that hedges the FX value exposure. Thus equity book value at time 0 is $8 million − 3 million = $5 million. The intrinsic value of MRT's equity is $9 million − 3 million = $6 million at time 0.

At time 0, SFAS 52 rules would allow only up to $2 million worth of MRT's euro-denominated debt to qualify as a net investment hedge; that is, the rules would allow only the amount equal to the book value of MRT's time-0 net investment in DEP. The MTM gains or losses on the $2 million of euro-denominated debt issued to hedge this net investment book value are taken to the AOCI account, matching the FX translation gain or loss on the net foreign investment. Like the FX translation gains/losses on the book value of the net foreign investment, the MTM gains/losses of this $2 million of euro-denominated debt bypass the current earnings statement.

The other $1 million worth of its euro-denominated debt does not qualify as a net investment hedge because it does not match to a book value of net foreign investment. This $1 million would be regarded under SFAS 52 as a *foreign currency transaction*. The MTM changes on $1 million of euro debt must figure into the computation of current reported earnings.

Assume the euro depreciates by 20% between time 0 and time 1. For clarity, we assume that MRT's net cash flow is paid out to shareholders as dividends. At time 1, the intrinsic value of MRT's net investment in DEP is $2.40 million, so that the intrinsic value of MRT as a whole is $8.40 million. The $3 million in euro-denominated debt is worth $2.40 million, so that the time-1 intrinsic value of MRT's equity is $8.40 million − 2.40 million = $6 million, the same as at time 0. The stability of the intrinsic value of MRT's equity is the point of using the euro-denominated debt as a hedge, as you learned in Chapter 6.

By SFAS 52 rules, the translation loss on MRT's net investment into DEP, $0.40 million, bypasses the current earnings statement and would be taken directly to the AOCI (CTA) account. There is also a gain of $0.40 million on the $2 million of MRT's euro-denominated debt that qualifies as a net investment hedge, and is thus also taken to the AOCI (CTA) account, offsetting the translation loss of $0.40 million on the net investment into the subsidiary.

The remaining $1 million of MRT's euro-denominated debt that does not match with the net investment book value is worth $0.80 million at time 1, representing an MTM gain (noncash) of $0.20 million. Since this portion of MRT's euro-denominated debt does not hedge a net investment book value and is thus considered a foreign currency transaction for accounting purposes, the $0.20 million gain must be reported in current earnings and will be taken to accumulated retained earnings.

The new book value of MRT's total assets is $7.60 million. Since the debt will appear on the reported balance sheet in US dollars as $2.40 million, the time-1 book value of MRT's equity is $7.60 million − 2.40 million = $5.20 million, which is equal to the time-0 book value of equity, $5.20 million, plus the addition to accumulated retained earnings of $0.20 million. Note that current reported earnings and book value of equity are higher by $0.20 million when the euro depreciates, the opposite direction of the firm's FX value exposure. This is because the real hedge position of $3 million exceeds the amount allowed as an accounting hedge, $2 million.

Exhibit 11.4 summarizes this example.

EXHIBIT 11.4 MRT Company (US Parent of DEP) Hedges with $3 million Actual Euro-Denominated Debt: FX Value Exposure (to the euro) of Investment in Subsidiary = 1

TIME-0 BALANCE SHEETS (US$)

Reported	Assets	Liabilities & Equity
	$2 million DEP	$3 million €-debt
	$6 million other	$5 million equity
	$8 million	$8 million
Intrinsic Value	Firm Value	Liabilities & Equity
	$3 million DEP	$3 million €-debt
	$6 million other	$6 million equity
	$9 million	$9 million

TIME-1 BALANCE SHEETS (US$)

Reported	Assets	Liabilities & Equity
	$1.60 million DEP	$2.40 million €-debt
	$6 million other	$5.20 million equity
	$7.60 million	$7.60 million
Intrinsic Value	Firm Value	Liabilities & Equity
	$2.40 million DEP	$2.40 million €-debt
	$6 million other	$6 million equity
	$8.40 million	$8.40 million

ABC Company is a US owner of the Eurozone subsidiary TZL. TZL's functional currency is the euro. From the US dollar perspective, ABC's net investment in TZL has an FX value exposure to the euro of 2. ABC has no currency swap positions; its current reported and intrinsic value balance sheets are shown in the accompanying table. ABC's euro-denominated debt does not qualify as a cash flow hedge, but ABC may use some of the euro-denominated debt as a net investment hedge up to the book value of its net investment in TZL. Assume that the euro appreciates by 10%. (a) What will ABC's time-1 reported and intrinsic value balance sheets look like? (b) Ignoring the impact of the FX change on current operating cash flow, what will be the impact on ABC's reported current earnings?

ABC Time-0 Balance Sheets (US$)

Reported	Assets	Liabilities & Equity
	$2000 TZL	$4000 €-debt
		$1000 AOCI
		$3000 other equity
	$6000 other	$4000 equity
	$8000	$8000

Intrinsic Value	Firm Value	Liabilities & Equity
	$2000 TZL	$4000 €-debt
	$6000 other	$4000 equity
	$8000	$8000

Answers: (a) The intrinsic value of TZL will increase by 2 × 10%, or 20%, so the time-1 intrinsic value is $2400. The book value of TZL increases by 10%, so the time-1 book value is $2200. In US dollars, the value of the $4000 in euro debt increases by 10% to $4400, both in book value and in intrinsic value. Thus, there is a $400 loss on the euro-denominated debt. Since $2000 of the euro debt qualifies as a net investment hedge, $200 of the $400 loss on the euro-denominated debt offsets the FX translation gain on the net investment book value of TZL, so the AOCI does not change. (b) Current reported earnings will be lower by $200, since only half ($2000) of the euro-denominated debt qualifies as a hedge, and thus the MTM gains on the nonqualifying portion go to current earnings. Ignoring taxes, this results in a drop in accumulated retained earnings (here part of "other equity").

ABC Time-1 Balance Sheets (US$)

Reported	Assets	Liabilities & Equity
	$2200 TZL	$4400 €-debt
		$1000 AOCI
		$2800 other equity
	$6000 other	$3800 equity
	$8200	$8200

Intrinsic Value	Firm Value	Liabilities & Equity
	$2400 TZL	$4400 €-debt
	$6000 other	$4000 equity
	$8400	$8400

The same results occur if MRT tries to hedge the FX value exposure with a short euro position in a currency swap that has a notional principal of $3 million, instead of with the euro-denominated debt. If MRT is otherwise all equity, the swap position is naked; if MRT couples the swap position with US dollar debt of $3 million, the company has synthetic euro debt. Either way, if the euro drops falls by 20%, the MTM gain on the swap position is $0.60 million. This gain is shown as an asset on MRT's reported balance sheet under SFAS 133. Since it is an economic gain, we also conceive of it on MRT's intrinsic value balance sheet.

At time 0, $2 million of the notional principal of the swap position qualifies as a net investment hedge under SFAS 133, while the other $1 million is regarded as a foreign currency transaction. If the euro drops by 20%, the MTM gain on the first $2 million ($0.40 million) matches the route of the FX translation loss on the net investment book value through to the AOCI (CTA) account, while the MTM gain on the other $1 million of notional principal ($0.20 million) is included in current reported earnings and goes to the accumulated retained earnings account. In effect, the accounting implications of the currency swap are the same as those of euro-denominated debt, by design of SFAS 133.

Exhibit 11.5 shows the swap scenario assuming that MRT has $3 million in US dollar debt. The off–balance sheet one-sided swap values are not shown, but the swap's MTM gain at time 1 is shown.

The MRT/DEP examples show that the MTM changes on a position that hedges FX value exposure can create FX accounting exposure. The FX accounting exposure in these examples is the MTM change on the portion of the hedge position that does not qualify for hedge accounting. That MTM change is a gain of $0.20 million, which we said is reported in current earnings and which we saw resulted in an increase in the reported book value of the firm's equity.

The reason for the FX accounting exposure in this case is that changes in intrinsic value cannot be accurately measured and thus cannot be reported on accounting statements. The impact of FX changes on the book value of the assets underlying an exposed investment are accounted for, but when the book value changes are not equal to the intrinsic value changes, some FX accounting exposure will result when the firm hedges the FX value changes.

Some companies may decide they do not want to hedge FX value exposure if it means creating FX accounting exposure, especially additional volatility in current reported earnings. Managers may be willing to tolerate real (intrinsic value) FX exposure rather than have FX accounting exposure. The managers may think that the market will mis-interpret the FX accounting exposure.[3]

Before SFAS 133, the accounting treatment for currency swaps, and thus synthetic foreign currency debt, was different from the accounting treatment for actual foreign currency debt. Accounting rules required the reporting of only realized gains or losses on derivatives, rather than the MTM gains or losses. For positions with longer maturities than the current reporting period, the MTM gains or losses were treated as contingent liabilities, required to be disclosed in the aggregate in the notes to the financial statements, but not required to be reported in current earnings or in balance sheet accounts. It was thus

---

[3]For survey evidence, see J. Graham, C. Harvey, and S. Rajgopal, "The Economic Implications of Corporate Financial Reporting," 2004, at http://papers.ssrn.com/sol3/ papers.cfm?abstract_id=491627.

EXHIBIT 11.5 MRT Company (US Parent of German Subsidiary DEP) Hedges with $3 million Short Euro Currency Swap Position: FX Value Exposure of Investment in Subsidiary = 1

TIME-0 BALANCE SHEETS (US$)

Reported	Assets	Liabilities & Equity
	$2 million DEP	$3 million $-debt
	$6 million other	$5 million equity
	$8 million	$8 million

Intrinsic Value	Firm Value	Liabilities & Equity
	$3 million DEP	$3 million $-debt
	$6 million other	$6 million equity
	$9 million	$9 million

TIME-1 BALANCE SHEETS (US$)

Reported	Assets	Liabilities & Equity
	$0.60 million swap MTM	$3 million $-debt
	$1.60 million DEP	
	$6 million other	$5.20 million equity
	$8.20 million	$8.20 million

Intrinsic Value	Firm Value	Liabilities & Equity
	$0.60 million swap MTM	$3 million $-debt
	$2.40 million DEP	
	$6 million other	$6 million equity
	$9 million	$9 million

possible for a firm to hedge FX value exposure with currency swaps and simultaneously avoid FX accounting exposure.

At one time, *currency-indexed debt* was another way for firms to avoid FX accounting exposure when trying to hedge FX value exposure. Currency-indexed debt is technically denominated in an issuer's base currency, but the interest and/or principal is a variable amount that is indexed on an FX rate. If both principal and interest are indexed in direct proportion to an FX rate, then currency-indexed debt is economically the same as foreign currency debt. Alternatively, currency-indexed debt is economically equivalent to synthetic foreign currency debt, constructed out of base currency debt and a currency swap. The PERLs discussed in Chapter 3 are an example of currency-indexed debt. If MRT were to have US dollar debt, with interest and principal indexed to the $/€ FX rate, this bond would behave economically the same as an actual euro-denominated bond. Such a bond would function as a hedge of the FX value exposure. Now, SFAS 133 makes clear that embedded derivatives like this must be accounted for separately as if they were stand-alone derivatives.

FX VALUE EXPOSURE VS FX ACCOUNTING EXPOSURE

In this section, to further compare FX value exposure and FX accounting exposure, we use several scenarios in which a firm's hedge position does not match the net investment book value and the nonmatching portion does not qualify for hedge accounting.

First, assume that XYZ Company has an FX value exposure of 0.40 to the euro because of its investment in Lenox SA, a subsidiary in the Eurozone with the euro as its functional currency. The intrinsic value of XYZ's net investment in Lenox is $10 million. We know that XYZ can use 0.40($10 million) = $4 million in euro-denominated debt to put on a hedge that eliminates its FX equity exposure (in intrinsic value terms).

As long as the book value of XYZ's net investment in Lenox is not less than $4 million, the full amount of the debt will qualify as a net investment hedge, since the debt amount would be less than the net investment book value. But there will be no hedge of the FX translation exposure on the portion of the net investment book value above $4 million. For example, assume that the book value of XYZ's net investment in Lenox is $6 million, higher than the principal of the euro debt that hedges the FX value exposure, $4 million. The translation gains or losses for the amount of the net investment book value not matched, which equals $6 million − 4 million = $2 million, will have to be reflected on XYZ's reported balance sheet as changes in the AOCI (CTA) account. Thus there will be an FX translation exposure, a change in the book value of the XYZ's reported equity whenever the FX rate changes. If the spot FX value of the euro rises, the book value of XYZ's equity increases, and vice versa. Current reported earnings are unaffected by FX changes, since the FX translation changes avoid the current earnings statement, and since the MTM changes on the euro-denominated debt qualify as a net investment hedge.

Exhibit 11.6 shows the time-1 balance sheets in this case for a 20% decline in the FX value of the euro. The book value of the net investment into Lenox drops from $6 million to $4.80 million. The FX translation loss on this net investment, $1.20 million, goes to the AOCI (CTA) account. The debt value drops from $4 million to $3.20 million. Since the entire debt qualifies as a hedge of net investment, the $0.80 million gain goes to the AOCI (CTA) account. Thus the net change in the AOCI (CTA) account is a drop of $1.20 million − 0.80 million = $0.40 million. Although there is no impact on current earnings, XYZ does have FX accounting exposure to the euro in the book value of its equity because of the changes in the AOCI (CTA) account.

What if XYZ decides to have $6 million in euro-denominated debt? This would eliminate the FX accounting exposure, but would create some FX equity exposure (in intrinsic value terms). The scenario in this case when the FX value of the euro drops by 20% is shown in Exhibit 11.7. There is no FX accounting exposure because the $6 million in euro debt is an exact hedge of the book value of XYZ's net investment in Lenox. But since more euro debt is used than is needed to hedge the FX value exposure, a negative FX equity exposure to the euro has been created.

Let us now consider an example of negative FX value exposure. A negative FX value exposure could characterize a foreign subsidiary that is an exporter of goods to the United States (see Chapter 5) or a competitor in the foreign market against a firm that exports from

EXHIBIT 11.6 XYZ Company (US Parent of Eurozone Subsidiary Lenox) Has $4 million Euro Debt: Lenox FX Value Exposure = 0.40; Lenox Book Value = $6 million

TIME-0 BALANCE SHEETS (US$)

Reported	Assets	Liabilities & Equity
	$ 6 million Lenox	$ 4 million €-debt
	$ 5 million other	$ 7 million equity
	$11 million	$11 million

Intrinsic Value	Firm Value	Liabilities & Equity
	$10 million Lenox	$ 4 million €-debt
	$ 5 million other	$11 million equity
	$15 million	$15 million

TIME-1 BALANCE SHEETS (US$)

Reported	Assets	Liabilities & Equity
	$4.80 million Lenox	$3.20 million €-debt
		$7 million common stock
		−$0.40 million AOCI
	$5 million other	$6.60 million equity
	$9.80 million	$9.80 million

Intrinsic Value	Firm Value	Liabilities & Equity
	$ 9.20 million Lenox	$ 3.20 million €-debt
	$ 5 million other	$11 million equity
	$14.20 million	$14.20 million

the United States (see Chapter 8). ABC Company is a US owner of SNC, a subsidiary in the Eurozone with the euro as its functional currency. Assume that the intrinsic value of ABC's net investment in SNC has a negative FX value exposure of −1.60 to the euro. In this case, ABC may use a long euro swap position to hedge the FX value exposure. But such a hedge position will not be regarded as a hedge of ABC's net investment under SFAS 52 and SFAS 133, because the MTM gains and losses on the swap position will move in the same direction as the FX translation gains and losses on the book value of ABC's investment in SNC. Similarly, the hedge position would not qualify as a cash flow hedge.

ABC's net investment in SNC has a book value of $2000 and an intrinsic value of $2000. Assume that ABC hedges at time 0 with an at-market long euro currency swap position with notional principal of $3200, which we know should hedge the FX value exposure because 1.60($2000) = $3200. Assume that the euro depreciates by 10%. The intrinsic value of ABC's net investment in SNC changes by −1.60(−10%), an increase of 16%, to $2320. The book value of ABC's net investment in SNC decreases by 10%, so the new book

EXHIBIT 11.7 XYZ Company (US Parent of Eurozone Subsidiary Lenox) Has $6 million Euro Debt: Lenox FX Value Exposure = 0.40; Lenox Book Value = $6 million

TIME-0 BALANCE SHEETS (US$)

Reported	Assets	Liabilities & Equity
	$ 6 million Lenox	$ 6 million €-debt
	$ 5 million other	$ 5 million equity
	$11 million	$11 million

Intrinsic Value	Firm Value	Liabilities & Equity
	$10 million Lenox	$ 6 million €-debt
	$ 5 million other	$ 9 million equity
	$15 million	$15 million

TIME-1 BALANCE SHEETS (US$)

Reported	Assets	Liabilities & Equity
	$4.80 million Lenox	$4.80 million €-debt
	$5 million other	$5 million equity
	$9.80 million	$9.80 million

Intrinsic Value	Firm Value	Liabilities & Equity
	$ 9.20 million Lenox	$ 4.80 million €-debt
	$ 5 million other	$ 9.40 million equity
	$14.20 million	$14.20 million

value is $1800. The FX translation loss of $200 on SNC is taken to the AOCI account. The MTM change on the long euro swap position is $2880 − 3200 = −$320. Reported current earnings and other equity are lower by $320, since the swap position is not viewed as a hedge of the net investment. Combining the translation loss and the MTM loss, book equity is lower by $520. The impact of the euro's drop on current earnings and book equity is negative, even though the impact on the firm's intrinsic value is positive. See Exhibit 11.8.

Next, consider briefly a domestic company that has no operating transactions in foreign currencies and has 100% of its assets and sales located in the United States and denominated in US dollars. Although the company's sales are assumed to be totally on US soil, its revenues are assumed to be sensitive to changes in the $/£ FX rate because of the actions of British competitors operating in the United States. That is, the company is assumed to have a competitive FX revenue exposure to the British pound.

The company wants to hedge its FX value exposure to the pound by having pound-denominated debt or a short pound currency swap position. But because the company has no pound-denominated foreign assets, the hedge does not qualify as a net investment

EXHIBIT 11.8 ABC Company (US Parent of Eurozone Subsidiary SNC) Hedges Long Euro Currency Swap; FX Value Exposure = −1.60

TIME-0 BALANCE SHEETS (US$)

Reported	Assets	Liabilities & Equity
	$2000 SNC	
	$6000 other	$8000 equity
	$8000	$8000
Intrinsic Value	Firm Value	Liabilities & Equity
	$2000 SNC	
	$6000 other	$8000 equity
	$8000	$8000

TIME-1 BALANCE SHEETS (US$)

Reported	Assets	Liabilities & Equity
	$1800 SNC	$ 320 unrealized MTM loss
		−$200 AOCI
		$7680 other equity
	$6000 other	$7480 equity
	$7800	$7800
Intrinsic Value	Firm Value	Liabilities & Equity
	$2320 SNC	$ 320 MTM loss
	$6000 other	$8000 equity
	$8320	$8320

−$320 included in current reported earnings

hedge. And because the company's cash flows are in US dollars, there is no way for the hedging strategy to qualify as a cash flow hedge of FX risk.

This is another case of MTM changes in instruments that hedge the intrinsic value of a firm having no matching changes in the book value of the firm's assets. It is therefore not possible to prove that these hedge positions are highly effective, and thus they will not qualify for hedge accounting. Then the changes in MTM values of the FX hedging instruments must be included in current earnings, with the undesirable side effect of increasing the volatility current earnings.

Finally, assume that the US parent's investment in a foreign subsidiary has an FX value exposure of 0 to the foreign currency, as in the case of Vulcan Materials in Chapter 6. With an FX value exposure of 0, the parent's intrinsic value would not change as FX rates change, and no hedging by the parent is necessary to protect the intrinsic value of its equity. Yet if the euro is the functional currency of the subsidiary, the parent is still subject to the same FX translation exposure as in the MRT example. Here it is useful for the parent that SFAS 52 does not require the translation gains or losses on the net investment in the subsidiary to be represented on the parent's current reported earnings. At the same time, the equity section of the parent's balance sheet does reflect the FX translation exposure through the AOCI account. Since the FX value exposure is 0, these FX translation changes do not have any economic meaning.

SUMMARY

Accounting rules for US companies for foreign currency transactions, financial reporting of accounts of overseas affiliates, and hedging with foreign currency debt and derivatives are set forth in SFAS 52 (1981) and in SFAS 133 (1998).

SFAS 52 permits firms to exclude the FX translation gains or losses on the book value of net investment in overseas assets from current reported earnings, although the changes do affect the book value of the firm's equity in the cumulative translation adjustment in the accumulated other comprehensive income account.

SFAS 133 generally requires that unrealized MTM changes on all FX derivatives positions appear as unrealized assets or liabilities. SFAS further requires that the MTM changes be included in the computation of current reported earnings, unless the position qualifies for hedge accounting.

The chief problem is that the FX changes do not affect intrinsic values the same way they affect book values. If a firm wants to hedge changes in its intrinsic value that occur because of FX changes, FX accounting exposure may occur. This FX accounting exposure may be evident only on the firm's reported balance sheet—for example, when the firm must account for FX translation changes for a foreign subsidiary that poses a relatively small FX value exposure. On the other hand, when a hedge position does not qualify for hedge accounting, there is an impact on the firm's reported current earnings. In such cases, the reported earnings are more volatile and may swing in the opposite direction from the firm's underlying FX exposure.

GLOSSARY

Accumulated other comprehensive income (AOCI): An equity account used to reserve valuation changes not considered as current earnings.

Cross-hedge: A hedging instrument denominated in a different foreign currency that is highly correlated with the actual currency of the FX exposure.

Cumulative translation account (CTA): Part of the AOCI account that reflects FX translation gains/losses.

Currency-indexed debt: Debt denominated in an issuer's base currency, but the interest and/or principal is a variable amount and indexed on an FX rate.

FX accounting exposure: The impact of FX changes on reported financial statements.

FX translation exposure: The impact of FX changes on the reported home currency values of foreign assets, liabilities, and income.

Functional currency: The currency in which a foreign entity's books are kept, chosen by the parent under SFAS 52.

Hedge accounting: Special rules that permit a company to avoid the normal accounting treatment when hedging, for the sake of achieving a matching of gains and losses in earnings.

Hedge effectiveness: A concept of SFAS 133 to measure the ability of a hedging instrument to match the gains/losses on the position being hedged.

Maquiladora: A foreign affiliate in a less developed country that uses cheap labor to assemble parts imported from the foreign market into products for a developed market.

Modified closing rate method: Under this method, all an affiliate's assets and liabilities are translated at the current spot FX rate and owners' equity is translated with historical rates. The resulting difference is booked in a special equity account called the *cumulative translation adjustment (CTA)*.

Temporal method: When the US dollar is the functional currency, any asset or liability that is carried on the affiliate's local currency books at fair value is translated at the current spot FX rate. In addition, any asset or liability of the foreign affiliate that is carried on the affiliate's local currency books at historical cost is translated into US dollars at the historical FX rate at the time the item was recorded.

Translation: The conversion of accounting items from one currency into another.

DISCUSSION QUESTIONS

1. According to the *efficient market hypothesis*, rational investors are able to see through accounting conventions used in reported financial statements, and to understand the firm's true economic situation. In this view, rational investors are believed to fully comprehend long-term FX exposure, even if FX accounting exposure shows up differently in reported current earnings and reported equity values. Discuss.
2. Why do managers sometimes think they should hedge their FX translation exposure, regardless of whether it is an accurate reflection of FX value exposure?
3. Assume that a US parent's FX value exposure to the euro, due to its foreign subsidiary, is 0, and the parent tries to hedge the FX translation gains/losses on book values by issuing euro-denominated debt. Discuss the implications.

PROBLEMS

1. Consider the MRT/DEP example in the text, but assume that MRT's FX value exposure to the euro from its investment in DEP is 0.80 (instead of 1). Assume that MRT employs 0.80($3 million) = $2.40 million worth of euro-denominated debt to hedge the FX value exposure of its $3 million intrinsic value net investment in DEP. How much of the euro-denominated debt can MRT count as a hedge under accounting rules? With the debt in place, does MRT have any FX translation exposure? Does MRT have any other FX accounting exposure? Is there any FX equity exposure (in intrinsic value terms)?
2. Assume that MRT's FX value exposure to its investment in DEP is 0.60 (instead of 0.80 in Problem 1) and that MRT employs 0.60($3 million) = $1.80 million worth of euro-denominated

debt to hedge the FX value exposure of its $3 million intrinsic value net investment. How much of the debt can MRT count as a hedge under accounting rules? With the debt in place, does MRT have FX translation exposure? Does MRT have any other FX exposure in the accounting sense? Is there any FX equity exposure (in intrinsic value terms)?

3. DTD Company is a US owner of TZL, a subsidiary in the Eurozone with the euro as its functional currency. From the US dollar perspective, DTD's investment in TZL has an FX value exposure of 1.60 to the euro. DTD has no currency swap positions, and the euro is assumed to depreciate by 10%. (a) What will DTD's new intrinsic value balance sheet and new book balance sheet look like under current accounting rules? (b) Ignoring the impact of the FX change on current operating cash flow, what will be the impact of the FX change on reported current earnings?

DTD Company Time-0 Balance Sheets (US$)

Reported	Assets	Liabilities & Equity
	$2000 TZL	$1000 €-debt
		$1000 AOCI
		$6000 other equity
	$6000 other	$7000 equity
	$8000	$8000
Intrinsic Value	Firm Value	Liabilities & Equity
	$2000 TZL	$1000 €-debt
	$6000 other	$7000 equity
	$8000	$8000

4. ABC Company is a US owner of SNC, a subsidiary in the Eurozone with the euro as its functional currency. From the US dollar perspective, ABC's net investment in SNC has an FX value exposure of −1.20 to the euro. Now ABC hedges its FX value exposure with a long euro currency swap position with notional principal of $3600. The swap is an at-market swap at time 0. Assume that the euro depreciates by 10%. (a) What will ABC's new intrinsic value balance sheet and new book balance sheet look like under current accounting rules? (b) Ignoring the impact of the FX change on current operating cash flow, what will be the impact of the FX change on reported current earnings?

ABC Company Time-0 Balance Sheets (US$)

Reported	Assets	Liabilities & Equity
	$3000 SNC	
	$5000 other	$8000 equity
	$8000	$8000
Intrinsic Value	Firm Value	Liabilities & Equity
	$3000 SNC	
	$5000 other	$8000 equity
	$8000	$8000

5. DOM Company is a purely domestic US company with no foreign sales or subsidiaries. At time 0, DOM expects operating cash flows of $1 million per year into perpetuity. The company's cost of capital is 10%, so the intrinsic value of the firm is $10 million, and the FX value exposure to the yen is 0.75. Assume that the FX rate at time 0 is 100 ¥/$. Assume that at time 0 DOM's intrinsic and book values are the same, $10 million. DOM has ¥750 million of 5% yen-denominated debt outstanding at par at time 0. Between time 0 and time 1, the yen appreciates by 20%. (a) If the operating cash flow at time 1 turns out to be $1 million, under current accounting requirements, what will be the current reported earnings? (b) What are the intrinsic and book values of DOM's equity at time 1?

ANSWERS TO PROBLEMS

1. There is no FX translation exposure. The MTM change on $2 million of the $2.40 million in euro-denominated debt will exactly offset the translation exposure of the $2 million book value of net investment in DEP. The remaining $0.40 million of euro-denominated debt is not regarded as a hedge in the accounting sense; thus MTM changes in this portion of the euro-denominated debt will affect reported current earnings each period. FX value exposure has been hedged.

2. Only $1.80 million of the $2 million book value of net investment is hedged in the accounting sense. The other $0.20 million is subject to FX translation exposure, meaning that the translation gains/losses will show in the AOCI account. There is no other FX exposure in the accounting sense and no impact on current reported earnings; FX value exposure has been hedged.

3. (a) The US dollar intrinsic value of the net investment in TZL will decrease by $1.60 \times 10\%$, or 16%. Thus the intrinsic value of TZL will decrease to $1680. The book value of TZL decreases by 10%, so the new book value is $1800. In US dollars, the value of the $1000 in euro-denominated debt decreases by 10% to $900, both in book value and in economic value. The FX translation loss of $200 on TZL is taken to the AOCI account, but is offset (partially) by the $100 gain on the euro-denominated debt, since the euro-denominated debt qualifies as a net investment hedge. (b) DTD's reported earnings will not change, since all of the euro-denominated debt qualifies for hedge accounting.

DTD Company Time-1 Balance Sheets (US$)

Reported	Assets	Liabilities & Equity
	$1800 TZL	$900 €-debt
		$ 900 AOCI
		$7000 other equity
	$6000 other	$7000 equity
	$7800	$7800
Intrinsic Value	Firm Value	Liabilities & Equity
	$1680 TZL	$ 900 €-debt
	$6000 other	$6780 equity
	$7680	$7680

4. (a) The intrinsic value of SNC will change by −1.20(−10%), or 12%. Thus the intrinsic value of SNC will increase by 12% to $3360. The book value of SNC decreases by 10%, so the new book value is $2700. In US dollars, the MTM value of the $3600 long euro swap position is $3240 − 3600 = −$360. The FX translation loss of $300 on SNC is taken to the AOCI account. (b) Reported earnings will be lower by $360, since a long swap position is not viewed as a hedge of the net investment (book value) or of the cash flows of SNC, and thus does qualify for hedge accounting.

DTD Company Time-1 Balance Sheets (US$)

Reported	Assets	Liabilities & Equity
	$2700 SNC	$360 unrealized MTM loss
		−$300 AOCI
		$7640 other equity
	$5000 other	$7340 equity
	$7700	$7700
Intrinsic Value	Firm Value	Liabilities & Equity
	$3360 SNC	$360 MTM loss
	$6000 other	$8000 equity
	$8360	$8360

5. (a) −$0.95 million. (b) The intrinsic value of DOM at time 1 is $11.50 million. Intrinsic equity value is $2.50 million; book equity value is $1 million.

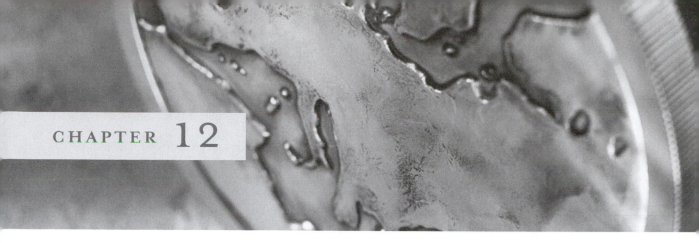

CHAPTER 12

OVERSEAS INVESTMENT DECISIONS

Overseas investment decisions should generally be made like any other investment decision: you discount an investment's incremental expected cash flows back to the present, using a cost of capital that reflects the risk. The investment's *net present value (NPV)* is the present value of the expected cash flows minus the outlay necessary to undertake the investment. If the NPV is positive, the investment should be accepted, because it will increase the intrinsic wealth of the firm's existing shareholders. If the NPV is negative, the investment should be rejected, because it would decrease the intrinsic wealth of the firm's existing shareholders.

This chapter contains examples of overseas investment decisions of three types. The first is a potential acquisition of a foreign firm by a US multinational. The second is a decision to relocate production capacity from one country to another. The third is an expansion proposal by an overseas subsidiary.

In overseas investment decisions, there is often the question about whether to consider the entire cash flow or only the portion repatriated. Our answer is immediate: consider the investment's entire cash flow, not just the portion to be repatriated. The reason is that even the portion reinvested overseas affects the intrinsic wealth of the investor, since the reinvestment increases the value the investment would bring if sold, and thus needs to be included in the analysis. So we consider an overseas investment's entire cash flow, not just the portion repatriated.

A more involved issue in overseas investment decisions is the choice of which of the two currency perspectives to use for the NPV analysis. In the home currency perspective, the analyst converts the expected foreign currency cash flows into home currency cash flows and then discounts them by using a cost of capital denominated in the home currency. In the foreign currency perspective, the analyst uses the cash flows denominated in the foreign currency and discounts them by using a cost of capital denominated in the foreign currency.

The typical advice tends to be that choice of currency perspective is irrelevant in cross-border valuation as long as we use consistent cash flow and cost of capital conversions across currencies. A critical condition behind this advice is an efficient foreign exchange (FX) market, in which FX rates are presumed to be correctly valued, and the best forecast of FX changes is implied in interest rates. For example, if the long-term risk-free rates in US dollars and euros are 6 and 4%, respectively, and if the linear approximation of the traditional uncovered interest rate parity (UIRP) condition holds, we can expect the euro to appreciate by 2% per year over the long term. This is called the equilibrium FX forecast because it is the forecast consistent with an equilibrium risk–return relation for all assets in integrated markets. The equilibrium FX forecast is the best FX forecast we can make, given an efficient FX market that correctly values the spot FX rate.

But FX rates are often thought to be misaligned (i.e., misvalued). In Chapter 2, we covered the idea of an overvalued yen or an undervalued euro. Misvaluations in FX rates might be due to central bank interventions or to the activities of speculators, but whatever the reason, they imply that one's best forecast of FX rate changes is different from the equilibrium forecast implicit in financial market rates. When a currency is overvalued, we forecast it to change at a rate lower than the equilibrium rate. When a currency is undervalued, we forecast it to change at a rate higher than the equilibrium rate.

You will see in this chapter that when managers' FX forecasts are not equal to equilibrium FX forecasts, the NPV analyses in the different currency perspectives lead to different results. Moreover, interpreting the different results requires some thoughtful consideration.

In the NPV analysis, let $E(O_{it}^\$)$ represent the expected cash flow in US dollars for investment i at time t. Let $k_i^\$$ represent the cost of capital in US dollars for investment i, depending on the risk. Let N be the number of years that cash flows are expected. In general, the present value in US dollars of the stream of expected cash flows for investment i is expressed as $V_i^\$ = \sum_{t=1,N} E(O_{it}^\$)/(1 + k_i^\$)^t$, which is the sum of the present values of each of the cash flows expected from year 1 through year N. Denoting the investment's initial outlay in US dollars at time 0 as $I_i^\$$, the NPV of the investment in US dollars is $V_i^\$ - I_i^\$ = \sum_{t=1,N} E(O_{it}^\$)/(1 + k_i^\$)^t - I_i^\$$. A similar framework can be specified from the perspective of the foreign currency.

For a while, we'll use a simple valuation framework according to which managers forecast a constant perpetual rate of change in the FX rate. This assumption allows us to use the constant growth model for valuation and to focus on some basic issues. Later in

EXHIBIT 12.1 EPC Cash Flow Statement (euros)

	1.00 $/€	0.80 $/€ ≡1.25 €/$
Revenues	€600	€600
Production Expense	360	360
Depreciation	40	40
EBIT	€200	€200
Taxes (20% × EBIT)	40	40
EBIAT	€160	€160
Add depreciation	40	40
After-tax operating cash flow	€200	€200

the chapter, we'll cover situations in which FX rates are forecasted to gradually converge to correct FX values.[1]

OVERSEAS ACQUISITION

The US multinational ABC is considering acquiring EPC, a company that produces and sells widgets in the Eurozone. EPC's revenues are generated in euros, and all production costs are stable in euros. EPC's current annual revenues are €600; production costs are €360; and depreciation is €40. At an assumed tax rate of 20%, EPC's current annual after-tax operating cash flow is €200. See Exhibit 12.1.

EPC's sales volume is not subject to economic exposure to FX changes in that output and selling price do not depend on FX rates. That is, EPC's FX revenue exposure to changes in the FX value of the US dollar (relative to the euro) is 0. Since its costs are stable in euros, EPC's operating cash flow has no FX operating exposure to the US dollar. Exhibit 12.1 also shows that a 25% appreciation of the US dollar (a 20% depreciation of the euro) would not affect EPC's cash flow in euros.

ABC's managers believe that the growth rate of EPC's expected cash flows in euros will be 4.5% indefinitely.

Let us first look at ABC's valuation of EPC from the perspective of US dollars. While ABC's managers expect a growth rate in EPC's euro cash flows of 4.5%, this is not the expected growth rate of EPC's cash flows when viewed from the US dollar perspective. There are two reasons for this. First the projected growth rate of EPC's cash flows when measured in US dollars depends on the forecasted rate of change in the FX value of the euro. Second, we must make an adjustment for any statistical interaction that exists between the euro cash flows and the FX rate. The second adjustment involves EPC's FX operating exposure and the FX volatility of the euro.

---

[1]Other aspects of foreign investment are presented in R. Click and J. Coval, *The Theory and Practice of International Financial Management* (Upper Saddle River, NJ: Prentice Hall, 2002).

EXHIBIT 12.2   EPC Cash Flow Statement (US dollars)

	1.00 $/€	0.80 $/€
Revenues	$600	$480
Production expense	360	288
Depreciation	40	32
EBIT	$200	$160
Taxes (20% × EBIT)	40	32
EBIAT	$160	$128
Add depreciation	40	32
After-tax operating cash flow	$200	$160

Equation (12.1) shows the relationship between the expected growth of the cash flows in US dollars, $g_i^\$$; the expected growth rate of the cash flows in euros, g_i^ϵ; the forecasted rate of change in the FX value of the euro, $E(x^{\$/\epsilon})$; asset i's FX exposure to the euro, $\xi_{i\epsilon}^\$$; and the FX volatility of the euro, σ_ϵ:

$$g_i^\$ = g_i^\epsilon + E(x^{\$/\epsilon}) - (1 - \xi_{i\epsilon}^\$)\sigma_\epsilon^2 \qquad (12.1)$$

The term $(1 - \xi_{i\epsilon}^\$)\sigma_\epsilon^2$ measures the statistical interaction between the cash flows and the FX rate changes, just as in the cost of capital conversion formula in Chapter 10. Since EPC's euro cash flows have no FX exposure to the US dollar, the FX operating exposure to the euro ($\xi_{i\epsilon}^\$$) is 1. Exhibit 12.2 verifies this, showing how a drop in the spot FX rate from 1 $/€ to 0.80 $/€, a 20% depreciation of the euro, would result in cash flow in US dollars from $200 to $160, a 20% decline.

What if ABC's managers forecast the FX value of the euro to appreciate at the rate of $E(x^{\$/\epsilon}) = 3\%$ per year? Let us further assume that σ_ϵ^2 is 0.015 (an FX volatility of about 0.122). Equation (12.1) tells us that EPC's expected cash flows, measured in US dollars, are forecasted to grow at the rate of $0.045 + 0.03 - (1 - 1)0.015 = 0.075$, or 7.5%.

We assume for now that the forecasted rate of change in the FX value of the euro of 3% is a constant, perpetual rate. Thus, since EPC's euro cash flows are expected to grow perpetually at 4.5%, and EPC's cash flows grow at a constant perpetual rate of 7.5% when measured in US dollars.

Given that investment i's US dollar cash flows are expected to grow perpetually at a constant rate, $g_i^\$$, and letting $E(O_i^\$)$ be the initial cash flow of the investment, the present value in US dollars of the cash flows may be expressed using the constant growth formula, as in equation (12.2):

$$V_i^\$ = \frac{E(O_i^\$)}{k_i^\$ - g_i^\$} \qquad (12.2)$$

EPC's owners are asking €5000 for the company. Given an assumed current spot FX rate of 1 $/€, ABC's investment outlay in US dollars would be $5000, and EPC's initial euro cash flow of €200 converts to $200. ABC estimates the cost of capital for EPC in US dollars as $k_i^\$ = 11\%$.

We can apply equation (12.2) to find the intrinsic value of EPC in US dollars, given ABC's managers' forecast of a perpetual euro appreciation of 3% per year: $200/(0.11 − 0.075) = $5714. The NPV of the investment would be $5714 − 5000 = $714. Given our assumptions, the acquisition of EPC will add $714 of intrinsic value to ABC's equity.

Consider the Eurozone firm DYA with current annual euro cash flow of €1 million, a projected perpetual growth rate of 3% per year, and an FX operating exposure of 2 when viewed in US dollars. The cost of capital for DYA in US dollars is 8.50%. XYZ Company, a US firm, is considering acquiring DYA. XYZ's managers forecast that the FX value of the euro will change by −0.50% per year into perpetuity. If the FX volatility of the euro is 10%, the current spot FX rate is 1.20 $/€, and DYA's owners are asking €25 million for the company, what is the NPV of XYZ's proposed acquisition of DYA in US dollars?

Answer: Since the current spot FX rate is 1.20 $/€, the initial euro cash flow of €1 million is converted to US dollars as $1.20 million. From equation (12.1), we see that the projected cash flow growth rate in US dollars is $0.03 + (−0.005) − (1 − 2)0.10^2 = 0.035$, or 3.50%. The intrinsic value of DYA to XYZ in US dollars is $1.20 million/(0.085 − 0.035) = $24 million. Since the outlay for the investment will require €25 million(1.20 $/€) = $30 million, the NPV of the proposed acquisition in US dollars is $24 million − 30 million = −$6 million.

CROSS-BORDER MERGERS AND ACQUISITIONS

A multinational will make a *foreign direct investment* (FDI) in an overseas plant to avoid tariffs or other foreign country import barriers, to engage in operational hedging, and so forth. The construction of a new facility is referred to as a *greenfield investment*. However, a cross-border acquisition or merger is often the preferred FDI mode of entry or expansion in foreign markets, where an existing local firm may be acquired by a multinational that wishes to avoid the construction time of a greenfield investment. Other reasons for foreign acquisitions include consolidating worldwide excess capacity, combining firms in fragmented industries ("roll-ups"), exploiting developed marketing channels, eliminating a competitor, achieving critical mass required for new approaches to R&D and production, obtaining an innovation (patent, knowledge, technology), or entering a market to exploit an innovation.

Since the mid-1980s, cross-border mergers and acquisitions (M&A) have accounted for about 25% of total M&A activity. Recent cross-border M&As have mostly been nonconglomerate, instead involving firms in the same industry (*horizontal M&A*) or along the supply/distribution chain (*vertical M&A*). In 1999, about 70% of all global

(continued)

M&As were horizontal. The major industries in which these horizontal combinations have occurred are the automobile, pharmaceutical, chemical, food, beverage, and tobacco industries, and more recently telecommunications and utilities. Some of the more well-known players include Daimler-Benz (Germany)–Chrysler (US); Vodafone (UK)–AirTouch Communications (US); British Petroleum (UK)–Amoco and ARCO (US); Alcatel (France)–DSC Communications (US); Deutsche Telecom (Germany)–Voice Stream Wireless (US); and Sony (Japan)–Columbia Pictures (US).

About 90% of cross-border M&A activity in 1999 occurred in developed countries. The great majority of global combinations have been between firms in the major western industrial countries. The foreign targets of US firms (outward US FDI) have been primarily located in the United Kingdom, Canada, and Europe. Japan is a relatively minor source of outward US FDI. British firms have been the source of the most acquisitions of US firms and in a wide variety of industries. Other acquirers of US firms come from Japan, Netherlands, Canada, Germany, France, and other European countries.

For the 25 largest cross-border transactions in history completed as of 2000, transactions involving US targets amounted to $305 billion, transactions involving US acquirers amounted to $105 billion, and transactions involving only foreign companies amounted to $230 billion. Figure 12.1 plots the relationship of FDI inflow and outflow between the United States and the rest of the world.

Source: This overview draws from Robert L. Conn, "International Mergers: Review of Literature and Clinical Projects," *Journal of Financial Education*, Fall 2003, 1–22, and Robert Feenstra, "Facts and Fallacies About Foreign Direct Investment," February 1998, in Martin Feldstein, ed. *International Capital Flows* (Chicago: University of Chicago Press and NBER, 1999, pp. 331–350). http://www.econ.ucdavis.edu/faculty/fzfeens/pdf/fdi2.pdf. Another source for international acquisition trends is the United Nations report *World Investment Report 2000: Cross-Border Mergers and Acquisitions and Development*.

PRODUCTION RELOCATION

ABC is considering relocating EPC's production from the Eurozone to the United States. The net investment outlay would be $2000 to buy a plant in the United States, less the proceeds from selling the plant in the Eurozone. Assume that at the current spot FX rate of 1 $/€, the production cost would be the same in the United States as in the Eurozone. Thus the current cash flow in US dollars would still be $200.

From the US dollar point of view, the relocation is anticipated to increase EPC's FX operating exposure to the euro from 1 to 2. EPC is more risky from the US dollar point of view because it has a higher FX operating exposure. Assume that EPC's cost of capital in US dollars will rise from 11% to 12% if the relocation is undertaken.[2]

---

[2]The theory for this is explained in Chapter 10. The cost of capital before the move, 11%, is consistent with a global CAPM, a 5% US dollar risk–free rate, a 4% global risk premium in US dollars, and an operating beta in US dollars of 1.50. If the FX global beta of the euro is 0.25, then the increase in FX operating exposure from 1 to 2 would cause the operating beta to increase to 1.75 [see equation (10.4)], and the cost of capital in US dollars to increase to 12%.

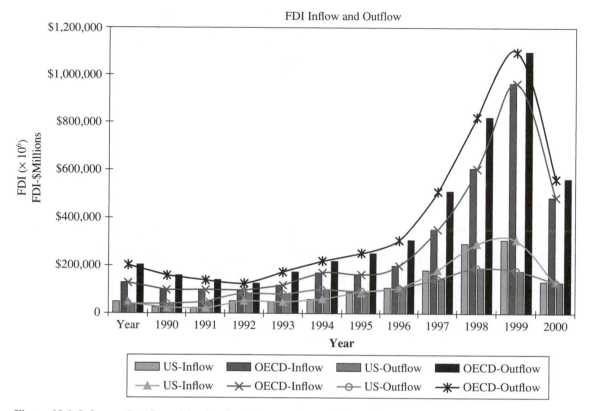

Figure 12.1 Inflow and outflow of foreign direct investment for the United States and for the other OECD countries. *Source*: OECD

The good news about the increase in FX operating exposure is that EPC's cash flows will be expected to grow faster when viewed in US dollars. Since ABC's managers forecast that the euro will appreciate by 3% per year, and since less of EPC's costs are in euros, EPC's cash flows are expected to grow in US dollars at $0.045 + 0.03 - (1 - 2)0.015 = 0.09$, or 9%.

Should the relocation be undertaken? As the cost of capital for EPC would change with the plant relocation, your NPV analysis of the proposed relocation should discount the expected cash flows of each alternative plant location using the appropriate cost of capital, rather than discount incremental cash flows. That is, we discount the cash flows (measured in US dollars) expected under the current (Eurozone) production arrangement using the *current* cost of capital. And we discount the cash flows (measured in US dollars) expected under the new (US) production arrangement using the *pro forma* cost of capital. If the present value of the expected cash flow from US production exceeds the present value of the expected cash flows from Eurozone production, after the proceeds from the sale of the Eurozone plant and the purchase of the US plant have been considered, the proposed relocation has a positive NPV and should be accepted.

We already know that EPC's intrinsic value in US dollars before the relocation is $200/(0.11 − 0.075) = $5714. EPC's intrinsic value in US dollars after the relocation would be $200/(0.12 − 0.09) = $6667. The NPV from the US dollar point of view is $6667 − 5714 − 2000 = −$1047. The relocation should not be implemented, because the NPV is negative.

Consider again the Eurozone firm DYA with euro cash flows that are initially €1 million and are projected to grow at the rate of 3% per year into perpetuity. The cash flows have an FX operating exposure of 2 when viewed in US dollars, since DYA sources some components from a plant in the United States. The cost of capital for DYA in US dollars is assumed to be 8.50%. XYZ Company, a US firm, is considering acquiring DYA. XYZ's managers forecast that the FX value of the euro will change by −0.50% per year into perpetuity. Assume tht the FX volatility of the euro is 10% and the current spot FX rate is 1.20 $/€. DYA's owners are asking €25 million for the company. If XYZ acquires DYA, it will build a plant in the Eurozone to supply all components currently being sourced from the United States. The new plant will cost €1 million. The relocation will not affect DYA's current cash flow or the cash flow growth rate in euros, but it will change the FX operating exposure to the euro to 1 and will reduce DYA's cost of capital in US dollars to 6%. Would this relocation affect the decision on XYZ's proposed acquisition of DYA in US dollars?

Answer: From equation (12.1), we see that the projected cash flow growth rate in US dollars is 0.03 + (−0.005) − (1 − 1)0.10² = 0.025, or 2.50%. Since the current spot FX rate is 1.20 $/€, the initial euro cash flow of €1 million is converted to US dollars as $1.20 million. The intrinsic value of DYA to XYZ in US dollars is $1.20 million/(0.06 − 0.025) = $34.29 million. Since the outlay for the investment will require €25 million(1.20 $/€) = $30 million and the cost of the plant relocation is €1 million(1.20 $/€) = $1.20 million, the NPV of the proposed acquisition plus production relocation in US dollars is $34.29 million − 30 million − 1.20 million = $3.09 million. XYZ should acquire DYA and move the plant to the Eurozone.

FOREIGN CURRENCY PERSPECTIVE

Let us now return to ABC's acquisition problem and perform an NPV analysis from the euro perspective. To find EPC's cost of capital in euros, $k_i^{\euro}$, consistent with its cost of capital in US dollars (11%), we use equation (10.2): $k_i^{\euro} = k_i^{\$} - E(x^{*\$/\euro}) + (1 - \xi_{i\euro}^{\$})\sigma_{\euro}^2$, where $E(x^{*\$/\euro})$ is the equilibrium expected rate of change in the FX value of the euro. We convert the cost of capital *not* using the managers' FX forecast, but rather using the equilibrium expected rate of FX change, even if it is different from the managers' FX forecast. The reason is that the cost of capital is a compensation for risk, regardless of the currency perspective of the cost of capital. We take the view that there is a single relationship between risk and *required* return for globally traded assets, even though any asset might be mispriced in one or more currencies. Only the equilibrium expected rate of change in the FX value of the euro preserves a consistent risk and required return relationship across different currencies for globally traded assets.[3]

Let's use the linear approximation of the traditional uncovered interest rate parity (UIRP) condition to estimate the equilibrium expected rate of change in the FX value of the euro, that is, with the risk-free interest rate differential, $r^\$ - r^\epsilon$. We assume that the risk-free interest rate in US dollars is 6% and the risk-free interest rate in euros is 4%. Thus the equilibrium expected rate of change in the FX value of the euro, $E(x^{*\$/\epsilon})$, is 2%.

Given our assumption that the US dollar cost of capital is 11%, equation (10.2) tells us that EPC's cost of capital in euros is $k_i^\epsilon = k_i^\$ - E(x^{*\$/\epsilon}) + (1 - \xi_{i\epsilon}^\$)\sigma_\epsilon^2 = 0.11 - 0.02 + (1 - 1)0.015 = 0.09$, or 9%. Now we adapt equation (12.2) to the euro denomination to find an intrinsic value for EPC in euros. Since the growth rate of EPC's cash flows in euros is the constant perpetual rate of 4.5%, $V_i^\epsilon = E(O_i^\epsilon)/[k_i^\epsilon - g_i^\epsilon] = €200/(0.09 - 0.045) = €4444$.

Given that €5000 is the price that EPC's owners require to sell the company, the investment outlay in euros would be $I_i^\epsilon = €5000$. ABC's NPV in euros of acquiring EPC would be $V_i^\epsilon - I_i^\epsilon = €4444 - 5000 = -€556$. Given the current spot FX rate of 1 $/€, the NPV analysis in euros says that the investment should not be made because the NPV is −$556.

Consider again the example of the Eurozone firm DYA with euro cash flows that are initially €1 million and are projected to grow at the rate of 3% per year into perpetuity. The cash flows have an FX operating exposure of 2 when viewed in US dollars. The cost of capital for DYA in US dollars is assumed to be 8.50%. XYZ Company, a US firm, is considering the acquisition of DYA. DYA's owners are asking €25 million for the company. Assume that the risk-free rate in US dollars is 5%, the risk-free rate in euros is 4%, the FX volatility of the euro is 10%, and the current spot FX rate is 1.20 $/€. Assume the linear approximation of the traditional UIRP condition for the equilibrium expected rate of change in the FX value of the euro. What is the NPV of XYZ's proposed acquisition of DYA in euros? Ignore the plant relocation possibility.

Answer: The equilibrium expected rate of change in the FX value of the euro is 5% − 4% = 1%. Using equation (10.2), the cost of capital for DYA in euros is $k_i^\epsilon = k_i^\$ - E(x^{*\$/\epsilon}) + (1 - \xi_{i\epsilon}^\$)\sigma_\epsilon^2 = 0.085 - 0.01 + (1 - 2)0.10^2 = 0.065$, *or 6.50%. The intrinsic value of DYA in euros is* €1 million/(0.065 − 0.03) = €28.57 million. *The NPV is* €28.57 million − 25 million = €3.57 million, *which is equivalent to $4.29 million at the current spot FX rate of 1.20 $/€.*

---

[3]See T. O'Brien, "The Global CAPM and a Firm's Cost of Capital in Different Currencies," *Journal of Applied Corporate Finance*, Fall 1999, 73–79.

INTERPRETING NPVS OF THE CURRENCY PERSPECTIVES

The NPV of ABC's proposed acquisition of EPC is $714 when the analysis is conducted in US dollars, but −$556 when the NPV analysis is conducted in euros. What is going on? Should ABC acquire EPC or not?

To address these questions, let us use the term "equilibrium NPV" to refer to the NPV found by conducting the analysis in euros, −$556 in the ABC example. The term "equilibrium NPV" is used because it is based on the cost of capital required by the global market's investors as compensation for risk and does not depend on managers' FX forecast. Again, to be consistent with an equilibrium model of risk and required return for all assets in the global financial market, we must use the equilibrium expected rate of FX change to convert the cost of capital across currencies. The equilibrium NPV could also be called the efficient FX market NPV.

The NPV we find in the US dollar analysis, $714 in the ABC example, differs from the equilibrium NPV in the euro analysis because the forecasted rate of FX change is not the same as the equilibrium expected rate of FX change. ABC's managers' forecast a 3% appreciation of the euro, while the equilibrium NPV in euros builds the equilibrium expected rate of 2% into an investment's cost of capital conversion between US dollars and euros.

If ABC's managers' FX forecast had been equal to the equilibrium expectation, 2%, EPC's expected cash flows, measured in US dollars, would be forecasted to grow at the rate of $0.045 + 0.02 − (1 − 1)0.015 = 0.065$, or 6.5%. The intrinsic value of EPC in US dollars would be $200/(0.11 − 0.065) = 4444. The NPV of the proposal would be then −$556, the equilibrium NPV we find when we conduct the analysis in euros.

Show that if the FX forecasted for the euro is equal to the equilibrium expected rate of change, the NPV analyses in US dollars and in euros give equivalent answers in the XYZ/DYA example.

Answer: From equation (12.2) we find that the projected cash flow growth rate in US dollars is $0.03 + 0.01 − (1 − 2)0.10^2 = 0.05$, or 5%. The intrinsic value of DYA to XYZ in US dollars is $1.20 million/(0.085 − 0.05) = $34.29 million. Since the outlay for the investment will require €25 million(1.20 $/€) = $30 million, the NPV of the proposed acquisition in US dollars is $34.29 million − 30 million = $4.29 million, the same as found when the analysis was conducted in euros.

We'll denote a project's NPV in the home currency analysis as $NPV_H^\$$, and we'll think of this NPV as consisting of two components. The first is the equilibrium NPV, denoted $NPV*^\$$. The second is the additional NPV that arises when the FX forecast is different from the equilibrium expected rate of change. We'll denote this component $NPV_{FX}^\$$. Thus we have equation (12.3):

$$NPV_H^\$ = NPV*^\$ + NPV_{FX}^\$ \tag{12.3}$$

For ABC's proposed acquisition of EPC, the equilibrium NPV in US dollars is –$556, and the home currency NPV is $714, so the FX forecast component, $NPV_{FX}^\$$, is $1270.

It is sometimes suggested that managers' FX forecasts be incorporated into the cost of capital conversion, but this approach would yield a misleading result. If the forecasted appreciation of the euro of 3% is incorporated into EPC's cost of capital in euros, instead of the equilibrium expected rate of 2%, ABC would estimate EPC's euro cost of capital to be 100 basis points lower, 8% instead of 9%. The NPV analysis, with a €5000 outlay, would show an NPV in euros of €200/(0.08 – 0.045) – 5000 = €714. Given the spot FX rate of 1 $/€, this NPV is equivalent to the home currency NPV found by conducting the analysis in US dollars, $714.

Note that this €714 is the NPV in euros *to a US dollar investor* (like ABC) with a 3% euro appreciation forecast, not to a *euro investor* with a 3% euro appreciation forecast. If euro investors want to buy EPC, they would base the valuation on the 9% cost of capital, which is the basic compensation for risk regardless of the FX forecast. And as we have shown, the equilibrium NPV of the acquisition proposal in euros is –€556.

Thus, converting an investment's cost of capital using an FX forecast that differs from the equilibrium rate may be misleading if we want to find an asset's intrinsic value from a foreign currency perspective.

EQUILIBRIUM NPV OR HOME CURRENCY NPV?

Which of the NPVs should be the basis of ABC's investment decision? There are two schools of thought. One school says to use the equilibrium NPV as the basis of the investment decision. Proponents of this position make several arguments. One is that managers should not be using FX forecasts that deviate from the equilibrium forecast. This argument is based on the efficient market notion that the financial market's information contains the best information. Managers should stick to managing their company instead of trying to forecast FX rates better than the financial market.

In the efficient FX market case, where the managers' forecasted FX change is equal to the equilibrium expected FX change, the two NPV perspectives will indeed lead to the same decision outcome, as long as the inputs to the analysis in the home currency are consistent with the inputs to the analysis in the foreign currency. In this case, it does not matter which currency is chosen for the NPV analysis.

The counterargument is that reports of FX misvaluation are common and easily observed, as we saw in Chapter 2. If the UIRP condition holds and implies that the euro should appreciate by 2% per year in equilibrium, and if we think the euro is currently undervalued, we will forecast the euro to appreciate at a rate higher than 2% per year. If we think the euro is overvalued, we'll forecast it to change at a lower rate than 2% per year. Proponents of using $NPV_H^\$$ rather than $NPV*^\$$ allow the level of the FX rate to influence their overseas investment decisions. Researchers have found that the level of overseas investment is related to the level of FX rates, consistent with the use of the home currency NPV approach. They have also found that the level of the acquisition premium is related to the FX rate in cross-border mergers and acquisitions.[4]

A second argument made by proponents of using the equilibrium NPV is that even if managers have an FX forecast that differs from the equilibrium expectation, they are better able to exploit it by using a financial market transaction instead of an investment like a foreign company acquisition. That is, in principle, ABC is better off investing the $5000 in a long-term risk-free euro-denominated bond than acquiring EPC.

To see this, recall that the euro risk-free rate is assumed to be 4%. Thus a €5000 investment in a euro-denominated risk-free bond will earn annual interest of $0.04(€5000) = €200$. In US dollars, the cost of capital for a risk-free euro asset is $r_f^€ + E(x^{*\$/€}) = 0.04 + 0.02 = 0.06$, if our assumption that the linear approximation of traditional UIRP condition holds. Basically, the linear approximation of the UIRP condition assumes that the FX risk is nonsystematic, so that a risk-free euro bond is "zero-beta" in US dollars. Thus the risk-free rate in US dollars, 6%, is the cost of capital for a risk-free euro bond in US dollars. From equation (12.1), ABC's managers forecast that the cash flows of the euro risk-free asset are projected to grow in US dollars at the rate of 3%, since there is no growth in the euro cash flows and no FX exposure to the US dollar.

Thus the intrinsic value in US dollars of investing $5000 in the risk-free euro bond is $200/(0.06 − 0.03) = 6667, and the home currency NPV is $1667, although the equilibrium NPV of the investment is zero. Thus the $1667 home currency NPV in US dollars of investing $5000 in a risk-free euro-denominated bond, given the forecast of a 3% per year appreciation of FX value of the euro, is higher than the $714 home currency NPV in US dollars of acquiring EPC. According to this analysis, the acquisition of EPC should be rejected in favor of an investment in the risk-free euro-denominated bond.

Proponents of using the home currency NPV counterargue that a financial market transaction like buying a euro-denominated bond is not a realistic alternative to a business investment decision. For one thing, investing in a euro-denominated bond is not consistent with ABC's business, while acquiring EPC is. For another, there are accounting implications for reported current earnings of the mark-to-market (MTM) changes in a financial transaction like the euro-denominated bond (or long euro currency swap position). See Chapter 11. ABC's managers are likely to want to avoid this volatility in reported earnings.

From the home currency perspective, acquiring EPC adds less intrinsic value ($714) than the euro-denominated bond ($1667), given the FX forecast of a euro appreciation at an above-equilibrium rate. But the acquisition of EPC may still be a more practical way for ABC's managers to add intrinsic value in light of their FX view.

---

[4]See R. Harris and D. Ravenscraft, "The Role of Acquisitions in Foreign Direct Investment: Evidence from the US Stock Market," *Journal of Finance*, July 1991, 825–844.

IMPACT OF HEDGING AND FINANCING DECISIONS

If ABC decides to acquire EPC on the basis of the $714 in US home currency NPV, the advocates of using the equilibrium NPV may bring out a third argument: that hedging the FX exposure of owning EPC will offset the benefits of the FX forecast, $NPV_{FX}^{\$}$. To hedge the future fluctuations in investment value due to FX changes (i.e., to hedge the investment's FX exposure to the euro), ABC could finance the $5000 acquisition cost with euro-denominated debt. This euro-denominated debt position is the mirror image of buying a euro-denominated bond. If owning the euro-denominated bond creates $1667 in intrinsic $NPV_{FX}^{\$}$, the euro-denominated debt position creates −$1667 in $NPV_{FX}^{\$}$ for ABC, more than negating the $714 of home currency NPV in acquiring EPC.

Of course, ABC's managers do not have to hedge the FX exposure of owning EPC if they don't want to. They can decide to acquire EPC without hedging, and the $NPV^{\$}$ will be $714. The managers might be willing to accept the FX exposure of owning EPC in light of the loss of NPV that hedging with euro-denominated debt would entail. Or, the managers could justify not hedging the FX exposure of EPC by arguing that FX exposure does not impact firm value in an efficient financial market. ABC's managers may be selective about market efficiency, believing the financial market is efficient in reflecting impact of FX exposure on firm value, even though they consider the FX market inefficient in valuing FX rates.[5]

Let's now look at an example of managers forecasting the FX value of the euro to change by less that the equilibrium rate. Say ABC's managers forecast an appreciation of the euro only $E(x^{\$/€}) = 1\%$ per year, below the 2% equilibrium rate. Now the growth rate of EPC's cash flows in US dollars is 5.5%, and the intrinsic value of EPC in US dollars is $200/(0.11 − 0.055) = $3636. Let's assume this time that EPC's owners are asking only €4000 for the firm, so the NPV of ABC's acquisition in US dollars is $3636 − 4000 = −$364. The intrinsic value of EPC in euros is still €4444, so the equilibrium NPV in US dollars is 1 $/€(€4444 − 4000) = $444.

The home currency NPV is negative because the euro is forecasted to appreciate at less than the equilibrium rate. Proponents of the equilibrium NPV approach would say to accept the investment, while proponents of the home currency NPV would advise rejecting it.

What if the acquisition is financed by euro-denominated debt? By issuing $4000 in euro-denominated debt, ABC will gain $800 in US dollar NPV. [The intrinsic value in US dollars of investing $4000 in the risk-free euro bond is $160/(0.06 − 0.01) = $3200, making the $NPV_{FX}^{\$} − $800.] If the acquisition is financed with euro-denominated debt, the proponents of the home currency NPV approach would agree with those who advocate the equilibrium NPV approach: accept the acquisition proposal.

---

[5]However, many academics now believe that hedging does enhance firm value. See K. Froot, D. Scharfstein, and J. Stein, "A Framework for Risk Management," *Journal of Applied Corporate Finance*, Fall 1994, 22–32, and René M. Stulz, "Rethinking Risk Management," *Journal of Applied Corporate Finance*, Fall 1996, 8–24.

The overall home currency NPV of the acquisition financed with euro-denominated debt would be −$364 + $800 = $546. There will be the added bonus that the debt will hedge the FX exposure that ABC takes on when it buys EPC.

If EPC's owners are asking €4500 instead of €4000, the equilibrium NPV is negative, 1 $/€(€4444 − 4500) = −$56. The home currency NPV is negative without the euro-denominated financing, $3636 − 4500 = −$864. By issuing $4500 in euro-denominated debt, ABC gains $900 in $NPV_{FX}^{\$}$, and the acquisition of EPC financed by euro-denominated debt has a positive overall home currency NPV, −$864 + 900 = $36. Proponents of the equilibrium NPV approach would say that ABC should reject the acquisition of EPC. They would argue that ABC could simply issue euro-denominated debt to exploit its forecast that the euro will appreciate at a lower rate than the equilibrium rate.

That is a reasonable argument in theory, but in practice SFAS 52 requires that the MTM gains and losses on the euro-denominated debt be included in the computation of reported current earnings unless the debt qualifies as a hedge. A similar requirement in SFAS 133 would pertain to a short euro currency swap position. Again, see Chapter 11. The use of euro-denominated debt or a short euro currency swap position for purposes other than hedging would thus make reported current earnings more volatile. ABC's managers may not consider these choices a viable alternative.

Issuing $4500 in euro-denominated debt to finance the acquisition not only creates a positive overall home currency NPV of $36, but the debt also qualifies as a hedge of ABC's net investment in EPC. This alternative does not create as much additional home currency for ABC's owners as would issuing euro-denominated debt on its own and not making the acquisition, but it avoids the drawback of adding volatility in reported earnings.

In the XYZ/DYA example (ignoring the production relocation analysis), the NPV in US dollars is −$6 million under XYZ's view that the euro will depreciate by 0.50% per year, but the equilibrium NPV in US dollars is $4.29 million. Proponents of the equilibrium NPV approach would say that XYZ should acquire DYA because the equilibrium NPV is positive. They would also say that XYZ can offset the negative $NPV_{FX}^{\$} = −\$10.29$ million by using euro-denominated debt or a short euro currency swap position. What is the overall US dollar NPV of XYZ's acquisition of DYA, given that XYZ hedges 100% of the FX value exposure of DYA with euro-denominated debt?

Answer: Since the FX value exposure of XYZ's investment in DYA is 2, and since its intrinsic value is $24 million, XYZ should have total euro-denominated liabilities (actual euro debt plus short euro currency swap position) of $48 million to eliminate FX equity exposure. Suppose XYZ borrows $48 million in euros (€40 million). At 4% per year, the annual interest expense is €1.60 million, which is equivalent to $1.92 million at the current spot FX rate of 1.20 $/€. XYZ believes that the interest expense, in US dollar terms, will decline by 0.50% per year. Since the US dollar risk-free rate is 5%, the present value of the liability in US dollars is $1.92/[0.05 − (−0.05)] = $34.91 million. This financing creates a positive home NPV for XYZ in the amount of $48 million − 34.91 million = $13.09 million. This NPV more than offsets the $NPV_{FX}^{\$}$ of the acquisition of DYA, −$10.29 million. The overall home currency NPV of the acquisition plus hedging with foreign currency debt is $13.09 million − $6 million = $7.09 million.

EXPANSION OF OVERSEAS CAPACITY

Now consider an investment proposal to expand EPC's production capacity in Eurozone. Assume that the expansion of production would require an investment outlay of €1000 and would increase EPC's output by 25%. Given the current spot FX rate of 1 $/€, EPC would thus generate an additional €40 in current after-tax euro cash flow. The growth rate in euro cash flows is still 4.50% and the euro is forecasted to appreciate at the perpetual rate of 3% while the equilibrium expected euro appreciation rate is 2%.

The NPV of the expansion proposal in euros is €40/(0.09 − 0.045) − €1000 = €800 − 1000 = −€200. The proposal's NPV in US dollars is $40/(0.11 − 0.075) − $1000 = $143. The proposal's NPV is negative in euros and is positive in US dollars. Should EPC accept or reject the expansion proposal?

If euro investors owned EPC, the answer would be to reject. If a US firm owns EPC, the positive NPV in US dollars suggests that the expansion proposal should be accepted. But the US owner should again consider the alternative of investing the $1000 outlay in a long-term risk-free euro deposit. The US dollar NPV of the euro-denominated deposit will be higher than the NPV in US dollars of EPC's proposed expansion of production, $143. The question for the US owner is again whether a position in the euro deposit is a realistic option. If not, then the expansion decision may make sense as a means for the US owner to exploit its FX forecast.

Consider the firm DYA with initial euro cash flows of €1 million that are projected to grow at the rate of 3% per year into perpetuity. The cash flows have an FX operating exposure of 2 when viewed in US dollars. The cost of capital for DYA in US dollars is assumed to be 8.5%. DYA is evaluating an investment proposal to expand production in the Eurozone. The forecasted rate of change in the FX value of the euro is assumed to be −0.50%, not the equilibrium expected rate, 1%. Assume that the expansion of production would require an investment outlay of €7 million and would increase DYA's output by 30%. Given the current spot FX rate of 1.20 $/€, DYA would thus generate an additional €300,000 in current after-tax euro cash flow. If euro investors own DYA, would they accept or reject the proposal? What about US dollar investors?

Answer: The NPV of the expansion proposal in euros is €300,000/(0.065 − 0.03) − €7 million = €8.57 million − €7 million = €1.57 million. The proposal's NPV in euros is positive. If euro investors own DYA, the answer would be to accept. The proposal's NPV in US dollars is $360,000/(0.085 − 0.035) − $8.4 million = $7.2 million − 8.4 million = −$1.2 million. If US investors own DYA, the negative NPV in US dollars means that the answer should be to reject.

MIGA AND OPIC

The *Multilateral Investment Guarantee Agency (MIGA)* was created in 1988 as a member of the World Bank Group to promote foreign direct investment into emerging economies to improve people's lives and reduce poverty. MIGA fulfills this mandate and contributes to development by offering political risk insurance (guarantees) to investors and lenders, and by helping developing countries attract and retain private investment. More information may be obtained from the agency's Web site: http://www.miga.org/.

The *Overseas Private Investment Corporation (OPIC)* is a development agency of the US government. OPIC helps US businesses invest overseas, fosters economic development in new and emerging markets, complements the private sector in managing the risks associated with foreign direct investment, and supports US foreign policy. By expanding economic development in host countries, OPIC-supported projects can encourage political stability, free market reforms, and US best practices. Because OPIC charges market-based fees for its products, it operates on a self-sustaining basis at no net cost to taxpayers. More information may be obtained from the Web site: http://www.opic.gov/.

*FORECASTS OF CORRECTIONS OF FX MISVALUATION

Let us now address valuation under a different approach to FX forecasting. Instead of forecasting a constant perpetual rate of FX change, suppose the current actual spot FX rate is 1 $/€ and the correct FX rate is 1.25 $/€, so the euro is currently undervalued (in terms of the US dollar) by 20%. What is the best forecast of future spot FX rates from this information? The answer depends on the rate at which we forecast the misvaluation to correct itself.

Let us first make the straw-man assumption that the misvaluation will be corrected immediately In this case, the forecasted spot FX rate for a year from now would be the same as the equilibrium expected FX rate if the current spot FX rate were the correct rate of 1.25 $/€. Thus, if the equilibrium expected rate of FX change is 2% per year, the forecasted correct FX rate for the next year would be 1.25 $/€(1.02) = 1.275 $/€. The forecasted correct FX rate for the following year would be 1.275 $/€(1.02) = 1.30 $/€, and so forth.

The reality, of course, is that actual FX rates tend not to correct misvaluations immediately. The process is gradual; the *prior year's* misvaluation will be corrected each year by a constant percentage. The correction rate for the US dollar value of the euro is denoted $c^{\$/€}$.

For example, assume $c^{\$/€} = 10\%$. Since the euro is presently undervalued by 20%, we forecast the euro to be undervalued a year from now by only 90% of 20%, or 18%. By the same token, our forecast for two years from now is that the euro will be undervalued by only 90% of 18%, or 16.2%, and so forth.

We can combine the forecasted correct FX rates and the percentage misvaluations to forecast actual FX rates. Given that the forecasted correct FX rate next year is 1.275 $/€, the forecasted actual FX rate for next year is 1.275 $/€$(1 − 0.18) = 1.046$ $/€. Given that the forecasted correct FX rate for the following year is 1.30 $/€, the forecasted actual FX rate is 1.30 $/€$(1 − 0.162) = 1.09$ $/€. In the first year, the spot FX rate is forecasted to increase from 1 $/€ to 1.046 $/€, a change of 4.6%. In the second year, the expected increase from 1.046 $/€ to 1.09 $/€ represents a change of 4.2%. The actual FX rate is forecasted to change at a nonconstant rate that gradually converges to the efficient FX market rate of change of 2%.

Although the actual FX rate is projected to change at a nonconstant rate, there is a useful pattern: The *difference* between the forecasted correct FX rate and the forecasted actual FX rate changes at a constant rate. The difference gradually diminishes, changing at the constant rate of approximately $E(x^{*\$/€}) - c^{\$/€}$. In our example, the difference starts at 1.25 $/€ − 1 $/€ = 0.25 $/€, declines to 1.275 $/€ − 1.046 $/€ = 0.229 $/€, and then to 1.30 $/€ − 1.09 $/€ = 0.21 $/€, and so on. The difference changes at a constant rate of approximately 2% − 10% = −8%.[6]

Assume that the equilibrium forecast is for the FX value of the euro to change at the rate of −1.50% per year. The current, spot FX value of the euro is 1 $/€, whereas the correct FX value of the euro is 1.25 $/€. Find the forecasted FX rates for the next two years, assuming that the misvaluation correction rate is 12% per year.

Answer: First, consider the "immediate correction" FX forecasts. The forecasted FX rate for next year would be 1.25 $/€(0.985) = 1.23125 $/€. The forecasted FX rate for the following year would be 1.23125 $/€(0.985) = 1.2128 $/€, and so forth. Since the euro is undervalued at the present time by 20% and since $c^{\$/€} = 12\%$, we forecast the euro to be undervalued a year from now by only 88% of 20%, or 17.6%. By the same token, we forecast the euro to be undervalued by only 88% of 17.6%, or 15.49%, two years from now, and so forth. Given that the forecasted correct FX value of the euro next year is 1.23125 $/€, the forecasted actual FX rate for next year is 1.23125 $/€(1 − 0.176) = 1.01455 $/€. Given that the forecasted correct FX value for the euro for the following year is 1.2128 $/€, the forecasted actual FX rate is 1.2128 $/€(1 − 0.1549) = 1.0249 $/€, since the euro is forecasted to be undervalued at that time by 15.49%.

---

[6]A gradual correction of an FX misvaluation by 10 to 15% per year is consistent with the consensus of empirical researchers that the half-life of convergence to parity is three to five years. This consensus is discussed in K. Rogoff, "The Purchasing Power Parity Puzzle," *Journal of Economic Literature*, June 1996, 647–668.

*ASSET VALUES AND CORRECTION OF FX MISVALUATION

When an FX misvaluation is projected to correct itself at a constant rate per year, and thus when managers forecast a nonconstant rate of FX change, the expected growth rate in a foreign investment's cash flows in US dollars is also not constant. For this reason, we assess an investment's value in US dollars, $V_i^\$$, in terms of two components.

The first component is the hypothetical value the investment would have in US dollars if the FX misvaluation were to correct itself immediately, denoted $V_{iC}^\$$. The $V_{iC}^\$$ is the present value of the stream of $E(O_{itC}^\$)$, where $E(O_{itC}^\$)$ represents the expected cash flow in US dollars for investment i at time t, assuming a correctly valued FX rate at time t. The expected growth rate in $E(O_{itC}^\$)$ is denoted $g_{iC}^\$$.

The second component of the intrinsic value, denoted $V_{iD}^\$$, is the present value of the difference between the cash flow in US dollars at the forecasted correct FX rate forecast and the cash flow in US dollars at the managers' actual FX rate forecast, given that the FX correction is expected to occur at the constant gradual rate, $c^{\$/\euro}$. This cash flow difference at time t is $E(O_{itC}^\$) - E(O_{it}^\$)$. The projected growth rate in this difference, denoted $g_{iD}^\$$, is a constant that is determined by a combination of the investment's efficient FX market cash flow growth rate in US dollars, $g_{iC}^\$$, and the rate of convergence of the actual FX rate toward the correct FX rate, $c^{\$/\euro}$. As a linear approximation, $g_{iD}^\$ = g_{iC}^\$ - c^{\$/\euro}$.

If the foreign currency is undervalued, $E(O_{itC}^\$)$ overstates the actual expected cash flow, $E(O_{it}^\$)$, and the cash flow difference is positive. Now $V_{iC}^\$$ will overstate the asset's value by $V_{iD}^\$$. If the foreign currency is overvalued, $E(O_{itC}^\$)$ understates the actual expected cash flow, $E(O_{it}^\$)$, and the cash flow difference is negative. Then $V_{iC}^\$$ will understate the asset's value by the absolute value of $V_{iD}^\$$, which is negative.

Putting the two components together, we have equation (12.4):

$$V_i^\$ = V_{iC}^\$ - V_{iD}^\$ \qquad (12.4)$$

Let us now see how this valuation approach works with some numbers in the EPC valuation. We assume that at the current spot FX rate of 1 $/€, the euro is currently undervalued by 20% (relative to the US dollar), so the correctly valued FX rate is currently 1.25 $/€. We assume the equilibrium expected long-term rate of change in the FX value of the euro is 2% per year. Because of the current undervaluation of the euro, the forecasted actual rate of FX change is *higher* now than 2%, but it is expected to converge gradually to the efficient FX market rate. We assume that the FX valuation correction is expected to take place at the constant rate of $c^{\$/\euro} = 10\%$ per year.

If 100% of the FX misvaluation were to correct itself immediately, EPC's first cash flow (€200) would be converted into US dollars at the current correct FX rate of 1.25 $/€, to get $250. The expected growth rate in EPC's cash flows, viewed in US dollars, is $g_{iC}^\$ = 6.5\%$ when the expected rate of FX change is the efficient FX market rate of 2%. Thus the hypothetical immediate correction value of EPC in US dollars would be $V_{iC}^\$ = \$250/(0.11 - 0.065) = \$5556$.

In US dollars, the difference between EPC's €200 initial euro cash flow at the current correct FX rate (1.25 $/€) and at the current actual spot FX rate (1 $/€), is

EXHIBIT 12.3 EPC Pro Forma Cash Flows (US dollars): Efficient FX Market Forecast = 2% Annual Appreciation of the Euro

	YEAR		
	1	2	3
Correct $/€ FX values	1.25 $/€	1.275 $/€	1.30 $/€
Forecasted actual $/€ FX rates	1.00 $/€	1.046 $/€	1.09 $/€
Immediate correction cash flow (6.5% growth)	$250	$266.25	$283.56
Cash flow difference (−3.5% growth)	$50	$48.25	$46.56
Forecasted actual cash flow	$200	$218.00	$237.00

$250 − 200 = $50. The difference between the correct FX rate cash flow and the actual forecasted cash flow (in US dollars) is projected to change at the constant rate of $g_{iD}^\$ = 6.5\% − 10\% = −3.5\%$ per year. Therefore, the present value of the differences is $V_{iD}^\$ = \$50/[0.11 − (−0.035)] = \$345$. This is the amount by which EPC's immediate correction value overstates its actual gradual correction value.

The US dollar value of EPC, using equation (12.4), is $V_i^\$ = V_{iC}^\$ − V_{iD}^\$ = \$5556 − 345 = \$5211$, lower than the value of $5556 if the FX misvaluation corrected itself immediately, to reflect the lower expected cash flows (since the FX correction is only gradual). Assume that EPC's asking price is €5000. As in the earlier example when the euro was forecasted to appreciate at a rate higher than the efficient FX market rate, the home currency $NPV_H^\$$ is positive, $5211 − 5000 = $211. The $NPV^{*\$}$ is 1 $/€(€4444 − 5000) = −$556, as before.

Exhibit 12.3 may help clarify the forecasted patterns of the FX rate and the US dollar cash flows. Note that the growth rate in the actual forecasted US dollar cash flow is 9% between years 1 and 2, and 8.7% between years 2 and 3. This growth rate continues to decline thereafter toward the long-run cash flow growth rate of 6.5%.

If the foreign currency is currently overvalued, the value of the investment, if the FX rate were to correct immediately, would be lower than the asset's US value, $V_i^\$$, and the difference between the immediate correction cash flow in US dollars and the actual cash flow in US dollars would be negative. Thus equation (12.4) applies, since the present value of the cash flow differences, $V_{iD}^\$$, is negative, and substitution of this result implies a higher value of $V_i^\$$ than $V_{iC}^\$$.

Assume that the correctly valued euro will change by an equilibrium expected rate of change of −1.50% per year. Thus, the long-run growth rate in EPC's cash flows, viewed in US dollars, is $g_{iC}^\$ = 3\%$. Continue to assume that the current spot FX rate of 1 $/€ and the correct FX rate is 1.25 $/€, representing an undervaluation of the euro by 20%. Assume that the misvaluation is anticipated to gradually correct itself by 12% per year. The current undervaluation of the euro, causes the forecasted rate of change to be higher than −1.50%, but it is expected to decline gradually toward −1.50% per year. Find the US dollar value of EPC.

Answer: If 100% of the FX misvaluation were to correct itself immediately, then EPC's first euro cash flow (€200) would be converted into US dollars at the current correct FX rate of 1.25 $/€, to get $250. Thus the hypothetical immediate correction value of EPC in US dollars would be $V_{iC}^{\$} = \$250/(0.11 - 0.03) = \$3125$. The difference between the correct FX rate cash flow and the actual forecasted cash flow (in US dollars) is projected to change at the constant rate of the $0.03 - 0.12 = -0.09$, or –9% per year. Therefore, the present value of the cash flow difference is $V_{iD}^{\$} = \$50/[0.11 - (-0.09)] = \$250$. The value of EPC in US dollars, found from equation (12.4), is $V_{i}^{\$} = V_{iC}^{\$} - V_{iD}^{\$} = \$3125 - 250 = \$2875$, less than the value if the FX misvaluation corrected immediately, to reflect the lower cash flows that must be anticipated because the FX correction is only gradual.

SUMMARY

This chapter presented an analytical framework for overseas investment decisions. We used examples of acquisitions, decisions to relocate production capacity from one country to another, and expansion proposals by overseas subsidiaries. In the relocation examples, we dealt with the potential cost of capital change due to the change in FX operating exposure.

The conventional statement is that an asset's value will be the same in one currency as in another, given the spot FX rate. Similarly, it is frequently asserted that it is irrelevant whether we analyze an overseas investment's NPV in the home currency or in the foreign currency, as long as we use consistent cross-border cash flow forecasts and costs of capital. These assertions are based on the assumption that the FX market is efficient and FX rates are correctly valued.

We asked how the possibility of an inefficient FX market affects decision making for overseas investments. When managers' FX forecasts differ from the equilibrium expected FX rates, should this affect their overseas investment decisions? We found that if managers' forecasted FX change differs from the equilibrium expected change, the two NPV perspectives may not result in the same decision. Then the question becomes how to interpret and use the NPV results from the two currency perspectives. In this environment, we showed how managers' FX forecasts might affect their investment and hedging and financing decisions.

This chapter has also shown a technique for valuation when projected cash flow growth rates are nonconstant in the case of an FX misvaluation gradually correcting itself at a constant rate.

GLOSSARY

Greenfield investment: The construction of a new plant or facility.

Horizontal M&A: Merger or acquisition involving firms in the same industry.

Multilateral Investment Guarantee Agency (MIGA): Organization connected to the World Bank that promotes foreign direct investment into emerging economies by insuring political risk.

Overseas Private Investment Corporation (OPIC): A development agency of the federal government to help US businesses invest overseas and foster economic development in new and emerging markets.

Vertical M&A: Merger or acquisition involving firms of a supply or distribution chain.

DISCUSSION QUESTIONS

1. In overseas investment decisions, should one consider an investment's overall cash flow or just the portion to be repatriated? Explain.
2. Discuss situations in which managers should consider the level of FX rates in overseas investment analysis.
3. Discuss situations in which managers should not consider the level of FX rates in overseas investment analysis.
4. Do you think managers incorporate their FX forecasts into international investment decisions?
5. Do you think managers *should* incorporate their FX forecasts into international investment decisions?

PROBLEMS

ABC is a US multinational company considering the acquisition of EPC, a company in the Eurozone. EPC's next cash flow in euros is projected to be €100, and subsequent cash flows in euros are projected to grow perpetually at a constant rate of 4% per year. From the US dollar point of view, EPC's FX operating exposure to the euro is currently 1.78 and the operating beta is 1. Assume that the euro has an FX global beta of 0 and a volatility of 0.08. Assume that the risk-free rate in US dollars is 5%, the risk-free rate in euros is 4%, and the risk premium on the global market portfolio (in US dollars) is 4%. Assume a current spot FX rate of 1 $/€. ABC forecasts that the euro will change by −1.2% (i.e., will depreciate by 1.2%) per year indefinitely into the future.

The equilibrium expected rate of change in the FX value of the euro, found by using the linear approximation of the traditional UIRP condition is 0.05 − 0.04 = 0.01, or 1%. Assuming the global CAPM, EPC's cost of capital in US dollars is 0.05 + 1(0.04) = 0.09, or 9%.

1. Find EPC's intrinsic value in US dollars, given the forecasted −1.2% rate of change per year in the FX value of the euro. Find EPC's intrinsic value in US dollars if the FX value of the euro is forecasted to change at the equilibrium expected rate.
2. EPC's owners are asking €2800 to sell the company. Should ABC buy EPC? What if the acquisition is financed by euro-denominated debt? Assume that the debt is risk free.
3. Regardless of your answer to Problem 2, assume that ABC acquires EPC. Some time passes and EPC now requests €1500 in additional capital to expand operations. The subsidiary has projected that the expansion will generate an incremental expected (after-tax) cash flow stream in euros that begins with €50 and grows perpetually at the constant rate of 4% per year. ABC has a new forecast that the euro will perpetually appreciate by 1.5% per year, but the equilibrium expected rate of FX change is still 1%. (a) What is the home currency NPV of the expansion proposal from the US dollar point of view? (b) What is the equilibrium NPV?
4. If the risk-free rate in US dollars is 5% and the risk-free rate in euros is 4%, what is the NPV of the expansion proposal in Problem 3 for financing with risk-free euro-denominated debt?

*5.   Assume that the equilibrium expectation is for the FX value of euro to change at the rate of 1% per year indefinitely. The current spot FX value of the euro is 1 $/€, whereas the correct FX value of the euro is 1.20 $/€. Find the forecasted FX rates for the next two years, assuming a misvaluation correction rate of 12% per year.

*6.   Consider EPC from Problem 1. Assume that a correctly valued euro would change by the equilibrium expected rate of change of 1% per year. Assume that the current spot FX rate of 1 $/€ and the correct FX rate is 1.20 $/€, representing an undervaluation of the euro by 16.67%. Anticipate that the misvaluation will gradually correct itself by 12% per year. Owing to the current undervaluation of the euro, the forecasted rate of change is higher than 1%, but it is expected to decline gradually toward 1% per year. Find the US dollar intrinsic value of EPC.

ANSWERS TO PROBLEMS

1.   Using equation (12.1), we find that EPC's cash flow growth rate in US dollars, given the -1.2% forecasted rate of change for the FX value of the euro, is $0.04 - 0.012 - (1 - 1.78)0.08^2 = 0.033$. EPC's intrinsic value in US dollars is $\$100/(0.09 - 0.033) = \$1754$. With the equilibrium FX rate of change of 1%, the expected growth rate of cash flows in US dollars is 5.5%. EPC's intrinsic value in US dollars is $\$100/(0.09 - 0.055) = \$2857$. Alternatively, we can use equation (10.2) to find the cost of capital for EPC in euros: $0.09 - 0.01 + (1 - 1.78)0.08^2 = 0.075$, or 7.5%. EPC's intrinsic value in euros is $€100/(0.075 - 0.04) = €2857$. Given the spot FX rate, the intrinsic value in US dollars is $2857.

2.   Investing $2800 in a risk-free euro-denominated bond would generate annual cash flow of $\$2800(0.04) = €112$. In US dollars, the cash flow would be forecasted to grow at -1.20% and the cost of capital would be 0.05. The NPV would be $\$1806 - 2800 = -\$994$. Financing the acquisition with euro-denominated debt would create $994 in intrinsic value for an acquirer whose forecast is for an FX depreciation of the euro of 1.2% per year. The NPV of the acquisition with euro-denominated debt is $\$1754 + 994 - 2800 = -\$52$. The acquisition proposal should be rejected even if it is financed with euro-denominated debt.

3.   (a) The first expected cash flow in US dollars is $€50(1 \$/€) = \$50$. The US dollar cash flows from the project would be expected to grow at the rate of $0.04 + 0.015 - (1 - 1.78)0.08^2 = 0.06$, or 6% per year. In US dollars, the intrinsic value of the expansion decision, using the forecasted FX rate change of 1.5%, is $\$50/(0.09 - 0.06) = \$1667$. The home currency NPV in US dollars is thus $\$1667 - 1500 = \$167$. (b) The NPV when the analysis is performed in euros is $€50/(0.075 - 0.04) - 1500 = -€71$. The equilibrium NPV in US dollars is $-\$71$.

4.   Investing €1500 into a risk-free euro asset at 4% will generate a cash flow of €60 per year. The growth rate in US dollars is expected to be 1.5%. The intrinsic value in US dollars is $\$60/(0.05 - 0.015) = \$1714$. The NPV is $214. So the NPV of issuing the risk-free euro-denominated debt is $-\$214$. ABC should not hedge the FX exposure of the expansion by financing it with euro-denominated debt.

5.   First, consider the immediate correction FX forecasts. The forecasted FX rate for next year would be $1.20 \$/€(1.01) = 1.212 \$/€$. The forecasted FX rate for the following year would be $1.212 \$/€(1.01) = 1.224 \$/€$, and so forth. Since the euro is undervalued at present by 16.67% and $c^{\$/€} = 12\%$, we forecast the euro to be undervalued a year from now by only 88% of 16.67%, or 14.67%. By the same token, we forecast that two years from now the euro will be undervalued by only 88% of 14.67%, or 12.91%, and so forth. Given that the forecasted correct FX value next year is 1.212 $/€, the forecasted actual FX rate for next year is $1.212 \$/€(1 - 0.1467) = 1.034 \$/€$. Given that the forecasted correct FX value for the following year is 1.224 $/€, the

forecasted actual FX rate is 1.224 $/€$(1 - 0.1291) = 1.066$ $/€, since the euro is forecasted to be undervalued by 12.91%.

6. From equation (12.1), the long-run growth rate in EPC's euro cash flows, viewed in US dollars, is $g_{iC}^{\$} = 0.04 + 0.01 - (1 - 1.78)0.08^2 = 0.055$, or 5.5%. If 100% of the FX misvaluation were to correct itself immediately, then EPC's first euro cash flow (€100) would be converted into US dollars at the current correct FX rate of 1.20 $/€, to get $120. Thus the hypothetical immediate correction value of EPC in US dollars would be $V_{iC}^{\$} = \$120/(0.09 - 0.055) = \$3429$. The difference between the correct FX rate cash flow and the actual forecasted cash flow (in US dollars) is projected to change at the constant rate of the $0.055 - 0.12 = -0.065$, or -6.50% per year. Therefore, the present value of the cash flow difference is $V_{iD}^{\$} = \$20/[0.09 - (-0.065)] = \$129$. The value of EPC in US dollars, from equation (12.4), is $V_i^{\$} = V_{iC}^{\$} - V_{iD}^{\$} = \$3429 - 129 = \$3300$, less than the value if the FX misvaluation corrected immediately, to reflect the lower expected cash flows due to fact that the FX correction is only gradual.

INDEX